AF757332

Implementing Environmental Law

THE IUCN ACADEMY OF ENVIRONMENTAL LAW SERIES

Series Editors: Kurt Deketelaere, *University of Leuven, Leuven, Belgium* and Zen Makuch, *Imperial College, London, UK*

As environmental law increases in importance as an area of legal research, this series brings together some of the most current research carried out by the IUCN Academy of Environmental Law, a global network of environmental law scholars. Each volume in the series addresses an important issue in the field and presents original research analysis and assessment, along with a much-needed synthesis of the state of environmental law. Directions as to the positive role that environmental law can play at a global level are also emphasized. This series provides essential reading for scholars throughout the world with an interest in cutting edge environment-related issues, and will no doubt play an important role in shaping future debate.

Titles in this series include:

Environmental Governance and Sustainability
Edited by Paul Martin, Li Zhiping, Qin Tianbao, Anel Du Plessis, Yves Le Bouthillier and Angela Williams

Poverty Alleviation and Environmental Law
Edited by Yves Le Bouthillier, Miriam Alfie Cohen, Jose Juan Gonzalez Marquez, Albert Mumma and Susan Smith

Local Climate Change Law
Environmental Regulation in Cities and Other Localities
Edited by Benjamin J. Richardson

Biodiversity and Climate Change
Linkages at International, National and Local Levels
Edited by Frank Maes, An Cliquet, Willemien du Plessis and Heather McLeod-Kilmurray

Global Environmental Law at a Crossroads
Edited by Robert V. Percival, Jolene Lin and William Piermattei

Water and the Law
Towards Sustainability
Edited by Michael Kidd, Loretta Feris, Tumai Murombo and Alejandro Iza

The Search for Environmental Justice
Edited by Paul Martin, Sadeq Z. Bigdeli, Trevor Daya-Winterbottom, Willemien du Plessis and Amanda Kennedy

Implementing Environmental Law
Edited by Paul Martin and Amanda Kennedy

Implementing Environmental Law

Edited by

Paul Martin

Professor, University of New England, Armidale NSW, Australia

Amanda Kennedy

Associate Professor, University of New England, Armidale NSW, Australia

THE IUCN ACADEMY OF ENVIRONMENTAL LAW SERIES

With the support of New Zealand Law Foundation

The Law Foundation NEW ZEALAND

Edward Elgar PUBLISHING

Cheltenham, UK • Northampton, MA, USA

© The IUCN Academy of Environmental Law 2015

All rights reserved. No part of this publication may be reproduced, stored in a retrieval system or transmitted in any form or by any means, electronic, mechanical or photocopying, recording, or otherwise without the prior permission of the publisher.

Published by
Edward Elgar Publishing Limited
The Lypiatts
15 Lansdown Road
Cheltenham
Glos GL50 2JA
UK

Edward Elgar Publishing, Inc.
William Pratt House
9 Dewey Court
Northampton
Massachusetts 01060
USA

Paperback edition 2017

A catalogue record for this book
is available from the British Library

Library of Congress Control Number: 2015935896

This book is available electronically in the **Elgar**online
Law subject collection
DOI 10.4337/9781783479313

MIX
Paper from
responsible sources
FSC® C013056

ISBN 978 1 78347 929 0 (cased)
ISBN 978 1 78347 931 3 (eBook)
ISBN 978 1 78347 930 6 (paperback)

Typeset by Columns Design XML Ltd, Reading
Printed and bound in Great Britain by TJ International Ltd, Padstow, Cornwall

Contents

List of contributors

Dr Robyn Bartel is a Senior Lecturer in Geography and Planning and a research associate of the AgLaw Centre at the University of New England. Robyn's fields of expertise are environmental law, regulatory theory and cultural geography.

Albert K. Butzel is the principal of Albert K. Butzel Law Offices in New York City. He has been counsel in a number of significant environmental litigations, including the Storm King Mountain and Westway MegaProject cases.

Javier de Cendra is Dean of IE Law School. He is also honorary senior lecturer at University College London Energy Institute and honorary senior fellow at UCL Faculty of Laws. His areas of research include climate change and energy law and policy.

Professor Donna Craig holds an appointment at the University of Western Sydney. Previously she was the co-director at the Macquarie University Centre for Environmental law. She researches and teaches environmental law and justice.

Meinhard Doelle is Professor of Law, and Associate Dean, Research, Schulich School of Law, Dalhousie University, and Director, Marine & Environmental Law Institute. Professor Doelle specialises in climate change, environmental law, and energy law.

Josefin Gooch is a researcher, teacher and doctoral candidate at Lund University. Her area of research includes transboundary water law and natural resource governance.

Wayne Gumley is a Senior Lecturer at the Monash University Faculty of Business and Economics. His areas of specialisation are environmental and natural resources law, corporate environmental responsibility and ecological tax reform.

Dr Cameron Holley is Senior Research Fellow (DECRA) at the Faculty of Law, the University of New South Wales. His areas of specialisation are water law and environmental law, with a focus on regulation and governance.

Tanya Howard is a doctoral student at the Australian Centre for Agriculture and Law at the University of New England. Her research focuses on improving institutional mechanisms for community engagement in natural resource governance.

Amanda Kennedy is the Deputy Director of the Australian Centre for Agriculture and Law at the University of New England. Her research interests are in the areas of environmental justice and land use governance.

William Lahey is Associate Professor of Law at the Schulich School of Law, Dalhousie University. His specialisations include law and regulation in environmental, health systems and energy systems governance and natural resources law and policy.

Andrew Lawson is a doctoral student at the Australian Centre for Agriculture and Law at the University of New England, specializing in governance issues in farming, rural communities, and the environment.

Dr Emma Lees is University Lecturer in Property and Environmental Law, Department of Planning Law, University of Cambridge. Her research focuses on land law, European and national environmental law, and planning law.

Professor Paul Martin is the Director of the Australian Centre for Agriculture and Law at the University of New England. His areas of specialisation are natural resource governance and rural social justice.

Molly Masterton is a recent graduate of the George Washington University Law School, where she served as a research assistant to LeRoy Paddock, Associate Dean for Environmental Studies, and focused on emerging issues in environmental and energy law.

Peter Noble is a director of the Australian Meat Processors Corporation and TAL's representative director on the UN EP FI Principles of Sustainable Insurance. His areas of interests are risk management, sustainability and the law.

Richard L. Ottinger is former Dean and now Dean Emeritus of Pace Law School. He served as a 26-year Member of Congress and chaired the House Energy Subcommittee. He chairs the Energy & Climate committee of the IUCN World Commission on Environmental Law.

Omondi Robert Owino is a doctoral candidate at the Faculty of Law, Bayreuth and an Advocate of the High Court of Kenya. He specialises in trans-boundary natural resource regulation and cooperation as well as energy law.

LeRoy Paddock is Associate Dean for Environmental Legal Studies at The George Washington University Law School. His areas of focus are environmental governance, environmental enforcement and aspects of energy law.

John Louis Parker is an environmental lawyer in the Hudson Valley, New York. He served as Regional Attorney for the NY Department of Environmental Conservation. His specialties include climate change, environmental justice and environmental regulatory issues.

Wang Pianpian holds environmental law degrees from Sun Yat-sen University and Pace University. She passed the Chinese Bar Exam in 2009. Pianpian is active in the business sector in carbon assets management and on environmental law in the context of climate change.

Grant Pink is an Adjunct Research Fellow (School of Law/Faculty of the Professions) at the University of New England. He is a recognised expert on environmental enforcement networks and is undertaking a PhD on environmental regulation.

Alistair Rieu-Clarke is a Reader in International Law at the Centre for Water Law Policy and Science, University of Dundee. He specialises on role and relevance of international law within the context of transboundary water resources management

Nicholas A. Robinson is University Professor for the Environment, and Emeritus Kerlin Professor of Environmental Law, at Pace University, whose environmental law programs he founded. A leader in IUCN since 1972, he lives along Hudson River.

Professor Gregory Rose is a member of the Australian National Centre for Ocean Resources and Security (ANCORS) and is Law Discipline Leader at the University of Wollongong. He specialises in international law focused on marine environment and on crime.

Taryn L. Rucinski is Environmental Law Librarian and Adjunct Professor of Law, Pace University School of Law. Ms. Rucinski graduated with her J.D. and certificate in environmental law from Pace in 2010; her research specialties include environmental and energy law.

Professor Solange Teles Da Silva is Professor of Law at the Mackenzie Presbyterian University and CNPq Fellow Research Productivity. Her areas of specialisation are environmental law, sustainable development and social environmental justice

Radina R. Valova received her J.D. from Pace Law School in 2012 and her LL.M. in 2013 in Land Use and Sustainable Development. She was the 2012–13 Pace Energy and Climate Center Ottinger Energy Research Fellow.

Marla E. Wieder is an Assistant Regional Counsel and Regional Criminal Enforcement Counsel with the U.S. EPA, Region 2. From 2000 through 2011 she served as an adjunct professor at Pace Law School. Her area of specialization is hazard waste.

Professor Wang Xi is the Director of the Natural Resources Law Institute of Shanghai Jiao Tong University. His areas of specialisation are environmental law and environmental governance.

Introduction: a jurisprudence of environmental governance?

Paul Martin and Amanda Kennedy

The history of science shows that the evolution of scholarly investigation follows two lines of development. The first is that innovations undergo a transformation from relatively low efficiency to higher efficiency as the discovery is refined and applied; implementation skill is gained through experience; and incremental inventions that improve on the original are brought to bear.[1] This phenomenon has been observed in many fields of knowledge. It is well illustrated by the trajectories of computer technology, psychological science, transport methods and in almost any other area of human endeavour where disciplined and purposeful development is applied.[2]

The second evolutionary pattern is that in most fields deepening of knowledge leads to differentiation into specialisations. This is illustrated by the physical sciences. Prior to the Scientific Enlightenment, religion, philosophy and science were intermixed. Gradually, subjective elements were excised from what was characterised as legitimate science. Philosophy, religion and science became distinct. These investigations evolved along different paths, as scholars and practitioners tackled increasingly specialist challenges. In science, what are now called chemistry and physics were originally intermixed, but gradually developed distinct epistemology and methodologies, as researchers pursued more specialised knowledge. Within physics, for example, there are epistemological differences between nuclear physics, planetary physics, and many esoteric and applied pursuits of principles and methods of this science. Over time sub-fields proliferate and become more knowledge-intense. They interact less with the parent field from which they evolve or

1 David Teece (1986).
2 Robert Schaller (1997).

with their sibling specialisations. Opportunities for creative recombination do not disappear, but become notable as boundary-spanning instances (particularly illustrated by Linus Pauling's two Nobel Prizes).[3]

The phenomena of evolution towards greater efficiency and differentiation are not only present in physical and experimental sciences. The evolution of economics into its specialisations such as microeconomics, behavioural economics, principal-agency economics and transaction cost economics is a useful illustration.[4] Similar patterns can be seen in psychology, sociology and other social sciences.[5] The same dynamics exist with the scholarly investigation of the science and philosophy of law ('jurisprudence').

These evolutionary patterns are the result of two forces. The first is adaptation to *external* challenges (such as community expectations of better performance from the products of scholarship), the infusion of knowledge from other fields, new technologies, novel methods of investigation, or a change to the broader context. The impact of climate change threats upon the scholarship and application science of mathematics, economics, ecological science, hydrology, coastal morphology, and many other fields illustrates the creative scholarly response to such external pressures. The need for useful knowledge, combined with infusions of methods from other disciplines, has driven investigation and discovery. The second driver is self-generating change from *within* a community of scholars, termed 'autopoetic' development.[6] Driven by curiosity, peer competition and collaboration, academic entrepreneurship and other internal causes (individual or collective), scholars self-generate questions and methods that feed innovations in epistemology.

In the evolution of environmental law these patterns and drivers of evolution can be seen. Environmental law as a distinct field of scholarship and practice was a response to external forces, including developments in ecological science and increasing public awareness, which drove political responses to these pressures. These external stimuli intersected with the sensibilities of lawyers, driving the creativity that has fostered many legal innovations. The subject matter of environmental law

---

3 Nobelprize.org, 'Linus Pauling – Facts' (2014).

4 Brian Loasby (2002).

5 Schultz and Schultz (2011); David Ashley and David Orenstein (2005); Kuper and Kuper (1996); Solomon and Higgins (1996).

6 Luhmann (1995).

has expanded to address many attributes of the natural world, diverse human interests and many ecosystem types.[7]

An important milestone of scholarly evolution is when the discipline identifies that a particular aspect of its work has become so specialist that it is worth recognising this cohort of investigators as pursuing distinct epistemologies. This book proposes that the investigation of the applied effectiveness of environmental law as a component of environmental governance systems is now deserving of that identification. The chapters in this volume highlight the distinctiveness of enquiries into the effective implementation of environmental law instruments. They suggest some of the unique research questions that might be pursued by a cohort of investigators pursuing a jurisprudence of the effectiveness of environmental law.

1. JURISPRUDENCE AND THE EVOLUTION OF ENVIRONMENTAL LAW

Modern environmental law scholarship pursues three types of enquiry that have distinct epistemologies. Scholars pursue different questions, use different methods and propose radically different types of solutions to environmental and social justice issues. They use varied theoretical frameworks to inform investigation within their specialisation. Given the nature of law, there is no hierarchy of importance between the sub-disciplines. The law is unique among public policy and social disciplines in integration of values and philosophy with the creation, interpretation and application of legal instruments, whilst needing to grapple with pragmatic challenges of improving the effectiveness, efficiency and fairness of natural resource governance.[8] Most other disciplines deal only with some aspects of the total challenge, and none have the same direct pathway to application that is a characteristic of the law.

These intersecting specialisations within environmental law scholarship are:

(1) 'Philosophical' jurisprudence. This incorporates a substantial amount of political argumentation. It is concerned largely with shaping the goals of environmental law and refining the values that should be incorporated in legal instruments. The emergence of

[7] Pūraitė (2012); Tarlock (2010); Tarlock (2003); Lazarus (1996); Winter (1989).

[8] See Martin and Craig, Chapter 1 below.

distinct theories of 'environmental jurisprudence' and environmental social justice illustrates evolution within this specialisation.[9]

(2) 'Instrumental' scholarship, focused upon doctrinal enquiry and legal instruments. The instruments upon which attention has been focused are judgements and statutes (viz. instruments of government). Increasingly private instruments such as market instruments and industry codes and standards are replacing or supplementing public instruments, though legal scholarship has been slow to come to grips with this development. Most mainstream environmental law scholarship is instrumentally focused.

(3) 'Operational' (or 'applied', or 'institutional') investigation, concerned with organisational structures and implementation. The focus is upon understanding and improving the efficiency, effectiveness, and fairness of instruments (measured partly against philosophical values). Effectiveness is concerned with moving law 'off the page', and thus this type of legal scholarship is more closely aligned to the empirical sciences than are philosophic or instrumental specialisations. However, because the law is concerned with applying social values, this jurisprudence must integrate aspects of both science and philosophy.

This book is designed to focus attention upon operational effectiveness and reform as a specialist field of jurisprudential enquiry. Research on implementation concerns phenomena observable in the real world, and this type of scholarship explores how these might be brought into alignment with phenomena envisaged in the idealised world proposed through legal philosophy, or the objectives that underpin legal instruments. The authors of the chapters in this book point to the uniqueness of the scholarly and practical issues that arise when the concern is the operational effectiveness of environmental law. Together the chapters allow insight into the real-world challenges and opportunities for innovation in the implementation of public and private legal arrangements. These arrangements are intended to advance the effective stewardship of natural resources, and improve fairness in the distribution of the costs and benefits of using and conserving the natural environment.

The idea for this book took root in 2012, with a proposal to the Research Committee of the IUCN Academy of Environmental Law for a workshop on implementation of environmental law. This took place in

---

[9] Westbrook (1993); Burdon (2012); Baber and Bartlett (2009); Riddell (2014) 21.

2013 at the Academy's annual Colloquium. More recent developments discussed below are indicative of a *zeitgeist*. This book is intended to respond to that movement by suggesting directions for scholarship that can assist in responding to the newly identified imperative for effectively implemented legal arrangements.

2. GOVERNANCE SYSTEMS OR LEGAL INSTRUMENTS?

A fundamental distinction in the investigation of effective implementation is between research of legal instruments and the investigation of systems of governance. The chapters variously deal with legal instrumental issues, public law and private contract, non-government 'voluntary' self-regulation, economic instruments, collaborative networks, power relationships in consultation processes, the effects of social and political dynamics, and many other causes of the effectiveness (or otherwise) of legal governance arrangements. Their suggestions of ways to improve effectiveness point to actions as diverse as the redesign of regulatory and international instruments, improving private contracts or market standards, better coordination of bureaucracies, new collaborative strategies, more sophisticated knowledge development and many other behavioural and organisational interventions. The net effect is to make it clear that diagnosis of effectiveness requires consideration of a complex mix of legal and non-legal matters, human and organisational behaviours, the multi-faceted contexts within which instruments operate, and pragmatic considerations such as economic resources and human capacity. In moving from a jurisprudence of instruments to a jurisprudence of implementation, there is a change of focus away from instruments towards the total system of governance where the law is a central, but not the overriding, consideration.

Governance is systemic. The IUCN World Conservation Congress defines governance as the '... interactions among structures, processes and traditions that determine how power and responsibilities are exercised, how decisions are taken, and how citizens or other stakeholders have their say in the management of natural resources – including biodiversity conservation' (IUCN WCC Resolution 3.012). It involves many participants including government officials, traditional authorities, self-government as well as non-government actors. It relies upon norms that may be formal or informal, and upon implementation organisations and structures. Governance systems vary between communities, and they constantly evolve. In some circumstances, there are intersecting or competing governance systems at work within or between jurisdictions. Thus, nation-state governance arrangements often intersect with private sector approaches including voluntary or supply chain codes; or with traditional and indigenous norms for conserving and using the natural world. For these reasons, the jurisprudence of effective implementation of environmental law requires novel methods to generate different types of insight to those sought from the other streams of environmental jurisprudence.

3. WHICH RULES ARE RELEVANT?

A central aspect of governance is the rules (or norms) which are at the heart of the system, but this raises the questions: 'whose rules' and 'what rules'? There are many rules that control how societies interact with the natural environment, how natural resources are accessed, used and transformed, conserved and how the cost and benefits from resources are distributed. This includes rules related to:

- The quality of natural resources such as the atmosphere, water, soil, climate;
- How all types of natural resources are allocated or used;
- Access to and benefit-sharing related to biodiversity;
- Energy generation; and
- All other activities with the potential for significant environmental impact.

Whilst legal judgments and regulations created by the nation-state and the community of states are fundamental to environmental law, private citizens (through agreements and self-government) also create rights and responsibilities to the natural world. The chapters in this volume discuss rules arising from international environmental conventions (e.g. bilateral or multilateral environmental agreements), national constitutions, statutes, judgments and rulings or administrative instruments. In the case of non-state governance the authors reference 'voluntary' collective arrangements and corporate self-standards. Whilst none of the chapters in this book focus upon traditional peoples' custodianship systems, the importance of customary law and other social norms must not be discounted as increasingly important in the scholarship of legal natural resource governance.

A taxonomy of rule types highlights various sources of authority, and that even non-state rules can be recognised by the nation-state in many ways. A listing of rule categories (based upon an unpublished methodology for the evaluation of the effectiveness of environmental law) shows the many different sources of natural resource institutions:[10]

(a) State-created formal rules, including constitutions, statutes, regulations, and administrative rules and plans.
(b) State-based judicial rules, which include judgments of courts and tribunals, and binding rulings of quasi-judicial authorities or agents of government.
(c) State-supported private (broadly consensual) rules, with the most common form of support for consensual arrangements being contract and property rights.
(d) International, bilateral, or multilateral treaties, conventions, and agreements. International arrangements have varying degrees of formal acceptance by nation states and communities.
(e) Spanning both nation-state law and international law are legal norms that have the status of being self-evident principles of law within a jurisdiction or in international jurisprudence, such as acceptance of the rule of law.
(f) Rules emerging from communities (in particular indigenous communities), often referred to as 'customary law'.

State-based formal rules, widely ratified international conventions, and principles endorsed by courts (such as equality before the law) are the most legally conventional. Un-documented norms and rules, including traditional rules for natural resource governance, vary in legal status but it is not legal status alone that determines their effectiveness in practice. The chapters illustrate that natural resources law consists of far more than rules. The quality and integrity of the arrangements for creating and implementing rules (institutions and processes) are critical. Understanding effectiveness in practice requires consideration of the quality, integrity, capacities and performance of political, legal, administrative and judicial bodies; and often of non-state agents. The functional capability and governance culture of participants in governance are also relevant to governance performance.

[10] Further detail is contained in Martin (forthcoming 2015).

4. CONCEPTUAL AND METHODOLOGICAL CHALLENGES

Major international environmental organisations are now signalling that significant improvements in the effectiveness of legal aspects of natural resource governance are essential. Their pronouncements indicate dissatisfaction with following the well-trod path of creating and interpreting international or intra-national legal instruments. The desire to focus far more upon effective implementation was signalled in the Rio+20 outcome document 'The Future We Want':[11]

> 19. We recognize that the twenty years since the Earth Summit in 1992 have seen uneven progress, including in sustainable development and poverty eradication. We emphasize the need to make progress in implementing previous commitments. We also recognize the need to accelerate progress in closing development gaps between developed and developing countries, and to seize and create opportunities to achieve sustainable development through economic growth and diversification, social development and environment protection. To this end, we underscore the continued need for an enabling environment at the national and international levels, as well as continued and strengthened international cooperation, particularly in the areas of finance, debt, trade and technology transfer, as mutually agreed, and innovation and entrepreneurship, capacity building, transparency and accountability. We recognize the diversification of actors and stakeholders engaged in the pursuit of sustainable development.

A parallel recognition that the focus of attention needs to turn from instruments to effective systems of governance has occurred within the IUCN with the emergence of the IUCN Natural Resource Governance Framework (NRGF). A key plank is a joint research program involving the World Commission on Environmental Law and the Environmental Law Centre in Bonn.[12] The IUCN program is intended to generate methodologies, constituting a 'basket of governance tools'. These tools will include methods to objectively review and improve the quality of legal arrangements so as to support more effective and fair natural

[11] UN General Assembly Resolution 66/288, adopted by the General Assembly on 27 July 2012.

[12] The initial step being to develop and test a method for objective evaluation of the effectiveness of legal arrangements, in collaboration with teams from Australia, Brazil, China, South Africa and New Zealand. This work forms part of a broader CEESP-led initiative.

resource governance. UNEP's Environmental Governance sub-programme,[13] the Memorandum of Understanding signed between UNEP and the International Organization of Supreme Audit Institutions (INTOSAI – Working Group on Environmental Auditing, WGEA), and the comments of a number of scholars, all point in the same direction. Even as this chapter was being drafted, the Chief of Staff of the Organisation of American States Secretary General, in announcing a major initiative with the United Nations Environment Programme, said 'it is our hope that this agreement will contribute to addressing the greatest challenge of our century: implementation'.[14]

Martin and Craig's chapter, 'Accelerating the evolution of environmental law through continuous learning from applied experience', highlights the methodological challenges for the academic community in providing the knowledge needed to improve the applied effectiveness of environmental law, to help to form a more powerful, less cumbersome and fairer environmental governance regime. Whilst acknowledging legitimate critiques of environmental law scholarship, they reject the idea that embracing scientific empiricism will provide a strong basis for sufficient improvement. Recognising that engaging with axiological issues is essential to shaping environmental laws that reflect social values and concepts of justice, they explain why a rigidly deductive scientific paradigm cannot be directly transposed into legal research. However, disciplined continuous improvement based upon objective understanding of empirical phenomena, and rejection of subjectivity as the basis for investigations, are also essential to improving the effectiveness of environmental law. For these reasons the integrity of deductive reasoning based upon empirical evidence is also important in pursuing deeper insights into how to make the law work better. They suggest that a constructive approach is to acknowledge that applied legal research requires a strategic framework rather than either a philosophic or a scientific one. In seeking real-world improvements, one dimension is factual where deductive reasoning drawing on objective evidence is essential. However, since the goals of the law are heterogenous and

---

13 'To achieve their environmental commitments and goals, States need strong legislative, political and judicial systems. UNEP will use its expertise in environmental policy and law to help States further develop these institutions, and enhance their ability to effectively participate in international negotiations.' See United Nations Environment Program (2009).

14 OAS Secretary General Chief of Staff Hugo De Zela on the signing of the Agreement on Environmental Rule of Law and Sustainable Development, 19 November 2014, Washington D.C.

dynamic, and the systems that produce outcomes are also multi-faceted and dynamic, it is not feasible to avoid the use of judgement in analysing applied legal arrangements and proposing improvements. As a result effective methods will have involved both objective and subjective elements, and the methods will have to be plural and pragmatic.

Xi, Ottinger, Robinson, Butzel, Wieder, Parker, Rucinski, Valova and Pianpian's chapter, 'Assessing environmental governance of the Hudson River Valley: application of an IPPEP Model', explores the nature of the politically dynamic relationship between the citizenry, elected officials, bureaucracy and the enterprise sector in shaping resource governance. They have used mathematical notation to emphasise the system interactions that occurred in a series of contests over resource use. The approach they use clearly points towards a methodology that focuses less upon the legal instruments that are involved in contests over governance, and far more upon the roles, institutions and political dynamics that enable legal tools to achieve socially valued outcomes. Their work highlights the significance of power as a feature of governance, suggesting the relevance of political theory to questions of legal natural resource governance. Whilst not explored in this chapter, the turbulent *realpolitik* that they document suggests that ideas from political economy, agency theories and other non-legal fields of investigation could fruitfully be used to build upon the dynamics that these authors have pointed towards.

Together these chapters point towards some insights about the methods that will be required for jurisprudence focused upon questions of effective implementation.

(1) Legal governance investigation is likely to be concerned with complex systems issues. This calls for a distinctive definition of scholarly issues and methods for investigation, but also points to the importance of fostering a rich relationship between doctrinal and philosophical jurisprudence.
(2) Research methods will need to enable a sophisticated understanding of political, legal, administrative, economic and social factors in determining what happens in practice. They will need to enable academic lawyers to understand more objectively and systematically the causes of environmental and social justice outcomes, so that they can propose more holistic strategies to improve effectiveness.
(3) The chapters suggest that methodological integrity in the research of effective systems of legal governance will draw upon the disciplines of empirical enquiry, but it is essential to avoid a

misleading distinction between 'scientific' and 'dialogic' methods. Different elements of this jurisprudence will require the use of combinations of deductive and inductive reasoning and a variety of analytical approaches.

(4) These chapters direct our attention towards methodologies that are distinct from those other disciplines but which draw upon many fields of enquiry, which are uniquely legal and which can bring philosophic and pragmatic concerns together into new epistemological structures. Because the underlying questions are about practical improvements in effectiveness, and since a scientific approach depends upon explicit theory, the methods will need to deliver both abstract knowledge and clear practical recommendations, and they will need to support new methods for evaluation of the utility of both types of knowledge.

5. INSTITUTIONAL ACCOUNTABILITY AND GOVERNANCE EFFECTIVENESS

The three chapters that follow explore the links between institutional structure and accountability. They also reflect some of the observations from the first two chapters, including the necessity to consider the *realpolitik* of implementation, and the function of multiple actors serving different intersecting roles within a system of governance where legal instruments are central but not deterministic of outcomes. The authors draw our attention to the ways in which legal arrangements are embedded in political systems and highlight how this impacts on accountability of actors and organisations, and thus upon creating strong motivations for implementation and for continuing improvement in effectiveness.

In 'Putting the train of environmental protection on track: Nova Scotia's experiment in using legislation to strengthen environmental governance', Doelle and Lahey provide an encouraging indication that innovative legal arrangements can provide an effective accountability framework for the legal, political, economic and other aspects of the total governance system. They discuss how Nova Scotia's parliament has created political accountability for environmental and economic outcomes through the Environmental Goals and Sustainable Prosperity Act 2007. That legislation makes the performance of government agencies in pursuing sustainability and related economic goals transparent, and builds political accountability. The example points to the important links between political dynamics and legal arrangements, and suggests that innovation through the law can be a foundation for systemic improvements in natural resource governance. The role of innovations in law to provide a more firm basis for political accountability, and the law's capacity to catalyse strategies that go well beyond purely legal considerations, are areas of potential investigation and improved practice.

A less heartening illustration of the practical importance of the links between legal instruments, constitutional arrangements and political dynamics is provided by Gumley in 'Has environmental impact assessment (EIA) lost credibility? Recent concerns from Australia and Canada'. This chapter demonstrates that the effectiveness of implementation of ratified international agreements within a federated structure is subject to many structural and political variables that go beyond the instruments themselves. Institutional arrangements and structural variables can undermine (or bolster) the effectiveness of any legal instrument. His discussion of the effectiveness of Australian biodiversity conservation laws introduced pursuant to the Convention on Biological Diversity[15] suggests that the lack of a strong framework for public accountability and transparency to supervise the performance of legal arrangements leaves it open for political actors to undermine the governance system. The example raises questions about the extent and ways in which political manipulation of 'non-law' factors (such as interstate administrative arrangements, budgets and internal management processes) can impact upon the effectiveness of legal arrangements and upon the rights of citizens. A deep comparative and historical analysis of the interactions between legal arrangements, bureaucratic structures and political dynamics would almost certainly reveal a number of ways in which the integrity and effectiveness of legal arrangements could be improved.

An aspect of the links between accountability and institutional structures is how the wording of legal instruments can radically alter the practical implementation of a broad legal principal. This issue is investigated by Lees in 'Contamination and the polluter pays principle'. She considers how the polluter pays principle has been legislated in Europe and the USA, leading to fundamentally different consequences in terms of accountability and remediation of pollution. In the version of the principle embodied in the US Environmental Protection Act 1990, a failure to trace the source of pollution to a particular polluter will result in an outcome of legal non-responsibility. Under these circumstances it is likely that either the general public or the environment will bear the harm. In the version used in the Environmental Protection Act 1990 the inability to trace specific causation results in the responsibility travelling

[15] Entered into force, 29 December 1993.

with ownership of the land, creating a strong 'stewardship' regime. A comparative law method that combines an investigation of different formulations of legal principles, the resultant allocations of risk accountability and the empirical consequences could provide important complementary insights to the doctrinal literature on regulatory design.

As was indicated by the preceding two chapters, embedded in structural considerations (such as the wording of legislation and the allocation of responsibility) are matters of distributive justice, as well as consequences for the protection and remediation of the environment. This indicates the importance of the links between the philosophical and the instrumental dimensions of governance, and matters of effectiveness in practice. Determining whether environmental law is effective or not implies an answer to the question 'effective in advancing what values?', and also that there be measures of the practical outcome of the application of the legal instrument. The combination of the philosophical and empirical questions points to the enormity of the task of objectively testing the effectiveness of legal principles, but it also points to why it is so important that this task be skilfully addressed.

It also highlights an important research issue. Economic concepts that have proven useful for the purpose of 'big picture' policy development may not transfer effectively into legal arrangements that are directly applied, and which have distributive (and therefore justice) effects. There has been negligible objective assessment in both law and economics of the 'meta-effectiveness' of economic instruments compared to regulatory or suasive approaches. *Ex ante* economic modelling cannot be considered to be as reliable as *ex post* empirical investigation. Examination of a particular instance cannot be considered to be the equivalent to a comprehensive investigation of the effectiveness of a variety of interventions under diverse circumstances. As with other effectiveness questions in environmental governance, objective findings would require consideration of what values are to be advanced, and what analysis (and therefore what data) would allow a meaningful answer to be given. However, the question is fundamentally important, because of the significant shift towards the use of economic instruments, supported by the implicit but empirically unproven view that the results of doing so are consistently more effective, efficient and fair than more traditional legal or social approaches.

Another area of legal governance where high expectations and achieved outcomes might be poorly aligned because of implementation issues is in public participation in environmental decision-making. The implementation challenges of public participation are carefully considered in 'Possible legal obligations to consult' by Howard and Teles Da

Silva. The chapter indicates that the high expectations of what legal requirements for public participation can do to improve the performance of environmental governance are not likely to be consistently achieved unless implementation issues are addressed. The first challenge identified in the chapter is instrumental: many regulated requirements are poorly specified. They allow for enormous variation in the interpretation of the purposes of participation. They fail to directly engage with the degree of power transfer that is intended through the legal requirement. This leaves the advocates of potentially environmentally or socially harmful developments largely free to select an interpretation suitable to their interests. In consequence, they are able to select from a wide array of methods that in effect alter the practical effects of the legal requirement. It is also possible for incompetence to create distortions, even when implementation of the legal principles is not frustrated by self-interest. In the absence of effective accountability mechanisms (such as merits and process review), and given the frequency with which the public lacks standing or capacity to contest the processes that are used or the outcomes of these processes, it ought not be surprising that the implementation of public participation principles is highly variable. The authors consider the situation in two 'non-Aarhus' jurisdictions, which confirm the significance of the challenges that they have identified.[16] If aspirations of legal requirements for public participation in natural resource governance are to be reliably satisfied, then it is likely that a more comprehensive approach to the integrity of implementation will be needed. Also, given that the purpose of many of these requirements is to protect the interests of the less powerful there is a strong social justice rationale for lawyers to pursue this empirical as well as philosophical investigation and to promote integrity mechanisms for public participation that will work reliably in practice.

---

[16] The United Nations Economic Commission for Europe (UNECE) Convention on Access to Information, Public Participation in Decision Making and Access to Justice in Environmental Matters (the 'Aarhus Convention') 2001. This convention seeks to implement Principle 10 of the Rio Declaration by granting to the public rights to information, participation and access to justice in environmental decision-making processes. For further discussion of the Aarhus Convention, refer to: Lee and Abbot (2003); Hartley and Wood (2005); Kravchenko (2007); Toth (2010).

6. WHAT DETERMINES THE EFFECTIVENESS OF INTERNATIONAL REGIMES?

Aspects of the four chapters we have just considered, which focus upon intra-national implementation of environmental governance regimes, are reinforced in the next four chapters where the concerns are bilateral and multilateral international regimes. As with the intra-national implementation of environmental law, issues of instrumental design, constitutional structures, power and politics all feature as matters impacting upon effectiveness.

In 'Implementing international water agreements', Rieu-Clarke and Gooch focus upon implementation of transboundary water governance. Their chapter begs the questions: 'what influences the implementation of transboundary agreements?' and 'what strategies are most likely to make such arrangements effective?' They argue that implementation could be considered at a procedural or substantive level. They highlight the difference between legal, behavioural, and problem solving effectiveness in international regimes. In considering effectiveness they point to the distinction between a political realist perspective (concerning imbalances in power relationships), or an interpretation of the dynamics as a 'collective action' problem. This interpretation of transboundary water management is mirrored in Owino's analysis of transboundary management of Lake Victoria ('Fouling Adam's Eden: a legal analysis of the collective action challenge in Lake Victoria'). In both cases the role of legal arrangements in determining applied outcomes is analysed within the context of political and power relationships. The effectiveness of instruments is largely seen as being determined by their 'fit' with economic and political (or in some instances military) contexts. In both instances the significance of the organisational structures and political and economic relationships that contextualise legal arrangements cannot be overstated.

These chapters support a view that understanding the effectiveness of a legal instrument requires an understanding of the extent to which its requirements respond to the degree of behaviour change that is needed. They also suggest that whilst procedural obligations are important, if the economic and political *status quo* runs strongly counter to the policy objectives then legal obligations that are specific are likely to be required. In this regard there is a resonance with Doelle and Lahey's example, which also indicates the importance of specificity and transparent evaluation of commitments. A research-based understanding of the problem of proportionality of the legal instrument to the challenge to be met could help reduce the tendency for political adoption of legal arrangements that are unlikely to work.

The chapters from Rieu-Clarke and Gooch, and Owino, point to the practical importance of the capacity of states to implement the commitments that they make. This is mirrored in other chapters, where the concern is not nation states but citizen capacity to do what is expected of them from the legal instrument. Below we refer to a model of behaviour where capacity is identified as one of the three fundamentals (alongside motivation and opportunity) governing environmental and pro-social behaviour of citizens. Regulatory process design is another area where there are significant opportunities for well-researched improvements, which would be likely to improve the overall effectiveness of natural resource governance.

Rose's chapter, 'Marine protection treaties in Antarctic Waters: fragmentation or coordination in international treaty implementation', directs our attention to the architecture of a variety of legal instruments that interact to constitute a framework for marine environmental governance. An issue that this chapter canvasses is the effect of complexity of legal architectures, due to the proliferation of legal instruments and implementation structures. The potential for competing norms, high transaction costs and resulting inefficiency or ineffectiveness is brought into focus. Rose highlights the co-existence of five distinct normative frameworks that intersect in the management of the Antarctic marine environment. These norms are translated into a dazzling array of instruments, with inconsistencies in their implementation and interpretation. To point this confusing situation out is not to suggest that the creation of these instruments is misguided. Rather, it focuses our attention upon the challenges of accountability and the transaction costs of implementation that arise in such situations, which are more common than not (as is pointed out in the later chapter by Martin and Noble). To minimise transaction cost and accountability failures, coordination regimes have been created, which include resource sharing through joint secretariats as well as information management. This points to the potential for bureaucratic innovation to improve effective implementation, even if architectural redesign is not feasible politically. Given the continuing chorus of criticism of environmental instruments as 'green tape' by the business sector, exploration of ways to reduce complexity and transaction costs whilst not derogating from substantive principles for environment protection would seem to be a fruitful pursuit.

De Cendra's chapter 'The effectiveness of instrument mixes in environmental law: insights from ship-source pollution' reflects the systems nature of implementation, and points explicitly to the behavioural dimension of legal governance. This chapter indicates a sound behavioural principle that the decisions that people take and the effectiveness of their actions are substantially determined by social and institutional contexts. This points to the need for analytic structures that can allow legal scholars and practitioners to better understand and take into account contexts in developing legal strategies. The chapter highlights the potential for an explicitly behaviouralist approach to the design and implementation of legal arrangements.[17] De Cendra analysis in effect considers the performance of a 'cocktail' of regulatory and market arrangements, which together should create a motivational framework of carrots and sticks. He considers how these arrangements in combination make it possible and relatively attractive for the potential wrongdoer to avoid the risks of penalty for unlawful discharges. Since the purposes of environmental governance are behavioural, an explicitly behaviouralist analysis of the role and function of environmental law alongside economic, social and other forms of intervention is appealing. There are signs of a fledgling suite of theories within the legal academic community that can help to 'plug' this jurisprudential gap. Other legal scholars have proposed concepts like 'smart regulation' and 'responsive governance', as well as various new forms of governance.[18] These emphasise different concepts that could together constitute an integrated framework for the design and testing of behavioural interventions, and suggest that the effectiveness of governance arrangements could be improved by harnessing different types of intervention arrayed systematically.[19] Other disciplines suggest the potential to facilitate a move by legal scholars into behavioural systems thinking. An example is from the recent publication *The behaviour change wheel: A new method for characterising and designing behaviour change interventions.*[20] That research draws on a meta-analysis of behaviouralist literatures and suggests the potential for an integrative framework for exploring how behavioural science, economics and legal governance systems might be drawn together in a coherent manner. It also highlights the intrinsically multi-disciplinary investigations that are likely to be needed in the pursuit of more behaviourally effective environmental laws. This is just one

---

17 See Kennedy (2010).

18 Gunningham, Grabosky and Sinclair (1998); Baldwin and Black (2008).

19 Noting that the systemic, multi-intervention approach proposed by such legal scholars does not fit well with the economic theory that a single intervention should be used for a single purpose.

20 Michie, Stralen and West (2011).

illustration that there is a rich crop of behaviouralist insights that could be harvested and applied in the service of more effective environmental laws.[21]

7. A FUTURE WORLD OF NETWORKED GOVERNANCE?

The final four chapters explore the increasing 'hybridity' of natural resource governance. Modern environmental governance involves many actors with different but intersecting roles. These include government organisations, private market certification schemes, traders in environmental services, corporations with internal and value chain environmental management systems, civil society activists, and consumers exercising their choice to 'buy green'. Together they constitute a system that combines economic, social and legal systems with the drivers of the behaviour of citizens and their organisations to change environmental and social outcomes. Non-government organisations like corporations and civil society groups are pivotal to the effectiveness of natural resource governance. The power of the marketplace and the political establishment, as well as social institutions (including religious and cultural organisations), in shaping how resources are conserved and used, surely cannot be discounted. This suggests that for contemporary environmental lawyers to focus heavily upon traditional regulatory arrangements and the functions of government, when so much 'real world' natural resource use and conservation behaviour is driven by private actors and by non-regulatory instruments, may be an unrealistic treatment of the realities of natural resource governance. These chapters highlight the hidden contest between government and private actors (commercial and citizen) over who will govern for the environment, and what instruments and strategies will prevail. They also reinforce the relevance of issues addressed in earlier chapters, including the need to reduce the counterproductive impacts of fragmentation and transaction costs, the importance of issues of capacity (including regulator capacity) and the need to focus upon improving the performance of an institutional system, rather than improving only the performance of a legal instrument.

The chapters by Holley and Lawson, 'Implementing environmental law and collaborative governance', and Paddock and Masterton, 'Private

[21] Garmestani (2014); Martin, Williams and Kennedy (2012); Kennedy (2010); Kennedy and Phromlah (2011).

environmental enforcement: using supply chain requirements to help assure better environmental outcomes', are complementary explorations of the increasingly important role of the private sector in regulation of environmental stewardship. Holley and Lawson point out that there are many situations where reliance upon central (government) action is likely to be sub-optimal because of limits to knowledge and authority, and because of the high transaction costs and barriers to effective supervision. Under such circumstances it is likely that decentralised mechanisms will be required. Environmental management issues such as diffuse source pollution, the management of rural and remote landscapes, or the harvesting of fugitive environmental resources such as fish demonstrate the transaction cost limits to traditional regulation, as well as limits to many types of economic incentives. Under such situations collaborative governance in its many different forms can be an efficient and effective alternative (or complement) to traditional approaches. Holley and Lawson use their empirical investigations to draw conclusions about when, where, and how such arrangements might create more effective public policy outcomes. They also point out opportunities for research to inform governance practice. A consideration they highlight is the behavioural power of self-standards, compared to externally imposed standards, due to psychological factors – this harks back to our earlier discussion of the potential for behavioural science to inform improved effectiveness of legal governance. They indicate that self-standards may motivate improvements that go beyond mere compliance with regulation. Their analysis is, however, also realistic in suggesting the limits to voluntary schemes, in particular the dangers of a lack of external supervision and accountability for the performance of industry self-standards. This is consistent with our observation that innovative approaches to natural resource governance, no matter what their form, are likely to require sound integrity mechanisms. A traditional function of government is to ensure that the instruments which are ratified for use are credible, by providing effective supervision and transparent reporting. The tradition of government oversight of private stock markets points to the potential for 'self-regulation' to be distinguished from 'non-regulation' through the use of government mandates, independent oversight and strongly enforced conditions to ensure integrity. The authors give examples of where governance collaboration is backed by government integrity mechanisms.

Paddock and Masterton identify that modern industry often involves complex multilevel international supply chains largely beyond the reach of national environmental laws. They highlight that private regulation and enforcement of private rules within supply chains are for this reason increasingly important mechanisms of governance. Martin and Noble, in

'Hybrid governance and "wicked" natural resource risks', independently consider similar issues but with a different orientation. Both chapters highlight the diverse drivers for private or self-regulation, and suggest that these often reflect far more pragmatic and more powerful drivers than 'mere' ethical concerns. Paddock and Masterton draw particular attention to the value of corporate reputation and risks to the social licence of the firm. Martin and Noble expand these drivers to include other economic and risk variables, and highlight how these diverse motivations tie into various aspects of corporate strategy and affect different functions and roles within a modern corporation. Paddock and Masterton provide a taxonomy of 'green' supply chain initiatives including certification and audit mechanisms, supply chain contracts, transparency mechanisms and closed loop approaches which strengthen disclosure. They also point to the role of information mechanisms such as life-cycle analysis as being increasingly important within the 'self-regulatory' arrangements of sophisticated industrial systems. Within this collaborative governance perspective on industry value chains the roles of government include facilitation, coordination, information dissemination and the use of purchasing power as an incentive for more effective self-governance. They point to the potential for a deeper relationship between government and industry, based upon a strategic response to the overall potential of industry supply chain stewardship structures, rather than the current largely *ad hoc* and tactical response to individual schemes.

This perspective echoes the arguments by Martin and Noble, who consider what is required to govern the increasingly vicious problem of complex trans-national risk. Based upon the history of environmental law, they explain that contemporary challenges are very different from the types of issue that were the focus of attention in the 1970s when an explosion in environmental law instruments was triggered. Contemporary (and future) legal governance will not only have to deal with the conventional type of issue where cause and effect are observable, and where governments have the jurisdictional rights and the institutional capacity to intervene effectively. It will also have to cope with complex system issues, notably new types of risk, where cause and effect transcend nation state jurisdictions and where the agencies of government are not likely to have sufficient technical knowledge (let alone authority and resources) to respond effectively. They point out that risk management concerns are not limited to risks from and to the environment. Public policy is also a high-risk venture, with failures in the form of non-adoption, ineffective design or execution or undesirable spillovers being frequent. There is a shared interest between government, industry and civil society to create policy solutions that are reliable politically, operationally and in terms of the fair distribution of costs and benefits. Martin and Noble propose an innovative partnership to integrate the capacity of the public and the private sector to respond to environmental (and social) risks. Crafting new governance relationships and making them work requires detailed investigation and careful negotiation, but could lead to more effective regimes. However, it is also possible that collaborations could result in weakened governance. Strategic hybridity and the supervision of the operation of innovative hybrids to ensure that they are effective is a scholarly topic that justifies more careful investigation.

The final chapter by Pink and Bartel, 'Regulators networks: collaborative agency approaches to the implementation and enforcement of environmental law', highlights a different aspect of collaborative governance: the potential of networks of regulators as a response to the need to accelerate learning to cope with regulatory complexity and coordination problems. As highlighted in previous chapters, contemporary natural resource regulation issues can be far more complex than those traditionally considered. The instruments and the implementation requirements are often diverse, and the resources available will generally not increase to reflect the increasing difficulty of regulation. Pink and Bartel highlight that traditional 'silos' of expertise may not cope effectively with the new types of natural resources governance challenges, particularly if the teams are small, isolated and under-resourced. As was also indicated by Martin and Noble, one way of responding is to pool knowledge and resources.

Pink and Bartel highlight that even within the regulatory sector, strategic alliances to tackle common interest problems are being used increasingly to improve the effectiveness of natural resource governance. They point to the need for governance systems to develop knowledge and other capabilities far more rapidly than they have typically had to in the past, so that they can cope with the accelerating changes in the legal, political and other context within which they must work. Their chapter provides information on different forms of hybrid structure and the variety of alternative strategies and network operations that are possible. The ideas they develop are rooted in a behavioural awareness of the effects of human and organisational capacity upon the performance of systems of governance. This links back to earlier observations about the desirability of developing a better structured and more comprehensive approach to understanding what capabilities of what people and organisations are needed to ensure effectiveness, and the development of more comprehensive institutional approaches to embed required capacity at the same time as creating new legal instruments.

8. SYNTHESIS AND POTENTIAL SCHOLARLY DIRECTIONS

Of course, it is not possible in this overview to do justice to the richness of the work of the authors whose chapters are featured. We have attempted to show that these diverse perspectives are all linked into a single topic: the scholarship that is needed to improve the applied effectiveness of legal arrangements for environmental governance. If indeed, as Hugo De Zela stated so clearly, implementation of legal instruments is the greatest governance challenge of this century,[22] then it justifies a concentrated and significant scholarly endeavour. It has been the purpose of this book to try to bring implementation issues to the forefront and to identify some of the dimensions of the jurisprudence that will be required to contribute to this worthy aim.

The chapters in this book demonstrate that a jurisprudence of environmental law implementation will be very different from the jurisprudence of legal philosophy, or of legal instruments. It will necessarily focus upon legal issues within the context of broader systems, and the contexts, that shape the outcomes of environment law interventions. It will also need to consider ways of combining different types of legal, economic, social and behavioural interventions into more effective 'cocktails', and paying attention to demonstrable results in terms of environmental protection, social justice, and economic efficiency.

The authors represented in this book have considered examples from many different countries and have focused upon a variety of environmental and governance issues. Their analyses suggest that there are many different ways to improve the effectiveness of legal arrangements to govern the environment. They have also pointed to the need to draw from a number of other disciplines, but to integrate these diverse methods into approaches that are well-designed to meet the needs of environmental law scholarship.

There are other dimensions to the implementation task that we have not considered, simply because of limits to space. Many of these are touched upon in environmental law publications, but they have not

---

[22] Organization of American States (2014).

generally been brought together as aspects of a coordinated jurisprudential field. Some of these include issues of judicial and legal culture and capacity; natural resource conflicts; indigenous peoples perspectives and governance frameworks; the effects of constitutional frameworks; and many others.

Environmental law is a form of behavioural management where society pursues continuous improvement. However, environmental law scholars do not draw upon a widely shared theory about what works and what does not, and do not have the types of institutional processes of peer review and joint theorising that are fundamental to scientific improvement. Faced with an array of issues, opportunities and epistemological choices there is a risk that investigations into effectiveness will become diffused and lose their focus and effectiveness. Indeed, we suggest that this is the current state of these enquiries within the environmental law academic community. We argue that it is essential: if the environmental law community is to rise to the challenge of improving the tangible effectiveness of legal arrangements for natural resource governance, then it will need a co-ordinated and powerful approach to investigating these diverse issues.

In many ways the timing could not be better for the creation of a distinct specialist jurisprudence of implementation of environmental law. A number of the most important international agencies have identified that it is essential that this challenge be met. The next challenge is to exploit this unique moment in time to create a concentrated and disciplined program of collegial investigation.

Finally, the editors wish to thank the Secretariat, the Research Committee and the Governing Board of the IUCN Academy of Environmental Law whose willingness to host a workshop on implementation of environmental law made it possible to advance this book far more efficiently than otherwise would have been possible. We would also like to thank Amy Cosby and Matthew Ryan, our editorial assistants. Finally, the editors would like to thank the New Zealand Law Foundation for their generous grant funding in support of the 2013 IUCN Academy of Environmental Law Colloquium held in Waikato. That support also contributed materially to the development of this book.

REFERENCES

Ashley D. and D. Orenstein (2005), *Sociological Theory: Classical Statements* (6th edn, London: Pearson Education).

Baber, W. and R. Bartlett (2009), *Global Democracy and Sustainable jurisprudence: Deliberative Environmental Law* (Cambridge, MA: MIT Press).

Baldwin, R. and J. Black (2008), 'Really Responsive Regulation' 71(1) *Modern Law Review* 59–94.

Burdon, P. (ed.) (2012), *Exploring Wild Law: The Philosophy of Earth Jurisprudence* (Adelaide: Wakefield Press).

Garmestani, A. *et al.* (2014), 'The Integration of Social-Ecological Resilience and Law in Garmestani, A. and C. Allen (eds) (2014) *Social-Ecological Resilience and Law* (New York: Columbia University Press).

Gunningham, N., P. Grabosky and D. Sinclair (1998), *Smart Regulation: Designing Environmental Policy* (Oxford: Clarendon Press).

Hartley, N. and C. Wood (2005), 'Public Participation in Environmental Impact Assessment – Implementing the Aarhus Convention' 25(4) *Environmental Impact Assessment Review* 319–40.

Kennedy, A. (2010), 'Using Community-Based Social Marketing Techniques to Enhance Environmental Regulation' 2(4) *Sustainability* 1138–60.

Kennedy, A. and W. Phromlah (2011), 'Behavioural Strategies to Support Climate Change Resilience' 10 *Environmental Taxation and Climate Change: Achieving Environmental Sustainability through Fiscal Policy* 79.

Kravchenko, S. (2007), 'The Aarhus Convention and Innovations in Compliance with Multilateral Environmental Agreements' 18 *Colorado Journal of International Environmental Law and Policy* 1.

Kuper, A. and J. Kuper (1996), *The Social Science Encyclopedia* (Abingdon: Taylor & Francis).

Lazarus, R. (1996), *The Making of Environmental Law* (Chicago: University of Chicago Press).

Lee, M. and C. Abbot (2003), 'The Usual Suspects? Public Participation under the Aarhus Convention' 66(1) *Modern Law Review* 80–108.

Loasby, B. (2002), *Knowledge, Institutions and Evolution in Economics* (Abingdon: Psychology Press).

Luhmann, N. (1995), *Social Systems* (Redwood City, CA: Stanford University Press).

Martin, P., J. Williams and A. Kennedy (2012), 'Creating Next Generation Rural Landscape Governance: The Challenge for Environmental Law Scholarship' in P. Martin *et al.* (eds) *Environmental Governance and Sustainability* (Cheltenham, UK and Northampton, MA, USA: Edward Elgar) 46–80.

Martin, P. *et al.*(forthcoming, 2015), *Developing a Structure for a Legal Component for the IUCN Natural Resource Governance Framework* (IUCN Environmental Law Centre and the World Commission on Environmental Law forming part of an IUCN ELC legal governance evaluation report).

Michie, S., M. van Stralen and R. West (2011), 'The Behaviour Change Wheel: A New Method for Characterising and Designing Behaviour Change Interventions' 6(1) *Implementation Science* 42.

Nobelprize.org, 'Linus Pauling – Facts' (*Nobel Media AB*, 2014) accessed 28 March 2015 at http://www.nobelprize.org/nobel_prizes/chemistry/laureates/1954/pauling-facts.html.

Organization of American States (2014), Press Release: OAS and UNEP Sign Agreement on Environmental Rule of Law and Sustainable Development (Organization of American States, 19 November) accessed 28 March 2015 at http://www.oas.org/en/media_center/press_release.asp?sCodigo=E-506/14.

Pūraitė, A. (2012), 'Origins of Environmental Regulation' 19(2) *Jurisprudence* 657–74.
Riddell, A. (2014), *Human Rights and the Environment* (Abingdon: Routledge Handbook of Environment and Society in Asia).
Schaller, R. (1997), 'Moore's Law: Past, Present and Future' 34(6) *Spectrum*, IEEE 52–9.
Schultz, D. and S. Schultz (2011), *A History of Modern Psychology* (Independence, KY: Cengage Learning).
Solomon, R. and K. Higgins (1996), *A Short History of Philosophy* (Oxford: Oxford University Press).
Tarlock, A.D. (2010), 'Environmental Law: Then and Now' 32 *Washington University Journal of Law and Policy* 1.
Tarlock, A.D. (2003), 'Is There a There in Environmental Law?' 19 *Journal of Land Use and Environmental Law* 213.
Teece, D. (1986), 'Profiting from Technological Innovation: Implications for Integration, Collaboration, Licensing and Public Policy' 15(6) *Research Policy* 285–305.
Toth, B. (2010), 'Public Participation and Democracy in Practice – Aarhus Convention Principles as Democratic Institution Building in the Developing World' 30 J. Land Resources & Envtl. L. 295.
United Nations Environment Program, Environmental Governance (2009), accessed 28 March 2015 at http://www.unep.org/pdf/brochures/EnvironmentalGovernance.pdf.
Westbrook, D. (1993), 'A Liberal Environmental Jurisprudence' 27 *UC Davis Law Review* 619.
Winter, G. (1989), 'Perspectives for Environmental Law – Entering the Fourth Phase' 1 *Journal of Environmental Law* 38.

1. Accelerating the evolution of environmental law through continuous learning from applied experience

Paul Martin and Donna Craig

Objective understanding of whether a legal instrument is effective involves consideration of the purposes of the instrument and its real-world effects. This is at least partly an empirical enquiry, similar to policy evaluation. It requires factual evidence of outcomes and data to underpin hypotheses about the causes of outcomes. These empirical enquiries must go beyond instrument design and the actions of legal agencies. Practical outcomes will often reflect context issues like social and cultural receptivity to legal arrangements, politics, economic capacity and impacts, and the dynamics of socio-ecological systems. As well, the resources invested to support a legal instrument, and the implementation strategy, are often determinants of success.

The question that this raises is whether our legal scholarship is suited to addressing implementation questions beyond doctrinal, procedural and philosophic/jurisprudential concerns. If legal scholarship is indeed concerned with improving the effectiveness of the environmental law system, this suggests the need for methodologies and knowledge that can illuminate the empirical questions: what works, when, and why?

In this chapter we consider arguments for and against a more empirical environmental law scholarship. We discuss a scholarship that grafts onto our discipline's concern for improving legal instruments (such as statutes, judgments) and values (rights, responsibilities and justice), a focus on the efficiency and effectiveness of the environmental governance system, and the role of empirical analysis as a basis for cumulative learning. We also consider the use and limits of the scientific method for driving improvement in the effectiveness of environmental law.

Implicit in a scholarly discipline is a shared theory of knowledge and methods (epistemology, methodology), and a collective effort to systematically improve these. Commentators on law's approach to advancing knowledge have suggested that particularly environmental law scholarship could be improved through an empirical scientific mode of investigation, with explicit theories as the basis for hypotheses testing on the basis solely of objective data, peer critique of methods and conclusions, and the minimisation of subjectivity in content matter. Others suggest that the exclusion of non-objective concerns will distort legal enquiry, given legal concerns like 'justice', 'fairness', 'weight of evidence', and 'motive'.[1] They point to the fact that many of the law's essential concerns (and many of its effects) are immeasurable. We suggest that a science/doctrine polarity is not constructive in practice.

We suggest that a constructive methodological path is to recognise that research on the effectiveness of environmental law is a strategic investigation rather than either a philosophic or a scientific one. The purpose is real-world improvements, and the variables in the state of the world include objective facts, subjective beliefs and dynamic systems that are changing even as they are investigated. The goals of the law are also heterogenous and dynamic. As a result, proposed real-world reforms must rely upon a mixture of deduction (conclusions following directly from analysis of data) and induction (conclusions informed by judgement), and they must anticipate a future that cannot be objectively deduced. Such analyses involve both objective and subjective elements, and the methods are plural and pragmatic. We suggest an integrative method that can help legal scholars tackle effectiveness, that does respect the objectivity dimensions of empirical scientific research but is not so narrow as to exclude the essential subjective aspects of the law.

1. METHODS AND PURPOSE(S) OF ENVIRONMENTAL LAW SCHOLARSHIP

Environmental law scholarship serves mixed purposes. It facilitates teaching; provides a context for teachers to advance their knowledge; and generates knowledge to improve environmental law outcomes, which are largely behavioural. Legal instruments and institutions are an important aspect of these investigations, but behaviour responds to many factors.

1 Hesselink (2009).

This suggests the need for an accepted theory of behaviour change within the discipline to underpin our investigations. This theory is lacking.[2]

Our scholarly enquiry should build understanding of behavioural outcomes from environmental law, taking account of other interventions (for example, economic and social interventions). Research should explore causal relationships and alternative legal, and other, strategies, taking account of the impacts of different contexts. A governance instrument that works in a wealthy jurisdiction with a strong rule of law is less likely to be effective in a jurisdiction struggling with poverty and weak governance.[3] An approach that works in an urban area may be inefficient in an area of sparse settlement. Beyond the legal instruments and institutions effectiveness might depend upon:

- the commitment and capacity of the implementation organisations;
- political and community support or opposition;
- synergies or conflicts between legal and other forms of intervention;
- context factors, including economic drivers, community attitude, the behaviour of the powerful and biophysical dynamics.

The weakest link in the chain of implementation will determine the effectiveness of that chain. Failure in any aspect can derail implementation. Many of these issues are not the subject of conventional legal research.[4] Some fall within the view of management or political scientists, economists, biophysical scientists, and behavioural experts. Thus any scholarly approach to improving environmental law implementation must involve insights from other disciplines, different types of research questions, and different methodologies to those of traditional legal scholarship.

---

2 An important behavioural dimension of our work is that the effectiveness of environmental law is less concerned with the control of aberrant individuals than with changing the norms of the larger population. For this reason, theories about law and behaviour that have developed through the study of crime are not likely to be of great value for our discipline.

3 Stavins (2001).

4 For an example of this expanded perspective see Lim (2012). See also Harding, Hendriks and Faruqi (2009); Hunter, Salzman and Zaelke (2011).

2. 'FOOD FOR THOUGHT' ON ENVIRONMENTAL LAW SCHOLARSHIP

Various authors, discussed later in this chapter, have raised significant questions about our methodologies and scholarly approaches. Most argue either for or against a scientific empiricist epistemology. An alternative is an epistemology that is neither purely discursive (doctrinal/ philosophical and inductive) nor scientific (empiricist and deductive). Rather a strategic epistemology that blends both forms of investigation and synthesis, focused upon finding pragmatic solutions for real world human behaviour challenges is needed. This goes beyond the mere pragmatism proposed for multi-method policy research,[5] and adopts the analytic structure of corporate and military intelligence gathering and decision-making. In this strategic epistemology, matters of values and belief (axiology) inform choices of direction, inductive choices are made about likely futures, scientific deductions are used to better understand central facts, and pragmatic choices are made about resources and plans. To frame our argument for such an approach, we begin by examining critical views about environmental law epistemology and methodology.

Professor Faure, at the 2009 IUCN Academy of Environmental Law Colloquium in Wuhan, considered empirical studies of implementation of environmental governance.[6] He proposed that the environmental law academy should embrace a serious concern for the effectiveness of legal instruments in our approach to research, through a more empirical and multi-disciplinary approach. He distilled themes about success/failure and instrument and technology design, based on the available empirical data.[7] He considered liability rules, regulation, command and control versus market instruments, taxation, emissions trading, and combinations.[8] In addition, he considered the significance of enforcement and implementation and suggested some principles about the use of empirical data:

> It is indeed crucial for any policy instrument, be it command and control or market-based, that the policy maker has clear ideas on the effects of the instruments chosen in practice. This requires *ex ante* consideration of the available empirical research since the choice of a particular instrument is often based on assumptions about its effects that may be merely theoretical.

5 Majchrzak (1984) 111.
6 Faure (2012).
7 Ibid.
8 Ibid.

> Good legal policy also requires serious *ex post* evaluation studies to examine whether a particular instrument or policy was indeed able to achieve the goals expected by the legislator.[9]

His ideas resonate with a critique of environmental law by Fisher, Lange, Scotford and Carlane in their paper 'Maturity and Methodology: Starting a Debate about Environmental Law Scholarship'.[10] This paper makes the 'very simple argument that environmental law scholarship can only come of age when scholars face the methodological challenges of environmental law research head on. This is because a lack of explicit and widespread discussion about methodology in environmental law scholarship has hampered the academic development of the subject and threatened the worth of environmental law as an intellectual discipline.'[11] They suggest that environmental law suffers from incoherence due to the relative newness of the field and the complexity of the issues (including the necessity of spanning disciplines) and assert that it has been difficult for the discipline to develop scholarly standards.

Whilst the criticisms themselves are empirically unsupported, the authors pose significant questions about methods and standards, and law's capacity to systematically improve the effectiveness of environmental governance. They describe four challenges: the speed and scale of change; the interdisciplinary nature of research and practice; the diversity of governance; and the multi-jurisdictional nature of environmental law.[12] These help to explain, but they certainly do not justify, research practices that lack scholarly integrity and which limit real advancement. The paper indicates the need for the discipline to reflect upon its research questions, methods, and institutional structures and for explicit debates about quality in environment law scholarship.

A study by McGrath, 'Does Environmental Law Work? How to Evaluate the Effectiveness of an Environmental Legal System,'[13] explores links between environmental law and environmental outcomes. In a scientifically ideal world this analysis would begin with a well-developed theory of causality accepted within the discipline. That theory would take into account the variables of instrument design, implementation institutions, context, resources and implementation strategy to allow prediction of outcomes. On that basis it would be possible to test the validity of

---

9 Ibid, 6.
10 Fisher *et al.* (2009).
11 Ibid, 214.
12 Ibid.
13 McGrath (2010).

the predictions and thus to refine theory and practice. In the absence of such a substantiated theory and methods for interpreting real-world outcomes, the author uses ambitious inference to pose a theory as a starting point. The history of economics and psychology (for example) indicates the necessity for such a starting step to facilitate the shift from broad assumptions to a validated theory of behaviour.

Using an approach drawn from natural resource policy, the study evaluates environmental law by reference to biophysical outcomes, using the 'pressure, state, response' logic. This brings into focus many difficulties in adopting an outcomes focused view of environmental law. One is articulating the relationships between the law, specific legal and administrative actions and the (third party evaluated) pressures, ecological conditions and biophysical system responses. Other variables, such as political contexts, social system dynamics, resourcing constraints and economics, were not analysed (reflecting the conventional treatment under this method of reporting). Whilst simplification is arguably essential for this type of policy analysis, the narrowing of causal considerations points to methodological challenges in theorising about complex environmental law issues.

McGrath discusses alternative approaches for evaluating the effectiveness of an environmental legal system.[14] The approaches vary in their objectives, terminology, and methods. Whilst all have intuitive validity none have been verified in a systematic way. He observes, consistent with other authors, 'that the majority of legal writing regarding environmental legal systems is descriptive, explanatory and interpretative rather than evaluative'[15] and provides illustrations supporting this point. On this basis he opts for his method. This analysis must ultimately come up against the problems of complex causality, context, and resourcing that will defeat pure scientific objectivity in any environmental law evaluation. Regardless of these limitations, it provides a pioneering contribution to understanding outcome causality in environmental law.

Environment law specific critiques of legal epistemology sit alongside broader critiques of the scientific integrity of legal scholarship.[16]

---

14 Ibid.

15 Ibid 13.

16 In relation to regulation as a particular form of environmental law, reference might be had to Driessen (2003). This study particularly highlights agency capture issues and the over-reliance on economic rationale in regulation as part of a general withdrawal from 'tough minded' environmental law under the influence of industry. Sparrow (2000) also takes a regulatory design and implementation perspective and evaluates in depth a number of concepts and

Herring[17] argues that a scientific approach to law, using specified questions, hypotheses, methods and testing based upon empirical data, is honoured in the breach. He provides a nuanced analysis of the potential overlaps and conflicts between legal doctrinal and theoretical research and the potential for legal research using the scientific method:

> The doctrinal scholar does not simply discover an aspect of the natural world. This scholar observes, organizes, and analyzes the law, and through this process, even if it is purportedly only descriptive in nature, participates in the human effort to construct the law and a particular society. She is not engaged only in the incremental discovery of what is. Rather, she is engaged in the incremental analysis of what is, and often the construction of what ought to be. By observing, explaining, analyzing and critiquing legal doctrine, the doctrinal scholar often attempts to channel, if not direct, the development of the law. The doctrinal scholar's participation in the process of constructing what is being studied (the law) differs markedly from the scientific scholar's process of discovery. Consequently, the legal scholar dedicated to the scientific method engages in scholarly projects that differ in nature from those of the doctrinal scholar.[18]

This reinforces our view (and that of other critics) that practical outcomes are distinct research matters, not subsets of doctrine or legal theory. A functionally complete scholarship must merge legal enquiry based upon discourse with enquiry based upon scientific empiricism. This synthesis of objectivity, subjectivity and a concern for pragmatic discussions mirrors key aspects of strategic decision-making.

Posner's discussion of the evolving nature of legal scholarship suggests the need for change in scholarly enquiry within the legal discipline.[19] He suggests a lack of self-reflection and self-criticism, highlighting causes such as the explosion of the amount of law, a decline in faith in the law and its autonomy, and the rising prestige of science as a basis for knowledge.[20] He concludes that a 'purely verbal, purely lawyer's scholarship, in which the categories of analysis are the same as, or very close to, those used by the judges or legislators whose work is being analyzed – a scholarship moreover in which political consensus is assumed and the

---

examples of regulation. He highlights issues such as agency capture and the increasing dominance of industry/economic rationales in the design and implementation of environmental and other regulation.

17 Herring (2006).

18 Ibid.

19 Posner (1987).

20 Ibid.

insights of other disciplines ignored does not fit comfortably into today's scholarly Zeitgeist.'[21]

Posner proposes to embrace new styles of interdisciplinary legal thought. The trajectory he maps indicates increasingly ambitious attempts to distill testable hypotheses from fragmented rules and judgments. Applying this to environmental law scholarship the challenge is in overcoming the 'noise' of everyday developments to identify underlying abstract concepts that can be identified (retrospectively) as the basis for objective hypotheses.[22]

Ulen sees a movement towards scientific empiricism within the legal discipline.[23] He argues that there are aspects of legal scholarship which are clearly 'scientific' but that there are material differences, notably, the absence of 'widespread and commonly accepted theoretical core or paradigm and accepted standards and methods of empirical or experimental verification'.[24]

Within (applied) policy studies, it is known that methods must cope with the multi-dimensional and dynamic nature of the variables, 'chaotic' politics, the pervasive effects of values and perception and the gap between theoretical and applied effectiveness.[25] Rittel and Webber characterised many environmental issues as 'wicked problems' having no definitive, optimal or objective answers.[26] Problem framing[27] to distill a clear specification of the desired goals is said to be critical to policy methods, but in environmental law goal clarity is problematic. The political process of law making can involve 'bundling' different and sometimes competing goals, to create compromised solutions. Apparently specific terms (such as 'precautionary principle', 'consultation', or 'intergenerational equity') mask many competing objectives. To decide *post hoc* that a particular version of plural goals is 'true' is a distortion that is common, and perhaps essential, to policy research in the same way that grand assumptions about behaviour and structure are essential to economic policy research. Methodology problems are not likely to be effectively solved by assuming away the messy realities, merely to create

21 Ibid, 773.

22 Interestingly, a thought process that mirrors thought processes of 'strategising', as described by Ohmae (1982).

23 Ulen (2002).

24 Ibid, 893.

25 Majchrzak (1984).

26 Rittel and Webber (1973).

27 Dovers (2005) 60.

the pretence of tractable 'scientific' research questions that fit available methodologies.

3. THE CHALLENGE OF EMBEDDED AXIOLOGY

Environmental law scholarship is more than functional and is not values-free. It advances social values that may (or may not) be held by the majority of a community. The scholarship of environmental law is often concerned with converting philosophical aspirations into tangible social arrangements. It often takes a stance upon issues of justice that is counter to the views of power holders. Axiology[28] is central to a discipline that is concerned with implementing norms and values. This mitigates against positivist methods which aim to strip out subjectivity. Lawyers' suspicion of empirical methods may reflect a visceral concern for the erosion of a philosophy of knowledge that has a real concern for justice.

Many sustainability principles reinforce the importance of values as the basis of environmental law rights and obligations:[29]

(1) inter-generational and intra-generational equity;
(2) the right to environmental quality;
(3) the obligation not to cause environmental harm;
(4) the precautionary principle;
(5) the common heritage of human kind;
(6) the polluter and user pays principles;
(7) obligation to prevent pollution;
(8) the right of public participation and access to information;
(9) environmental impact assessment of projects and proposals likely to have significant environmental impacts.

Some of these (viz. (2), (4), (6), (8) and (9)) have legal expression in conventions, standards, national laws and environmental indicators. Others are advancing towards law. Legal pluralism, law and anthropology and customary law scholarship are important in developing a richer understanding of law as a normative system, with a potentially interesting intersection between empirical and philosophical research.

Whilst acknowledging that a positivist empirical model will not properly accommodate the transformative role of environmental law, even

---

28 The scholarship of ethics and values.
29 Harding *et al.* (2009) 31–7.

in this aspect of our scholarship scientific objectivity could advance transformative aims. Environmental law scholars often seek to develop social justice through instruments such as Agenda 21, the Rio Principles and the Millennium Development Goals.[30] This type of environmental law advocacy relies on assumptions that legal instruments, such as the principles in the Aarhus Convention, will improve participation and thereby sustainability outcomes. Whilst observation suggests that in many situations these approaches have been useful, observation also suggests that often the transfer of real power has not occurred. It is an empirical question whether, when and how real empowerment occurs. Reed rightly suggests that there is inadequate research on the relationship between participation by stakeholders, social learning and behavioural change.[31]

4. CAN (AND SHOULD) OUR SCHOLARLY APPROACH BECOME MORE 'SCIENTIFIC'?

Standing apart from arcane debates about the scientific method, an appropriate definition of the essence of the scientific method for the purposes of legal scholarship is provided by an eminent legal institution:

> The United States Supreme Court has laid out a four-step inquiry regarding whether testimony should be accepted as 'science.' In *Daubert v. Merrell Dow Pharmaceuticals, Inc.*, the Court established these four steps:
>
> - The theoretical underpinnings of the methods must yield testable predictions by means of which the theory could be falsified.
> - The methods should preferably be published in a peer-reviewed scholarly journal.
> - There should be a known rate of error that can be used in evaluating the results of the assertions.
> - The methods should be generally accepted within the relevant scientific community.[32]

Finding a basis for a shared theorising and empirical testing in our field is not easy. Environmental law scholarship copes with diverse issues (such as various aspects of water, air, pollution, mining), heterogeneous legal systems within different jurisdictions and different legal instruments and governance structures. Implementation occurs in varied ecological,

---

30 United Nations Department of Economic and Social Affairs Division for Sustainable Development (2012).

31 Reed (2008).

32 Ibid, 881.

political, economic and social contexts. These characteristics push our scholarship towards being descriptive rather than analytic.[33] This results in a lack of explicit research questions, limited descriptions of causal hypotheses, and a failure to test outcomes against specific predictions. Our academic discourse uses argumentation focused around values, instruments and to a lesser degree institutional arrangements, rather than hypothesis based empiricism. This reflects the absence of a common ground for more universal research questions, theory, and comparative data and methods.

Disciplines tend to evolve towards increasing specialisation and heterogeneity. During the Enlightenment, fields of science that now have distinct questions and methodologies were unified. Over time astronomy, physics and chemistry evolved into specialisations, and thence into distinct sub-fields. Early biology (like much environmental law research today) was descriptive (viz. Linneaus), then observational of empirical facts (viz. Darwin) before branching out into experimental methods. Disciplinary boundaries also tend to blur as ideas from one field lead to discoveries in another and thence into integrated methods. The iconic demonstration is the Nobel Prize winning work of Linus Pauling that integrated physics and chemistry to identify radical insights into the biology of plants and thence the foundations of molecular biology.

Such evolutions within disciplines have a strong social impact, as Kuhn documented with his work on scientific revolutions.[34] As suggested by a commentator from another discipline (geography):

> Learned societies are under substantial pressure to find new structural solutions in promoting the continuing development of their respective disciplines. The mission hasn't changed. Scholarly associations are still charged with guiding, from a discipline's perspective, the process of problem articulation, theory generation, data handling, and knowledge content organization. But as each society pursues its role of disciplinary core and boundary definition, in an age of interdisciplinary thought and communication, it runs the risk of becoming overly defensive in warding off the perceived encroachment of other disciplines.[35]

Environmental law scholarship is evolving into plural forms, pursuing distinct questions using different forms of enquiry. The term 'environmental law' is a 'category of concealed multiple reference' as defined by

---

[33] Posner (1987) 761–80; Fisher *et al.* (2009) 213–50.
[34] Kuhn (1996).
[35] Cohen (1988).

Stone: a single term embracing many distinct meanings.[36] Figure 1.1 highlights the interaction between traditional (discursive) methods and more recent (more empirical) concerns.

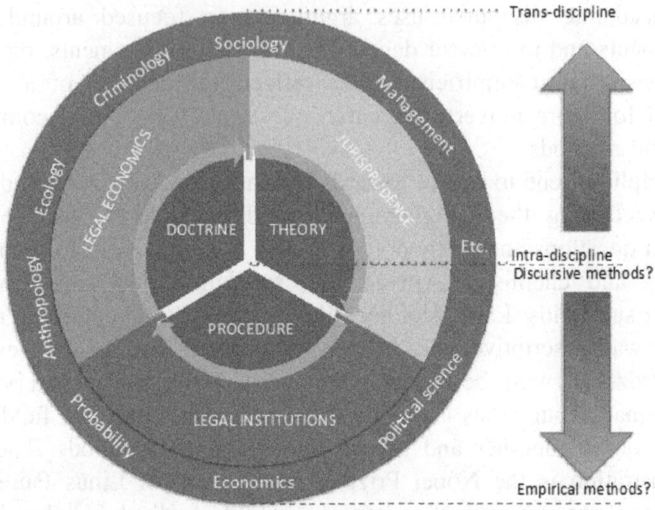

Figure 1.1 The diverse methods of environmental law research

At the heart of legal scholarship is doctrine and theory, but procedural tactics and legal outcomes are intertwined. Often the outcomes of law reflect the procedural skills of the lawyer more than doctrine. The methods used to explore these central themes are the mainstream of legal scholarship.

'Surrounding' these intra-disciplinary issues are areas that cannot be fully characterised as purely doctrinal or empirical. Three stand out: jurisprudence, legal institutional studies and legal economics. The methods are often discursive and abstract, but can be informed by empirical considerations (for example the use of models as economic argumentation).[37] Jurisprudence tends towards methods akin to legal discourse but informed by philosophic concepts that may be capable of general application. The outer circle in Figure 1.1 represents where legal culture and methods are most likely to intersect with many other

[36] Stone (1964), particularly Ch. 7.

[37] There is sometimes a misleading assumption that models are empirical rather than a specialised form of discourse. Models are merely mental constructs of a more complex reality, which may or may not reliably reflect that reality.

disciplines. Environmental law scholars often engage with these diverse fields, depending upon the applied issues with which they are concerned.

This poses many challenges for legal scholarship. To illustrate: Sparrow notes, in relation to regulation, that:

> The topic of regulatory reform touches an alarming number of established academic disciplines. To deal with the subject in a comprehensive way would demand mastery of criminal justice, compliance psychology, public regulation, public administration, public management, organizational theory, political science, institutional analysis, program evaluation, economic, crime prevention, sociology, criminology, regulatory law, and the emerging risk sciences. To speak with any authority, perhaps academic commentators should also be required to know the particular sciences relevant to each regulatory field: biology, chemistry, and physics (for environmental protection); industrial engineering and industrial hygiene (for occupational safety and health); toxicology, radiology, and medicine (for public health).[38]

The journey from the centre to the outer circle involves a shift from discourse towards empiricism. Many advances are likely to span theories and methodologies. For the scholar, it suggests the need for many skills, knowledge, methodologies and research projects. Given the limits to an individual's capacity, this pushes our research away from legal traditions of individual enquiry towards multi-disciplinary teams. This is a methodological, managerial and sometimes personal challenge.

We do not wish to trivialise the dangers of going down a methodologically plural pathway. Law is a discipline where values are pivotal. Many issues cannot be dissected into simple questions or clearly enunciated hypotheses amenable to empirical tests. Many of the key questions are multi-faceted. Simplifying the issues to fit an empirical methodology is not likely to represent a significant advance. Karl Popper suggests that:

> Long-term prophecies can be derived from scientific conditional predictions only if they apply to systems which can be described as well-isolated, stationary, and recurrent. These conditions are very rare in nature, and modern society is surely not one of them.[39]

Rarely are socio ecological-legal systems neither messy nor bordering on chaotic, and environmental governance issues present 'vicious' analytical challenges. The risk of elevating methodological purity over practical utility in coping with complexity ought not to be dismissed. We need a new approach that combines the strengths of traditional jurisprudence

---

38 Sparrow (2000) XVII.

39 Popper (2002) 457.

with the strengths of traditional science. It should not be a case of adopting one in preference to the other, but a matter of finding an integrative approach that suits the realities of environmental law and its social purpose.

5. GENERATING AN EPISTEMOLOGY OF IMPLEMENTATION

Scientific method is a disciplined foundation for systematic improvement across many fields. Originally concerned with learning about physical phenomena (that is, the physical sciences) these fundamentals have also proven to be useful in metaphysical enquiry concerned with human behaviour and abstract notions such as values (that is, the social sciences).

Enlightenment ideas reflected the research questions of the time. The focus of attention was upon discoveries in the physical world. The fundamental endeavour was to dethrone subjective, religious belief as 'science' – to de-legitimise axiological enquiry. This was achieved through an epistemology that prioritised proof based upon empirical assessment of physical phenomena. Empiricism became entrenched as (indeed synonymous with) the scientific method. As demands for reliable knowledge expanded from physical phenomena to metaphysical concerns, the 'social sciences' emerged. Whilst some social sciences embraced the methodological positivism of the physical sciences, practical concerns and philosophical movements suggested limits to the universality of the positivist mode.

Post-positivism attempted to deal with the constraints of methodological positivism, notably its inability to cope well with subjectivity. Post-positivist methods brought a greater awareness of subjectivity and context, a new language for discussing research and knowledge and the recognition of qualitative methods as scientifically legitimate. This trend towards research of non-measurable phenomena as legitimate data from which valid theory can develop, has led to the development of 'pragmatic' research approaches. These largely reject the ontological purity expectations of earlier methodologies, accepting that both qualitative and quantitative methods can yield valid knowledge. An aspect of these developments is that the values of the researcher and the research subjects can be legitimate aspects of research, re-legitimising 'axiology' alongside methodology in some (but not all) disciplines. However, the re-legitimising of subjectivity is far from completely accepted in science, nor is the role of beliefs and subjective conclusions the same as it was prior to the enlightenment. Subjectivity remains suspect as a basis for disciplined enquiry, for very good reasons.

Environmental law has also evolved. Much of the pioneering environmental law scholarship emerged in the 1960s, where the focus was upon creating doctrine and establishing practice. The concern of legal scholarship was upon the inner circle of doctrine, theory and procedure. In this context it was hard to see how methodological positivism could be truly relevant to environmental law.

Gradually, the middle circle of jurisprudence, legal economics and institutional research evolved towards critical reflection. We can trace an increasingly plural conception and a recognition of the legitimacy of diverse theoretical perspectives (for example, environmental jurisprudence or the application of ecological economics to environmental regulation). Embracing a greater concern for outcomes and implementation issues will move the focus of some scholarship towards empiricism upon which to base theories about what works and what does not under various circumstances. With the advent of pragmatic methodology, which can incorporate value and values (axiology), comes the possibility of bringing aspects of environmental law scholarship into alignment with contemporary understandings of the scientific method.

The editorial of Environmental Governance (the book resulting from the 2009 Colloquium of the Academy of Environmental Law) put forward the following challenge:

> It is clear that our scholarship will have to expand further, so that we can marry to good doctrinal approaches a new set of methods to provide comprehensive and sophisticated governance solutions to a world increasingly in need of them. This will involve moving to a systems framework, and deepening our thinking about instruments and institutions. This can only be done if we can draw upon the knowledge that exists in economics, social sciences and the biophysical natural sciences, but without submerging laws concern for social justice and the lawyers learned scepticism about simple solutions to complex problems.[40]

A significant reason for accepting this challenge is because the scientific method imposes a structured approach to continuous improvement. Whilst the sharing of jurisdiction-specific examples allows scholars to draw their own inferences, this is a poor replacement for a discourse based on clearly specified research questions, hypotheses and tests of validity.

---

40 Ibid, xxxi.

A second reason for adjusting our thinking about epistemology and methodology is that a 'non-science' approach limits our ability to fruitfully interact with empirical disciplines, and to take leadership in the development of the knowledge that is necessary for more effective environmental governance. The culture of the law, with its recognition of values as vitally important to the practical resolution of social challenges, brings an important dimension to the policy and practice of sustainability. This would probably not be sufficiently advanced by 'scientific' or 'economic' disciplines.

History suggests that the success of any legal intervention is far from assured. The strategic variables can be interpreted through many disciplinary lenses.[41] A variety of approaches has emerged in the social policy sciences that can help us to understand these issues. These include action research, grounded theory, engaged research including participative systems modelling, narrative enquiry, qualitative and quantitative survey methods, citizen juries, meta-analysis of prior studies, case studies or triangulation using different enquiries to bridge the gap between problem 'messiness' and scientific rigour. A focus on implementation requires objective measurement of outcomes and evaluation of causes (of which the operation of the law is one component).

Policy research is characterised by a pragmatic mix of methods, as a response to complexity. Pragmatism does not mean a lack of commitment to objective evidence, but it reflects that purer forms of the scientific method are often not realistic. Ann Majchrzak, in her book on methods

---

[41] This is well illustrated by Professor Faure's examination of the empirical data. 'The empirical research does not necessarily point in the direction of strongly favouring either command and control or market-based instruments. Rather it shows that the effectiveness of the instruments depends to a large extent upon the particular design … Command and control is dependent upon public enforcement, which may, at least in Western Europe) be weak, giving rise to low expected sanctions *ex ante*. However, studies equally show that for taxation instruments the tax rate is not always efficiently set. Taxation has been shown to be effective only where an effective monitoring and enforcement system applies. In that respect, command and control and market-based are not that much different: both will need effective monitoring and enforcement systems. Strong laws and efficient institutions are a fundamental requirement regardless of instrument choice.' 'The studies show that it may not be possible to argue that one particular instrument is "best" or "optimal". In most cases, a combination of instruments may be indicated. An important point for further research is to look for "optimal mixes" policy instruments. These may also to a large extent depend upon country-specific characteristics."(Faure (2012) 16–17).

for policy research,[42] defines five characteristics of policy research that, in part, resonate with research on applied environmental law. She suggests that such research is intrinsically multidimensional, uses an 'empirico-deductive' method that is (or ought be) focused upon variables that are malleable with intervention (rather than those which cannot be effected), responds to the needs of the users and incorporates values.[43] She highlights methods including 'focused synthesis', based upon literature and interviews, as well as secondary analysis of field experiments, qualitative methods, surveys, case studies, cost benefit and cost effectiveness analysis. Majchrzak argues that a combination of different methods is needed. In an interesting aside she states:

> Unless the finding is both politically and statistically significant, it is probably not worth noting.[44]

This reflects the dichotomy of policy research, where good and comprehensive investigations combine scientific deduction and empirical integrity with the messy, chaotic and subjective calculus of real-politik and human values. At least in the investigation of environmental law reform, to suggest that research has integrity only where it limits the exercise of the researcher's judgement about moral or social values, likely future contexts or the projected behaviour of people and organisations would be absurd. These are all unavoidable part of the effectiveness concerns of environmental governance. Even in relation to objective matters, it is unrealistic to exclude some subjective judgement and estimation, because there are many dimensions to the questions of anticipated performance of a legal instrument, and these factual dimensions are dynamic and context dependent. The law reform researcher is faced with the choice of excluding axiological and non-deducible variables that are significant to real-world outcomes, or using estimation in the absence of the resources and methods to investigate all the many aspects that might be empirically tractable in theory but not in practice.

Many questions about environmental law scholarship do however invite more scientific empirical investigation:

- To what extent, and under what conditions, do different forms of legal intervention work in achieving environmental and social justice outcomes?

---

42 Majchrzak (1984).
43 Ibid, 18–20.
44 Ibid, 69.

- To what extent and under what conditions are market instruments, or social interventions like education programs, likely to be more effective than traditional legal interventions?
- How and under what conditions can market or other interventions be synergistic with legal interventions, to secure outcomes that are 'greater than the sum of the parts'?
- What legal or institutional arrangements do enable effective community engagement and participation, including benefit sharing, in natural resource governance?

We do not have accepted theories within the discipline for these issues, upon which to base testable hypotheses. We should expect that initial theories about such issues would be context contingent, with limited predictive value – the history of science suggest that this is so with most initial theories. The earliest theories in sciences (such as physics or chemistry) were metaphysical speculation based upon observation rather than upon rigourous science. The same can be said of the social sciences such as economics or psychology. The normal pathway towards reliability is from early stage ('pre-paradigmatic') theories that are inefficient, towards mature understanding based upon the accumulation of experience and experimentation.[45] However, the march of science suggests that even with a limited initial theory, it is possible to develop specific testable hypotheses and over time to evolve greater robustness and 'generalisability'. There is no reason why environmental law could not embark upon such a synthesis using heuristics reflecting experience as a starting point.

6. A POTENTIAL INTEGRATIVE FRAMEWORK?

We have argued that whilst there is a legitimate concern about how integrity will be assured in our scholarly pursuit, the perceived science/non-science polarity is deceptive. Applied environmental law involves a complex mix of factual matters amenable to empirical scientific methods, axiological issues where discourse and reason are the investigative tools, and matters of values weighting and predictions where judgement (informed by reason and data) is the investigative mechanism. For applied environmental law the true goal is not the pursuit of knowledge *per se*, rather it is improved social justice and ecological sustainability outcomes within a socio-economic system that places emphasis upon

---

[45] Teece (1986); Abernathy and Utterback (1978) 44–7.

wealth. At this level the aim of legal research is not scientific (the pursuit of knowledge as an end) but pragmatic (the pursuit of knowledge for applied ends). Finally we have observed that governance outcomes are the result of complex socio-ecological systems rather than legal arrangements alone.

We conclude that an effective scholarship of implementation will have to: adopt a pragmatic approach, use mixed methods and embrace axiology but with scientific standards of integrity and structured improvement. We will need new integrative frameworks because our purpose is real-world social and ecological improvement. Merely adding knowledge will be insufficient to deliver outcomes which go beyond knowledge alone.

Finding applied solutions to human problems of dynamic complexity is a core pursuit of strategy, where dynamic and poorly understood variables determine the outcome of policy action. Kenichi Ohmae's 'The Mind of the Strategist' distills the thought processes of successful strategists. From investigation of complex reality the strategist distills their own 'theory of the world' about relationships and drivers of the relevant system. They use this to determine priorities for intervention.[46] Experience tests whether these judgements are reliable. Achieving clarity based upon investigation of what is causally important, judging where intervention is likely to be effective in a future context is a necessary choice, and determining what actions will achieve the desired goal, are essential in an integrated framework. The elements of this strategic epistemology (as distinct from scientific epistemology) seem relevant to framing our approach to a disciplined investigation of applied environmental law. Table 1.1 outlines some questions that are posed for applied environmental law, and possible methodological implications for environmental law research.[47] This table is focused upon investigation of law reform, but similar issues arise in investigation of the performance of legal governance arrangements.

Accepting that environmental law instruments are often ineffective or can create perverse outcomes,[48] it is important that we can systematically learn from experience. Approaches to learning from experience are reflected in widely used approaches such as 'The Scientific Method', the

---

46 Ohmae (1982).

47 For a detailed discussion of a strategic architecture for sustainability research see Martin and Verbeek (2006).

48 The statement can equally be applied to market instruments, property rights, communal action and social persuasion. There is no meta-research that conclusively supports the conventional.

Table 1.1 Questions and methods in applied environmental law

Environmental governance strategic questions	Methodological dimensions of the question
PURPOSE: What is the policy objective of the proposed legal intervention?	The more ambiguous the purpose of a legal intervention, the less precise will be the investigation and the possible research conclusions. However, oversimplification of complex purposes will reduce the reliability of the conclusions. Research of the 'policy objective' question can involve consideration of social needs and preferences (empirical research and philosophical discourse), evaluation of statements of purpose and policy (documentation), analysis of political preferences and dynamics (empirical, documentary and discourse analysis); and the functional needs underpinning the need for action (social, ecological, economic research). Synthesis will involve weighing diverse interests and values (judgement). Investigation might also be required about whether a legal intervention will be more or less effective than interventions (nil-action, market instruments, or social interventions like education). Methods for investigation might include historical analysis, discourse, benefit/cost analysis, systems analysis and modelling.
CONTEXT: What are the context variables and how might they impact on outcomes?	Since context is everything outside the phenomena being considered, the starting point is to determine what is relevant and feasible to investigate. This is a judgement (possibly informed by methods like systems mapping). Context is dynamic, so descriptive research ('what is the context') will yield insufficient information to determine likely impacts on strategies to be implemented over time. Forecasting methods include unaided judgement, scenario methods, expert panels or community research (for example, futures Delphi research), or modeling. Context spans topics including the socio-ecological system, economics, cultural issues, political dynamics, technological trajectories and the functioning of ecological systems under biophysical and use assumptions. There are many research methods for these aspects. A first level of context is the organisational or institutional context of the possible intervention, in particular the capacity and commitment of the implementing agencies. Organisational and political research methods are relevant. A second level of context is the community or group whose behaviours are to be changed by the proposed intervention. How they might react involves considerations like attitude and values (social research), political dynamics (political methods), patterns of incentive (economic systems), and their capacity to respond to the interventions (economic and human capacity analysis).

Environmental governance strategic questions	Methodological dimensions of the question
RESOURCES: Can (and will) sufficient resources be deployed to support the intervention?	Resources, not conceptual brilliance, largely determine the outcomes of strategy.[49] The capacity of the responsible agency to implement is an important consideration, but the capacity of the targeted community to respond suitably is also critical. Strategic resource analysis has three main concerns: determining what resources are required, deciding whether (and how) they can be secured, and managing logistics. This involves financial aspects (accounting, budgeting and economics), human capacity (human resource management), and organisational systems (logistics, systems management, general management).
STRATEGY: What activities and allocation of resources will result in achievement of our goals, given likely conditions?	This decision is where analysis and judgement are integrated. Environmental law strategy (unlike military or management) lacks decision-making frameworks to support choices such as: (1) Choosing between a legal or another form of intervention; or (2) determining the complementary cocktail of legal and other interventions; or (3) deciding between potential legal instruments (public law, private law) or design characteristics. The available methods generally rely on discourse and individual judgement.
IMPLEMENTATION and IMPROVEMENT: Who most do what, when and how to achieve effective implementation? And how will we learn from implementation experience, to improve outcomes.	Various forms of planning provide methods for analysing the implementation of legal governance. An important consideration is methods of continuous improvement/adaptation based upon objective analysis of outcomes.

Deming 'System of Profound Knowledge', which transformed into 'Total Quality Management', or 'Adaptive Management'. All share a commitment to the disciplined use of objective data about outcomes to fuel continuous improvement.

Complex 'wicked problems' do require diverse, pragmatic methods for scholarly investigation. It is also true that environmental law must engage with issues where many aspects are immeasurable and so the scientific ideal of objectivity is limited. However, these characteristics of our scholarship do not alter the fact that all research requires a disciplined framework to ensure the integrity and generalisability of findings. Legal

[49] For classical illustrations of this see Von Clausewitz (1873) and Tzu (1910). In commercial strategy, resource concepts of the firm and corporate strategy mirror this perspective.

research focused on outcome effectiveness should reflect to the fullest extent possible the integrity mechanisms of science – clear articulation and transparency of methods and data, identification and disclosure of the limits of generalisability of conclusions and proper peer review. It is, we think, in the pursuit of scientific standards of integrity rather than a direct application of the scientific method, where some of the criticisms of our scholarly approach are most telling. Regardless of methodology, in all cases the scientific safeguards of integrity should be considered essential. This is not yet the case, but it is achievable.

REFERENCES

Abernathy, W. and J. Utterback (1978), 'Patterns of Industrial Innovation' 10(7) *Technology Review* 40.

Cohen, S. (1988), 'A Question of Boundaries: The Response of Learned Societies to Interdisciplinary Scholarship' (American Council of Learned Societies Occasional Paper No. 5).

Dovers, S. (2005), *Environment and Sustainability Policy: Creation, Implementation and Evaluation* (Sydney: Federation Press).

Driessen, D. (2003), *The Economic Dynamics of Environmental Law* (Cambridge, MA: MIT Press).

Faure, M. (2012), 'Instruments for Environmental Governance: What works' in P. Martin *et al.* (eds) *Environmental Governance and Sustainability* (Cheltenham, UK and Northampton, MA, USA: Edward Elgar).

Fisher, E. et al. (2009), 'Maturity and Methodology: Starting a Debate about Environmental Law Scholarship' 21(2) *Journal of Environmental Law* 213.

Harding, R., C. Hendriks and M. Faruqi (2009), *Environmental Decision-Making: Exploring Complexity and Context* (Sydney: Federation Press).

Herring, D. (2006), 'Legal Scholarship, Humility and the Scientific Method' 40 *University of Pittsburg School of Law Working Paper Series*.

Hesselink, M. (2009), 'A European Legal Method? On European Private Law and Scientific Method' 15 *European Law Journal* 20.

Hunter, D., J. Salzman and D. Zaelke (2011), *International Law and Policy* (4th edn., Sydney: Foundation Press/Thompson Reuter).

Kuhn, T. (1996), *The Structure of Scientific Revolutions* (Chicago: University of Chicago Press).

Lim, M., 'Legal and Institutional Requirements for the Effective Management of Transboundary Resources in the Pamir Mountains of Central Asia: A Comparative Study of Water and Biodiversity' in R. Warner and S. Marsden (eds), *Transboundary Environmental Governance in Inland, Coastal and Marine Areas* (Farnham: Ashgate Publishing).

Majchrzak, A. (1984), 'Methods for Policy Research' in L. Bickman and D. Rog, *Applied Social Research Methods* (Vol. 1, Thousand Oaks: Sage Publications).

Martin, P. and M. Verbeek (2006), *Sustainability Strategies* (Sydney: Federation Press).

McGrath, C. (2010), *Does Environmental Law Work? How to Evaluate the Effectiveness of an Environmental Legal System* (Staarbrücken, DE: Lambert Academic Publishing).

Ohmae, K. (1982), *The Mind of The Strategist: The Art of Japanese Business* (New York: McGraw Hill Professional Publishing).

Popper, K. (2002), *Conjectures and Refutations: The Growth of Scientific Knowledge* (Abingdon: Routledge).

Posner, R. (1987), 'The Decline of Law as an Autonomous Discipline' 100(4) *Harvard Law Review* 761.

Reed, M. (2008), 'Stakeholder Participation for Environmental Management: A Literature Review' 141 *Biological Conservation* 2417.

Rittel, H. and M. Webber (1973), 'Dilemmas in a General Theory of Planning' 4 *Policy Sciences* 155.

Sparrow, M. (2000), *The Regulatory Craft: Controlling Risks, Solving Problems, and Managing Compliance* (Washington, DC: The Brookings Institute).

Stavins, R. (2001), *Experience with Market-Based Environmental Policy Instruments: Discussion Paper 01-58* (Washington DC: Resources for the Future).

Stone, J. (1964), *Legal System and Lawyers' Reasonings* (Redwood City, CA: Stanford University Press).

Teece, D. (1986), 'Profiting from Technological Innovation: Implications for Integration, Collaboration, Licensing and Public Policy' 15 *Research Policy* 285.

Tzu, S. (1910), *The Art of War*, translated by L. Giles (Project Gutenberg).

Ulen, T. (2002), 'A Nobel Prize in Legal Science: Theory, Empirical Work and the Scientific Method in the Study of Law' 4 *University of Illinois Law Review* 875.

United Nations Department of Economic and Social Affairs Division for Sustainable Development (UNDESASD January 2012), *Sustainable Development in the 21st Century: Review of Implementation of Agenda 21 and the Rio Principles Synthesis.*

Von Clausewitz, C. (1873), *On War* (N. Trubner).

2. Assessing environmental governance of the Hudson River Valley: application of an IPPEP model

Wang Xi, Richard L. Ottinger, Nicholas A. Robinson, Albert K. Butzel, Marla E. Wieder, John Louis Parker, Taryn L. Rucinski, Radina R. Valova, and Wang Pianpian

Compliance with environmental law faces difficulties in all nations. This chapter seeks to define a methodology for assessing the requisites for determining whether or not a given state or nation is likely to succeed in protecting the environment. Studies at Shanghai Jiao Tong University have produced a model, described below as 'Interactions of Parties in Process of Environmental Protection (IPPEP)'. The methodology of IPPEP permits evaluation of how governmental, economic and non-economic public values interact.[1] The IPPEP Model was tested in evaluating five case studies from the Hudson River Valley, in New York State (USA). The test shows that the IPPEP Model is a useful tool for understanding and assessing environmental governance in any given geographical or administrative area.[2]

[1] The model is a qualitative instrument that uses an algorithmic notation to help to illustrate.

[2] An extensive research article, elaborating on the themes of this paper, at 31(1) *Pace Environmental Law Review* (Winter 2014).

1. THE IPPEP MODEL

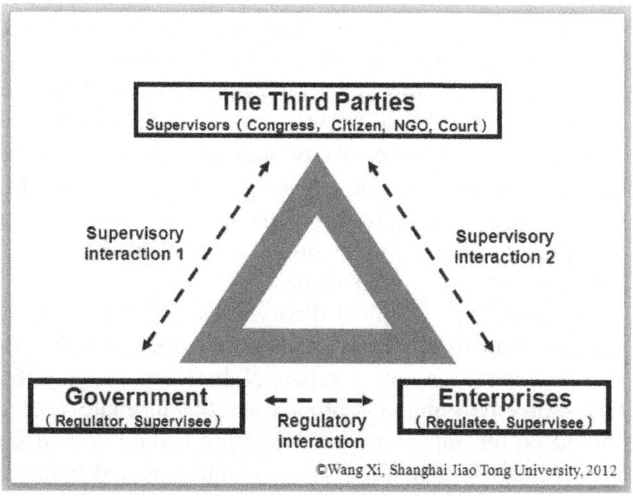

The IPPEP Model refers to the situations of mutual influence among the parties when they develop, utilise or protect the environment. Environmental legislation establishes the rules for protection of ecological systems and public health. When all parties respect and observe this legislation, their relationships are in balance with each other. The equilateral triangle in the diagram expresses the Model.

Figure 2.1 IPPEP model of party implementation responsibilities

There are three parties or major players in the process of environmental protection: (1) government, being the state's executive authority (which regulates and is subject to supervision or oversight by others in doing so); (2) economic enterprises (which are regulated, and often influence governments as well), and (3) The 'Third Parties' (such as citizens and environmental non-governmental organisations (NGOs), Courts and Congress), provide oversight and supervise the governmental regulatory and economic enterprise parties.

Where the government is closely supervised by the Third Parties, the dynamic of environmental compliance tends to enforce environmental protection norms effectively. Where, however, economic enterprises are favoured by government, less environmental enforcement may result. Only intervention by the Third Parties can restore these balanced relationships, realising the goals of environmental laws. Typically, the public or NGOs appeal to the courts, or to local or national legislatures, to secure supervision of regulators and enterprises in order to assure their compliance with environmental laws.

The essence of balanced environmental governance, illustrated through the IPPEP model, is cooperation, exchange and a positive sum game. This is highly consistent with the concept and goal of sustainable development. 'In a very real sense … political action is viewed essentially as a means through which the "power" of all participants may be increased, if we define "power" as the ability to command things that are desired by the public. To be justified by the criteria employed here, collective action must be advantageous to all parties. In the more precise terminology of modern game theory, the utility or economic approach suggests that the political process, taken in the abstract, may be interpreted as a positive-sum game.'[3]

As a matter of political theory, these three sets of parties promote the improvement of environmental quality and maximise their own interests at the same time, by 'exchange' between these different interests. In terms of environmental protection, the ultimate goal of all the parties should be the same, that is, achieving economic and social development in a condition of harmonisation of humans and nature. The interactions, including regulatory interactions and supervisory interactions, all should produce 'positive sum' or 'win-win' results.[4] Environmental legislation, as a pillar of sustainable development, provides the framework within which these interactions occur. When all the major parties get what they want by doing the 'exchanges' in the environmental protection process, the process is a positive sum game, and the goals of the legislation are attained.

The significance of these interactions to implementation of environmental laws is well illustrated by case studies of actions to protect the Hudson River in New York State against a variety of threats from pollution and adverse development proposals from both private parties and government entities. The means employed to protect the river, the actors and obstacles are described in the case studies described below. The foundations of United States environmental protection law were established in the resolution of these Hudson River cases.

2. THE SCENIC HUDSON CASE

For nearly a century, the Hudson has witnessed a struggle concerning its environment between government, enterprises and the public. Today, organisations such as the Environmental Consortium of Colleges and

---

3 Buchanan and Tullock (2004) 22–3.

4 This paragraph is translated from Xi (2012) 13–14.

Universities of the Hudson River[5] study ambient environmental conditions and assess new challenges. NGOs educate about sustainable land development practices and ordinances. Because of the environmental controversies in the Hudson River Valley, there is a well-documented and substantial record, which can be accessed to apply the IPPEP Model. The authors selected five cases for the IPPEP Model analysis.

In 1963, Consolidated Edison Company of New York (Con Edison) announced its plan to build a new power generating station at Storm King Mountain on the Hudson River. Storm King is one of the most beautiful and dramatic sites along the Hudson, rising directly out of the River in a sheer wall of granite and rounding 500 feet above the water to reach 1,500 feet at its peak. Con Edison proposed to construct a pumped storage hydroelectric plant, which would have been the largest pumped storage plant in the world. A large reservoir was to be constructed by damming a valley behind the Mountain 1,000 feet above the river. The powerhouse and upper reservoir would be connected by a two-mile-long tunnel.

Con Edison's announcement launched a struggle that marked the underpinning of modern environmental law in the United States. Before, conventional wisdom rarely questioned the need for an increased energy supply, which appeared central to a robust economy and a higher standard of living. Yet, the courts held that supplying electricity had to be balanced against the conservation of nature. After seven court decisions and an aborted start of construction, Con Edison finally faced the reality that the Storm King plant was unlikely to be built. Ultimately, Third Parties met with enterprises directly to settle in 1980.[6] The Storm King case and other power plant controversies were described by *The New York Times* as a 'Peace Treaty for the Hudson'.[7]

The Scenic Hudson decision by Judge Paul Hays of the Federal Court of Appeals,[8] upheld the rights of the public to demand that the licensing authority give equal consideration to factors such as recreation, fishing and appreciation of natural beauty, along with the need for electricity. It opened the courts to citizen suits to protect the environment. Alternatives to the proposed pumped storage project, which would have fewer environmental impacts (such as using natural gas turbines), had to be

---

5 Website: http://www.environmentalconsortium.org/ (accessed 29 March 2015).

6 Sandler and Schoenbrod (1981) 2–3.

7 New York Times (1980) 24.

8 *Scenic Hudson Preservation Conference v Federal Power Commission* (1972) 407 U.S. 926.

considered. The public's non-economic rights were given appropriate weight, off-setting the prior exclusive focus on economic factors.

NGOs began to make comparable complaints about fossil fuel power plants, and contested proposals for these and other new power plants. The several years of litigation and 'battle fatigue' over the Storm King case prompted the parties to negotiate a settlement of all these disputes together. The result was a reasonable balance of power among the parties where potentially major concessions could be made on all sides. Mediation offered an opportunity to reset the IPPEP balance and resolve the economic and environmental differences between parties.

3. THE HUDSON RIVER EXPRESSWAY CASE

Two proposals to build superhighways in the Hudson River Valley provide comparable IPPEP insights. Before the passage in 1969 of the National Environmental Policy Act (NEPA) and section 4(f) of the Department of Transportation Act, the process of weighing the costs and benefits of constructing a highway usually was not a matter of public debate. Administrative agencies 'made decisions about highway placement, location, scope, and type' with the scientific data provided by technical experts, and emphasised engineering concerns and technical feasibility rather than human impact. With the public disclosure required by NEPA, the public had an opportunity to access the relevant information that might influence the final decision; and NGOs could sue to force the agencies to take required actions when they failed to comply with NEPA or other statutory requirements.

The first highway case predated NEPA, and showed why enactment of this law was required. In the 1960s, New York Governor Nelson Rockefeller decided to construct The Hudson River Expressway along the shore of the Hudson River in Westchester County, half way between Manhattan and across the River from Storm King. It would have closed two village marinas, two bathing beaches and Kingsland Point Park, disrupted ecological conditions in the River, and cut people off from access to the shore of the river. Despite executive decisions that ordered establishment of the expressway, it was never built.

The Hudson River Expressway (the 'Expressway') case[9] is a hallmark of third-party success in protecting the environment, despite the powerful

[9] Unless otherwise noted, all information in this section derives from Talbot (1972).

efforts of the Federal and State governments, their agencies and regulators, and private enterprise to complete the roadway. Multiple Third Parties were involved in this case, including the NGOs, municipal governments, courts, and the federal Congress through a Member of Congress, Richard Ottinger, a co-author of this paper. Governor Rockefeller had aligned all federal and state regulators in support of the expressway, and had the support of economic enterprises such as construction companies that would have built the expressway.

The Expressway was officially proposed as a solution to traffic congestion, and private enterprise was eager to move the project through the regulatory process.

The Hudson River Valley Commission, which Governor Rockefeller had established in 1968 as a planning agency responsible for evaluating large developments in the Valley, was also strongly in support of the Expressway. Other agencies and government entities supporting the project were the U.S. Army Corps of Engineers ('Corps') and the U.S. and New York State Departments of Transportation.

Rather than conducting its own review of risks to aquatic species in the portions of the Hudson River most likely to be impacted by the Expressway, the Department of Transportation simply relied on a memorandum prepared by a New York State Conservation Department fisheries biologist, who was given a mere three weeks to prepare his report. Ultimately, the New York State Legislature approved allocating part of the riverbed for the construction of the Hudson River Expressway in 1965. This set the stage for New York's application for and receipt of dredge and fill permits from the Corps.

In response, several third parties – the Sierra Club, the Village of Tarrytown, and Citizens' Committee of the Hudson Valley – sought a judicial injunction to prevent the Corps from granting the permit to New York State. The Second Circuit Court of Appeals, reversing a District Court decision, ordered a trial on the Third Parties' claims.[10] Attorney David Sive, one of the 'fathers' of environmental litigation in the USA, then won a complete court victory for these Third Parties.[11] The court held that the Corps issued the dredge and fill permit in violation of the 1899 Rivers and Harbors Act.

While the Court's decision terminated the Hudson River Expressway project, New York tried to seek Congressional approval to alter the law to

---

[10] Ibid.

[11] Sandler and Schoenbrod (1981) (noting that all the utilities except Niagara Mohawk agreed to this provision).

allow the project. However, U.S. Representative Richard L. Ottinger won Congressional opposition to the project. He persuaded Representative John Dingell, Chair of the Federal House Subcommittee on Fisheries and Wildlife Conservation, to convene a Congressional hearing on the Hudson River Expressway. The Committee was extremely critical of the agencies involved, finding that New York State and the Department of the Interior gave only cursory reviews to the project proposal and its potential impacts to the region. Thus, in combination with the efforts of NGOs, local municipalities, the federal courts, and the legislative committee these Third Parties were able to preserve the environmental integrity of the Hudson River and uphold the rule of law.

4. THE WESTWAY CASE

A comparable battle was waged off of Manhattan Island, in the lower Hudson River. Four decades ago, the 'Westway' was abandoned after a 14-year controversy. This event was marked as 'one of the great citizen victories of our time',[12] and illustrates again how 'Third Parties', NGOs and the courts achieved environmental protection in the face of opposition by the private enterprises aligned with powerful government agencies.

The original West Side Highway ('elevated way'), from West 72nd Street south to Chambers Street in New York City, was constructed between 1927 and 1931. As time passed, the decayed situation of the West Side Highway became serious. In order to tackle the challenge of excessive traffic as well as to satisfy conformance with a local development plan, New York City proposed to build the 'Westway' in 1971. It would have transformed the Hudson River waterfront to a great extent.

There were two opposite views on the Westway Project at that time. The government of New York City, the NY State Department of Transportation (NYSDOT), New York Chamber of Commerce and Industry and many enterprises (shipping, building trades, theaters, trucking, and labour unions) all held that the Westway Project was critical to the economic survival of Manhattan and to create employment. The opposition was from community residents, civic and environmental groups maintaining that the government's decision improperly favoured development geared toward the car, not mass transit or the pedestrian, and would exacerbate air pollution and destroy important fishery habitat.

12 See Robbins (2010).

Westway was a project proposed by the government, supported by private enterprise, and yet opposed successfully by NGO third parties through legal action in the courts, upholding the laws that required protection of the environment. In this case, the role of government, as indicated by the IPPEP model, is complex. It must regulate, 'as trustee of a public trust for the benefit of the people' to minimise the damages brought by urban developments, and functions also as the economic enterprise project applicant and proponent.

As the regulator, to grant the permit to dredge and fill in the Hudson, the Army Corps has a legal obligation to consult the public and balance environmental with other interests. The Corps must provide for protection of 'fish and wildlife values'. Since the project may have 'significant' effects on the environment, the Corps must prepare an Environmental Impact Statement (EIS). In addition, the Corps must cooperate and consult with other administrative agencies to obtain further information to enable a reasonable decision. The regulations demand that the Corps give full consideration to the views of the agencies such as the Fish and Wildlife Service (FWS) and the National Marine Fishery Service (NMFS) on fish and wildlife matters, and to the U.S. Environmental Protection Agency (EPA).

The Corps issued the permit without abiding by its legal duties. The Corps relied on other agencies' environmental review, discounted the views of other federal agencies, and failed to make findings of fact regarding issuing the landfill permit despite the fact that 'the conclusions in the Final EIS were virtually the opposite of those in the Draft EIS'.[13] The Corps did not provide a substantive explanation for this drastic change that could affect the final permit decision.

To redress the government's failures, the Hudson Riverkeeper, Sierra Club, and other NGOs sought review by the courts. The Federal Second Circuit Court of Appeals, affirming judgment by the District Court, held that the Corps, the FHWA and the NYSDOT had neither developed the FEIS report 'in objective good faith' nor was it 'consonant with proper scope of review and proper view of obligations' to consider the aquatic impact in the candidate location.[14] The Court required the Corps to set forth 'a rational basis' to justify its decision.[15] The Court found that the Corps failed to provide a trustworthy and reasonable *post-hoc* analysis of the change 'from "significant adverse impact" [on striped bass habitat] in

---

[13] *Sierra Club v United States Army Corps of Engineers* (1984) 732 F.2d 253.

[14] Ibid 1462.

[15] Ibid 1050.

the Draft EIS to the "minor impact" in the Final EIS'. The Court remanded the permit matter back to the Corps and required the FHWA and the Corps 'to make their own independent evaluations' of the fisheries in order to decide whether to issue the landfill permit.[16] Unable to demonstrate how it could protect the environment in order to obtain the Corps permits, New York City abandoned promoting construction of Westway. The IPPEP balance was restored.

5. THE PCB CONTAMINATION CASE

The next case study is not about preventing future harm, but restoring environmental quality by legal mandates to clean up past pollution, under a federal hazardous waste law known as the 'Superfund'.[17] Two hundred miles of the northern reach of the Hudson are classified by the EPA as a 'Superfund' site requiring remediation due to contamination by polychlorinated biphenyls (PCBs). When completed, this remediation will be one of the most expensive cleanups in the U.S. Together with the New York State Department of Environmental Conservation (DEC), the EPA has held General Electric (GE), the polluting enterprise, responsible for not only the cleanup but also for the governments' costs.

PCBs were widely used as a fire preventive and insulator in the manufacture of electrical devices, like transformers and capacitors, because of their ability to withstand exceptionally high temperatures. When PCBs are released into the environment, they create a hazard to human health and render fish exposed to them inedible. During a 30-year period ending in 1977, when the EPA banned the discharge of PCBs in United States waters under the Clean Water Act, GE had discharged some 1.3 million pounds of PCBs into the Hudson River. PCBs were discharged daily in plant cleanup water from GE's capacitor manufacturing plants located in the towns of Fort Edward and Hudson Falls, New York and became bound in the river sediments. The EPA listed the Hudson on its list of the nation's most contaminated hazardous waste sites identifying the GE PCB contamination.

Despite the contamination, the EPA in 1984 initially chose not to deal with this contamination and issued a 'No Action' decision regarding the GE site. NGOs immediately protested, enlisting political leaders to support them. In 1989, the EPA announced its decision to initiate a detailed Reassessment Remedial Investigation/Feasibility Study (RI/FS)

---

16 Ibid 1048.

17 Environmental Protection Agency (2014).

of the contamination, effectively reversing its September 1984 'No Action' decision. In the subsequent decade, the Hudson was witness to an expansive, emotionally-charged public controversy over the cleanup of a site. GE, which was a potentially responsible party for dozens of contaminated sites across the country (including several other water bodies), argued vehemently that the River should be, in essence, allowed to clean itself up. GE opposed the EPA's remediation decisions. Following continuous public pressure, in February 2002, the EPA issued a thorough Record of Decision (2002 ROD), which selected the final cleanup plan for the Site.

Third Parties were essential for bolstering the EPA's enforcement against GE. Under public pressure, the EPA observed its regulatory duties and provided for extensive community/public participation. For example, a Technical Assistance Grant provided funding for the NGO, Scenic Hudson, to educate communities along the Hudson River to understand the technical details of the Reassessment and participate in the decision-making process. In addition, the EPA established a comprehensive Community Interaction Program (CIP). Public hearings sought public comments. By the end of the public comment period, nearly 73,000 separate individual comments had been submitted on the Proposed Plan. The EPA responded to 274 sets of public comments.

A number of NGOs, including Riverkeeper, Scenic Hudson and Clearwater, banded together and spoke with one voice for the Hudson. They enlisted elected officials to support them in pressing the EPA for a strong clean-up. Some other NGOs did not favour an active remedy, such as Citizen Environmentalists Against Sludge Encapsulation (CEASE) and Farmers Against Irresponsible Remediation (FAIR), and they coordinated their public participation and legal efforts with GE, and at times with industry lobbying groups.

Although NGOs were the key Third Party actors, the courts were essential. Over the years, there have been numerous lawsuits by both NGOs and GE (or GE-financed groups) and 'friend of the court' or *amicus* briefs filed in related proceedings. The courts required disclosure of documents showing how GE was lobbying federal leaders to prevent the EPA's enforcement. In 2011, the U.S. Supreme Court refused to hear appeals from GE, effectively ending the regulatory controversy that had spanned over a decade. Without strong Third Party support for the regulator, EPA, the clean-up could not have advanced. This case study demonstrates the necessity of empowered citizens and the courts. The clean-up continues.

6. THE INDIAN POINT NUCLEAR POWER PLANTS CASE

The Indian Point nuclear power plants involve a continuing controversy in which the Third Parties have as yet been unable to succeed in their efforts to close the plants.

The electrical generating facility ('Indian Point') contains two active nuclear power plants and one deactivated plant, all built by the Consolidated Edison Corporation (Con Edison); the plants are now owned by the Entergy Corporation ('Entergy'). The plants are located on the Hudson River above a geological fault situated 40 miles north of New York City. Indian Point has been in operation since the mid- to late-1970s. The plant's two operating reactors, Units 2 and 3, collectively have a capacity of over 2,000 megawatts. Since its beginning, the plants have used cooling water from the Hudson, killing trillions of fish as they withdrew and discharged many millions of gallons of water. These fish kills led the Hudson River Fishermen's Association to demand measures to safeguard fish. When the screens installed to save fish failed to operate effectively, the Riverkeeper and others, including the Attorney General of the State of New York, demanded that the power plants be closed when their initially authorised period of operations came to an end. Today, the Third Parties are seeking to require that Entergy close the power plants.

Pursuant to U.S. law governing nuclear power facilities, Indian Point is currently in the process of applying to renew its operating licenses for an additional 20 years. A heated public debate is underway regarding whether or not Units 2 and 3 should be permitted to continue operating. Public outcry against Indian Point has focused on environmental, safety and, since 9/11 in 2001, terrorism vulnerability concerns, while advocates for maintaining the plant as operational point to its important contribution to providing electricity to the greater New York City area with almost no greenhouse gas emissions in its operation. Third Parties invoked their powers under NY State law and federal law to demand environmental safeguards from Entergy. The Governor of New York has now called for closing of the plants and the State's DEC has denied the plants water quality permits required under the Clean Water Act for use of essential cooling water for the plants; this decision is being appealed. Pursuant to the Atomic Energy Act, the Nuclear Regulatory Commission (NRC) is the agency responsible for issuing licenses to operators of nuclear power plants. The Atomic Safety and Licensing Board of the NRC conducts the licensing hearings, acting as a quasi-judicial body, holding open hearings with many procedures like courts, including the filing of motions, the involvement of interveners, presenting of evidence, and a formal record appealable to the federal courts. States and NGOs may participate as interveners. The states, however, retain decision power over the need for plants and environmental quality.

The role of the NRC as a presumably neutral regulator is complicated by the fact that its members often view public participation as a hindrance to efficient relicensing. As a result, NRC Boards frequently attempt to reduce the scope of the NRC's environmental oversight. When President Obama was campaigning in 2008, he called the NRC 'a moribund agency ... captive of the industry that it regulates'.[18] This illustrates an inherent conflict between the public's interest in participating meaningfully in the process, and the Nuclear Regulatory Commission's interest in maintaining greater control over the proceedings favouring the end result of granting a license to operate.

While several NGOs petitioned for intervener status in the Indian Point license renewal hearings, only two organisations and one New York State entity were granted such status: the New York State Department of State (DOS), acting as a representative of the State's interests in the matter, and two NGOs, Riverkeeper and the Hudson River Clearwater Sloop, Inc. (HRCS).

The importance of Third Parties as interveners is essential to strengthening observance of environmental legal norms, particularly in such cases as this, where the federal government and the enterprise have shared interests. Third Parties are able to bring issues to light that members of the general public cannot uncover or challenge on their own due to lack of resources and technical knowledge. In addition, because the nuclear power enterprises applying for relicensing do not always submit all of the documents or information necessary for the NRC to make a truly informed decision, third parties have the power to compel the applicants to submit – and the NRC to consider – additional environmental information. For example, the DOS alleged in its intervention petition that Entergy did not update its final safety analysis reports (FSAR) as required, which made it impossible to determine the safety of the plant. The NGOs also filed a joint challenge to Entergy's report on the environmental harms associated with spent fuel pool leaks, alleging that Entergy and the NRC had failed to visually inspect nearly half the surface of the pool liner.

---

18 See http://www.thenation.com/video/159308/nuke-lobby-has-us-regulatory-commission-their-pocket (accessed 29 March 2015).

The NRC has come under heavy criticism for permitting the nuclear industry to hold sway over its decision-making. One former NRC Chairman resigned, questioning the agency relicensing of all nuclear facilities.[19] NRC Commissioners usually are appointed because of their support for nuclear power rather than for environmental protection.

It is important to note that in the present case it may take years for the NRC to make a final decision regarding the relicensing of Indian Point Units 2 and 3. As such, the success of the Third Parties in securing denial of Entergy's license renewal application remains to be determined. Whatever the NRC does, there will be undoubtedly be court cases to challenge its decision. Since the 1960s it has been apparent that, viewed through the IPPEP triangle's three sectors, the balances between the parties are skewed. The NRC defers to Entergy and 'business as usual'. The legal process is weak and, as the IPPEP analysis would predict, the environmental harm continues, with significant ongoing fish mortality.

7. THE FUNCTIONS OF IPPEP MODEL INDICATED BY THE CASE STUDIES

These five case studies on Hudson River conservation indicate that the IPPEP Model can be a useful tool for understanding and assessing environmental governance, whether within a small community or a larger administrative region such as a county, a state or province, or for an entire country. IPPEP visually guides researchers to explore the political and legal relationships among the three major 'parties' in the process of safeguarding environmental quality. The relationship represented by the three sides of the triangle is mutually influencing. The IPPEP Model is an equilateral triangle suggesting a required symmetry. A good IPPEP will be achieved when all the three categories of parties properly play their legitimate role in the environmental protection process. When all the parties are essentially in compliance with environmental law and other related laws, they reach a balance in their rights and duties in environmental matters. This is effective at securing observance of relevant laws, and may be termed 'good IPPEP'.

The model helps researchers to identify the legal framework under which the parties interact. Those laws can be divided into two categories. One is environmental law, both substantive rules and procedures for public participation. The second category comprises all the other laws

---

19 Wald (2013).

related to environmental protection, including the Constitution, the law of torts, administrative law and procedural rules governing court practice.

The IPPEP Model helps researchers to observe how the legal framework for environmental protection functions. For example, in the Scenic Hudson case, the issue of standing was a key issue in the related litigation. This litigation resulted in progressive development of the rule on standing and made it more adapted to the need of contemporary environmental public interest litigation. It is interesting to see that in almost all the five case studies a federal permit and related laws are at the center of the controversies.

Lastly, the model can be used for assessing the soundness of environmental governance. For understanding this function the authors have developed an algorithmic notation expression of the IPPEP Model (see Figure 2.3). As applied to each of the five case studies, the formulae may be set forth as follows:[20]

$$(-\text{R}) + (-\text{E}) + (\text{NGO} + \text{J, changing R}) = \text{Q}$$

In the Storm King Case, the FPC (appears as '–R') was obligated to consider recreational concerns and scenic beauty in deciding whether or not to issue a license under the Federal Power Act. It had failed to comply with its obligations. The NGO in this case is Scenic Hudson. It filed a lawsuit to the court to challenge the FPC's decision, which was upheld by the court. The wider significance of the Storm King decision is that it opened the courts to citizen suits to protect the environment. With a strong participation of environmental NGOs and a court decision in favor of environmental value, the regulator was forced to respect the environmental value.

$$(-\text{R}) + (-\text{E}) + (\text{NGO} + \text{C, changing R}) = \text{Q}$$

In the Hudson River Expressway Case, the Corps, as the primary representative of the government role (appears as '– R'), issued the dredge and fill permit to New York State in violation of the 1899 Rivers and

[20] The meanings of the capital letters in the formulae are the following respectively. **Q:** Environmental Quality or the goals that the environmental legislation seeks have observed; **– Q:** Poor environmental quality and environmental legislation not observed; **R:** Strong environmental regulator; **– R:** Weak environmental regulator; **– E:** Polluting enterprise; **J:** Court in favor of environment; **– J:** Court not in favor of environment; **– NGO:** Ineffective NGO participation or no NGOs at all; **G:** Good environmental governance; **– G:** Poor environmental governance; **C:** Congressional action.

Harbors Act. The Sierra Club and other citizen groups challenged the decision through a lawsuit. The federal District Court ruled in favour of the plaintiffs and further expanded the scope of third-party standing that was previously established in the Storm King case.

$$(-\text{R}) + (-\text{E}) + (\text{NGO} + \text{J, changing R}) = \text{Q}$$

In the West Side Highway Case, the Corps (appears as '– R') issued the permit without abiding by environmental protection and other administrative requirements. The Sierra Club, as the representative of citizen groups invoked the judicial procedure and its challenge was upheld by the court. The Westway Project was stopped.

$$\text{R} + (-\text{E}) + \text{NGO} + \text{J} = \text{Q}$$

In the PCB Contamination Case, the government, pressured by the Third Parties, acted on concerns for environmental protection.

$$(-\text{R}) + (-\text{E}) + (-\text{NGO}) = -\text{Q}$$

In the Indian Point Nuclear Power Plant Case, the NRC (appears as '– R') is closely aligned with the nuclear power plant entity in interest and defers to 'business as usual', rather than order measures to better protect the environment. Also, the NRC has complicated procedural requirements for the hearings that impede public participation. As a result, only two NGO organisations and one New York State entity were granted standing for license renewal hearings. In addition, inadequate legal resources and expert knowledge frequently limits citizen groups' participation.

A contributing factor in the ineffectiveness of federal and state regulatory agencies in some cases is that the regulators responsible for decision-making not infrequently come from industries that are either being directly regulated or have an interest in the outcome. Additionally, federal and state regulators may return to be employed by those very same industries after leaving government service, often at high salaries. This 'revolving door' can compromise the integrity of decision-making by regulators. For example, the NRC has been widely criticised for being too closely tied to industry and for the revolving door between agency and public sector jobs.[21]

The case studies make clear that Third Parties play a key role in safeguarding good environmental governance. The environmental NGOs

21 See, e.g. Zeller (2011).

and the people they represent, together with their access to scientific information about environmental problems and their direct experience with pollution and other environmental degradation, prompts government or courts to demand effective compliance with environmental laws and regulations. The contribution of their knowledge improves governmental decision-making. NGOs, such as Scenic Hudson, can petition legislatures to hold public hearings investigating environmental problems. In addition, NGOs, such as the Hudson Riverkeeper, can bring law suits to invoke judicial oversight. NGOs can induce the legislature to exercise oversight. They can require the regulator to do its assigned job and break the de facto control that economic enterprises exercise over the regulators. Often local governments, such as towns or villages, can act to protect their residents and the local environment, much like an NGO, although sometimes they will take parochial views such as at Indian Point where the village of Buchanan sought to keep jobs for local power plant works.

Figure 2.2 summarises the interactions among the major parties in the five case studies.

Category	Regulators	Enterprises	The Third-Parties Case
Scenic Hudson Case	-Federal Power Commission Inactive	-- Consolidated Edison Company of New York Inactive	--Citizen Groups (i.e: Scenic Hudson) --News Media --The Court Active
Hudson River Expressway	--U.S. Environmental Protection Agency --U.S. Army Corps --U.S. Department of Interior --The government of New York State Inactive	N/A	--Citizen Groups (i.e: Scenic Hudson) --The Court --The Congress Active
Westway Case	--The government of New York City --U.S. Army Corps Inactive	N/A	--Citizen Groups (i.e: Sierra Club) --The Court Active --News Media Inactive
The PCB Contamination Case	--U.S. Environmental Protection Agency --New York State Department of Environmental Conservation --U.S. Department of Interior --U.S. Department of Commerce Active	General Electric Co. Inactive	--Citizen Groups --The Court --News Media Active
Indian Point Nuclear Power Plants Case	--Nuclear Regulatory Commission Inactive --The New York State Department of State Active	Entergy Corporation Inactive	--Citizen Groups --News Media Active

Notes: Inactive, means inactive in environmental protection; Active, means in environmental protection.

Source: Wang (2013).

Figure 2.2 Major parties and their roles in Hudson River Conservation

It should be pointed out that the courts are not uniformly in favour of protecting the environment. They are, instead, focused on ensuring that regulators and economic enterprises obey the law. Thus, when NGOs show that the laws to protect the environment are being violated, the courts may enforce the laws, with the result that the environment is protected, as in the case of the Hudson River Expressway and Westway projects. However, when the law leaves discretion to the regulator, and violations of the law are hard to identify, the courts may not upset the decisions of the regulator, even when the regulator and the economic enterprise appear to be closely aligned, as in the case of the Indian Point Power Plant controversy. Conversely, when some local governments sought to overturn the EPA decisions to require GE to clean up the PCB contamination of the upper Hudson River, the courts deferred to the EPA decision, which had the result of upholding environmental protection.

It should also be pointed out that the legislative body, Congress or a state or provincial legislative body, can play a key positive or negative role in the political and legal processes of environmental protection. For example, Congress can use its investigatory powers to require the disclosure of scientific information and to overcome deficiencies of the regulatory authorities or misconduct by economic enterprises. Such legislative oversight may stimulate the regulators to act with integrity to enforce environmental law, or stimulate the Congress to amend environmental statutes to strengthen or weaken their environmental protection provisions in ways that the regulator and economic enterprise must obey, including making it easier or harder for NGOs to seek judicial enforcement. In all these examples, the media disseminates information to the public, and furthers environmental education.

Based upon the case studies, the IPPEP model can be expressed by the notation shown in Figure 2.3.

8. CONCLUSIONS

Very important conclusions can be derived from the Hudson River case studies as illustrated by the IPPEP Model, that in the United States the achievement of effective implementation of environmental laws has required the existence of independent NGOs granted by law the power to sue polluters and the government agencies responsible for enforcement of the laws in order to assure compliance with the laws; and the existence of an independent judiciary empowered by law to order polluters and government agencies to abide by the laws.

1. (R) + (− E) = G

2. (− R) +(− E) = (− G)

3. (− R) + (− E) + (NGO , changing R) = G

4. (− R) + (− E) + (NGO + J , changing R) = G

5. (− R) + (− E) + (− NGO) + (− J) = − G

6. (− R) + (− E) + NGO + C (changing R or law) = G

R: Strong environmental regulator
− R: Weak environmental regulator
− E: Polluting enterprise
J: Court in favor of environment
− J: Court not in favor of environment
− NGO: Ineffective NGO participation or no NGOs at all
G: Good environmental governance
− G: Poor environmental governance
C: Environmental Congress

Source: These formulae were jointly designed by Nicholas Robinson (Pace U. USA), Wang Xi (SJTU, CN), Richard Ottinger (Pace U. USA), and Wang Pianpian (Pace U. USA) in July 2013.

Figure 2.3 A formula expression of the IPPEP model

The applicability of these conclusions to other jurisdictions will need to be adapted to their legal systems. But it is clear everywhere that to simply rely on regulators to provide effective implementation of laws is insufficient. The regulators inevitably become too subject to the influence of the polluters or developers subject to the regulations, either through corruption or by the political pressures to favour economic development over environmental protection to the extent of ignoring environmental laws even if that means jeopardising the health and safety of the citizenry. So there must be provided some means such as demonstrated in the Hudson River cases of holding regulators responsible and allowing the affected citizenry to require them and the offenders to observe the law.

Any jurisdiction that is serious about providing the environmental protections in the laws it has passed has to provide for the effective implementation of those laws in some manner to achieve the results equivalent to those demonstrated in the Hudson River cases.

The IPPEP Model is an analytic tool applicable at all scales, from small governments to large ones, from a central government to a federal one, and without regard for the political form of government. Based upon the Hudson River case studies, the authors developed the general formula expression of the IPPEP Model. It is hoped that more environmental law scholars will use it to assess environmental governance in different given parts of the Earth.

Over time, the Model will doubtless be refined and enhanced. But in its early application, the Hudson River Valley case studies offer ample examples of how the Model can be used to effectively assess environmental governance.

REFERENCES

Buchanan, J. and G. Tullock (2004), *The Calculus of Consent: Logical Foundations of Constitutional Democracy* (Ann Arbor, MI: University of Michigan Press).

Environmental Protection Agency (2014), 'Hudson River Cleanup website', accessed 29 March 2015 at http://epa.gov/hudson/cleanup.html#quest1.

New York Times (1980), 'Peace Treaty for Hudson' *New York Times* (20 December 1980).

Robbins, T. (2010), 'Westway, the Highway That Tried to Eat New York, Defeated 25 Years Ago This Week' (*The Village Voice Blog*, 1 October 2010), accessed 29 March 2015 at http://blogs.villagevoice.com/runninscared/2010/10/westway_the_hig.php.

Sandler, R. and D. Schoenbrod (eds) (1981), *Hudson River Power Plant Settlement* (New York: New York University School of Law).

Talbot, A. (1972), *Power Along the Hudson: The Storm King Case and the Birth of Environmentalism* (New York: Dutton).

Wald, M. (2013), 'Ex-Regulator Says Reactors are Flawed', *New York Times* (8 April).

Xi, W. (2012), 'Legal Protection for Interactions Between Parties in the Cause of Environmental Protection' 1 *Journal of Shanghai Jiao Tong U. (Philosophy & Social Sciences)* 13.

Zeller, T. (2011), 'Nuclear Agency is Criticized as Too Close to Its Industry' *New York Times* (7 May).

3. Putting the train of environmental protection on track: Nova Scotia's experiment in using legislation to strengthen environmental governance

Meinhard Doelle and William Lahey

1. INTRODUCTION

In a 2008 article entitled 'A Train Without Tracks', Annecoos Wiersema argues that new governance approaches to environmental challenges lack substantive direction.[1] New governance approaches have focused on process and on engaging non-state actors in the design and implementation of responses to the environmental challenges we face. There are many good reasons to engage non-state actors through effective processes, including: the complexity of the challenges; the social license that is associated with transparency and public engagement in decision-making; the role that collaboration with non-state actors can play in compensating for limited government resources and expertise; and the improved compliance that is expected with laws and broader policies that are developed through collaborative processes.

Wiersema, however, argues that this shift of focus from substance to process has come at a price. Using the image of a train without tracks, Wiersema makes the point that a focus on process, without clear environmental goals against which the results of these process-oriented approaches to governance can be measured, risks compromising the very purpose of environmental governance. Governance, at best, becomes a consensus building process among non-state actors with a diverse range of interests. At its worst, the process moves environmental protection toward the lowest common denominator. It can even become a rationale for government inaction, and a tool for those resistant to effective

[1] Wiersema (2008).

environmental regulation. The definition and achievement of environmental objectives is left too much to the interests, capacity and commitment of self-interested non-state participants.

Wiersema suggests that legislation can play an important role in fixing this problem. At the time Wiersema wrote her article, the Canadian province of Nova Scotia was experimenting with legislation to address some of the shortcomings in environmental governance Wiersema identified. This legislation was the Environmental Goals and Sustainable Prosperity Act, commonly called EGSPA in Nova Scotia.

This chapter explores Nova Scotia's experience with EGSPA since 2007 and considers what lessons it may have to offer. It concentrates on two innovations inherent in EGSPA. The chapter explores opportunities to combine new governance arrangements with legislative efforts to hold governments to account for ensuring that the underlying objectives are met. A second innovation explored is the effort in EGSPA to integrate environmental protection with economic well-being.

The first two sections of the chapter provide some basic context and offer an overview of EGSPA. This is followed with an assessment of the performance of the Act between 2007 and its five-year review in 2012. In the final sections of the chapter, the 2012 amendments are contrasted against what could have been done to improve the Act. This analysis is a basis to offer some concluding comments on what other jurisdictions might take from the Nova Scotian experience.

2. THE CONTEXT FOR THE DEVELOPMENT OF EGSPA

Nova Scotia's history of environmental governance is not unlike many jurisdictions in the developed world. First generation efforts in the 1970s and 1980s consisted mainly of permissive approval-based approaches that sought to regulate releases without discouraging industrial development.[2] Environmental assessment legislation was introduced in the late 1980s.[3] In the 1990s, in the wake of the 1992 Rio Conference, Nova Scotia became one of the first Canadian provinces to adopt comprehensive environmental protection legislation, the Environment Act, which replaced most of the issue specific environmental legislation adopted in

---

[2] See Doelle (1996). See also, Peter Mushkat (2000).

[3] Environmental Planning and Assessment Act (1989) c 149.

the 1970s and 1980s.[4] This Act instituted a comprehensive environmental approvals process that was typical of command and control regulation. At the same time, it reflected shifts in approaches to environmental governance that are now generally associated with 'New Governance'. For example, the Act contemplated the use of a broader range of governance tools in addition to regulation, informed by concepts such as sustainable development, pollution prevention and waste reduction, shared responsibility between governments and others, government's catalytic role, cooperative partnerships, stewardship, the polluter-pay principle, and the active development of environmental technologies.[5]

Along these 'New Governance' lines, the Environment Act established a provincial round table on Environment and Economy and included a legislative commitment to achieving a goal set by the Canadian Council of Ministers of the Environment (CCME) of reducing waste going to the landfill by 50 per cent by 2000.[6] Effective management of solid waste became a focus of provincial environmental efforts and Nova Scotia became the first province to meet the CCME goal.

In the years preceding the EGSPA, the Nova Scotia government became interested in integrating environmental protection and economic prosperity, by pursuing economic opportunities that had direct environmental benefits, and by protecting Nova Scotia's environmental capital to ensure long-term prosperity.[7] The basis for this approach was set out in a 2006 document *Opportunities for Sustainable Prosperity*.[8] EGSPA was introduced a year later. It created a framework for combining a strong economy with a clean environment by integrating environmental protection and economic prosperity. In a relatively poor province that has traditionally depended on extractive industries, this implied stronger environmental protection as well as higher levels of economic performance. EGSPA set out specific environmental goals with firm timelines that would contribute to the achievement of 'sustainable prosperity'. While a few of these goals were developed specifically for EGSPA, many were drawn from existing policy positions of the provincial government.

---

[4] Environment Act (1994–95), c 1.

[5] Ibid, s 2.

[6] Ibid, s 93(1).

[7] For discussion of the political and policy context, see Lahey and Doelle (2012) 5.

[8] Nova Scotia Department of Economic Development (2006).

A number of these were goals on which little progress was made prior to their incorporation into EGSPA.[9]

3. THE ORIGINAL VERSION OF EGSPA

The original version of the Act came into force on 7 June 2007.[10] At the heart of the *Act* was the long-term objective of integrating environmental sustainability and economic prosperity, as articulated in section 4(1):

> 4 (1) The long-term environmental and economic objective of the Province is to fully integrate environmental sustainability and economic prosperity and to this end to
>
> (a) demonstrate international leadership by having one of the cleanest and most sustainable environments in the world by the year 2020; and
>
> (b) provide certainty to all sectors of the economy through the Government's economic development strategy entitled Opportunities for Sustainable Prosperity and establish clear environmental goals while improving the Province's economic performance to a level that is equal to or above the Canadian average by the year 2020.[11]

The *Act* enumerated 21 short- and medium-term goals, established a process to monitor and report on the implementation of these goals, and created authority for the adoption and implementation of additional measures to meet the long-term objective.

The 21 goals are set out in subsection 4(2) of the Act.[12] Many of the goals address substantive targets on issues including: greenhouse gas (GHG) emissions; air pollutants; energy sources and use; solid waste disposal rates; wilderness protection and conservation; and waste-water treatment and drinking water quality standards. Others stipulate process-related targets

---

[9] For example, the development of a comprehensive water management strategy was foreshadowed in the Department of Environment's work on a drinking water strategy: see Lahey (2005). Similarly, a number of goals were previously included in the 'Green Plan' adopted by the Province in 2003: see Nova Scotia Department of Natural Resources (2005) and Nova Scotia Department of Environment and Labour (2003). Goals relating to air emissions and energy policy were previously agreed to by Nova Scotia through the Canadian Council of Ministers of the Environment or the Conferences of the New England Governors and Eastern Canadian Provinces.

[10] Environmental Goals and Sustainable Prosperity Act (2007), c 7 (EGSPA).

[11] EGSPA, s 4(1).

[12] Ibid, s 4(2).

such as the requirement to develop strategies, policies or regulations on resource management, wetlands, brownfield re-development and government procurement.

The goals can be roughly grouped into five categories. One category embraces goals pertaining to air emissions, including: emission reductions of NO_x by 20 per cent by 2009 as compared to 2000; mercury emissions by 70 per cent by 2010 compared to 2001; SO_2 emissions by 50 per cent by 2010 compared to 2001; and GHG emissions by at least 10 per cent by 2020 compared to 1990. This category also includes goals requiring the adoption by Nova Scotia of Canada-wide standards established by the CCME on ground-level ozone and fine-particulate matter and the adoption of provincial standards for new vehicles on GHG and air pollution emissions, all by 2010.

A second, overlapping category of goals, particularly given the reliance of Nova Scotia's electricity system on fossil fuels, includes goals tied to the energy sector. One of these required new residential dwellings built in or after 2008 to display an EnerGuide rating. A closely related goal demanded that all new dwellings built in or after 2011 have an EnerGuide rating of 80. A third goal in the energy category required 18.5 per cent of Nova Scotia's energy to be from renewable sources by 2013.

The third category of goals deals with water. The grouping includes the development of a comprehensive water resource management strategy by 2010, the application of at least primary treatment to all wastewater treatment discharge by 2017, the compliance of all municipal public drinking water supplies with provincial standards by 2008, and the establishment by 2009 of a policy to prevent net loss of wetlands.

The fourth category of goals addresses resource conservation and management. Specific requirements include: the adoption, by 2010, of strategies to ensure sustainability of natural capital in forests, mining, parks, and biodiversity; the legal protection of wilderness areas equal to 12 per cent of Nova Scotia's land mass by 2015; and the development, by 2010, of regulatory tools to stimulate redevelopment of contaminated lands. This category also includes the goal of limiting waste disposal to 300 kg per person by 2015.

The fifth category consists of two goals that relate to the responsibility of government to 'put its own house in order', and to lead by example. The first of these goals required the Province to adopt a sustainable procurement policy by 2009. The second required the Province to construct a 'government facility' to serve as a 'demonstration facility in accordance with a leading standard for building efficiency and sustainability'.

Most of the goals were designed with environmental protection in mind. This is consistent with the underlying concept of EGSPA: that long term economic prosperity depends on environmental stewardship. The Act was, however, clearly concerned with both economic prosperity and environmental protection. The 21 environmental goals were explicitly linked to a single long-term objective: 'to fully integrate environmental sustainability and economic prosperity'.

There were (and continue to be) clear economic opportunities associated with a number of the goals. The province had created employment through solid waste reduction efforts in the 1990s.[13] It has stressed the economic benefits associated with renewable energy production and with energy efficiency and conservation efforts.[14] The Act was based on seven principles that were as much about the economy as the environment, including, the principle that 'the management of goals for sustainable prosperity, such as emission reduction, energy efficiency programs and increasing the amount of legally protected land will preserve and improve the Province's environment and economy for future generations'.[15]

The Act was heavily weighted towards environmental protection and, specifically, to the 21 environmental goals. Not surprisingly, these were the focus during the first five years of the Act's operation, with respect to implementation and annual reporting.

The EGSPA accountability mechanisms are basic. The Act obliged the Minister of Environment to carry out an annual review of progress and to table a report in the House of Assembly.[16] The Minister was, until 2012, required to seek the advice of the Nova Scotia Round Table on Environment and Sustainable Prosperity on each annual report.[17] The annual reviews are required to consider the implementation of the targets, as well as their adequacy in meeting the long-term objective in section 4(1). The Minister is required to ask the Round Table to carry out 'a comprehensive public review of this Act and the regulations every five years after this Act comes into force' and to submit to the Minister 'a report with recommendations for amendments and improvements in the

---

13 Walker (2004).

14 Nova Scotia Department of Energy (2009) (Nova Scotia's 2009 Energy Strategy); Nova Scotia Department of Energy (2007). Department of Energy (2010) (Electricity Plan); Wheeler and Melvin (2008); Adams and Wheeler (2009) (Wheeler).

15 EGSPA, s 3(2)(g).

16 Ibid, s 6(1).

17 Environment Act, s 6(3); An Act to amend Chapter 1 of the Acts of 1994–95, the Environment Act, SNS 2006, c 30.

implementation of this Act'.[18] Although goals calling for new strategies and policies imply consultations with the public, the requirement that the five-year review be a public review is the only express provision for public participation in the implementation of the Act.

The Act assigns responsibility for implementation of the goals to the government of Nova Scotia. Some goals were more directly within the control of the government than others. The substantive goals, such as the reduction of GHG emissions, required action from other levels of government and from non-state actors, including Nova Scotia's privately owned power utility, major industries and the general population. Other goals that focused more on policy than the meeting of a specific substantive target were more within the control of the provincial government, though many involved extensive stakeholder consultations. Ultimately, the Act makes the provincial government responsible for implementation.

The powers granted in the Act to take additional measures were allocated to the Governor in Council, not to any particular Minister.[19] These powers consist of broad authority to pass regulations, to develop programs, and to enter into agreements with other governments or non-state actors.[20] This approach reflected the idea that integration of environmental and economic policy can only happen optimally on a government-wide scale.

On the other hand, as noted, the Minister of Environment alone is responsible for reporting to the House of Assembly on implementation of the Act. Most of the goals established by the Act fell within the mandate of the same Minister under Nova Scotia's Environment Act.[21] Thus the Act has been largely implemented as environmental legislation in the context of environmental policy.

In keeping with the focus of this chapter on the role of goal-setting legislation such as EGSPA in an age of 'New Governance', it is worth noting that EGSPA can be characterised as an example of the 'soft law' associated with New Governance. Under the Canadian law of justiciability,

---

[18] EGSPA, s 6(2).

[19] Under the Canadian system of Westminster governance, the Governor in Council effectively means the cabinet of the ruling government.

[20] EGSPA, ss 5, 7–9.

[21] Environment Act.

a court would be unlikely to entertain an action based on an alleged breach of the Act.[22]

The Act aligns with 'New Governance' in two other respects. In significant measure it seeks to achieve its objectives through a range of soft instruments, including a 'comprehensive water resource management strategy', a 'natural resources strategy', and a 'policy of preventing net loss of wetlands'. Even where the Act prescribed a substantive outcome, such as 18.5 per cent renewable energy by 2014, it left the methods to be used entirely to the implementation process. Second, with a few exceptions, EGSPA creates goals that government can only achieve through processes that include non-state actors. Most could not be implemented without a plan or a process developed and implemented in collaboration with a diverse range of non-state actors. In these respects, EGSPA shares the view of New Governance that environmental protection depends as much or more on multi-party governance as it does on government.

4. ASSESSMENT OF THE ORIGINAL EGSPA

EGSPA's performance to date is considered in three steps. First, the performance of EGSPA on the original 21 environmental goals is assessed. Second, its impact on the integration of environmental and economic governance is considered. Third, EGSPA's impact on environmental governance in Nova Scotia is evaluated.

It is important to have Nova Scotia's changing political situation in mind when evaluating the impact that EGSPA has had on environmental governance. In 2009, a majority government formed by the New Democratic Party (NDP) replaced the minority conservative government that had enacted EGSPA. In respect of the essentially non-justiciable EGSPA, this political change has meant that Nova Scotia's experience under the Act sheds light on the role that legislation such as EGSPA can play in maintaining effort on a program of environmental policy-making across governments.[23]

---

22 *Friends of the Earth v Canada (Governor in Council)* 2008 FC 1183; *Lexogest Inc. v Manitoba (Attorney General)* [1993] MJ No 54; *Canadian Union of Public Employees v Canada (Minister of Health)* 2004 FC 1334.

23 The strength of the conclusions in this regard is limited by the fact that the NDP would be regarded by many in a Nova Scotia context to be stronger on environmental protection than was the Progressive Conservative government it replaced. A change in government in 2013 to the Liberal Party should offer

4.1 Performance on Specific Environmental Goals

The quantitative track record with respect to the original 21 goals is impressive. Of the 15 goals due before 2012, seven were achieved on time, one was achieved early, and four were achieved late. In other words, 12 of 15 goals (80 per cent) have been achieved and more than 50 per cent have been achieved on time. Of the three that have been missed, one (the labeling of new dwellings with an EnerGuide rating) was subsumed in a later more important goal (the achievement of a specified EnerGuide rating by all new dwelling), bringing the 'achieved' rate to 87 per cent.

One missed goal continues 'in progress', but has been largely accomplished (universal implementation of higher municipal water quality standards) while the third (reduction of mercury emissions by 70 per cent) was deferred by the government.[24] This latter goal is the only instance where government has given itself a different timeline from that in the Act. It is unfortunate that the government did not amend the Act in this regard, or consult with the Round Table before changing the timeline. In changing the target date government did acknowledge the obligation to achieve the goal.

In short, none of the goals have been ignored or abandoned while the solid majority has been implemented early, on time, or modestly behind schedule. It is disturbing that the unachieved goals relate to drinking water quality and the reduction of mercury emissions – two goals connected directly to human health. The municipal drinking water goal is largely accomplished. The government has proposed to deal with the mercury reduction on a different timeline by a renewable energy target that goes beyond the one in the Act.[25] On the positive side of the equation, EGSPA has played a crucial role in tipping the balance in favour of decisive action on policy objectives that were of doubtful status prior to EGSPA. The leading example of this is the soon to be accomplished goal of bringing wilderness areas equal to 12 per cent of landmass under legal protection.[26]

---

further opportunity to consider the role of legislation in ensuring environmental policy goals survive changes in governments.

[24] Sierra Club Canada (2010); Province of Nova Scotia (2010a).

[25] Government of Nova Scotia (2012).

[26] Ibid, 2 and 4.

4.2 Performance on Integrating Environmental and Economic Governance

EGSPA purports to be about more than the achievement of discrete environmental goals. It also purports to be about the integration of environmental and economic governance. While there are broad references in the *Act* to the role that other sectors of society will play, the operational focus of the *Act* is on the role that government plays as maker of environmental and economic policy. The question arises: has the implementation of EGSPA produced greater integration of environmental and economic policy-making within the Nova Scotia government?

Evaluating EGSPA's impact in this more diffuse respect is more difficult than evaluating its impact in terms of the implementation of the 21 goals listed in subsection 4(2). In its five-year review of the Act, the Round Table concluded that limited or uncertain progress has been made under EGSPA on integrating environmental and economic policy-making, either in respect of the implementation of the specific EGSPA goals or more broadly.[27] The contribution that EGSPA has made in this aspect can be evaluated from the perspective of whether EGSPA can be said to have been administered with integration as an objective, and from the perspective of EGSPA's broader influence on matters relevant to EGSPA's objective of policy integration.

From the perspective of how EGSPA has been administered, there is little evidence that policy integration has been aggressively pursued. Judging by the annual reviews, implementation of the Act has been overwhelmingly limited to the achievement of 21 discrete environmental goals.

As to whether EGSPA has had a broader influence on integration between environmental and economic policy-making, there is some evidence of this broader influence. The work carried out by the Department of Energy to produce climate change and renewable energy strategies was completed under the framework of the general principles and objectives laid out in EGSPA.[28] The same can be said of the work carried out under the Act by or under the direction of the Department of Natural Resources to create strategies for sustaining natural capital in forestry, mining, parks and biodiversity.[29] Economic implications or benefits have also been significant influences of the work of the

---

[27] Janowitz (2012).

[28] Wheeler and Melvin (2008); Electricity Plan; Nova Scotia Department of Energy (2009).

[29] Nova Scotia Department of Natural Resources (2011).

Department of Environment in meeting EGSPA goals in water resource management and wetland protection.[30]

Despite these examples of integrative policy-making the overall picture is one in which the overriding objective of integrated policy-making seems not to have been significantly advanced, under the framework of EGSPA. Instead, EGSPA was largely administered as environmental legislation. In fact, in 2010, the NDP government replaced *Opportunities for Sustainable Prosperity* with an economic development strategy that gave less prominence to the role that environmental sustainability would play.[31]

Recently, the 'One Nova Scotia Commission' has produced a sweeping report on the current state and future prospects of the Nova Scotia economy that calls for fundamental change on multiple fronts to reverse decades of economic and population decline.[32] The report includes a 'backgrounder' on 'Green Economic Growth and Social Sustainability' that mentions EGSPA but neither EGSPA nor the broader concept of green economy are discussed in the report. On the other hand, it is interesting that without citing EGSPA as a precedent, the Commission recommends enshrining the fundamental goals of economic policy in legislation.

4.3 Impact on the Process of Environmental Governance

The implementation of EGSPA has entailed stakeholder engagement in the development of new policies or strategies in natural resources, energy, water resource management, wetland protection, waste reduction and on other topics. No comprehensive analysis of these processes of engagement has been carried out. It can be assumed that most were effectively conducted, given the results, the absence of public controversy and the fact that the five-year review of EGSPA did not reveal concern about the processes used.

The clear exception is the process to develop a new forestry policy under the umbrella of the natural resources strategy which was itself developed under EGSPA. As argued by Duinker, this process served to accentuate and deepen divisions among forestry stakeholders, undoing improvements in relationships made through the Colin Stewart Forestry Forum, which developed a plan independently of EGSPA to achieve the

[30] Nova Scotia Department of Environment (2010); Nova Scotia Department of Environment (2011).

[31] Province of Nova Scotia (2010a).

[32] Nova Scotia Commission on Building Our New Economy (2014).

wilderness conservations goals that were incorporated into EGSPA.[33] According to Duinker, bad process produced a policy of ‘split the difference’ outcomes on contentious issues like clear-cutting that left few satisfied and that made little sense from forestry management or sustainability perspectives. His conclusions suggest that EGSPA produced a process that was completed on time at the expense of taking the time to achieve understanding and consensual accommodation of core interests.

The broader process criticism of EGSPA is that it has been implemented in a way that largely limits the engagement of the public and stakeholders to the implementation of the specific goals. With the exception of the five-year review, there has been no broader engagement on the Act as a whole or on its core premise – that higher environmental protection and a stronger economy can become mutually reinforcing objectives. Tirone *et al.* argue the Act assumes an alignment with the values of Nova Scotians that may not be accurate and that the Act cannot be expected to accomplish its larger objective unless this alignment exists or is created.[34] Their scepticism may be supported by the developments in economic policy-making that have followed EGSPA that have largely ignored or given only minimal attention to EGSPA and the philosophy on which it is based.

5. THE 2012 AMENDMENTS TO EGSPA

At the conclusion of the five-year legislative review in 2012, the NS government passed amendments to EGSPA. The amendments were generally in line with recommendations of the Round Table.[35] They responded to some of the key challenges during the first five years of implementation, without fundamentally changing the nature of the Act. The amendments include some significant structural changes to the Act and some new goals.

On the structural side, the overall objectives of the Act have been revised. The target of environmental and economic leadership on a global scale by 2020 has been replaced with a more realistic and measurable goal of continuous improvement in measures of social, environmental and economic indicators of prosperity. There is also now a more explicit recognition of the importance of integration in the stated objectives of the

33 Duinker (2012).

34 Tirone, Gallant and Sykes (2012) (Tirone).

35 The Round Table carried out public consultations as part of its five-year review of the Act.

Act. The Mi'kmaq concept of 'Netukulimk', which parallels the concept of sustainable development, has been incorporated into the Act's foundational principles. The basic approach of meeting the long-term objective of integrated prosperity and environmental protection through the establishment of clear and specific individual goals, however, remains. The language of sustainable prosperity has been retained and extended – whereas the Act previously spoke of environmental goals, it now refers to 'goals for sustainable prosperity'. In many ways, the emphasis on the integration of environmental goals with economic ones, has been reinforced.

On the procedural side of the equation, the Minister of Environment is no longer under an obligation to consult with the Round Table in preparing the annual report, which must be tabled in the House of Assembly. He or she is now obligated to consult with the Ministers of other key departments. This should create a stronger context for integration of the operation of the Act into the wider functioning of government. The scope of the annual reports has also been expanded. They now encompass not only the goals laid out in the Act but the 'regulations and activities of all provincial departments relating to sustainability'. The role of the Round Table in conducting a comprehensive public review every five years has been retained.

Key among the changes to the Act is the addition of goals. A first category of new goals is generally in line with the approach taken in the original Act, a focus on environmental objectives. Among these are revised goals on reducing mercury emissions (to replace the one previously missed) and on transitioning to renewable energy (to reflect NDP policy previously announced independently of the Act).

The scope of the Act was expanded by three new goals that are heavily economic in their thrust. One goal calls for an energy framework that advances the economic, social and environmental benefits of energy efficiency and productivity, sustainable transportation, increasing reliance on renewable energy, replacement of coal and oil with natural gas and energy innovation. A second goal deals with the increase of local food production. A third goal calls for a green economy strategy. Each of these goals, and especially the green economy goal, is as much an economic goal as an environmental goal. All three goals offer opportunities to connect environmental and economic performance, and all have important social implications.

The overall impact of these amendments, therefore, is a shift away from the initial focus on environmental goals to more integrated goals, and toward the integration of environmental, social and economic well-being. As such, these amendments have the potential to respond to one of the shortcomings identified with the original EGSPA, that while government's performance of the specific goals was impressive, there was limited evidence of resulting integration of environmental protection with economic prosperity.[36]

Other criticisms of the Act, however, remain unanswered. The government generally avoided setting new targets in areas where the initial goals have been met, and it only set a small number of new targets. As a result, most of the goals now stated in the Act are completed goals. Only minor changes were made to the mandate or composition of the Round Table. The Act remains silent on the process to develop mandated strategies or policies and the role of the public in these processes. The role of the public in the broader administration of the Act has also not been enhanced. Government self-evaluation remains the primary compliance tool. It should be noted that in each of these respects, the new EGSPA largely reflect the conclusions and recommendations of the Roundtable based on its five-year review.

6. LESSONS FOR THE DESIGN OF GOAL ORIENTED LEGISLATION

Based on the experience to date, EGSPA has had a positive impact on environmental governance in Nova Scotia. It is also clear that there is room for improvement. We have identified opportunities to strengthen EGSPA – and legislation like EGSPA – in the following areas:

(1) Updating and developing new goals on an ongoing basis rather than just during the legislative five year review.
(2) The value of effective public engagement in the administration of the Act and activities undertaken to meet the goals of the Act.
(3) The importance of ensuring good process, particularly for the implementation of goals related to policies and strategies.
(4) The potential role of an independent commissioner for sustainable prosperity.

6.1 Updating and Developing New Goals

Nova Scotia's experience with EGSPA shows that legislating environmental goals can help to ensure diligence by government in meeting

36 Janowitz (2012).

stated goals. Under EGSPA, this has been the experience not only for goals that are largely internal to government but also for goals developed through multi-stakeholder processes that can only be implemented with the contribution of non-state actors. It follows that our first recommendation for improving EGSPA – and similar legislation – is that it should have a built-in mechanism for evaluating, changing and adding to the goals to ensure the Act is focusing attention on a continuing basis on the right goals for achieving the objectives of environmental governance.

The rudiments of such a mechanism can be found in the Act. The Act confers authority on government to make regulations that establish additional goals to those contained in the Act itself. The annual report of the Minister of Environment to the legislature provides an opportunity for evaluation of the continuing appropriateness and adequacy of existing goals. The existing machinery has, however, not been used, not even when Nova Scotia has moved beyond the goals stated in the Act, as it did when the NDP government increased Nova Scotia's renewable energy target to 40 per cent from the 18 per cent stated in EGSPA. The five-year review resulted in the addition of new goals but otherwise left in place the original goals, many of which have been completed.

Later, we suggest that reviewing and proposing changes to existing goals or the adoption of new goals could be one of the primary responsibilities of a new officer called the Commissioner for Sustainable Prosperity. The Round Table could play an important role in the process, including by contributing to the annual reporting process, a role it had before the 2012 amendments. The ongoing review of the adequacy of goals presents a good opportunity for public engagement with the Act as a whole and with its overall administration. At the same time, public engagement, effectively conducted, would be critical to the effectiveness of whatever process is created for reviewing and updating goals; for one thing, it could help to ensure buy-in for the goals and the Act.

Legislation such as EGSPA which purports to connect specific goals to larger and overarching outcomes such as the integration of environmental governance with economic prosperity should specify, at least in general terms, the criteria for evaluating the contribution that specific goals are expected to make to these larger objectives. This evaluation should be a key variable in determining whether goals are retained, dropped, changed or added. This could help to ensure that the process of goal-setting is not only keeping the train of environmental governance on *some* track but on the *right* track for reaching desired destinations. In the process, it could build understanding of the role that legislated goal-setting can and cannot play in achieving larger outcomes such as sustainable prosperity.

6.2 Public Engagement

As stated above, the only provision made in EGSPA for public participation is the description of the five-year review by the Round table as a 'comprehensive public review'. The five-year review that was completed in 2012 included a public consultation process. Public and stakeholder consultations have also been part of the processes used to complete the policies and strategies required under the Act on water management, wetland protection, and natural resources management.

More effective public engagement in all aspects of the Act should be at the heart of any effort to strengthen the Act's contribution to environmental governance in Nova Scotia. To do so would make the Act a more effective instrument for combining the strengths of new governance approaches to environmental governance with the importance of holding governments accountable for ensuring that environmental governance leads to ultimate policy objectives. We consider it useful to distinguish between public engagement in administration of the Act and public engagement in activities that are undertaken to meet specific goals.

With respect to the administration of the Act, public engagement will be critical in at least two respects. First, it is an essential tool in motivating government to continue to take compliance with the specific goals and the overall objective of the Act seriously. The more the public is engaged in the administration of the Act, the less likely it is that governments will be tempted to make choices in favour of other government objectives that may conflict with the effective implementation of EGSPA. Second, the public can contribute directly to the effective administration of the Act, including the enhancement of existing goals and their implementation and the identification of new goals. The combined effect would be a more engaged and informed public that is more likely to be invested in the Act, and a government that is more motivated to pursue the goals and objectives because it knows that the public is supportive. This would address the assessment of Tirone *et al.*, that the effectiveness of *EGSPA* is constrained to the extent that the substance of the Act is misaligned with the values that inform the environmental attitudes and behaviours of Nova Scotians.[37]

---

[37] Tirone (2012).

6.3 Ensuring Good Process

In this section, attention shifts from the general value of public engagement to the need for good process, particularly for policy development. Experience in Nova Scotia and elsewhere has demonstrated time and time again the value of good process. As Duinker points out in the context of forest policy, good process can be critical to achieving an effective outcome, particularly with respect to goals that point to a strategy, policy or regulation rather than a substantive outcome.[38]

Duinker argues that the goal of public engagement should be informed consensus. We take this to mean something different than consensus supporting the lowest common denominator, a consensus that effectively addresses the substantive issues. In other words, good process is about building as much consensus as is reasonably possible on how to most effectively achieve a clearly stated objective. It is not about just doing what everyone can agree to do, and it is not about policy development that ignores the views and values of the public and key stakeholder.

We conclude based on the academic literature and our own experience that good process results in a better end product, be that a new wetland policy, a water strategy, or a green economy strategy.[39] This is particularly important for goals that are stated in such a manner that they can be achieved without serving the goal of sustainable prosperity. The goal to develop a wetland policy, for example, should be met in a manner that maximises long-term net benefits to the province by identifying opportunities to integrate environmental protection with economic and social prosperity. Good process is critical to ensuring the goals are met in a manner that will maximise sustainable prosperity, integration, and long term benefits to Nova Scotians.

Equally important, good process builds support for the substance of what is being developed, ensuring more effective implementation. As pointed out by Tirone, we cannot assume that the general public supports either the specific goals in EGSPA or the overall objectives of integration and sustainable prosperity. Public engagement is an opportunity to build support and to diffuse opposition.

One of the lessons learned from the first five years of EGSPA is that a goal to develop a policy or strategy with a firm timeline can lead to bad process and less than desired substantive outcomes, even when the intentions are good. For this reason, it is important for legislation such as

---

38 Duinker (2012).

39 Duinker (2012). See also Diduck and Sinclair (2012); Sinclair and Diduck (2001).

EGSPA to be clear about the elements of good process, and the importance of good process. One way to assist this would be to establish criteria for good process in the legislation; criteria against which processes utilised to meet the goals in this Act can be measured.

Principles of good process can be found in the public engagement literature.[40] Duinker refers to the desired process as a principled negotiation process, and considers it as a form of participatory democracy, as distinct from representative and deliberative democracy.[41] He notes that an acceptable process is increasingly one that participants are involved in designing. This leads to the conclusion that the criteria that should guide implementation of legislation such as EGSPA would include principles of transparency, access to information and decision-makers, inclusiveness, active engagement in decision making, and an effort to build consensus where possible. The criteria could be established in the Act, or the Act could set the stage for their development in regulations as long as their role in the Act was clearly set out. With either approach, the role of legislation would be to prescribe fundamental principles such as transparency, inclusiveness, and the basic rules of engagement. It would leave the specific design of processes for specific goals to those directly responsible for those goals.

6.4 Commissioner for Sustainable Prosperity

The role we propose for a commissioner in relation to EGSPA would be a more proactive and cooperative role than has traditionally been the case for such officers, at least in Canada. The leading Canadian example of a commissioner in the environmental field is the federal Commissioner for the Environment who operates as part of the Auditor General's Office. Like other audit officers, the Commissioner seeks to ensure accountability of the federal government for environmental responsibility through after-the-fact audits that result in published reports. The Commissioner plays an important role in making government decisions on the environment open to public scrutiny. The model has its limits however. For example, reports of the Commissioner on the federal government's failure to implement its commitments on climate change have been

---

40 See, for example, Sinclair and Diduck (2009) and Connor (2001).
41 Duinker (2012) 64.

ignored by the current Conservative government and its Liberal predecessor. More broadly, relationships between governments and auditors general unavoidably tend in the adversarial direction.[42]

What we have in mind is an office charged with overseeing independent research on sustainable prosperity in Nova Scotia. The focus of the office would be on getting things done by figuring out how they can be done (through a transparent and objective process) rather than on getting things done by after-the-fact criticism when goals are missed (probably with little recognition of the difficulties involved in implementing goals).

Our reasoning is multifaceted, but has two essential elements. First, it is an approach that is possible and likely to produce results given the growing track record of follow-through on goals articulated in EGSPA and the progress that EGSPA has made in becoming a continuing part of the governance framework in Nova Scotia, regardless of which party is in power. Second, it has the potential to address the key obstacle to this follow-through to date, which is not political resistance but, as in the case of mercury emissions, uncertainty about feasibility, consequences and implementation options as economic and technological circumstances evolve.

In addition to having a role in commissioning research, the office could be given responsibility (and resources) for managing public engagement processes and/or leading the annual and five-year reviews with input from the Roundtable. Consistent with the purpose and scope of EGSPA, the focus of the mandate should be on how Nova Scotia is doing rather than how the government is doing under the Act.

The idea would be to build an institutional infrastructure that carries minimal risk of taking the administration of the Act in an adversarial direction, with the resistance to the Act that this would be likely to engender. The impressive performance under the Act to date does not warrant an adversarial role for a commissioner in Nova Scotia. On the other hand, an institution that brings arms-length transparency and independence on the administration of the Act through a mandate that is more about assisting with implementation than it is with enforcing would be consistent with the governance philosophy embedded in the Act. It would also help to ensure that the role the Act appears to have played in keeping the process of environmental governance on track is consolidated, strengthened and expanded.

The issues which Nova Scotia is seeking to address under the concept of sustainable prosperity are complex and likely to be among the defining

---

42 Savoie (2008).

issues of our and future generations. The creation of a Commissioner for Sustainable Prosperity would ensure an independent voice and a source of expertise on these critical and complex issues. The collaborative model we are proposing for the Commissioner will help to assure citizens that governments will follow through on their environmental commitments at the same time giving citizens a dependable avenue for participating in the Act's development. The creation of this independent voice will serve these functions naturally, without this having to be the primary focus of the position.

7. CONCLUSION

For new governance approaches to be effective in the environmental field, it is critical that the engagement and empowerment of non-state actors does not diminish government accountability for achieving clearly stated objectives of environmental governance. Experience in Nova Scotia suggests that a legislative framework which includes clear and specific goals of environmental governance can serve an important role in holding governments accountable for ensuring that new governance approaches do not come at the price of environmental progress. The combination of power sharing and active, constructive engagement of non-state actors through new governance approaches on the one hand, and clear goals that hold governments accountable for meeting stated policy objectives on the other hand, can offer an effective combination of 'bottom up' and 'top down' approaches.

Based on Nova Scotia's experience, this approach may require the following to be effective:

- a conducive political context, including support for the objectives and the legislative mechanism across political lines;
- a clear statement of the overall objective, such as sustainable prosperity or the integration of environmental protection, and economic and social wellbeing;
- specific, well designed goals with clear timelines set in legislation;
- regular review of the adequacy of the goals, including through an institutional mechanism that enjoys the benefits of independence and specialised expertise;
- accountability of the government as a whole and relevant departments;
- transparency about the status of the goals and the process for meeting them; and

- active, ongoing and constructive public engagement at multiple levels.

With these elements in place, legislation that codifies the goals of environmental governance and the accountability of government for achieving those goals can significantly enhance environmental governance. It has the potential to serve as a counterweight to the tendency in an age of 'New Governance' to emphasise the process of environmental governance over its substance. In other words, in the terms suggested by Annecoos Wiersema, legislation like EGSPA can help to keep the train of environmental governance on track when it is conducted under the diffuse principles and modalities of New Governance. The lesson from the Nova Scotia experience, however, is that careful design in light of local conditions is critical to the success of such an approach, particularly given the need to balance political support with accountability.

REFERENCES

Adams, M. and D. Wheeler (2009), *Stakeholder Consultation Process for a Renewable Energy Strategy For Nova Scotia* (Final Report to Government of Nova Scotia, 28 December).

Connor, D. (2001), *Constructive Citizen Participation: A Resource Book* (Connor Development Services Limited).

Department of Energy (2010), *Renewable Electricity Plan: A path to good jobs, stable prices and a cleaner environment* (Government Policy Document, April).

Diduck, A. and A. Sinclair (2012), 'Public Participation in Environmental Assessment: The Case of the Nonparticipant' 29(4) *Environmental Management* 578.

Doelle, M. (1996), 'Nova Scotia' in A. Lucas and R. Cotton (eds) *Canadian Environmental Law* (2nd edn, London: LexisNexis Butterworths 1996).

Duinker, P. (2012), 'In Search of Compass and Gyroscope: Where Were Adaptive Management and Principled Negotiation in Nova Scotia's Forest-Strategy Process' 35 *Dalhousie Law Journal* 55.

Government of Nova Scotia, *Environmental Goals and Sustainable Prosperity Act: Progress Report 2012* (Progress Report, 2012).

Janowitz, M. (2012), *Report to the Minister of Environment Regarding The Environmental Goals and Sustainable Prosperity Act (EGSPA)* (Round Table on Environment and Sustainable Prosperity Report, 30 March).

Lahey, W. (2005), *A Drinking Water Strategy for Nova Scotia: Final Report* (Interdepartmental Drinking Water Management Committee Final Report, 2005).

Lahey, W. and M. Doelle (2012), 'Negotiating the Interface of Environmental and Economic Governance: Nova Scotia's Environmental Goals and Sustainable Prosperity Act (2012)' 35 *Dalhousie Law Journal* 3.

Mushkat, P. (2000), *Guide to Environmental Law for Nova Scotians* (2nd edn, Halifax: Legal Information Society of Nova Scotia).

Nova Scotia Commission on Building Our New Economy (2014), *Now or Never: An Urgent Call to Action for Nova Scotians* (The One Commission Report, February).

Nova Scotia Department of Economic Development (2006), *Opportunities for Sustainable Prosperity* (Nova Scotia Government Economic Growth Strategy).

Nova Scotia Department of Energy (2007), *Nova Scotia's Renewed Energy Strategy and Climate Change Action Plan* (Consultation Paper: October).

Nova Scotia Department of Energy (2009) *Toward a Greener Future: Nova Scotia's 2009 Energy Strategy* (Government Policy Document, January).

Nova Scotia Department of Environment (2010), *Water for Life: Nova Scotia's Water Resource Management Strategy* (Province of Nova Scotia Strategy Paper, 23 December).

Nova Scotia Department of Environment (2010) *Nova Scotia Wetland Conservation Policy* (Province of Nova Scotia Policy Paper, September).

Nova Scotia Department of Environment and Labour (2003), *Towards a Sustainable Environment* (Strategy Document of Province of Nova Scotia).

Nova Scotia Department of Natural Resources (2005) *Green Plan: Progress towards a sustainable environment* (Strategy Document for Province of Nova Scotia).

Nova Scotia Department of Natural Resources (2011), *The Path We Share: a Natural Resources Strategy for Nova Scotia 2011–2020* (Province of Nova Scotia Strategy Paper).

Province of Nova Scotia (2010a), *Province to hold NS Power accountable for new mercury emissions caps* (Province of Nova Scotia, 9 December).

Savoie, D. (2008), *Court Government and the Collapse of Accountability in Canada and the United Kingdom* (IPAC Series in Public Management and Governance, Toronto: University of Toronto Press).

Sierra Club Canada (2010), 'Nova Scotians will pay the price for giving NS Power a pass on mercury regulations' (26 July), accessed 29 March 2015 at http://www.sierraclub.ca/en/node/2763.

Sinclair, A. and A. Diduck (2001), 'Public Involvement in EA in Canada: A Transformative Learning Perspective' 21(2) *Environmental Impact Assessment Review* 113.

Sinclair, A. and A. Diduck (2009) 'Public Participation in Canadian Environmental Assessment: Enduring Challenges and Future Directions' in K. Hanna (ed.), *Environmental Impact Assessment Process and Practices in Canada* (2nd edn, Oxford: Oxford University Press).

Tirone, S., K. Gallant and K. Sykes (2012), 'Environmental Goals and Sustainable Prosperity Act: And the People of the Province: EGSPA's Social Deficit' 35 *Dalhousie Law Journal* 71.

Walker, S. *et al.* (2004), 'Executive Summary' in *The Nova Scotia Solid Waste-Resource Accounts* (Genuine Progress Index: Measuring Sustainable Development Report).

Wheeler, D. and H. Melvin (2008), *Stakeholder Consultation Process For An Administrative Model For DSM Delivery in Nova Scotia* (Final Report, 10 April).

Wiersema, A. (2008), 'A Train Without Tracks: Rethinking the Place of Law and Goals in Environmental and Natural Resources Law' 38 *Environmental Law* 1239.

4. Has environmental impact assessment (EIA) lost credibility? Recent concerns from Australia and Canada

Wayne Gumley

1. INTRODUCTION

A central theme of sustainable development is the need to integrate economic and ecological considerations in decision making.[1] One of the earliest and most widely adopted strategies for this purpose was the inclusion of environmental impact assessment (EIA) within development approval processes. EIA was envisaged as a catalyst for 'productive and enjoyable harmony between man and his environment'.[2] However, this bold vision has proved to be elusive as our economic system has not yet found an effective way to integrate environmental values, and EIA processes alone do not impose any obligation to prioritise environmental protection. As a result, negative environmental impacts of a development proposal are usually outweighed by economic objectives when making project approval decisions.[3]

Meanwhile, the indicators of unsustainable development continue to grow, with the global ecological footprint of human society now exceeding bio-capacity by more than 50 per cent.[4] This growing ecological crisis might suggest a more rigorous approach to EIA is required. Recent

[1] World Commission on Environment and Development (1987) (WCED 1987) 62; United Nations Conference on the Environment and Development (1992) (UNCED 1992) ('The Rio Declaration'), which recognised EIA as a fundamental principle contributing to sustainable development (at Principle 17).

[2] As stated in the preamble to the US National Environmental Policy Act of 1969 (42 U.S.C. 4321 *et seq.*).

[3] Jay et al. (2006); Macintosh (2004); Bonyhady and Macintosh (2010).

[4] World Wildlife Fund (2012).

regulatory developments in Australia have been aligned more to the contrary, with concerted efforts being made to by-pass and weaken current EIA processes. The main driver of this trend has been persistent lobbying by industry groups like the Business Council of Australia for reductions in 'green tape' to ease compliance costs for business.[5] In 2012 the Council of Australian Governments (COAG) yielded to these pressures by announcing a proposal for 'streamlining the process for approval of major projects, through accreditation of state assessment and approval processes' to replace most of the EIA functions currently conducted by the Commonwealth Government.[6] In October 2013, the newly elected Commonwealth Government announced a 'One-Stop Shop' for development approvals to be implemented through a range of new bilateral agreements.[7] This chapter will consider the legitimacy of the One-Stop Shop proposals as a response to perceived problems with the current project approval processes. It will firstly describe the original rationale for EIA and then review the current range of EIA processes implemented by Commonwealth, State and Territory governments across Australia.

2. WHAT IS ENVIRONMENTAL IMPACT ASSESSMENT?

The recognised purpose of EIA is to 'inform decision making and result in appropriate levels of environmental protection and community well-being'.[8] Thus EIA does not prioritise environmental outcomes in development approval processes, but enables decision-makers to balance adverse environmental impacts against wider economic and social objectives.[9] The first national EIA process was introduced by the United States in the National Environmental Policy Act of 1969 (NEPA).[10] This landmark legislation arose from concerns over major infrastructure projects conducted by Federal agencies such as the Bureau of Public Roads[11] and US Army Corps of Engineers, in which environmental

---

5 Business Council of Australia (2012).

6 Council of Australian Governments (2012a).

7 Hunt (2013).

8 International Association for Impact Assessment and Institute of Environmental Assessments (1999).

9 Elliott and Thomas (2009) 13.

10 National Environmental Policy Act of 1969 (42 U.S.C. 4321 et seq.) (NEPA).

11 Weingroff (1996).

considerations were often given little thought.[12] NEPA was notable for its bold purpose, which espoused an emerging global environmental ethic:

> To declare a national policy which will encourage productive and enjoyable harmony between man and his environment; to promote efforts which will prevent or eliminate damage to the environment and biosphere and stimulate the health and welfare of man; to enrich the understanding of the ecological systems and natural resources important to the Nation ...[13]

The essence of NEPA was a legislative requirement for US federal government agencies to provide a detailed statement on environmental impacts for 'all major federal action significantly affecting the quality of human environment'.[14] For this purpose, federal actions included activities requiring federal permits or federal funding. The main objective was better public participation in the decision making process. NEPA also established the Council on Environmental Quality to develop and promote national environmental policies and goals.[15]

NEPA-style legislation has now been adopted throughout the world. However, NEPA did not prescribe the procedures required in EIA. In the USA these were at first developed through administrative procedures and the courts, and later elaborated through regulations.[16] In most jurisdictions, EIA is now fairly standardised, and commonly includes the following elements:[17]

(1) A determination by a regulatory agency on the need for an EIA ('screening') and the range of environmental and social impacts that must be assessed ('scoping').
(2) A draft EIA report prepared by the project proponent including a detailed description of the proposed action, the current baseline environmental conditions, an evaluation and prediction of impacts, and appropriate strategies for management and mitigation of the

---

[12] Caldwell (1998).

[13] NEPA, s 2 (42 USC § 4321). Statements to similar effect were subsequently adopted in multilateral declarations of international law such as the 1972 Stockholm Declaration, the 1982 World Charter for Nature and the 1992 Rio Declaration.

[14] NEPA, s 102 (42 USC § 4332).

[15] NEPA, s 202 (42 USC § 4342).

[16] Council of Environmental Quality Regulations (1978) 43 FR 55994, 29 November 1978; see also Caldwell (1998).

[17] Elliott and Thomas (2009) 23; Wood (2002).

expected impacts (including alternative ways to achieve the project objectives).

(3) A consultation process with local community and other stakeholders, seeking comments upon the proposal and the draft report, to be incorporated into a final EIA Report.

(4) A decision to allow or disallow the proposal (with or without conditions), based on the findings of the final EIA Report, made by a designated regulatory agency.

(5) Follow up measurement and monitoring of the actual impacts of the completed project by the proponent and/or relevant regulatory agencies, after the project is completed.

Within this broad framework, the specific procedural requirements and terminology applied at each stage can vary widely from one jurisdiction to the next. The potential for environmental impacts to influence project approval decisions generally depends upon the quality and breadth of data revealed by the process as well as the weight given to those impacts against other priorities such as the economic outcomes of the project.

3. EIA IN AUSTRALIA

3.1 Commonwealth Government Processes

The Australian Commonwealth Government followed the U.S. example in 1974, by introducing a legislated EIA process under the Environment Protection (Impact of Proposals) Act 1974 (Cth) ('the EPIP Act'). At this time there were concerns about controversial infrastructure projects carried out by State Government agencies, including the notorious flooding of Lake Pedder by the Tasmanian Hydro Electricity Commission in 1972, and various State-approved ventures which threatened World Heritage sites, such as sand mining at Fraser Island in Queensland.[18] Like NEPA, the EPIP Act was directed at projects requiring approval by the Commonwealth Government (typically export-oriented projects, projects relating to defence operations and projects affecting Commonwealth marine areas) as well as projects supported by Commonwealth funding. The EPIP Act prompted several major public inquiries on environmental matters[19] and also fostered the development of some important ground

[18] Fowler (1982).

[19] Including the Ranger Uranium Inquiry, the Fraser Island Sand Mining Inquiry and Shoalwater Bay Inquiry.

rules for the rapidly evolving field of environmental law, such as the standing rule in public interest litigation.[20]

However, the EPIP Act differed from NEPA in several important aspects. The Honourable Moss Cass, as Minister for the Environment and Conservation who introduced the legislation, was wary of problems that had emerged with NEPA:

> In developing the impact statement procedure we have noted difficulties that have accompanied its use in the United States. These have largely stemmed from mandatory requirements for statements and from procedures which result in too frequent a resort to the courts. We hope to avoid these difficulties, firstly, by making the impact statement requirement discretionary so that we can concentrate on the most significant proposals and, secondly, by incorporating the requirement into the normal process of governmental decision making.[21]

As a consequence, the EPIP Act provided the 'Action Minister' wide discretion in screening and scoping decisions, based upon 'Administrative Procedures' that were specifically designed to be non-reviewable.[22] This meant that the ultimate effectiveness of EPIP was highly dependent upon the environmental stance of the political party controlling the government at any particular time. Thus, in 1975, when the conservatives led by Malcolm Fraser replaced the Australian Labour Party government led by Gough Whitlam, the application of the EPIP Act was significantly restricted.[23] Eventually the scope of the Act was further weakened by amendments to the Administrative Procedures in 1987.[24]

3.2 Inter-jurisdictional Conflicts

Most Australian State governments initially perceived the Commonwealth EPIP Act as an unjustified encroachment upon State sovereignty over the development of natural resources within their borders. This prompted various alternative forms of EIA to be separately established in all States and Territories within a short span of time (by Queensland and Tasmania in 1974, Victoria in 1978, NSW in 1979, South Australia in 1982, NT in 1984, Western Australia in 1986 and the ACT in 1991).

---

20 *Australian Conservation Foundation v Commonwealth* (1980) 146 CLR 493.

21 Cass (1974).

22 Padgett and Kriwoken (2001).

23 Fowler (1996).

24 Commonwealth of Australia (1987).

After Australia ratified the World Heritage Convention in 1974, several State governments also mounted legal challenges against proposals for listing under the Convention of sites within State boundaries, particularly the South West Forests of Tasmania and Wet Tropics Rainforests of Queensland.[25] The major outcome of these challenges was a strong affirmation by the High Court that the Commonwealth had power to legislate broadly upon on environmental protection under various constitutional heads including external affairs, corporations and people of any race.[26] This protracted period of Commonwealth-State conflict was eventually ended by the 1992 *Intergovernmental Agreement on the Environment* ('the IGAE'),[27] under which the Commonwealth agreed to limit its regulatory actions to a restricted range of 'matters of national environmental significance' (primarily based upon Australia's international treaty commitments). The IGAE also provided the foundation for a major overhaul of all Commonwealth environmental legislation which ultimately included replacement of the EPIP Act and a range of other Commonwealth Acts by the Environmental Protection and Biodiversity Conservation Act 1999 (Cth) with effect from 16 July 2000 ('the EPBC Act'). Whilst these changes represented a significant retreat from the environmental field by the Commonwealth, the EPBC Act provided several clear advantages over the former EPIP Act. In particular, the new Act placed the Commonwealth Minister for Environment at the centre of decision making on environmental assessment and approval instead of the relevant department's Action Minister,[28] adopted the 'principles of ecologically sustainable development' as guiding criteria[29] and provided specific statutory criteria to 'trigger' an assessment by reference to certain 'matters of national environmental significance' (NES), which now include:[30]

(1) World Heritage properties;
(2) National Heritage places (from 23 Sep 2003);

---

[25] Boer (1992).

[26] Ibid. The breadth of Commonwealth legislative power was more recently affirmed in *New South Wales v Commonwealth* [2006] HCA 52 (14 November 2006); the 'WorkChoices' case.

[27] Commonwealth of Australia (1992b).

[28] Environmental Protection and Biodiversity Conservation Act 1999 (EPBC), ss 75, 87.

[29] Ibid, ss 3A, 136.

[30] Ibid, at Division 1 of Part 3.

(3) wetlands of international importance (under the Ramsar Convention);
(4) threatened species and ecological communities;
(5) migratory species;
(6) nuclear actions (including uranium mining);
(7) Commonwealth marine areas;
(8) the Great Barrier Reef Marine Park; and
(9) water resources affected by coal seam gas and large coal mining developments (from 22 June 2013).

In addition to these specific matters, the Act also provides for assessment of actions by Commonwealth agencies and actions involving Commonwealth land or Commonwealth Heritage places overseas.[31]

The EPBC Act assessment and approval process is normally commenced by 'referral' of a proposed action to the Commonwealth Minister for Environment.[32] Once a matter is referred, the Minister must decide whether the proposed action is a 'controlled action',[33] and if so, what type of assessment approach will be used.[34] The onus to make a referral is driven by civil and criminal penalties that apply if a project proponent takes a 'controlled action' without approval.[35] Flexible standing rules are also provided for interested third parties to seek an injunction restraining a breach of the Act.[36] If a State or Territory government has decided to conduct its own EIA for the same matter, the Commonwealth Minister can allow assessment by an accredited State or Territory assessment process. This latter option may also be provided by bilateral assessment agreements under which the final project approval decision must still be made by the Commonwealth Minister.[37] In addition to the project-based EIA, the EPBC Act also provides for strategic assessments, on a wider 'landscape scale' for classes of actions carried out in accordance with an

---

[31] Ibid, Division 2 of Part 3.
[32] Ibid, s 68.
[33] Ibid, s 75.
[34] Ibid, Part 8. Under s 87 the Minister can choose one of six possible assessment approaches including assessment on referral information, assessment on preliminary documentation, Public Environment Report (PER), an Environmental Impact Statement (EIS), a Public Inquiry (PI) or assessment by an accredited assessment process.
[35] Ibid, Parts 3, 18 and 19.
[36] Ibid, s 475.
[37] Ibid. s 475.

endorsed policy, plan or program.[38] These may cover a given geographical region, cumulative impacts, or a given industry sector (for example, logging, mining, electricity). Recent examples include Melbourne's urban growth boundary and the Browse Basin liquefied natural gas hub (West Kimberley, WA).[39]

Many writers have questioned whether the EPBC Act has led to better environmental outcomes.[40] The record shows that very few projects referred under the Act have been refused approval, and most suffer only minor modification. Part of the explanation can be found in the narrow scope of matters covered by the Act, which has been described as a 'worrying retreat' for Commonwealth involvement in environmental protection.[41]

The EPBC Act envisages the addition of new matters of NES from time to time. However, this power has been exercised very sparingly to date, with the only additions being matters of national heritage added in 2003, the Great Barrier Reef Marine Park in 2009 and most recently, water resources affected by coal seam gas and mining in 2013. The first statutory review of the Act, led by Dr Allan Hawke, received numerous submissions recommending additional new matters, including greenhouse emissions, inland waters, land clearing, invasive species, ecosystems that are not yet threatened and so on.[42] The Hawke Review recommended just two additional matters; being 'ecosystems of national significance' (Recommendation 8) and an interim greenhouse trigger for actions resulting in emissions above 500,000 tonnes (Recommendation 10). Neither recommendation has been adopted to date.

One of the most significant exclusions from the matters of NES is forestry activities carried out under Regional Forest Agreements (RFAs).[43] It was agreed in the 1992 National Forest Policy Statement that the protection of biological diversity in forest areas would be provided for under the RFAs and State forestry codes.[44] However, public interest

---

38 Ibid, Part 10.
39 Australian Government (2014a).
40 Macintosh (2004); Godden and Peel (2007); McGrath (2006); Tridgell (2013).
41 Mould (1998).
42 Hawke (2009) 100-101.
43 EPBC, s 38.
44 Commonwealth of Australia (1992a).

litigation over forestry activities in Tasmania and Victoria has demonstrated that clear-felling is regularly carried out under RFAs with little or no consideration for the habitat of listed threatened species.[45]

4. STATE AND TERRITORY EIA PROCESSES

Notwithstanding the historic importance of the Commonwealth Government EIA processes, and the specific role of the Commonwealth concerning matters of NES, a much broader range of environmental impacts outside the scope of the EPBC Act are left for assessment and regulation by State or Territory governments. These include impacts such as air and water pollution, noise, natural resource depletion, greenhouse emissions and impacts on non-listed species and non-threatened ecosystems. These State and Territory based EIA processes are carried out as an integral part of various development approval processes for urban and regional planning, transport, water and energy supply infrastructure. EIA processes are also implicit in various statutory licensing schemes in sectors such as mining, agriculture, fisheries, forestry and industrial pollution and waste management. A table in the Appendix to this chapter provides a summary of the principal legislation providing for EIA across all Australian jurisdictions noting responsible agencies, triggers and decision criteria, public participation in scoping and the various levels of assessment. This table indicates significant levels of inconsistency and duplication in EIA procedures across all Australian jurisdictions. One key difference is the governing agencies, with some administered under environmental protection legislation (for example, WA and Qld), whilst others are part of planning law and development approvals (ACT, NSW, Qld, SA and Tas) and some separated as a stand-alone EIA schemes (Vic and NT). The legislative objectives of the responsible agencies vary widely, with some promoting environmental protection, whilst others focus on promoting economic development. There is also wide variation in key elements such as the triggers for an assessment, criteria for screening and scoping, opportunities for public participation and the final decision making responsibility. In 1991, the Australian and New Zealand Environment and Conservation Council (ANZECC) released a report on a 'National Approach' to remove duplication and inconsistency across

---

[45] See, for example, *Brown v Forestry Tasmania (No 2)* [2006] FCA 1729; *Environment East Gippsland v VicForests* [2010] VSC 335.

Australian jurisdictions.[46] Under the IGAE in 1992, all Australian governments committed themselves to a number of key principles to provide a national approach.[47] The 2009 Hawke Review also emphasised that a national approach was desirable, whereby the Commonwealth could provide leadership to the States and Territories through five key processes: harmonisation, accreditation, standardisation, simplification and oversight.[48] In particular, the Review recommended that the Commonwealth should harmonise its practices with State and Territory regimes, focus on accreditation, facilitate uniform regulatory systems between those regimes, provide simplification through streamlined EIA processes and oversight by engaging in performance monitoring of accredited systems.[49]

Regrettably, the IGAE commitment to a national approach has not been fulfilled, as State and Territory EIA processes have continued to evolve independently. Some State processes appear to be tending away from best practice with new 'fast track' alternatives for major infrastructure projects recently introduced in Victoria, and major overhauls of approval processes in Queensland and NSW.[50] Meanwhile, at the Commonwealth level, the Hawke Review recommendations for harmonisation and streamlining of Commonwealth EIA and greater accreditation of State and Territory processes have evolved into the 'One-Stop Shop', which proposes a major reduction in the Commonwealth's role. Before considering the COAG proposal, it is worth noting that 'duplication' of government responsibility is not necessarily a bad thing in a Federal context, where checks and balances may be highly desirable. As Hollander puts it: 'duplication, overlap and redundancy perform a useful function in a complex policy domain such as the environment where the science is uncertain and the politics fraught'.[51]

---

46 Australian and New Zealand Environment and Conservation Council (1991).

47 Elliot and Thomas (2009) 126; Australian and New Zealand Environment and Conservation Council (1996).

48 Hawke (2009) 63.

49 Hawke (2009) 63, and Recommendations 4 and 27.

50 See, Major Transport Projects Facilitation Act 2009 (Vic); Sustainable Planning and Other Legislation Amendment Act (No. 2) 2012 (Qld); New South Wales Government (2013); Hasham (2014).

51 Hollander (2009).

5. COAG'S 'ONE-STOP SHOP'

COAG's objective is to lower costs for business and improve competition and productivity by reforming 'duplicative and cumbersome environment regulation; streamlining the process for approvals of major projects' and 'improving assessment processes for low risk, low impact developments'.[52] Under this proposal, the Commonwealth would work with the States and Territories to 'fast-track the development of bilateral agreements for accreditation of State assessment and approval processes ...' and a draft framework of standards for accreditation of environmental approvals to support these reforms was later released.[53] However, in December 2012, COAG announced that the proposed reforms would be delayed due to 'significant challenges that have emerged in developing accreditation arrangements that provide consistency for business and assurance to the community that high standards will be met and maintained'.[54] It appears that these 'significant challenges' arose from a belated realisation that State processes were highly variable and far from satisfactory to meet EPBC Act requirements, thus creating potential for even greater uncertainty in development approvals.[55] Some of these problems were clearly foreshadowed by the Hawke Review, which broadly supported bilateral agreements as mechanisms for reducing duplication and streamlining processes in principle, but also noted widespread concerns about the quality of assessments completed by State governments, and the need to ensure 'the transparency of, public engagement in, and appeal rights in relation to assessments performed under a bilateral agreement'.[56] A 2009 Senate Inquiry into the Operation of the EPBC Act raised similar concerns and recommended that particular regard must be paid to 'the transparency of, public engagement in, and appeal rights in relation to assessments performed under a bilateral agreement, compared to the conditions that would have existed had the assessment been performed under the EPBC Act'.[57]

Despite these widespread concerns, the new Coalition Government revived the One-Stop Shop proposal shortly after the Federal election in

---

52 COAG (2012a).

53 Australian Government (2012).

54 Council of Australian Governments (2012b).

55 Taylor and Coorey (2012).

56 Hawke (2009) 65.

57 Australian Network of Environmental Defender's Offices (2009) Recommendation 6.

September 2013. On 16 October 2013, the new Minister for the Environment, Greg Hunt, announced a framework for achieving this goal, whereby participating States or Territories would enter a *Memorandum of Understanding* (MOU) followed by negotiation of an *approval* bilateral agreement within 12 months.[58] All States and Territories have now signed MOUs to guide implementation of this approach,[59] aiming to 'lift the use of a single accredited assessment process to 100%'. The MOUs provide a two-stage process whereby State Governments will firstly amend existing assessment bilateral agreements to more specifically address matters of NES, in order to provide a stronger basis for State *assessment* of proposals impacting upon those matters.[60] The second stage envisages that the Commonwealth will sign off on 'approval bilaterals' to enable final approval decisions with regard to EPBC Act matters to be made by State and Territory governments. At the time of writing, all States and Territories have made significant progress towards the completion of approval bilaterals but none have been finalised.[61]

6. FLAWS IN THE COAG APPROACH

COAG approved the One-Stop Shop approach just a few months after the Federal election in 2013, based primarily upon a ten-page Discussion Paper prepared by the Business Council of Australia (BCA).[62] The BCA claimed that the costs and delays associated with EIA are significant, citing an estimate that all industries have incurred up to $820 million over the life time of the EPBC Act (since 2000). Whilst this aggregate figure may seem large when spread across all projects the average cost estimate per project is from $30,000 to $100,000.[63] Expenses of this magnitude are fairly modest within major project budgets which can run into the billions. In any case, for most major projects impact assessment costs would be necessarily incurred as a matter of normal risk management practice. If unforeseen social or environmental impacts are caused by a project after it commences, the proponent could face catastrophic financial liabilities and severe reputational harm. Legal liabilities may

58 Hunt (2013).
59 Abbott (2013).
60 For example, see Commonwealth of Australia (2013b), Clause F (Roles).
61 Australian Government (2014b).
62 Business Council of Australia (2012).
63 Ibid, 6, citing Macintosh (2004); Macintosh, Fear and Cummings (2009).

arise in the form of penalties and prosecution for breaching environmental laws, as well as potentially huge common law liabilities for economic losses suffered by shareholders and third parties who suffer consequential losses. The danger of fast tracking and cost cutting in major projects was well demonstrated by the BP Limited Deepwater Horizon oil rig explosion and oil spill in the Gulf of Mexico in April 2010. BP is still negotiating its way through tens of billions in liability arising from this disaster which killed 11 men and devastated the Louisiana coastline.[64] The chairman of a National Academy of Engineering investigation into that disaster stated that:

> A large number of decisions were made that were highly questionable and potentially contributed to the blowout of the Macondo well ... Virtually all were made in favor of approaches which were shorter in time and lower in cost. That gives us concern that there was not proper consideration of the tradeoffs between cost and schedule and risk and safety ... officials of the minerals service, which was reorganised after the accident and renamed the Bureau of Ocean Energy Management, Regulation and Enforcement, had failed to put in place the oversight and the procedures that could have prevented the blast and saved lives.[65]

Disasters of this type demonstrate why a robust EIA process coupled with strong regulatory oversight should be an essential prerequisite for all development projects. The focus for any EIA reforms should be on improving the long term outcomes for the business sector and the whole community, not just short term cost and delay suffered by project proponents. This view of wider perspective of the role of EIA is supported by international best practice principles such as the United Nations Global Compact, which recommends that 'Businesses should support a precautionary approach to environmental challenges'.[66] It is also supported by industry associations like the International Council on Mining and Metals (ICMM), which has established ten 'Sustainable Development Principles' that member companies are expected to implement and measure their performance against.[67] Many leading financial institutions have committed to the Equator Principles to promote 'sound environmental management practices' for large infrastructure and industrial projects.[68] Where funds are sought for projects with potential for

---

64 The Associated Press (2014).
65 Broder (2010).
66 United Nations (2000) Principle 7.
67 International Council on Mining and Metals (2003).
68 Equator Principles Association (2013).

significant adverse environmental and social risks, the Equator Principles require proponents 'to conduct an assessment process to address, to the Institution's satisfaction, the relevant environmental and social risks and impacts of the proposed Project'.[69]

With regard to delay, the BCA view is overly simplistic. In most cases the time frame for completion of EIA obligations is largely in the hands of the proponent, who controls when the development approval process is commenced, and when the gathering of evidence for impact assessment purposes will commence. Assessment processes are often lengthy due to the intrinsic difficulties and uncertainties involved in assessment of ecosystem impacts, but are often delayed at the whim of the proponent, due to changing commercial considerations and variations to the project. Approval decisions have also been delayed where proponents fail to provide sufficient information on relevant environmental impacts.[70] A recent Senate Inquiry found that the Business Council of Australia could name only one project in which Commonwealth involvement delayed approval of a project. That was the Traveston Dam proposal, where scientific evidence obtained by the Commonwealth Minister's office showed that, contrary to the proponent's assessment, the project would have unacceptable impacts, and thus the alleged delay was totally vindicated.[71] It is difficult to see how the One-Stop Shop reforms will overcome the need for lengthy and careful independent investigation of environmental impacts in such cases.

7. THE DOUBTFUL INTEGRITY STATE AND TERRITORY PROCESSES

The One-Stop Shop approach places great faith in the integrity of State and Territory EIA processes. Whilst it is beyond the scope of this chapter to analyse all State and Territory EIA processes in detail, guidance has been provided by Bonyhady and McIntosh through a series of in-depth case studies which demonstrate fundamental weaknesses across all Australian jurisdictions.[72]

In Victoria, a case study by Brad Jessup on the Port Phillip Bay Channel Deepening Project highlighted the 'brief and ineffectual' legislative scheme for EIA under the Environment Effects Act 1978 (Vic),

69 Ibid, Principle 2: Environmental and Social Assessment.
70 Australian Network of Environmental Defender's Offices (2013) 4.
71 Australian Senate (2013) Chapter 2, para 2.31.
72 Bonyhady and Macintosh (2010).

which was first introduced over 40 years ago. That Act gives the Minister for Planning complete discretion in the screening and scoping stages. Ministerial guidelines provide criteria to trigger assessments, but these are not enforceable and are often ignored, allowing the process to be mismanaged and manipulated.[73] As a result, many highly contentious major projects have been approved in Victoria without any significant EIA process, including the CityLink tunnels under the Yarra River, the Albert Park Grand Prix Circuit, the North-South pipeline and the DualGas power station. Projects that have faced EIA processes in Victoria have exposed fundamental weaknesses in the state process, such as narrow scoping, arbitrary procedures, conflicts of interest between the State as a proponent and assessor, pre-emption of the outcomes, failure to consider alternatives, and suppression of community involvement.[74] The Wonthaggi Desalination Plant provides a salutary lesson on what can go wrong in the absence of a comprehensive and inclusive assessment process. In that project the fundamental question of whether a desalination plant was the best solution to Melbourne's water supply problem was outside the scope of assessment. This contributed to an outcome where Victorian households will pay over $18 billion for a facility that has no present use.[75] Despite this bitter experience in the water sector, the Victorian Government recently introduced the Major Transport Projects Facilitation Act 2009 (Vic) to fast track EIA processes for 'major transport projects'. This Act enables the Planning Minister to take over approval decisions under a wide range of other legislation including environmental protection functions under the Planning and Environment Act 1987, Heritage Act 1995, Environment Protection Act 1970, Flora and Fauna Guarantee Act 1998, National Parks Act 1975, Wildlife Act 1975 and the Forests Act 1958. The Act also significantly restricts appeal or review of the Minister's decision. Ironically, the lack of public participation and transparency under this new process may expose the Victorian Government to risks of legal action. The $6–8 billion East West tunnel recently approved under this fast track scheme is currently being challenged on the basis that statements by the government about the claimed benefits of the project are actionable as 'misleading or deceptive conduct'.[76]

In New South Wales, a case study by Jemilah Hallinan examined Part 4 of the Environmental Planning and Assessment Act 1979 (NSW),

---

73 Jessup (2010).
74 Ibid.
75 Victorian Auditor-General (2009–10) 41.
76 Gordon (2014).

which she described as a robust process, with features of best practice including specific requirements for public consultation and concurrence by other relevant agencies (to support integrated decision-making), appeals on the merits to the specialist Land and Environment Court, as well as third party enforcement and open standing provisions for judicial review.[77] In 2005, an additional 'fast track' process was introduced in Part 3A of the NSW Act, to cover 'critical infrastructure' and major projects of State significance. The EIA trigger and scoping under Part 3A were highly discretionary, public participation and appeal rights were reduced and some projects could be assessed and approved merely on the basis of a 'concept plan'.[78] In the face of extensive criticism of Part 3A, in 2013 the NSW Government released a White Paper and draft legislation that proposes a complete overhaul of planning approvals with greater emphasis on public consultation at the strategic planning level, rather than at the 'back end' of project approvals.[79] However, the draft legislation was significantly amended by a coalition of minor parties in November 2013, and the NSW Government has subsequently stated it will seek reform using existing legislation.[80]

In Queensland, a case study by Larissa Waters describes three alternative pathways for EIA in that State.[81] The most common assessment process applied to 'significant projects' under the State Development and Public Works Organisation Act 1971 (Qld). Mining and petroleum projects may be assessed under the Environment Protection Act 1994 (Qld), whilst the highest level of assessment was applied under the Integrated Planning Act 1997 (Qld), which dealt with accredited assessment of controlled actions under the EPBC Act (and the bilateral agreement). Waters found that the significant projects process was 'almost completely discretionary' with no mandatory requirements to consider environmental impacts unless the matter was a controlled action subject to assessment under the EPBC Act. Her description of the Traveston Dam project suggests that the Queensland process can be manipulated and outcomes pre-empted for political purposes.[82] More recently, the Integrated Planning Act 1997 was replaced by a new Sustainable Planning Act 2009, which Chris McGrath describes as, 'a

---

77 Hallinan (2010).
78 Bateman (2013).
79 New South Wales Government (2013).
80 Hasham (2014).
81 Waters (2010) 125–59.
82 Ibid.

complex piece of legislation which in substance makes quite limited changes'.[83]

Similar concerns have been detailed in case studies from Western Australia (by Hannes Schoombee re the Gorgon Gas Project), South Australia (by Rob Fowler re the Penola Pulp Mill), Tasmania (by Andrew Macintosh and Michael Stokes re the Gunns Pulp Mill), Northern Territory (by Kirsty Howey re the McArthur River Mine) and the ACT (by James Prest re the Gunghalin Drive Freeway).[84]

8. CAN STATE AND TERRITORY PROCESSES SATISFY AUSTRALIA'S INTERNATIONAL OBLIGATIONS?

Australia has made a wide range of environmental commitments under numerous international agreements covering matters such as World Heritage, Ramsar wetlands, endangered species, migratory species and marine pollution. As a party to the 1992 Rio Declaration it has also made a broad commitment to undertake EIA in relation to all proposals 'likely to have a significant adverse impact on the environment', not just matters of NES.[85] Under the One-Stop Shop proposal there will be a continuing need for a Commonwealth assessment and approval process for development projects outside State or Territory jurisdictions (for example, proposals relating to Commonwealth territory, Commonwealth actions and Commonwealth marine areas).

The current EPBC Act process has many features that have been designed to meet Australia's international obligations, which are not consistently found in the State and Territory schemes. These include clear statutory triggers, greater transparency, greater scope for public participation, stronger review rights and other stakeholder remedies, and a higher level of administrative support and enforcement. Under the One-Stop Shop MOUs each of the eight State and Territory governments have undertaken that they will separately reform their EIA processes to satisfy EPBC Act requirements (and these will operate alongside the ongoing Commonwealth assessment processes that will continue to be

83 McGrath (2011) 31.

84 Bonyhady and Macintosh (2010).

85 UNCED (1992) Principle 17 and see also Hunter, Salzman and Zaecke (2002) 432.

needed for projects outside State or Territory jurisdiction). Thus developers will face a new wave of complexity, uncertainty and inconsistency in EIA processes across nine separate jurisdictions.

A deeper long-term concern is various compromises to EIA standards contained in the MOUs, including reliance upon 'common streamlined terms of reference'[86] and soft commitments to ensure that impacts are assessed 'to the greatest extent practicable',[87] which clearly contradict the stated aim of maintaining high environmental standards.

It is difficult to see how the 'significant challenges' identified in the early stages of the One Stop Shop proposal have been resolved.[88] In order to meet their MOU obligations the States and Territories must find the political will and financial resources to significantly upgrade existing EIA processes. However the prevailing attitude is one of 'competitive federalism' where States and Territories effectively compete to attract investment at the expense of environmental protection,[89] as indicated by recent expressions of rivalry between Queensland and NSW with regard to coal seam gas developments.[90] State and Territory governments have also significantly compromised their EIA responsibilities by severely downsizing environmental agencies over the last few years.[91]

Given this 'race to the bottom' mindset, there is every chance that future development projects will be vulnerable to many new causes for delay and legal challenges on constitutional or administrative law grounds due to inadequate community consultation and inadequate consideration of international law commitments.[92] Australia's reputation in international affairs is already at a low point following recent expansion of coal seam gas processing plants adjacent to the Great Barrier Reef, which prompted UNESCO's World Heritage Committee to consider placing the Reef on the List of World Heritage in Danger.[93]

One of the most obvious problems with the One-Stop Shop proposal is the increased likelihood of conflicts of interest when State agencies assess impacts on matters of NES. Principles of natural justice and good governance require a clear separation between government decision makers and parties that hold an economic interest in a project. For many

86 Commonwealth of Australia (2013a) para 6.4.
87 Ibid 6.1.
88 Taylor and Coorey (2012).
89 Commonwealth of Australia (2013a) para 2.47.
90 Bajkowski (2014).
91 Dunckley and McCullough (2013).
92 Fowler (1996); Gardner (1994).
93 The World Heritage Committee (2013).

major projects, a State or Territory will be the approval body for the project whilst also being a significant beneficiary, either as a proponent (either directly or through a State owned corporation), or as a recipient of royalty revenue.[94] This potential for conflict was clearly identified by the Business Council of Australia when it raised concerns that a 12-month delay to an export coking coal mine could cost the Queensland Government $170 million in revenue.[95] This example also reveals a very narrow view of economic value of major projects that often prevails in the business sector, which can be quite contrary to the broader public interest and intergenerational equity. A failure to develop coal reserves immediately would merely defer government revenue, not create a loss. And of course, if the coal is developed immediately there would be a permanent loss to the natural capital, which the resource industry never likes to recognise. It also ignores the beneficial longer term consequence of deferral that the economic value of non-renewable natural resources is likely to increase in future, as the resources become increasingly scarce.

9. IS EIA IN AUSTRALIA STILL CREDIBLE?

The chequered history of EIA processes in Australia prompts the question whether EIA has outlived its usefulness as the primary legal mechanism for minimisation of environmental impacts by major development projects? Bonyhady has pointed out that despite the popularity of EIA there is an enduring 'dearth of information' regarding its environmental benefits and cost effectiveness.[96] Tridgell has concluded that the EPBC Act has contributed to some significant environmental outcomes but only minimal gains in most areas.[97] However, these assessments may be harsh, given the modest original objectives of EIA; to involve the public in decision-making through consideration of public comment *before* an environmental impact statement is finalised and *before* any decision is taken on the proposal concerned.[98] There was never any promise of optimal environmental outcomes, merely a process for transparent and well-informed decision-making.

---

94 Australian Conservation Foundation (2013).

95 Business Council of Australia (n 5) 6; Macintosh, Fear and Cummings (2009).

96 Bonyhady (2010) 1–15.

97 Tridgell (2013).

98 Caldwell (1998); Cass (1974).

Over the last few decades Australian governments seem to have focused on EIA as the primary stamp of environmental credibility for development activities. During the same period, competition policy reforms have promoted a 'small government' mind-set that places greater focus upon privatisation of infrastructure, self-regulation and market based instruments instead of direct regulation.[99] This trend has contributed to a significant shift in staff and financial resources away from environmental agencies responsible for EIA.[100]

With diminishing government resources applied to EIA there is greater reliance upon the proponent, or consultants paid by the proponent, to provide the majority of the evidence of impacts and project alternatives. Submissions to the Hawke Review pointed out that information from those sources is more likely to support the proposal as local community stakeholders have limited financial capacity to provide expert evidence to the contrary.[101] A related problem is the lack of accountability and very limited scope for legal challenges to the various decisions made during the course of EIA, particularly the threshold decisions on whether a matter requires EIA and the choice of assessment method.[102] Even where legal challenges are possible, the general cost of public interest litigation may be prohibitive to community based litigants. These financial barriers include a possible obligation to provide an undertaking as to damages when seeking interlocutory orders, and security for costs in the event that the legal challenge is unsuccessful.[103]

Most of the problems with EIA identified in this chapter have been previously considered at great length by the final report of the Hawke Review in 2009. The One-Stop Shop proposal almost completely ignores the Hawke Review. Instead of acting upon the findings of that comprehensive review process, COAG has hastily adopted a fast-track approach delegating assessment of EPBC Act matters to the States and Territories based upon unsubstantiated claims that this will reduce cost and delay, whilst satisfying Australia's international obligations. COAG has completely failed to recognise well-grounded concerns about the conflicts of interest and poor performance of State and Territory governments that have plagued development approvals in the past. COAG has also failed to provide any clear mechanism to ensure that States and Territories will

---

99 Hilmer (1993); Australian Government (2006).

100 Brodie (2014); Dunckley and McCullough (2013).

101 Australian Network of Environmental Defender's Offices (2001).

102 Hawke (2009) para 15.61.

103 Ibid paras 15.86–15.115.

provide sufficient resources to properly administer their new responsibility for assessing matters of NES.

In conclusion, it is clear that the credibility of EIA processes in Australia is set to be greatly undermined by the One-Stop Shop reforms as proposed by the MOUs. If the business community is truly concerned about inefficiency and duplication in development approvals it should recognise that a proper assessment of matters of NES cannot be avoided, and delegating this task to under-resourced State and Territory agencies may be highly counter-productive. A far better starting point for EIA reform would be to exert pressure upon all States and Territory governments to adopt a uniform EIA process based upon 'best practice' in Australia, such as the current EPBC Act model. Once the States and Territories have demonstrated that they can lift their EIA processes to the EPBC Act level, the delegation of EPBC Act matters will be far less problematic. It should also be recognised that the EPBC Act process is not perfect. In order to enhance the overall integrity of information that is relied upon by decision-makers in designing a new uniform EIA process, many of the Hawke recommendations need to be revisited. In particular the recommendations to expand public participation,[104] enhance the use of expert evidence,[105] and extend review rights[106] deserve early attention.

Harmonisation of State EIA regulation is not a radical suggestion. Increasing harmonisation has been a normal progression in many other fields of Australian law, such as corporation law,[107] consumer law,[108] industrial relations[109] and occupational health and safety.[110] As environment and sustainability issues have increasingly involved national and international dimensions, the time is ripe for harmonisation of Australian EIA processes, but this should only proceed in accordance with the long-term public interest in environmental protection, and not short-term industry perspectives.

---

104 Hawke (2009) Chapter 14.
105 Ibid para 16.7.
106 Ibid Chapter 15.
107 Barrett (2012).
108 Nottage (2009).
109 Mitchell *et al.* (2010).
110 Johnstone (2008).

REFERENCES

Abbott, The Hon. Tony, MP (2013), *Media Release Friday 13 Dec 2013; All States and Territories sign up for the one-stop shop.*

Associated Press (2014), 'Appeals Court Upholds BP Oil Spill Settlement' *The New York Times* (10 January), accessed 30 March 2015 at http://www.nytimes.com/2014/01/11/business/energy-environment/appeals-court-upholds-oil-spill-settlement.html.

Australian and New Zealand Environment and Conservation Council (1991), A National Approach to Environmental Impact Assessment in Australia and Background Paper (Canberra: Australian and New Zealand Environment and Conservation Council).

Australian and New Zealand Environment and Conservation Council (1996), Guidelines and Criteria for Determining the Need for and Level of Environmental Impact Assessment in Australia (Canberra: Australian and New Zealand Environment and Conservation Council).

Australian Conservation Foundation (2013), *Submission on Draft Bilateral Agreement between the Commonwealth and the State of Queensland* (Melbourne: Australian Conservation Foundation).

Australian Government (2006), *Rethinking Regulation; Report of the Taskforce on Reducing Regulatory Burdens on Business*, accessed 30 March 2015 at http://www.pc.gov.au/research/completed/regulation-taskforce/report/regulation-taskforce2.pdf.

Australian Government (2012) Draft Framework of Standards for Accreditation of Environmental Approvals under the Environment Protection and Biodiversity Conservation Act 1999, (July 2012); accessed 10 April 2015 at: http://www.environment.gov.au/system/files/resources/0bfc6fde-8e57-4017-bea7-8a856bd7d2d5/files/accreditation-standards-framework.pdf.

Australian Government, Strategic assessments website (2014a), accessed 30 March 2015 at http://www.environment.gov.au/epbc/assessments/strategic.html.

Australian Government, 'Bilateral Agreements' (2014b), accessed 30 March 2015 at http://www.environment.gov.au/protection/environment-assessments/bilateral-agreements.

Australian Network of Environmental Defender's Offices (2009), *Submission to the Independent Review of the Environment Protection and Biodiversity Conservation (EPBC) Act 1999* (Submission No. 189).

Australian Network of Environmental Defender's Offices (2013), *Submission on Draft Bilateral Assessment Agreement between Queensland and Australian Governments.*

Australian Senate (2009), *Report of the Standing Committee on Environment Communications and the Arts* (18 March).

Australian Senate (2013), *Report of the Standing Committee on Environment and Communications* (12 March).

Bajkowski, J. (2014), 'Queensland Flames NSW over Coal Seam Gas Output' *Government News* (29 April) accessed 30March 2015 at http://www.governmentnews.com.au/2014/04/queensland-flames-nsw-coal-seam-gas-output/.

Barrett, R.I. (2012), 'Towards Harmonised Company Legislation – "Are We There Yet"?' 40 *Federal Law Review* 141.

Bateman, B. (2013), 'A New Planning System for New South Wales' (Clayton Utz Insights), accessed 30 March 2015 at http://www.claytonutz.com/publications/edition/23_may_2013/20130523/a_new_planning_system_for_new_south_wales.page.

Boer, B. (1992), 'World Heritage Disputes in Australia' 7 *Journal of Environmental Law and Litigation* 247.

Bonyhady, T. (2010), 'Introduction' in Bonyhady, T. and A. Macintosh (eds), *Mills, Mines and other Controversies: The Environmental Assessment of Major Projects* (Sydney: The Federation Press, 2010).

Bonyhady, T. and A. Macintosh (eds), *Mills, Mines and other Controversies: The Environmental Assessment of Major Projects* (Sydney: The Federation Press, 2010).

Broder, J. (2010), 'Report Faults BP and Contractors for Rig Explosion and Spill' *The New York Times* (17 November), accessed 30 March 2015 at http://www.nytimes.com/2010/11/18/us/18BP.html?hp.

Brodie, J. (2014), 'Environmental Job Cuts Risk a Repeat of Gladstone Failures' *The Conversation* (13 May), accessed 30 March 2015 at http://theconversation.com/environmental-job-cuts-risk-a-repeat-of-gladstone-failures-26491.

Business Council of Australia (2012), *Discussion Paper for the COAG Business Advisory Forum* (Melbourne: Business Council of Australia).

Caldwell, L.(1998), *The National Environmental Policy Act: An Agenda for the Future* (Bloomington, IN: Indiana University Press).

Cass, D. (1974), *Second Reading Speech on the Environment Protection (Impact of Proposals) Bill 1974* (Parliament of Australia).

Commonwealth of Australia (1987), *Environment Protection (Impact of Proposals) Act 1974 – Order under section 6.*

Commonwealth of Australia (1992a), *Intergovernmental Agreement on the Environment* (1992a) *(the 'IGAE')*, accessed 30 March 2015 at http://www.environment.gov.au/about-us/esd/publications/intergovernmental-agreement.

Commonwealth of Australia (1992b), *National Forest Policy Statement; A New Focus for Australia's Forests* (1992b).

Commonwealth of Australia (2013a), *Bilateral Agreement between the Commonwealth of Australia and The State of New South Wales.*

Commonwealth of Australia (2013b), *Memorandum of Understanding Agreement between the Commonwealth of Australia and Queensland Government.*

Council of Australian Governments (2012a), Communiqué of Meeting held 13 April (Canberra).

Council of Australian Governments (2012b), *Communiqué of Meeting held December 2012* (Canberra).

Dunckley, M. and D. McCullough (2013), 'Victoria cuts 4000 public service jobs to save surplus' *Australian Financial Review* (22 Oct), accessed 30 March 2015 at http://www.afr.com/p/national/victoria_cuts_public_service_jobs_crr2mab9c5SDr0NTLZ8GsI.

Elliott, M. and I. Thomas (2009), *Environmental Impact Assessment in Australia; Theory and Practice* (Sydney: The Federation Press).

Equator Principles Association (2013), *The Equator Principles III 2013*, accessed 30 March 2015 at http://www.equator-principles.com/resources/equator_principles_III.pdf.

Fowler, R.J. (1982), *Environmental Impact Assessment, Planning and Pollution Measures in Australia* (Canberra: Dept. of Home Affairs and Environment).

Fowler, R. (1996), 'Environmental Impact Assessment: What Role for the Commonwealth? – An Overview' 13 *Environmental and Planning Law Journal* 246.

Gardner, A. (1994), 'Federal Intergovernmental Co-operation on Environmental Management: A Comparison of Developments in Australia and Canada' 11(2) *Environmental and Planning Law Journal* 104.

Godden, L. and J. Peel (2007), 'The Environment Protection and Biodiversity Conservation Act 1999 (Cth): Dark sides of virtue' 31 *Melbourne University Law Review* 106–45.

Gordon, J. (2014), 'Supreme Court to be asked for ruling on East West Link' *The Age* (22 April), accessed 30 March 2015 at http://www.theage.com.au/victoria/supreme-court-to-be-asked-for-ruling-on-east-west-link-20140421-370hs.html.

Hallinan, J. (2010), 'New South Wales and the Sandon Point Development' in T. Bonyhady and A. Macintosh (eds) *Mills, Mines and other Controversies: The Environmental Assessment of Major Projects* (Sydney: The Federation Press)

Hasham, N. (2014), 'NSW set to deliver radical changes to planning under existing law' *Sydney Morning Herald* (28 February), accessed 30- March 2015 at http://www.smh.com.au/nsw/nsw-set-to-deliver-radical-changes-to-planning-under-existing-laws-20140228-33oss.html.

Hawke, A. (2009), *The Australian Environment Act: Independent Review of the Environment Protection and Biodiversity Conservation (EPBC) Act 1999 Final Report* (Canberra: Commonwealth of Australia).

Hilmer, F.G., (1993) *Independent Committee of Inquiry into National Competition Policy* (Australia). National Competition Policy: Report by the Independent Committee of Inquiry. AGPS.

Hollander, R. (2009), 'Rethinking Overlap and Duplication: Federalism and environmental assessment in Australia' (2009) 40 (1) *Publius* 136–70.

Hunt, The Hon. Greg, MP (2013), 'One-stop shop approved by Government' *Media Release – Minister for the Environment* (16 October).

Hunter, D., J. Salzman and D. Zaecke (2002), *International Environmental Law and Policy* (2nd edn, Sydney: The Foundation Press).

International Association for Impact Assessment and Institute of Environmental Assessments (1999), *Principles of Environmental Impact Assessment Best Practice* (Fargo, ND: International Association for Impact Assessment).

International Council on Mining and Metals (2003), *ICMM Sustainable Development Framework* (London: ICCM).

Jay, S. *et al.* (2006), 'Environmental Impact Assessment: Retrospect and Prospect' 27 *Environmental Impact Assessment Review* 287.

Jessup, B. (2010), 'Victoria and the Channel Deepening Project' in T. Bonyhady and A. Macintosh (eds) *Mills, Mines and other Controversies: The Environmental Assessment of Major Projects* (Sydney: The Federation Press).

Johnstone, R. (2008), 'Harmonising Occupational Health and Safety Regulation in Australia: The First Report of the National OHS Review' *Journal Of Applied Law And Policy* 35.

Macintosh, A. (2004), 'Why the Environment Protection and Biodiversity Conservation Act's referral, Assessment and Approval Process is Failing to Achieve its Environmental Objectives' 21 *Environmental and Planning Law Journal* 288.

Macintosh, A., J. Fear and J. Cummings (2009), 'The EPBC Survey Project: An Overview of the Results' 3 *National Environmental Law Review* 36.

McGrath, C. (2006), 'Swirls in the Stream of Australian Environmental Law: Debate on the EPBC Act' 23(3) *Environmental and Planning Law Journal* 165–84.

McGrath, C. (2011), *Synopsis of the Queensland Environmental Legal System* (Brisbane: Environmental Law Publishing).
Mitchell, R. *et al.* (2010), 'The Evolution of Labour Law in Australia: Measuring the Change' 23 *Australian Journal of Labour Law* 1–31.
Mould, H. (1998), 'The Proposed Environment Protection and Biodiversity Conservation Act' 15(4) EPLJ 275–86.
New South Wales Government (2013), *White Paper: A new planning system for NSW.*
Nottage, L. (2009), 'Consumer Law Reform in Australia: Contemporary and Comparative Constructive Criticism' (2009) 9(2) Queensland U. Tech. L. & Just. J. 111.
Padgett, R. and L. Kriwoken (2001), 'The Australian Environment Protection and Biodiversity Conservation Act 1999: What Role for the Commonwealth in Environmental Impact Assessment?' 8 AJEM 25.
Taylor, L. and P. Coorey 2012, 'Bid to Cut Green Tape Bogged Down in Detail' *Sydney Morning Herald* (6 December), accessed 30 March 2015 at http://www.smh.com.au/federal-politics/political-news/bid-to-cut-green-tape-bogs-down-in-detail-20121205-2avve.html.
The World Heritage Committee (2013), *Committee Decisions 37 COM 7B.10, Great Barrier Reef (Australia)* (N 154).
Tridgell, S. (2013), 'Evaluating the effectiveness of the Environment Protection and Biodiversity Conservation Act 1999 (Cth): 2008–2012' EPLJ 245.
United Nations (2000), *UN Global Compact.*
United Nations Conference on the Environment and Development (1992), *Declaration of the Conference held at Rio de Janiero from 3 to 14 June 1992 ('the Rio Declaration')*.
Victorian Auditor-General, 'Victorian Auditor-General's Report on the Annual Financial Report of the State of Victoria, (2009–10)', accessed 30 March 2015 at http://www.audit.vic.gov.au/publications/2010-11/20100710-AFR-report.pdf.
Waters, L. (2010), 'Queensland and the Traveston Crossing Dam' in T. Bonyhady and A. Macintosh (eds), *Mills, Mines and other Controversies: The Environmental Assessment of Major Projects* (Sydney: The Federation Press, 2010).
Weingroff, R. (1996), 'Federal-Aid Highway Act of 1956: Creating the Interstate System' 60(1) *Public Roads.*
Wood, C. (2002), *Environmental Impact Assessment: A Comparative Review* (2nd edn, Abingdon: Routledge).
World Commission on Environment and Development (1987), *Our Common Future* (Oxford: Oxford University Press).
World Wildlife Fund (2012), *Biodiversity, Biocapacity and Better Choices* (Living Planet Report).

APPENDIX

Table 4A.1 A table comparing key aspects of Australian EIA processes

Key legislation in each jurisdiction	Responsible agencies	EIA trigger and decision criteria	Public participation in scoping	Levels of assessment*
Commonwealth Environment Protection and Biodiversity Conservation Act 1999	Cth Dept of Environment (formerly Sustainability, Environment, Water, Population and Community)	Proponent referral if a significant impact on matters of NES	Discretionary (only for PER/EIS)	RI, PD, PER EIS, PI, AP
Australian Capital Territory Planning and Development Act 2007	ACT Planning and Land Authority	Prescribed Impact Track or Discretionary	No	EIS, PI
New South Wales Environmental Planning and Assessment Act 1979#	NSW Dept of Planning and Infrastructure	Designated developments or Discretionary	No	EIS
Northern Territory Environmental Assessment Act 1982	NT Environment Protection Authority	Discretionary	Yes	PER, EIS
Queensland State Development and Public Works Organisation Act 1971 Sustainable Planning Act 2009 Environment Protection Act 1994	Qld Dept of State Development Infrastructure and Planning, Qld Dept of Environment and Heritage Protection Qld Dept of Environment and Heritage Protection	Discretionary	Yes	EIS

South Australia				
Development Act 1993	Sth Aust Dept of Planning and Local Government	Discretionary	No	PER, EIS, DR
Tasmania				
Land Use Planning and Approvals Act 1994 Environmental Management and Pollution Control Act 1994 State Policies and Projects Act 1993	Tas Environment Protection Authority Tasmanian Planning Commission	Prescribed categories or Discretionary	No	EER, DPEMP IIS, IS
Victoria				
Environment Effects Act 1978 Planning and Environment Act 1987 Major Transport Projects Facilitation Act 2009	Vic Dept of Planning and Community Development	Discretionary	Discretionary	EES, PI IMP, CIS
Western Australia				
Environment Protection Act 1986	WA Environment Protection Authority	Discretionary	Discretionary	API, PERev

Notes: *** Levels of assessment**

AP – Accredited Process
API – Assessment of Proponent Information
CIS – Comprehensive Impact Statement
DR – Development Report
DPEMP – Devpt Proposal and Env Mgmt Plan
EER – Environment Effects Report
EES – Environment Effects Statement
EIS – Environmental Impact Statement
IIS – Integrated Impact Statement
IMP – Impact Management Plan I
S – Impact Statement
PD – Preliminary Documentation
PER – Public Environment Report
PERev. – Public Environmental Review
PI – Public Inquiry
RI – Referral Information

Source: #NSW White Paper – 'A new planning system for NSW' and draft planning legislation was released 16 April 2013.

5. Contamination and the polluter pays principle

Emma Lees

The two contaminated land liability regimes in force in the UK embody the polluter pays principle in differing fashions. The Environmental Liability Directive (ELD) sees the polluter pays principle as an exclusionary principle of liability: the polluter should pay, and no one else. The Environmental Protection Act 1990 (EPA) interprets the polluter pays principle as just one of the possible justifications for liability to clean up land. This chapter argues that the latter interpretation is to be preferred. Not only does this better embody the justice inherent in the polluter pays principle, but it also better recognises the distinct nature of principles in law. This chapter uses these two regimes as a vehicle to explore the meaning of the polluter pays principle as a principle of liability.

1. INTRODUCTION

The Environmental Liability Directive (ELD)[1] is a self-proclaimed embodiment of the polluter pays principle. It punishes those who pollute and does not touch those where no causal link can be established between pollutant and activity. It also prevents pollution, and calls on the polluter to pay for such a 'pre-emptive strike'. Its main aim is to internalise the costs of polluting. In doing so it regulates those who cause contamination of land. This directive runs alongside the Environmental Protection Act 1990, Part 2A (EPA), and the national law contaminated land provisions therein, established by the Environment Act 1995. These provisions embody a more sophisticated understanding of what it means

[1] Directive 2004/35/EC of the European Parliament and of the Council of 21 April 2004 on environmental liability with regard to the prevention and remedying of environmental damage (Environmental Liability Directive – ELD).

to make a polluter pay, and what other reasons there might be to ensure that an individual or company pays to clean up land which has become contaminated. A comparison between the philosophies behind these regimes begins to demonstrate why the polluter pays principle is not and cannot be the only justification for action to clean up land, and also why regulation based on an 'exclusionary' interpretation of this principle is inevitably limited in its scope. A more nuanced understanding of the justice inherent in 'clean land' leads to a deeper understanding of principled regulation designed to tackle this problem.

This chapter will demonstrate this by considering the key provisions of the two regimes, to outline their overall shape. From here it is possible to develop a clearer understanding of how the philosophies that make up these regimes have been represented in their provisions. The philosophies themselves will then be looked at in more detail. In particular, the stewardship aspect of the contaminated land provisions contained in the EPA will be compared with the purely polluter pays philosophy in the ELD. This will allow an examination of how the polluter pays principle is understood within each regime. The purpose is to suggest that the principle can and should be supplemented with other principles – that it should not be understood as an exclusionary principle of liability. The polluter pays principle states that polluters should pay. It does not say that those who are not polluters should not be made to pay. The ELD does not recognise this: the EPA does. This simple point should help with the development of a more sophisticated formulation of the polluter pays principle which in turn should be useful when designing, implementing and interpreting regimes attempting to deal with diffuse, historical and widespread contamination of land.

2. THE ENVIRONMENTAL LIABILITY DIRECTIVE

The ELD itself establishes, in its own words, a 'framework [for] environmental liability'.[2] As such, it is neither sector nor 'target' specific in that it is not limited to a particular activity, nor to damage a single environmental receptor, but rather covers the gamut of potentially harmful activities. It also attempts to both prevent damage being caused by these activities and imposing penalties on those who do cause such damage. Such damage, as defined in article 2, relates to water damage, land damage and damage to protected species. The last of these of course

---

2 ELD preamble, [3].

is linked with the Habitats[3] and Birds Directives[4] and depends upon those for their classification of protected species.[5] Water is defined in the Water Framework Directive.[6] Only 'land damage' is therefore seen as a standalone concept, unrelated to other EU legislation. This in itself arguably makes the land aspect the most interesting part of the ELD, since damage to these other receptors is arguably already remedied by the existing European legislation in place designed to protect them.

Damage, defined again in article 2, is 'a measurable adverse change in a natural resource or measurable impairment of a natural resource service which may occur directly or indirectly'. This very broad definition of damage is, however, mitigated by the fact that, with the exception of damage done to protected species,[7] only certain activities can attract liability under the ELD.[8] These activities tend already to require permits.[9] A full list of them can be found in Annex III of the ELD. There is a clear overlap with many of the existing provisions, such as environmental permitting schemes,[10] which already attempt to control these potentially damaging operations. The result of this is that the ELD overlaps with, and attempts to close gaps between, other existing regimes. It is to this extent a 'fill-in' piece of legislation, the main aim of which is to mop up damage not covered elsewhere. It addresses this by focusing on damage with an identifiable cause. It does not therefore cover diffuse pollution.[11]

Where such damage has occurred, the ELD provides that the operator should remediate such damage,[12] or pay for such remediation to occur.[13] If the damage has not yet occurred, but is likely, the ELD allows for

---

[3] Council Directive 92/43/EEC of 21 May 1992 on the conservation of natural habitats and of wild fauna and flora.

[4] Directive 2009/147/EC of the European Parliament and of the Council of 30 November 2009 on the conservation of wild birds.

[5] ELD, art 2(1)(a).

[6] Directive 2000/60/EC of the European Parliament and of the Council establishing a framework for the Community action in the field of water policy (Water Framework Directive).

[7] ELD, art 3(1)(b).

[8] ELD, art 3(1)(a).

[9] Environmental Damage (Prevention and Remediation) Regulations 2009, SI 2009/153 explanatory note at para. 7.5.

[10] In the UK context, Environmental Permitting Regulations (England and Wales) 2010, SI 2010/675.

[11] ELD, art 4(5).

[12] ELD, art 6.

[13] ELD, art 8.

preventive action also.[14] The provisions, however, only apply to prospective damage, and cannot be used to remedy damage that occurred before the directive came into force.

Beyond this, little guidance is given to the member states as to the precise mechanisms that should be used to implement this directive. The general principle, however, is clear. Damage to water, land and protected species, as defined, caused by particular economic activities, as listed, must be remediated by the polluter or at the cost of that polluter. If the damage has not yet occurred, that polluter must pay to ensure that preventive action is taken. A more explicit embodiment of the polluter pays principle as an exclusionary reason for liability is difficult to imagine. As will be seen, however, this directive does not in fact represent the best understanding of that principle.

The directive is directly transposed into UK law by the Environmental Damage (Prevention and Remediation) Regulations 2009.[15] The provisions are largely a repetition of the provisions of the directive itself and therefore more useful guidance can be derived, in terms of the practical application of the regime, from the accompanying documents. As is stated at paragraph 7.5 of the explanatory note,[16] the drafters of the regulation recognised that the purpose of the new directive was to 'penalise and require remediation for damage to the environment'. This explicit link between penalty for action, and liability to remediate, is central to the ELD and to its implementation into national law.

3. THE ENVIRONMENTAL PROTECTION ACT 1990

By contrast, the EPA establishes the method by which historical contamination in the U.K. is remediated, but can also be used to tackle prospective damage. The regime was established in order to tackle the historical problem of contamination on the basis of a white paper entitled 'Paying for Our Past'.[17] The title of this paper alone demonstrates that the EPA proceeds on a different footing from the ELD. The regime operates by placing duties on local authorities to survey the local area for contaminated land.[18] If contaminated land is found, defined according to

---

[14] ELD, art 5.

[15] Environmental Damage (Prevention and Remediation) Regulations 2009, SI 2009/153.

[16] Ibid explanatory note at para 7.5.

[17] UK Government (1993).

[18] EPA, s 78B(1).

the presence of a substance in, on or under the land, which is causing significant harm, or is posing a significant risk of significant harm,[19] then the local authority falls under a duty to remediate that land.[20] In doing so they are entitled to require that appropriate persons either carry out these remediation works or pay for these works.[21] There are two classes of appropriate person:[22] Class A persons – those who caused or knowingly permitted that substance to be in, on, or under the land,[23] and Class B persons, the owner or occupier of the land for the time being.[24] Liability will only fall onto a Class B person if there is no Class A person.[25] Thus, liability falling onto polluters is prioritised, but polluters are not the only potential actors in the regime. The local authority is also entitled if it sees fit to carry out the remediation itself and pay for such action also.[26]

Once again, in very general terms, the structure of the regime is relatively simple. The primary responsibility for solving the historical problem of contaminated land lies with the local authority. The local authority then has some discretion to determine the extent to which a polluter, if one can be found, must remediate the land or pay for that remediation to take place. If no polluter can be found, then once again the local authority is able to determine whether responsibility for remediation should fall onto the shoulders of the owner or occupier of that land.

Both regimes therefore tackle the problem of contamination, albeit that one does so prospectively, the other, largely, retrospectively. There is overlap between the regimes, but they do not cover exactly the same ground. The underlying problem in each however is the same. Where land is damaged, who should fix that damage, and why? The answer given to these questions is, for both regimes, reached by an appeal to the polluter pays principle, but the understanding of that principle present in the regimes is very different.

---

19 EPA, s 78A(2).
20 EPA, s 78E(1).
21 EPA, s 78N.
22 EPA, s 78F.
23 EPA, s 78F(2).
24 EPA, s 78F(4).
25 EPA, s 78F(4).
26 EPA, s 78N.

4. THE POLLUTER PAYS PRINCIPLE

Before examining the place of the principle within the provisions, it is first necessary to establish what is meant by the polluter pays principle and what the parameters of this principle are. The principle was first articulated by the OECD in 1972.[27] That incarnation of the principle was an economic principle recommending that the costs of pollution be internalised by state action.[28] 'As originally propounded, the PPP is *not* a liability principle, but rather is a principle for the 'allocation of the costs of pollution control'.[29] As a principle of environmental justice however it can be articulated as a justification for state action to impose liability onto an individual relying on causation rather than fault. As Lee argues, 'the polluter pays principle, notwithstanding its primarily economic rationale, could just as easily rest on intuitive notions of justice (it is "fair" that the polluter pays)'.[30] Thus the justice inherent in the principle is that causation can suffice for liability regardless of fault in the context of environmental liability.

There is an important ambiguity inherent in statements of the polluter pays principle as a principle of liability based in justice. This ambiguity relates to whether or not the principle excludes liability for other groups of persons. As a principle of economics, the principle requires the internalisation of the costs of pollution, and as such must, at the very least, steer against government or victim contributions to the cost of the pollution. In short, for the polluter pays principle to work as an economic principle, it must be exclusionary. As Stevens highlights, the principle is 'a cost allocation or non-subsidisation principle intended to guide governments in addressing domestic pollution'.[31] The polluter pays principle as a guide to regulation of the market demands that the government not distort the market by the introduction of subsidies. The polluter has to pay, and no one else must pay.

As a principle of justice however, the polluter pays principle does not need to be interpreted in this exclusionary fashion. Some do interpret it in this way. As Larson argues, 'the core of the principle derives from the fundamental, fair, and logical proposition that the parties who generate pollution, not the government, should bear the cost of abatement'.[32]

---

27 Organization for Economic Cooperation and Development (1972).
28 Stevens (1994) 578.
29 Gaines (1991) 468.
30 Lee (2009) 267.
31 Stevens (1994) 578.
32 Larson (2005) 545.

Larson also highlights that this approach to the principle is also adopted by the European Commission: 'the Commission argues, the polluter pays principle demands that the actor whose conduct is inherently dangerous to the environment bear the risk of damage caused by their conduct, rather than the victim of the damage or society at large'.[33] This, as will be seen below, is reflected in the manner in which they have incorporated the principle into the liability regime. At points too the U.K. Government appears to have taken this approach to the principle. As Tromans has highlighted, in a 1994 White Paper, the principle was described as: 'mak[ing] those who cause environmental damage face the costs of control in full, without subsidy'.[34] In the view of this author, however, this approach is inappropriate when treating the principle as a principle of liability. There are two key strands to the argument that sees the principle as a principle of liability as different in shape from the principle which guides economic policy.

First, when transformed from a question of effective policy, to a question of justifiable liability, invoking the principle requires an understanding of the justice behind its operation. It is clear that at times, '[i]ts economic roots are often forgotten when the principle is invoked in a legal context',[35] and a more open understanding of the transformations that must be made to the principle when it is integrated into law, will also allow for a more thorough understanding of the principle as a principle of liability. This demands that the justification behind the principle be examined. Once this takes place, it is clear that causation ought not to be the only reason for liability. This relates also to the difficulty with the principle in terms of the normative label of polluter. As Pederson has highlighted, 'a general problem with the polluter pays principle is to identify who the polluter actually is. Although this might seem obvious, this question is also relevant to environmental justice and the norms of ethics and social justice inherent in the concept of environmental justice'.[36] As a result, when considering the polluter pays principle as a principle of liability, it is necessary to engage with wider considerations of justice.

Secondly, when considered as a legal principle, rather than a policy guide, the principle must be treated, like all legal principles, as merely an argument in a particular direction which can and should be balanced

---

33 Ibid, 559.

34 U.K. Government, *This Common Inheritance* (Cm. 1200) para 1.25 cited in Tromans (1995) 785.

35 Gaines (1991) 469.

36 Pederson (2010) 40.

against, and coupled with, the other legal principles relevant to a particular decision. This approach to principles is highlighted by Fisher,[37] relying on Dworkin,[38] and is particularly relevant in the environmental context where the lack of scientific certainty makes calculations on the basis of justice more difficult, arguably, than elsewhere.[39] In short, as a principle of liability, the polluter pays principle cannot stand alone and nor can it be divorced from the particular context in which it is being used, and the particular role assigned to it.

In this particular context therefore, in addition to being an expression of environmental justice, at least to a certain extent, the principle is also a principle justifying regulatory intervention in relation to land use. It must therefore be given a concrete meaning in this context. Furthermore, in the EU context the justice inherent in the polluter pays principle also becomes a legitimacy issue as a result of the fact that the principle is present in the treaty provisions.[40] Thus, Union action is justified on the basis of the principle as a result of the mandate given to the Union to enforce it. This, no doubt, motivates the drafters of such regimes to give shape to the regimes on the basis of this principle. It also encourages a limited understanding of the principle, however, since the principle is ranked alongside the other EU environmental principles alone, rather than more generalised conceptions of justice, as expressed for example in the notion of stewardship. All of these factors are relevant to an understanding of how the polluter pays principle should be understood in the context of contaminated land. When considered in this way, it is clear that here the principle should not be conceived of as an exclusionary principle of liability.

Thus, it is important to see the polluter pays principle not only as a principle of economic policy, but as having a second role as a principle of environmental justice. When considered in this way it becomes even clearer that the polluter pays principle cannot exclude liability based upon other, equally valid, explanations as to what constitutes a 'just' imposition of a burden to remediate or account for environmental degradation. Understanding justice from a distributive perspective requires that not only goods be distributed appropriately, but that burdens too be shared. To treat the polluter pays principle as exclusionary is to conceive of the polluter pays principle as the only relevant criterion by which any distribution of burdens should be shared throughout the

37 Fisher (2010) 41.
38 Dworkin (1977) 26.
39 McEldowney and McEldowney (2011). See also Fisher *et al.* (2009).
40 Treaty on the Functioning of the EU, article 191.

community. In addition, if the concept of environmental justice is taken further to include elements such as 'distribution, recognition, capabilities, and procedural justice'[41] it is clear that any 'just' system for the distribution of environmental liabilities must take into account not just causation, but also capability to prevent degradation and so on. The polluter pays principle, in itself, does not express the totality of reasons for the imposition of liability for environmental harm. Rather, it is simply one justification amongst many, and when considered as a principle of law, this is how it should be treated.

Amongst much else, this means that the polluter pays principle cannot and ought not to exclude burdens imposed on the basis of stewardship. The EPA's conception of stewardship is discussed below. Stewardship in this sense is an obligation binding upon those with rights in or over land to use and protect that land in such a way as to advance the interests of future generations, or at least not to damage those interests, whilst also giving the right-holder the ability and duty to use the land for the benefit of the current generation as well.[42] Notions of stewardship explain, on the basis of a Rawlsian conception of justice,[43] that it is unjust for one generation to prioritise its own needs over those of future generations. Distribution is therefore expressed not only geographically across living persons, but also temporally, across future (and indeed past) generations. Such a conception of 'environmental justice' is one which again argues against treating the polluter pays principle as the only reason for the imposition of liability. Instead, those who currently have rights in land, whether or not they have caused that land to be in a poor state, can become liable to remediate that land under the conception of justice expressed in duties of stewardship.

5. THE POLLUTER PAYS PRINCIPLE EXPRESSED IN THE ELD

The ELD, however, does interpret the polluter principle as an exclusionary principle of liability, and it is this which provides the biggest limitation on both the scope of the regime, and in the extent to which it can fully address the justice inherent in 'clean land'. The reliance on this philosophy is apparent from even a cursory glance at its provisions, and the preamble in particular.

41 Schlosberg (2007) 7.
42 Lochery (2011) 39–45.
43 Rawls (2005) 274.

In the preamble, references to the polluter pays principle are repeated often. For example in paragraph one, reliance on the principle is used as a justification for Union action in this form. Paragraph two takes a similar approach. The specific relevance of the polluter pays principle to environmental issues is called upon in paragraph 11 of the preamble. The most significant exploration of the principle within the preamble however is to be found at paragraph 13. The text of this entire paragraph is worth reproduction here, as this is the understanding and specific implementation of the principle represented by the ELD.

> Not all forms of environmental damage can be remedied by means of the liability mechanism. For the latter to be effective, there needs to be one or more identifiable polluters, the damage should be concrete and quantifiable, and a causal link should be established between the damage and the identified polluter(s). Liability is therefore not a suitable instrument for dealing with pollution of a widespread, diffuse character, where it is impossible to link the negative environmental effects with acts or failure to act of certain individual actors.

What this paragraph does, ultimately, is to highlight the limitation of the polluter pays principle as a mechanism to allocate liability. Damage must be established, and a causal link must be apparent to an individual. 'Diffuse' pollution is not caught by the principle. The purpose of the explanation in this paragraph is to assist in the identification of who can be a polluter, but it does not address the more fundamental question as to whether or not it might be justified to intervene where a particular person cannot be causally linked to the contaminating substance, but where nevertheless there are reasons in justice as to why liability should be imposed.

In the provisions themselves, the polluter pays principle is again expressed in the causation requirements articulated in article 3(1) and most importantly in article 4(5). That provision states that: '[t]his Directive shall only apply to environmental damage or to an imminent threat of such damage caused by pollution of a diffuse character, where it is possible to establish a causal link between the damage and the activities of individual operators.' Thus not only is the 'aim' of the regime restricted to directly attributable damage, but the scope of the regime is also explicitly limited in this way. Article 8(1) then implements the 'pays' part of the principle in stating that the operator is responsible for the costs of remediation and prevention. The simple structure of the regime is, in essence, a simple reproduction of its philosophy. Most importantly, and perhaps because of its role in overlapping with myriad other regimes, the provisions, however, make no comment on how land damage is to be remediated where the pollution cannot be causally linked to a particular individual or individuals. Liability of this type, as understood by the ELD, would not be justified according to the polluter pays principle because the polluter pays principle prevents state or private subsidisation of the costs of pollution.

6. THE POLLUTER PAYS PRINCIPLE AND STEWARDSHIP IN THE EPA

The ELD does not, and because of the way the polluter pays principle is understood by the European institutions, cannot, impose liability where an individual did not cause a contaminating substance to be in, on, or under land. The EPA, however, has a more sophisticated understanding of the way in which the polluter pays principle interacts with other principles of environmental justice, such as stewardship.

This is seen most clearly, in terms of policy, in the statements made by John Gummer in the House of Commons in support of the Environment Bill. He argued that: '[i]t is our responsibility not to lay similar costs on future generations if we are to proceed with the growth which all of us want to achieve today',[44] and again: '[t]hat is because we are concerned not just for this generation, but for future generations. Our concept [is] of continuity and of passing on to the next generation something better than we have received in the past'.[45] His consideration of responsibility to future generations, and to ourselves, expresses the fact that there are good reasons grounded in environmental justice as to why liability might be imposed on those who are not labeled as polluters. Liability becomes removed from notions of responsibility. This is a difficult move to make in a system which relies heavily on fault-based liability principles. When understood from the principle of moral responsibility for damage being passed on to others whether or not it was caused by us, however, imposing costs onto non-polluters appears justified.

Within the regime itself, the statutory guidance is binding.[46] Again, this guidance demonstrates that the primary objectives of the regime are not to ensure that the polluter who caused damage is made to pay for that damage, but rather than the damage is remediated: 'The overarching objectives of the Government's policy on contaminated land and the Part 2A regime are: (a) To identify and remove unacceptable risks to human

44 Gummer (1995) Col 36.
45 Ibid, Col 48.
46 EPA, s 78YA.

health and the environment. (b) To seek to ensure that contaminated land is made suitable for its current use'.[47] In this regime, unlike the ELD therefore, the polluter pays principle is a principle of liability, but it is not also the aim of the regime. The regime does not set out to ensure that polluter pays. It is therefore less about internalising the cost of pollution, and more about ensuring that the effects of pollution are remediated. This remediation can therefore be justified on the basis of one or more principle of liability, but only if the polluter pays principle can be seen as silent on the question as to whether it is justified to impose liability elsewhere.

There is no doubt of course that the polluter pays principle is part of the regime, but it is a more complicated regime with a more sophisticated basis for liability. It is suggested here that in addition to expressing the polluter pays principle, the EPA also expresses the principle of stewardship. The argument that the EPA represents an important, albeit necessarily modified, version of stewardship has been presented in more detail elsewhere.[48] For the purposes of this chapter it is necessary only to note the key features of the regime that, whilst based in part on the polluter pays principle as expressed in the liability of Class A persons, contains a sophisticated understanding of how environmental justice operates in the context of contamination on land, especially where that contamination is historical.

It recognises this by imposing what is essentially a modified duty of stewardship onto the owner of land such that if there is a problem with that land the owner, and not the state, is 'first in line' to foot the costs of remediating that land. It achieves this by imposing two potential duties onto the owner of land. The first duty, which will come into play where there is a Class A person or where the local authority determines that it will carry out the remediation works itself, is a duty to grant rights of access onto the land.[49] The property rights of the owner do not take priority over the objective of remediation of the contamination and as such their ownership rights are therefore burdened with the weak duty to allow clean-up of the land to take place. Thus even in the 'polluter pays' scenario, the owner of the land himself is obliged by virtue of this obligation to engage in the remediation process. The EPA recognises that there are limitations even in a Class A scenario on what the polluter pays principle as a principle of liability can achieve in isolation. Secondly, in

---

47 DEFRA (2012) 1.4.
48 Lochery (2011).
49 EPA, s 78G.

cases where there is no Class A person, the owner or occupier for the time being becomes potentially liable under the regime[50] and if a remediation notice is served upon them they will commit a criminal offence if they do not comply with it.[51] The regime therefore imposes onto such owners a non-optional course of conduct, that is, to remediate the land to a pre-set standard. The non-optional nature of this obligation, where it comes into play, is a burden on the owner's rights in their land. This too is an expression of the justice inherent in stewardship of land, and is a burden on property rights.

What this means is that the EPA in the context of contaminated land recognises what the ELD does not – the importance of property rights to the question of remediation, and the central role that non-polluting owners can and should play in remediation of contamination. The philosophy as expressed in the House of Commons and in the White Paper therefore is mirrored in the shape of the provisions in this regime.

7. A CRITICAL COMPARISON OF THESE PHILOSOPHIES

The position is therefore as follows: both regimes prioritise the polluter pays principle as a principle of liability dictating who ought, in the first instance, to pay for or carry out remediation works to remedy damage to land by contaminating substances. Both regimes achieve this by imposing liability based on a casual link between polluter and contaminating substance. The EPA, however, unlike the ELD, in deference to the limitations of the polluter pays principle, backs up its understanding of the justice inherent in the clean-up of contaminated land to include liability as a fall-back position onto the owner or occupier of land for the time being through the imposition of modified stewardship obligations onto such owner/occupiers. The ELD, concerned as it is only with prospective contamination does not provide a solution to the possibility that the polluter may not exist or cannot be found, but rather only acknowledges the difficulty of diffuse pollution. Its simplistic understanding of the polluter pays principle means that it cannot impose liability in cases of diffuse pollution. The EPA, however, can. It can do this because it relies not on the polluter pays principle as a principle

50 EPA, s 78F(4).
51 EPA, s 78M.

which dictates who ought not to pay for pollution, but rather as a principle expressing who ought to pay for pollution.

It was highlighted above that it is preferable that the polluter pays principle be understood as not excluding liability for others where it is being conceived of as a principle of liability in the environmental land use context. It is only by considering the principle as merely one justification for liability that the importance of stewardship can be brought to the fore. In the land use context in particular, the principle of stewardship provides an important, and often overlooked principle of liability. In particular, in the context of contaminated land also, the notion of stewardship reveals an important reality about contaminated land. The clean-up of the land is of benefit to those with rights in that land to a greater extent than it is of benefit to the state or the public as a whole. It is also of greater benefit to those future persons who will have rights in the land than it will be to future generations in general. This imbalance in improvement, which arguably does not apply to other forms of diffuse pollution, such as air pollution, means that there is an important additional layer of factors to be considered. This reality is obscured if the polluter pays principle is understood in such a way as to rule out other reasons for liability.

When the polluter pays principle is unpacked, two different situations emerge in the contaminated land context. One is where there is no identifiable causal link between an individual and contamination. Such diffuse pollution is clearly not caught by the polluter pays principle and there would be other principles in play to assist in designing a regime to impose liability in cases of diffuse pollution, such as stewardship. The second situation is where, for example, there is a clear polluter who does not have rights in the relevant land, and the right-holder in the land who will receive a windfall in terms of land values if the land is remediation. Again, the polluter pays principle can tell us that there is a good justification for imposing liability onto the polluter, but it does not provide a justification for the windfall that will thus be granted to the holder of the rights in land. Reliance on the polluter pays principle when improperly understood therefore produces a potentially unjust allocation of liability.

As a result, the understanding of the polluter pays principle that is expressed in the EPA is not only to be preferred in terms of the definition of the polluter pays principle, as outlined above, but also in terms of environmental justice in general. This is because the EPA allows for the benefits and burdens of liability to be allocated across different groups as a discretionary decision-maker sees fit. This flexibility is a better expression of how legal principles operate. This more flexible approach is at the very heart of the policy expressed in the statutory guidance accompanying the EPA: the aim is '[t]o ensure that the burdens faced by individuals, companies and society as a whole are proportionate, manageable and compatible with the principles of sustainable development'.[52]

8. CONCLUSION

Tromans has argued that, 'the polluter pays principle is multi-faceted and elusive. It can mean almost anything one wishes it to mean, yet in practice it is meaningless until one descends to the basis of designing a liability system'.[53] The elusive nature of the principle is highlighted once it is considered in the context of such liability systems. It is important, however, to unpack reliance on this principle. Once this task is undertaken, it becomes clear that the EPA better expresses not only the justice within the polluter pays principle itself in that it is clear that it does not see it as an exclusionary principle of liability, but also therefore achieves a better balance in terms of environmental justice as a whole. It recognises that land use regulation in particular can and should incorporate notions of stewardship to account for the imbalance of benefits and burdens that arise when individuals have private rights to land. The principle of stewardship which is expressed in the EPA is not a violation of the polluter pays principle of environmental law, but rather can act hand in hand with notions of causal liability in a way which best accords with the justice not just of causing harm, but also of the responsibilities which come with having rights in land. The exclusive focus on the polluter pays principle at the European level has meant that the ELD fails to acknowledge the central role that those with rights in land can and should play in the remediation of the contaminated land. The polluter pays principle is not the end of the story. Once this is better recognised, contaminated land issues can be better tackled.

REFERENCES

Council Directive 92/43/EEC of 21 May 1992 on the conservation of natural habitats and of wild fauna and flora.

DEFRA (2012), *Environmental Protection Act 1990: Part 2A – Contaminated Land: Statutory Guidance* (London: DEFRA).

---

[52] DEFRA (2012) 1.4.

[53] Tromans (1995) 790.

Directive 2000/60/EC of the European Parliament and of the Council establishing a framework for the Community action in the field of water policy.

Directive 2004/35/EC of the European Parliament and of the Council of 21 April 2004 on environmental liability with regard to the prevention and remedying of environmental damage.

Directive 2009/147/EC of the European Parliament and of the Council of 30 November 2009 on the conservation of wild birds.

Dworkin, R. (1977), *Taking Rights Seriously* (London: Duckworth).

Fisher, E. (2010), *Risk: Regulation and Administrative Constitutionalism* (Oxford: Hart Publishing).

Fisher, E. *et al.* (2009), 'Maturity and Methodology: Starting a Debate about Environmental Law Scholarship' 21 *Journal of Environmental Law* 213.

Gaines, S. (1991), 'The Polluter Pays Principle: From Economic Equity to Environmental Ethos' 26 *Texas International Law Journal* 463.

Gummer. J. (1995), House of Commons Hansard, 18 April 1995, Vol 258, Col 36.

Larson, E. (2005), 'Why Environmental Liability Regimes in the United States, the European Community, and Japan Have Grown Synonymous with the Polluter Pays Principle' 38 *Vanderbilt Journal of Transactional Law* 541.

Lee, M. (2009), '"New" Environmental Liabilities: The Purpose and Scope of the Contaminated Land Regime and the Environmental Liability Directive' 11 *Environmental Law Review* 264.

Lochery, E. (2011), 'Does the Contaminated Land Regime Impose Stewardship Obligations on Owners of Land?" LLM Thesis, University of Dundee.

McEldowney, J. and S. McEldowney (2011), 'Science and Environmental Law: Collaboration Across the Double Helix' 13 *Environmental Law Review* 169.

Organization for Economic Cooperation and Development (1972), *Guiding Principles Concerning International Economic Aspects of Environmental Policies,* (Annex Doc C(72)128, 26 May).

Pederson, O. (2010), 'Environmental Principles and Environmental Justice' 12 *Environmental Law Review* 26.

Rawls, J. (2005), *Political Liberalism: Expanded Edition* (New York: Columbia University Press).

Schlosberg, D. (2007), *Defining Environmental Justice: Theories, Movements and Nature* (Oxford, Oxford University Press).

Stevens, C. (1994), 'Interpreting the Polluter Pays Principle in the Trade and Economic Context' 27 *Cornell International Law Journal* 577.

Tromans, S. (1995), 'High Talk and Low Cunning: Putting Environmental Principles into Legal Practice' 9 JPEL 779.

U.K. Government (1993), *Paying for Our Past* (London: Department for the Environment, White Paper).

6. Possible legal obligations to consult

Tanya Howard and Solange Teles Da Silva[1]

Public participation is an increasingly important feature of environmental governance. Obligations upon government or project developers to "consult" appear in legislative arrangements and government policies of many countries. Environmental law and social justice scholars propose that consultation or community engagement (which we collectively term 'public participation') can adjust power imbalances, particularly for marginalised and Indigenous people, ensure better informed decisions, and improve communication between power-holders and citizens.[2] The extent to which these aspirations are achieved through the implementation of legal obligations is an important environmental and social justice question, given the significance of the aims and the sometimes vulnerability of those whose interests are involved.

In this chapter we explore some challenges of ensuring effective public participation through legal requirements. We consider the problem of ensuring integrity and effectiveness given a high degree of variability that is due in part to the imprecision of terminology and in part to the concealed flexibility in the methods that might be used to implement any legal requirements. We also consider the relationship between dominant democratic structures that give decision-making power to elected government and its institutions, and an aspiration for local participative democracy. We consider the issue of variability and challenges of safeguarding integrity through case studies in two jurisdictions, Brazil and Australia.

---

[1] The authors acknowledge the advice and assistance of Professor Paul Martin in the preparation of this paper.

[2] Adams and Hess (2001); Eversole (2011); Lockwood *et al*. (2009); Holley (2010) 360.

1. PARTICIPATIVE CONCEPTS AND THEIR IMPLICATIONS FOR GOVERNANCE

Terms such as participation, consultation, collaboration, partnership, public, citizen and community are often used synonymously.[3] 'Public participation' and variants like 'consultation' or 'engagement' mean many different things, depending on circumstances and processes.[4] When these words appear in legislation, policy documents or implementation guidelines, they are rarely specified in detail or given a conceptual framework.[5] Scholars who research these different terms are most likely to come from linguistic or sociological disciplines, and the debates are often esoteric in terms of the application of a legal instrument.[6] However in fundamental issues of empowerment and integrity of decision-making, it is worth taking the time to consider how these synonymous terms might impact on legal requirements to bring community voices into natural resource governance.

Arnstein's Ladder of Citizen Participation is the foundation work for classifying and theorising community participation, and highlights eight levels, grouped in three categories: non-participation, tokenism and citizen control.[7] Although the academic field has moved on, the 'classification still proves a useful correction to naive and untempered enthusiasm for public participation',[8] and reminds us that 'citizen participation is a categorical term for citizen power'.[9]

This question of citizen power is a significant policy consideration for designing processes that range from 'manipulation' (an exercise of power upon people), through 'consultation' (shared power), to 'citizen control' (citizens holding power).[10] Another way to assess how citizen power is codified in policy design is by asking whose interests are being prioritised?

A related consideration is the choice of participatory techniques, and how they are implemented.[11] Each has implications for power relationships, and information flows. This can covertly privilege particular voices

---

3 Whitman (2008); Berner, Amos and Morse (2011).
4 Brackertz and Meredyth (2009); Margerum (2008) 487.
5 Berner, Amos and Morse (2011); Brackertz and Meredyth (2009).
6 Brugnach et al. (2011).
7 Arnstein (1969).
8 Fung (2006).
9 Arnstein (1969).
10 Fung (2006); Dryzek (2000).
11 Rowe and Frewer (2005); Bishop and Davis (2002).

and interests. A failure of the legal system to require that the substantive purposes of participation are respected can mean that *procedures* and *compliance* become the focus, leading to a 'tick the box' mentality.[12] With inadequate clarity or inappropriate processes the status quo can be reinforced even if power transfer is a policy goal that has driven participation requirements.[13]

Related to this are the possible risks of participative processes, for citizens as well as proponents. For proponents of a development, community empowered processes involve the potential that their preferred initiatives will be set aside, or significantly modified. Citizens who participate genuinely in a deep engagement process may invest hours, days or weeks in the process, and this time and emotional commitment is diverted from alternative 'investment'. Should the outcome not satisfy their needs, this good faith investment is wasted.[14] Given the contingencies of process design and potential manipulation, community politics, and the emotional costs that can be involved, the citizen risks of participating in an engagement process around a contentious issue can be very high.

If community members find their expectations disappointed, this increases the likelihood of withdrawal from legal processes, perpetuation of conflict and undermining of the 'virtuous' principles that public participation rests upon.[15] These implementation dynamics raise questions of environmental and social justice.[16]

How can environmental law address these systemic problems? This chapter suggests that by balancing procedural and administrative requirements with substantive commitments to public participation, gradual changes to practices can be strengthened by a shift in expectations and norms.[17] International principles of public participation and environmental governance provide overarching frameworks for negotiating this balance, and should be used as roadmaps for reform.[18]

This chapter examines how international frameworks are influencing institutional responses in Australia and Brazil, using case studies of national and intra-national legislation. The analysis takes a vertical slice

---

12 Beierle (1999); Irvin and Stansbury (2004).

13 Kirk and Reeves (2011); Bell *et al.* (2013).

14 Markell (2006); Peterson (2011).

15 Koontz and Thomas (2006); Reed (2008).

16 Martin and Shepeard (2011); Gross (2008) 130.

17 Kirk and Blackstock (2011); Visseren-Hamakers (2013); Woolgar and Neyland (2013).

18 Jendroska (2013); Dellinger (2012); Werksman and Foti (2011).

of legislation, policy and practice, to see how principles are translated into on-ground experiences.[19] It concludes with suggestions for future developments that could improve the integrity of existing natural resource governance mechanisms for public participation.

2. THE CASE STUDY COUNTRIES

Australia and Brazil provide interesting contrasts on this topic, sharing similarities of political design but with different formal rules for public participation and indigenous recognition. Both countries are members of the United Nations and have signed Agenda 21, the Rio Declaration on the Environment and the re-statement of these goals at Rio+20.[20]

Politically, the countries are federated systems with representative democratic procedures of elections and referenda. The countries have similarities of history and politics, experiencing European colonialism, immigration and significant impacts on indigenous populations. Both countries are geographically vast. Australia is an island continent with a sparse population, and a largely arid environment. Brazil is world renowned for the Amazon rainforest and its environmental and cultural biodiversity. It has actively promoted the role of civil society through global leadership.[21]

The environmental issues of both countries are linked to their colonial past and conditions of international trade. A reliance on natural resources to drive economic growth has seen both countries embrace land clearing, pastoral production and mineral extraction, with associated environmental impacts upon biodiversity, erosion and water pollution. The social and cultural impacts of these natural resource issues are experienced differently and the institutional framework of each country informs how community voices are heard in decision making around these issues. This chapter draws on a tradition of comparative analysis to examine the different ways that emerging modern democracies such as Australia and

---

[19] Howard (2014) 1.

[20] United Nations Environment Programme (1992), 'Agenda 21'; United Nations General Assembly (1992), 'Rio Declaration on Environment and Development'; United Nations General Assembly (2012a), 'Rio+20: The Future We Want'.

[21] United Nations General Assembly (2012b), 'Rio+20 concludes with big package of commitments for action and agreement by world leaders on path for a sustainable future'.

Brazil deal with issues such as resource management, conflict, corruption and social and environmental justice.[22]

3. ENVIRONMENTAL PUBLIC PARTICIPATION IN AUSTRALIA

Australia is a constitutional monarchy, with colonial links to Britain. The country is governed as a Federated coalition of six States and two Territories that are united under the foundation law of the Australian Constitution.[23] In terms of community participation, the federated system and the role of local government institutionalises a politically decentralised approach.[24] Such decentralisation is seen by some as a strategy for increasing community participation,[25] suggesting that a federal system can be a pathway for more local participatory governance. However, critical constitutional analysis suggests that this may also create multiple veto points for reform, obscure lines of accountability, and privilege organised 'representative' lobbies rather than the citizenry.[26]

The Australian Constitution does not contain a Bill of Rights. There are no protections for the community's role beyond participation in democratic processes, such as referendum, plebiscite and compulsory voting in elections at all levels of government. Thus, legal requirements for participatory processes arise (if at all) in specific legislation, generally at a state level. There is no over-arching legal principle of participation, nor is there a history of legal enforcement of good quality participatory process in Australian law.[27] Although 'community' is regularly referred to in the objects of legislation there is seldom a precise identification of the specific 'community', nor substantive or procedural rights to address

---

[22] Wogan (2014); Fountain, Libânio and Lane (2011); Berndt and Tomkins (2013); Rocha (2014); Andreoli *et al.* (2002).

[23] Commonwealth of Australia Constitution Act (1900).

[24] Steelman (2010).

[25] Ostrom and Cox (2010).

[26] Miller (2012).

[27] Recently in NSW community consultation requirements became a trigger for suspension and revocation of a controversial coal seam gas exploration license. A High Court challenge has since overturned this ruling, resulting in claims for compensation from the company, and threats of ongoing civil disobedience from the community. This is one example of the challenges that face the institutional framework in designing and enforcing public participation requirements. See: AAP (2014a); Hasham (2014).

unsatisfactory community participation other than the limited rules under administrative law.

As a signatory to Agenda 21, Australia has made a formal commitment to strategies for achieving the environmental and social principles of the framework. In 1992 the Intergovernmental Agreement on the Environment was developed to formalise environmental responsibilities for governments across the federation.[28] While the Agreement incorporates '*ecologically sustainable development*', the Environmental Policy principles ratified in the Agreement make no mention of participation.

After a period of around two decades of historically record investments in the environment, government funding for natural resource management is now declining. National conservation and environmental management programs are under review, with a growing emphasis on market-based strategies.[29] Conflict over land use has resulted in tensions between government, community and private industry over policy and resource developments.[30] Recent investigations have linked vested interests with development decisions that have serious environmental impacts, where community concerns were overridden by corrupt administrative action.[31] Attempts to manage natural resources across jurisdictional boundaries have been challenged by politicisation and community opposition,[32] limiting the ability of government to deliver natural resource management outcomes.[33]

This latter point is important to note at three levels. First, we should recognise that local decision-making can compete directly with the decision-making structures of formal democracy. Second, local participation processes may lack the integrity mechanisms and safeguards of formal democratic processes. Third, sometimes what the local citizenry wants may run counter to the interests of the broader community or the environment.

In contrast to Brazil, the pre-settlement presence of Australia's indigenous Aboriginal people is not recognised in the Constitution. At the time of settlement prevailing British legal principles categorised Australia as being un-owned (*Terra nullius*). Gradually, through constitutional

---

28 Council of Australian Governments (1992), *Intergovernmental Agreement on the Environment* (Australian Government).

29 Australian Government (2012); Australian Government (2014).

30 Barbour (2014); Guilliat (2014); Woods (2014).

31 Nicholls (2013); ABC News (2014).

32 Gray (2011); Hussey and Dovers (2007).

33 National Water Commission (2013); Rawlins, Gramenz and Haxton (2014).

change in 1967 and High Court rulings,[34] the legal status of Australian Aboriginal people has been elevated. However, whilst there are *sui generis* obligations to consult with Aboriginal people over issues such as mining on their lands or on disturbance of cultural heritage, there is as yet no constitutional recognition of the first Australians, nor any overarching requirements to consult or respect their interests.

Nationally and in each state there are legal arrangements to ensure access to information. The *Federal Freedom of Information Act* (1982) rests on the belief that 'a community that is better informed can participate more effectively in the nation's democratic processes'. In line with commitments made under Agenda 21, transparency and information provision are entrenched in legislation at both the Federal and State level, with additional mechanisms for investigation into corruption or issues of public importance (for example the *Royal Commissions Act* 1902 (Cth)).

Public consultation periods, invitations to make submissions, online discussion forums or public display of plans are commonly required public participation processes.[35] Although these activities provide information to the public and offer (restricted) channels for feedback, it is often unclear what impact these processes have on decision-making.[36] The required processes generally sit at the instrumental or functional end of community engagement scales,[37] and do not tend towards the transformational or empowerment strategies from participatory democratic theory.[38] Deeper engagement processes, while being more time-intensive, unpredictable and expensive are considered to be best suited for addressing complex issues.[39]

In Australia there is limited recourse for community members who wish to challenge the integrity or quality of a public participation process. While some legislation may require administrative review of processes, this is largely a procedural compliance requirement. For example, development applications under the New South Wales (NSW) planning system[40] must evidence public notification, display and comment periods, and in some cases establishment of community consultative committees. As another example, under the NSW *Local Land*

---

34 *Mabo* and others v Queensland (No 2) (1992).
35 Rowe and Frewer (2004).
36 Brackertz and Meredyth (2009).
37 Buchy and Race (2001); Bishop and Davis (2002).
38 Bishop and Davis (2002).
39 Ostrom and Cox (2010).
40 *Environmental Planning and Assessment Act 1979* No 203.

Services Act 2013,[41] external third party audits allow assessment against community ownership and customer satisfaction criteria; however, this function cannot be triggered by community members.[42]

4. ENVIRONMENTAL PUBLIC PARTICIPATION IN BRAZIL

Brazil is a federal presidential constitutional republic, formed by the union of 26 federal states and the Federal District, and 5,570 municipalities. Similarly to Australia, its political and administrative organisation comprises the Union, the federal states, the Federal District and the municipalities, all of them autonomous. The Constitution addresses fundamental principles, rights and guarantees; the organisation of the State and its powers (legislative, executive and judicial); defense of the State and democratic institutions; rules for taxation and budget; economic and financial order; social order; general provisions and temporary constitutional provisions.[43]

The Constitution was adopted after a period of military dictatorship (1964–1979) and a democratic transition period (1979–1988). It enshrined the principle of participatory democracy[44] and incorporated provisions that promote participatory governance.[45] The Constitution includes mechanisms of popular participation such as plebiscite and referendum. It also creates a popular mechanism to draft laws (art 14, inc III) and cooperation between associations in municipal planning (art 29, inc XII). Public participation is required by the Constitution in social security, health and education.

Under the 1988 Constitution, the Union (Federal level), Federal States and Federal Districts have concurrent authority to legislate on environmental matters. Specific issues – water, energy, mining and nuclear

---

41 *Local Land Services Bill* 2013.

42 The *Local Land Services Bill* 2013 replaced the Catchment Management Authority Act 2003 resulting in new regional land management bodies commencing 1 January 2014. The oversight and audit function provided by the Natural Resources Commission in the previous Act has been adapted to meet the needs of the new Local Land Services organisations.

43 This constitution has also 83 amendments (at 5 August 2014).

44 Reis (2014). See the documentary movie: *O Dia que Durou 21 Anos*, Camilo Tavares and Flavio Tavares, Pequi Filmes [2012].

45 For example, para 3 of art 37 states that 'the law shall regulate the forms of participation of users in governmental entities and in entities owned by the Government'. Avritzer (2008).

activity – are reserved to the Union; that can, however, allow States to legislate. Municipalities can legislate on local issues and territorial planning; they can also supplement federal and state legislation. In this sense Federal law establishes a minimum standard that can be reinforced at the State or Municipal level, dealing with regional or local specificities.

Mechanisms of environmental public participation were established at the Federal level under Law 6938/81, the National Environmental Act. This law created The National Environment Council ('*Conselho Nacional do Meio Ambiente*' – CONAMA), a consultative and deliberative organ of the National Environment System that made popular participation possible in federal environmental policies.[46] CONAMA, as a deliberative organ, approved a number of resolutions defining environmental norms and standards at the Federal level that must be observed for all the federal entities – states, Federal District and municipalities – as minimum standards. It has also approved resolutions establishing environmental impact assessment and public hearings.

Public participation has increased alongside growth in the number of environmental associations. The National Front of Ecological Action at the National Constituent Assembly (NCA) acted to insert the right to a balanced environment in the Federal Constitution of 1988 (art. 225). It also enshrined new Indigenous rights (arts. 231 and 232), including the duty to consult Indigenous communities in the case of exploitation of water resources or mines in their territories (art 231, par 3). Brazil has ratified ILO Convention 169, a legally binding international instrument which deals with the rights of Indigenous and tribal peoples. It requires consultation with these people on issues that affect them, such as development projects and also questions of governance.[47]

Under some federal laws, public access to environmental information is guaranteed – Federal Law n. 10.650 of 2003 – and social participation in the environmental field is required. Two mechanisms of social participation are used in pursuit of these laws: (a) collegiate bodies to ensure public participation such as CONAMA; the National Council of

---

46 Mirra (2011) 67.

47 Courtis (2009). However, advocates query to what extent this obligation has turned into a mere checklist or is simply ignored: see the work of The Interamerican Association for Environmental Defense (AIDA) a non-government organization focused on environmental governance, available at http://www.aida-americas.org/sites/default/files/Brazil%20UNHCR%20SIDE%20EVENT%20ENG%20march% 202014_final.pdf.

Water Resources (*Conselho Nacional de Recursos Hídricos*) and the National Technical Commission of Biosecurity (*Comissão Técnica Nacional de Biossegurança*);[48] and (b) public participation in the drawing up of plans and programmes: for example, the National Plan of Waste or Urban Master Plans.

In order to strengthen mechanisms for dialogue between the state and civil society, the federal government has adopted a *National Policy of Social Participation*.[49] This policy aims to embed social participation as a method of government and it organises bodies and mechanisms of social participation. It defines civil society as citizens, social groups ('*coletivos*'), social movements (institutionalised or not), their networks and their organisations.

In environmental protection, the Constitution creates a legal regime (art 225) which imposes upon Government and the community the duty to defend and preserve the environment. In this sense it also creates a platform for public participation.[50] For exploitation of water and minerals on Indigenous lands, the Constitution establishes a mandatory procedure for decision-making participation by affected communities.

However, despite constitutional guarantees and other legislation intended to ensure participation, there are still implementation questions about the *quality* of participation achieved, the *impact* of this participation on government decisions and community satisfaction with the outcomes. While procedures for participative natural resource governance are legislated, community participation is affected by economic and social restrictions, also concentrating power in existing elites.[51] Case studies suggest that participation depends on the social and economic situation of the affected community, as well as on the quality of environmental resources and the characteristics of properties located nearby the project.[52]

---

[48] There are structural differences between these councils and also different quorums for approval of their decisions.

[49] Federal Decree n. 8.243 2014.

[50] Mirra (2011) 101–21.

[51] Fonseca and Bursztyn (2009).

[52] Assunção, Bursztyn and Abreu (2010).

5. IMPLEMENTATION CASE STUDIES

The preceding sections have outlined some challenges of participatory process in natural resource management, and have described the legal frameworks in Australia and Brazil. We have suggested that:

(1) Regardless of jurisdiction, there is a significant conceptual and practical gap between the aspirations of public participation and the implemented reality achieved through the law. This is in part because the terms used have many possible interpretations, and in part because the choices of processes and process quality (which are largely left unspecified in legislation) leave a great deal of latitude for the proponents of proposals to shape the process. It is also in part because of the lack of detailed integrity mechanisms in either jurisdiction, for legal oversight and continuous improvement to take place.

(2) Within any democratic system, there is a potential tension between the authority of elected parliaments and their executive agents and the aspiration for local participatory decision-making. There are significant issues of process and integrity that can arise. The two jurisdictions have taken a different structural approach to embedding community participation in environmental decision-making. Brazil has well-developed structures requiring and implementing public participation in many environmental decisions or in decisions impacting upon first nations peoples, though there is still substantial latitude for variation in implementation even whilst following formal requirements. Australia does not have the same depth of institutional formalisation of requirements for public participation, relying largely upon specific provisions in particular issue legislation. It allows a substantial degree of latitude in how the many different forms of participatory requirement are implemented.

Given these conclusions we now consider how structural concerns impact 'at the front line' upon public participation. Our aim is only to illustrate the extent of variation that is possible in both jurisdictions, in terms of process choice and substantive participation by citizens. The case studies are not intended to prove whether the processes used do or do not result in effective participation, or whether the law guarantees integrity in the design and implementation of public participation. A more in-depth, larger study would be needed to explore these issues. We believe the case studies do illustrate that existing legal arrangements allow a great deal of proponent discretion in the choice and implementation of process. In each case the specific participatory requirements arise from laws related to a particular environmental issue, and it is necessary to describe the specific framework of rules within which the participatory requirement is embedded.

An Australian Case Study: Rural Wind Farm Development

This case study contrasts examples of community participation approaches for the same natural resource issue (wind farm development) within the same state planning system.

Wind farm development is regulated under the *Environmental Planning and Assessment Act* 1979 No 203. Nested within the Act are the draft NSW Wind Farm Guidelines which

> have been prepared to ensure effective consultation with local communities and to deliver improved consistency, transparency and rigour in the planning assessment process. (Department of Planning & Infrastructure 2011)

Beyond information provision through display and notification requirements, a Community Consultative Committee (CCC) is the specific community participation mechanism prescribed by the Guidelines. The governance requirements focus on transparency procedures such as publishing minutes online and the responsibilities of members and the proponent. The proponent bears all costs associated with running the committee, and must appoint a neutral, independent chair. The Guidelines specify minimum procedural requirements for community engagement, and how compliance with these conditions will be assessed. Appendix D (*Information to include in an EIS*) suggests that 'effective' consultation will result in clear documentation of the procedures undertaken, embedding a procedural compliance version of what constitutes 'effective consultation'.

Two case studies of these community participation mechanisms for wind farm developments illustrate the extent to which process choices and substantive commitments to community engagement are interdependent.

The first case was a volunteer community initiative run by a Consortium of stakeholders, to develop a community wind farm. Seed funding was obtained for a feasibility study. A key output was community-negotiated design principles for the planning and operation of a potential community-owned wind farm. These principles have become significant for the Consortium, providing legitimacy but involving duties of accountability to the community of the region. The community has been fully involved in the design of the project principles, and has shaped the major decisions without an external proponent forcing a design upon the community.

However, this deeply participative process has created expectations for the project that challenge the capacity of the Consortium as it attempts to move from project design to project realisation. These expectations are not connected to the legal requirements of wind farm project development. Whilst in a substantive sense the approach seems to reflect genuine and authentic levels of community participation, it is unclear whether this will satisfy the procedural requirements of the NSW planning system and the wind farm Guidelines. The Consortium members did not see their community engagement activities as matters of legal compliance, but as core to the social and environmental objectives of the project.

The alternative example is a case where community engagement is viewed as a compliance requirement rather than as part of a philosophical commitment. It involves a small energy business focused on achieving development approval in order to sell on a viable wind-farm project. The proponent established a Community Consultative Committee in line with the requirements of their approval, issued under the Guidelines. Due to difficulties in finding a suitable independent Chairperson (required by the Guidelines), the proponent contracted a consultant to fill this role, incurring operational costs but also creating a debate within the committee about the integrity of the mechanism. Difficulties in determining the purpose and scope of the Committee, and this question of integrity, have resulted in suspicion and distrust within the Committee. Committee participants interviewed were unsure of the purpose, questioned their actual influence, and demonstrated little awareness of frameworks for effective community participation.

These two case studies reinforce our observations that under the rubric of 'engagement' or 'participation' there is an enormous variety of possible processes. These allow for a great variation in the substantive outcomes of the process. It is interesting to observe that in these examples, the more deeply engaged approach may not satisfy the procedural legal requirement, whereas the compliance approach is most likely to allow the proponent to jump the legal hurdle.

Embedding participatory practice in legislation and policy may suggest a changing culture of engagement, but implementation is the key test of whether a new norm of community engagement is realised. Mere procedural requirements seem unlikely to adequately address the implementation issues illustrated by these examples: a compliance culture, diverse processes of engagement, and a focus on project approval. However, formalising minimum procedures can focus attention on principles of transparency, inclusiveness and accountability, and possibly contribute to more effective community participation. The examples suggest that legal procedural requirements are necessary but far from sufficient to ensure substantive community participation.

Brazilian Case Study: Troubled Implementation

Recent developments in Brazil suggest tension between advancing ideals of community consultation and a desire to pursue government and economic development agendas. The aim of the 2014 National Policy of Social Participation is, among others, to consolidate social participation as a 'method of government' and to develop mechanisms for social participation accessible to historically excluded and vulnerable social groups. It organises participatory mechanisms that already exist. The decree defines as mechanisms of public participation: a council of public policies, a committee of public policies, national conferences, a federal public ombudsman, a table of dialogue, forum inter-councils, public hearings, public consultations and a virtual environmental for social participation. It also establishes that the organs and entities of the federal government should prepare an annual implementation report for this policy. However, there is pressure from conservative sectors of Congress to stop implementation of this decree.[53] The National Policy was adopted by Federal Decree n. 8.243 of 2014 and the conservative bloc argues that this policy could not be adopted by a decree. The Chamber of Deputies has already approved the policy, canceling this federal decree on 28 October 2014, and it will be voted on in the Senate.

In Brazil some participative mechanisms have a deliberative character and a binding force. For example, at the federal level, CONAMA, a structured council that has an important role in developing environmental policy, demonstrates 'its democratic character and its significant social representation'.[54] Nevertheless at the local level, the Brazilian Institute of Geography and Statistics (IBGE) show that in 2008 47.6 per cent of Brazilian Municipalities had municipal environmental councils, a key mechanism for community participation. However this procedural step

---

[53] At the National Congress the opposition is trying to approve the Project of Legislative Decree n. 1491 2014 to stop the application of the Federal Decree n. 8.243 2014.

[54] Cappelli (2003) 288.

(establishing a municipal environmental council) does not necessarily translate into actual participation. Only 33.8 per cent have met at least once in the last 12 months.[55] In reality the functioning of these councils depends on the degree of democratisation at the Municipality level. The composition and operating rules for such institutional arrangements are also significant for the effectiveness of participation, including issues of balance and representation of interests, and how the deliberation process operates.[56]

There are also participative mechanisms that are consultative, and have no binding force. These generally involve public hearings and consultation. The National Policy of Social Participation seeks to integrate participation and decision-making, proposing that there be a commitment to respond to the proposals received.

For both types of process, if the decision-maker does not follow the legal procedures for social participation a judge can annul the decision that may result from the flawed process.

However, having such a legal requirement does not necessarily mean that decision-makers will comply automatically with the requirement. As a result, the community may be either disenfranchised or forced to take legal or political action to see their rights enforced. An example is citizen participation in the approval of genetically modified crops. The National Technical Committee of Biosecurity ('*Comissão Técnica Nacional de Biossegurança*' – CTNBio) can hold a public hearing before genetically modified crops are approved for commercial release. In November 2013 CTNBio denied the request for a public hearing in the case of commercial release of genetically modified corn and soybeans resistant to the herbicide 2,4-D, requested by the Federal Prosecutors, Brazilian Consumer Defense Institute (IDEC) and the representatives of consumers on this committee.

The Brazilian examples indicate that even when there are reasonably strong formal requirements in place, achieving substantive decision-making involvement for the community is far from guaranteed. As with the Australian instances, legal requirements tend to enforce procedural compliance rather than moving processes upwards along Arnstein's notional ladder. The challenge of improving the implemented quality of participatory processes, and in particular to ensure that these processes do translate into influence on decisions, remains.

---

[55] Instituto Brasileiro de Geografia e Estatística (IBGE) (2008).

[56] For example, at the National Technical Committee of Biosecurity the quorum for approving the genetically modified organisms has changed from a qualified majority of 2/3 to an absolute majority.

6. CONCLUSION

Moving beyond good intentions to realised outcomes is a serious challenge for most aspects of natural resource governance, including achieving effective community participation.[57] Ineffective reform can create frustration and increase the risk of community disengagement by generating opportunities to participate that do not, in practice, shape decisions or drive change.[58] There continues to be great difficulty in linking stated intentions to achieved outcomes.[59] This suggests the need for more nuanced understanding of concepts like community, representation and participation,[60] which overlap in environmental governance discourses.[61]

The gap between aspiration and achievement can be seen in the cases presented here. Diverse instruments such as the substantive commitment of Brazil's National Policy of Social Participation and the procedural requirements of the Draft NSW Wind Farm guidelines are subject to similar questions about how to make them work consistently well in practice.

Within these environmental governance systems, it remains difficult for communities to challenge environmental decisions on the basis of an unsatisfactory engagement process. In Australia, vague concepts of community involvement are procedurally limited, and rarely sufficient for decisions to address power imbalances or insincere actions.[62] In Brazil, greater legal support for effective participation does not always ensure better implementation. Reform must focus on creating a firmer connection between the intent of the law and how it is put into practice, and address issues of legitimacy and accountability.

Existing laws provide an avenue to enable more rapid progress[63] towards institutionalising new norms of community participation.[64] Responses to the significant efforts of the public to participate in governance must be prioritised to ensure that the best advantage and learning is gained from these responses, but also to ensure that there is an ongoing rationale for making this effort, as it is generally agreed that

---

57 Gunningham (2009); Martin, Kennedy and Williams (2012).
58 Banisar *et al.* (2011); Lewanski (2013).
59 Margerum (2008).
60 Rockloff and Moore (2006).
61 Lane (2005).
62 Shepheard and Martin (2011); Lingard (2012).
63 Ross (2010).
64 Becker (2010).

'disillusionment is a potential risk with processes that … generate disappointing results'.[65]

Future Research: Considering a 'Duty to Consult'

The case studies presented in this chapter suggest that reforms must balance procedural and administrative requirements with substantive commitments to public participation. Attempts to improve the intersection of human rights with environmental governance ultimately require that 'institutional reform and substantive norm development must proceed hand-in-hand'.[66]

To improve, we need to create institutional triggers for review that move us away from a mere compliance 'tick the box' approach. This requires changing legal objectives to include definitions of community; clear directions about how community input will be prioritised in making difficult decisions; and explicit avenues for appeal by community members.

Considering how environmental law can contribute to this evolution of norms suggests the creation of a legal 'duty to consult'. The form of this duty, where in the legal framework it might be situated, and what rationalisation could be developed to support such a duty, are important considerations.

Duties that are linked to purely procedural compliance mechanisms are likely to be inadequate, as they reinforce entrenched power dynamics and place onerous burdens of proof on those who wish to challenge the integrity or authenticity of these procedures. For a duty to have real teeth, it must give standing to those who are part of the affected 'community'.

Further research is needed to consider how ambitious reforms could combine procedural and substantive instruments to elevate a new norm of community participation in democratic decision-making.[67] This would require not only the design of compliance and integrity mechanisms, but in recognition of the implementation gap identified in this chapter, a concerted effort to test this duty by empirical methods, in the spirit of continuous improvement.

---

65 Werksman and Foti (2011).

66 Abbott and Marchant (2010).

67 The UNECE Convention on Access to Information, Public Participation in Decision-making and Access to Justice in Environmental Matters (Aarhus Convention) suggests a pathway for reform in this vein.

REFERENCES

AAP (2014), '"Degrees in activism" put brake on growth' *The Australian* (Melbourne, 15 October), accessed 31 March 2015 at http://www.theaustralian.com.au/news/degrees-in-activism-put-brake-on-growth/story-e6frg6n6-1227090673642.

ABC News (2014), 'Metgasco referred to ICAC' ABC News (ABC online, 15 May), accessed 31 March 2015 at http://www.abc.net.au/news/2014-05-15/government-suspens-metgasco-licence-at-bentley/5454442.

Abbott, K. and G. Marchant (2010), 'Institutionalizing Sustainability across the Federal Government' 2 *Sustainability* 1924.

Adams, D. and M. Hess (2001), 'Community in Public Policy: Fad or Foundation?' 60 *Australian Journal of Public Administration* 13.

Andreoli, S.B. *et al.* (2002), 'Age-at-first-registration in Schizophrenia: A Comparison of Mental Health Registers from Australia and Brazil' 54 *Schizophrenia Research* 277.

Arnstein, S.R. (1969), 'A Ladder Of Citizen Participation' 35 *Journal of the American Institute of Planners* 216.

Assunção, F., M.A. Bursztyn and T. Abreu (2010), 'Participação social na avaliação de impacto ambiental: lições da experiência da Bahia' 10 *Confins – Revue Franco-bresilienne de geographie*, accessed 31 March 2015 at http://confins.revues.org/6750.

Australian Government (2012), 'Caring for our Country Review' (*Australian Government*, 2014), accessed 10 April 2015 at http://smtp.auricht.com/docs/aclep/c4oc_report_on_review_2012_a.pdf.

Australian Government (2014), 'Have your say on the National Landcare Programme' (*Australian Government*, 2014), accessed 10 April 2015 at http://www.nrm.gov.au/funding/nlp/index.html.

Avritzer, L. (2008), 'Instituições participativas e desenho institucional: algumas considerações sobre a variação da participação no Brasil democrático' (2008) 14 *Opin Publica* 43.

Banisar, D. *et al* (2011), *Moving from Principles to Rights: Rio 2012 and Ensuring Access to Information, Public Participation, and Access to Justice for Everyone* (Washington, DC: World Resources Institute).

Barbour, L. (2014), 'No New Money for Landcare Groups' ABC Rural (ABC online, 30 May), accessed 31 March 2015 at http://www.abc.net.au/news/2014-05-30/landcare-grants-no-money/5488998.

Becker, M.A. (2010), 'Russia and the Arctic: Opportunities for engagement within the existing legal framework' 25 *American Universities International Law Review* 225.

Beierle, T.C. (1999), 'Using Social Goals to evaluate Public Participation in Environmental Decisions' 16 *Review of Policy Research* 75.

Bell, D. *et al.* (2013), 'Re-visiting the 'Social Gap': Public Opinion and Relations of Power in the Local Politics of Wind Energy' 22 *Environmental Politics* 115.

Berndt, A. and N.W. Tomkins (2013), 'Measurement and Mitigation of Methane Emissions from Beef Cattle in Tropical Grazing Systems: A Perspective from Australia and Brazil' 7 Suppl 2 *Animal* 363–72.

Berner, M.M., J.M. Amos and R.S. Morse RS (2011), 'What Constitutes Effective Citizen Participation in Local Government? Views from City Stakeholders' 35 *Public Administration Quarterly* 128.

Bishop, P. and G. Davis (2002), 'Mapping Public Participation in Policy Choices' 61 *Australian Journal of Public Administration* 14.

Brackertz, N. and D. Meredyth (2009), 'Community Consultation in Victorian Local Government: A Case of Mixing Metaphors?' (2009) 68 *Australian Journal of Public Administration* 152.

Brugnach, M. *et al.* (2011), 'More is not always Better: Coping with Ambiguity in Natural Resources Management' 92 *Journal of Environmental Management* 78.

Buchy, M. and D. Race (2001), 'The Twists and Turns of Community Participation in Natural Resource Management in Australia: What is Missing?' 44(3) *Journal of Environmental Planning and Management* 293.

Cappelli, S. (2003), 'Acesso à justiça, à informação e participação popular em temas ambientais no Brasil' in M. Leite and M. Dantas (eds), *Aspectos Processuais do Direito Ambiental* (Rio de Janeiro: Forense Universitária).

Council of Australian Governments (1992), *Intergovernmental Agreement on the Environment* (Canberra: Australian Government).

Courtis, C. (2009), 'Notes on the Implementation by Latin American Countries of the ILO Convention 169 in Indigenous Peoples' 6 Sur, Rev int direitos human 52.

Dellinger, M. (2012), 'Ten Years of the Aarhus Convention: How Procedural Democracy Is Paving the Way for Substantive Change in National and International Environmental Law' 23 *Colorado Journal of International Environmental Law & Policy* 309.

Dryzek, J.S. (2000), *Deliberative Democracy and Beyond: Liberals, Critics, Contestations* (New York) Oxford University Press 2000), ch 1.

Eversole, R. (2011), 'Community Agency and Community Engagement: Re-theorising Participation in Governance' 31 *Journal of Public Policy* 51.

Fonseca, I. and M. Bursztyn (2009), 'A banalização da sustentabilidade: reflexoes sobre governança ambiental em escala local' 25 *Sociedade e Estado* 17.

Fountain, C., P. Libânio and G. Lane (2011), 'Differences Between the Engineering Cultures of Australia and Brazil' (MetPlant Conference, Perth, August).

Fung, A., 'Varieties of Participation in Complex Governance' 66 *Public Administration Review* 66.

Gray, J. (2011), 'Water Trading and Regulation in Australia' in Saddy, A. and A.M. Linares (eds), *Infrastructure Law: A Study of Regulated Markets* (Rio de Janeiro: Lumen Juris).

Gross, C. (2008), 'A Measure of Fairness: An Investigative Framework to Explore Perceptions of Fairness and Justice in a Real-Life Social Conflict' 15 *Research in Human Ecology* 130.

Guilliat, R. (2014), 'How a row over land clearing left compliance officer Glen Turner dead' *Weekend Australian* (Melbourne, 13 September), accessed 31 March 2015 at http://www.theaustralian.com.au/news/features/how-a-row-over-land-clearing-left-compliance-officer-glen-turner-dead/story-e6frg8h6-1227055190971.

Gunningham, N. (2009), 'Environment Law, Regulation and Governance: Shifting Architectures' 21 *Journal of Environmental Law* 29.

Hasham, N. (2014), 'Coal seam gas company licence cancelled after alleged breaches' The Sydney Morning Herald (Sydney, 15 October), accessed 31 March 2015 at http://www.smh.com.au/business/mining-and-resources/coal-seam-gas-company-licence-cancelled-after-alleged-breaches-20141014-115tqr.html#ixzz3GGxdwTxC.

Holley, C. (2010), 'Public Participation, Environmental Law and New Governance: Lessons for Designing Inclusive and Representative Participatory Processes' 27 *Environmental and Planning Law Journal* 32.

Howard, T. (2014), 'From International Principles to local Practices: A Socio-Legal Framing of Public Participation Research' *Environment, Development and Sustainability* 1.

Hussey, K. and S. Dovers (eds) (2007), *Managing Water for Australia: The Social and Institutional Challenges* (Collingwood, VIC: CSIRO).

ILO Convention 1969, Declaration on the application of Principle 10 of the Rio Declaration on Environment and Development (2012).

Instituto Brasileiro de Geografia e Estatística (IBGE) (2008), *Perfil dos municípios brasileiros: gestão pública 2008* (Rio de Janeiro: IBGE).

Irvin, R.A. and J. Stansbury (2004), 'Citizen Participation in Decision Making: Is It Worth the Effort?' 64 *Public Administration Review* 55.

Jackson, S. and J. Morrison (2007), 'Indigenous Perspectives in Water Management, Reforms and Implementation' in K. Hussey and S. Dovers (eds), *Managing Water for Australia: The Social and Institutional Challenges* (Collingwood, Vic: CSIRO).

Jendroska, J. (2013), 'Public Participation in Environmental Decision-Making: Interactions between the Convention and EU Law and Other Key Legal Issues' in M. Pallemaerts (ed.), *The Aarhus Convention at Ten: Interactions and Tensions between Conventional International Law and EU Environmental Law* (Groningen: Europa Law Publishing).

Kirk, E.A. and K.L. Blackstock (2011), 'Enhanced Decision Making: Balancing Public Participation against "Better Regulation" in British Environmental Permitting Regimes' 23 *Journal of Environmental Law* 97.

Kirk, E.A. and A.D. Reeves (2011), 'Regulatory Agencies and Regulatory Change: Breaking out of the Routine' 13 *Environmental Law Review* 155.

Koontz, T.M. and C.W. Thomas (2006), 'What Do We Know and Need to Know about the Environmental Outcomes of Collaborative Management?' 66 *Public Administration Review* 111.

Lane, M. (2005), 'Public Participation in Planning: an intellectual history' (2005) 36(3) *Australian Geographer* 283.

Lewanski, R. (2013), 'Institutionalizing Deliberative Democracy: the 'Tuscany laboratory'' (2013) 9(1) *Journal of Public Deliberation* 10.

Lingard, K. (2012), 'The Impact of the Law on Consultation Practices and Purposes: A Case Study of Aboriginal cultural Heritage Consultations in NSW' *International Journal of Rural Law and Policy*.

Lockwood, M. *et al.* (2009), 'Governance Principles for Natural Resource Management' (2009) 23 Soc Nat Resour 986.

Margerum, R.D. (2008), 'A Typology of Collaboration Efforts in Environmental Management' (2008) 41 *Environmental Management* 487.

Markell, D.L. (2006), 'Understanding Citizen Perspectives on Government Decision Making Processes as a Way to Improve the Administrative State' 36 *Environmental Law* 651.

Martin, P., A. Kennedy and J. Williams (2012), 'Creating Next Generation Rural Landscape Governance: The Challenge for Environmental Law Scholarship' in P. Martin *et al.* (eds) (2012), *Environmental Governance and Sustainability*, IUCN Academy of Environmental Law Series (Cheltenham, UK and Northampton, MA, USA: Edward Elgar).

Martin, P. and M. Shepeard (2011), 'What is Meant by the Social License?' in J. Williams and P. Martin (eds) (2011), *Defending the Social License of Farming: Issues, challenges and new directions for agriculture* (Collingwood, Vic: CSIRO).

Miller, L.L. (2012), *(Mis)Understanding American Federalism: On Constitutions, Collective Action, Competition and Quiescence* (Oxford: The Foundation for Law, Justice and Society).

Mirra, Á.L.V. (2011), *Participação, processo civil e defesa do meio ambiente* (São Paulo: Letras Jurídicas).

National Water Commission, *Murray–Darling Basin Plan implementation: initial report* (Canberra: National Water Commission, 2013).

Nicholls, S. (2013), 'ICAC: mining licence corruption 'almost inevitable' in NSW' *The Sydney Morning Herald* (Sydney, 30 October), accessed 31 March 2015 at http://www.smh.com.au/nsw/icac-mining-licence-corruption-almost-inevitable-in-nsw-20131030-2wf2y.html.

O Dia que Durou 21 Anos (2012), Camilo Tavares and Flavio Tavares, Pequi Filmes.

Ostrom, E. and M. Cox (2010), 'Moving beyond Panaceas: A Multi-Tiered Diagnostic Approach for Social-Ecological Analysis' 37(4) *Environmental Conservation* 451.

Peterson, N. (2011), 'Excluding to Include: (Non)participation in Mexican Natural Resource Management' 28 *Agriculture and Human Values* 99.

Rawlins, J., E. Gramenz and N. Haxton (2014), 'Wild Rivers Declarations for Stewart Basin, Archer and Lockhart Ruled Invalid' *ABC News* (ABC online, 17 June), accessed 31 March 2015 at http://www.abc.net.au/news/2014-06-17/queensland-government-wild-rivers-declarations-declared-invalid/5529148?WT.mc_id=newsmail.

Reed, M. (2008), 'Stakeholder Participation for Environmental Management: A Literature Review' (2008) 141 *Biological Conservation* 2417.

Reis, D. (2014), 'A ditadura faz cinquenta anos: historia e cultura politica nacional-estatista' in D. Reis, M. Ridenti and R. Motta (eds), *A ditadura que mudou o Brasil: 50 anos do golpe de 1964* (Rio de Janeiro: Zahar).

Rocha, C. (2014), 'Globalization of Spiritism: Tracking Flows between Australia and Brazil in John of God Religious Movement' 52 *Revista de Antropologia* 571.

Rockloff, S. and S. Moore (2006), 'Assessing Representation at Different Scales of Decision Making: Rethinking Local is Better' (2006) 34 PSJ 649.

Ross, A. (2010), 'It's Time to Get Serious – Why Legislation is Needed to Make Sustainable Development a Reality in the UK' 2 *Sustainability* 1101.

Rowe, G. and L.J. Frewer (2004), 'Evaluating Public-Participation Exercises: A Research Agenda' 29(4) *Science, Technology & Human Values* 512.

Rowe, G. and L.J. Frewer (2005), 'A Typology of Public Engagement Mechanisms' 30 *Science, Technology & Human Values* 251.

Shepheard, M. and P. Martin (2011), 'Using the Moot Court to Trial Legislation about Land Stewardship' 28(2) *Land Use Policy* 371.

Steelman, T.A. (2010), *Implementing Innovation: Fostering Enduring Change in Environmental and Natural Resource Governance* (Washington, DC: Georgetown University Press).

United Nations Environment Programme, 'Agenda 21' (*United Nations*, 1992), accessed 31 March 2015 at http://www.unep.org/documents.multilingual/default.asp?documentid=52.

United Nations European Commission on the Environment (1998), UNECE Convention on Access to Information, Public Participation in Decision-making and Access to Justice in Environmental Matters (Aarhus Convention).

United Nations General Assembly, 'Rio Declaration on Environment and Development' (1992), accessed 31 March 2015 at http://www.un.org/documents/ga/conf151/aconf15126-1annex1.htm.

United Nations General Assembly (2012a), 'Rio+20: The Future We Want', accessed 31 March 2015 at http://www.un.org/en/sustainablefuture/

United Nations General Assembly (2012b), 'Rio+20 concludes with big package of commitments for action and agreement by world leaders on path for a sustainable future' accessed 31 March 2015 at http://www.un.org/en/sustainablefuture/pdf/rio20%20concludes_press%20release.pdf.

Visseren-Hamakers I.J. (2013), 'Partnerships and Sustainable Development: the Lessons Learned from International Biodiversity Governance' (2013) 23 *Environmental Policy and Governance* 145.

Werksman, J. and J. Foti (2011), 'Improving Participation in International Environmental Governance' (UNEP Perspectives).

Whitman, D. (2008), '"Stakeholders" and the Politics of Environmental Policymaking' in J. Park, K. Conca and M. Finger (eds), *The Crisis of Global Environmental Governance: Towards a New Political Economy of Sustainability* (Abingdon: Routledge).

Wogan, J.B. (2014) 'Lessons in Gun Control from Australia and Brazil', accessed 31 March 2015 at http://www.governing.com/topics/public-justice-safety/gov-gun-control-lessons.html.

Woods, P. (2014), 'Residents lock the gate on coal' *The Gympie Times* (Gympie, 10 September), accessed 31 March 2015 at http://www.gympietimes.com.au/news/residents-lock-the-gate-on-coal/2381379/.

Woolgar, S. and D. Neyland (2013), 'Structures of Governance' in S. Woolgar and D. Neyland (eds), *Mundane Governance* (Oxford: Oxford University Press).

7. Implementing international water agreements

Alistair Rieu-Clarke and Josefin Gooch

1. INTRODUCTION

There are estimated to be 276 transboundary river and lake basins, which cover nearly half of the Earth's land surface.[1] These river and basin areas are home to 40 per cent of the world's population, and are shared by 145 States.[2] A number of facts emphasise the significance of transboundary water resources: 39 States have more than 90 per cent of the territory that is within transboundary basins; 20 rivers are shared by five or more States; and a number of the world's most important transboundary waters are shared by even more States. These include the Danube (17 States), the Congo (13 States), the Nile (12 States), the Niger (10 States), and the Amazon, Rhine and Zambezi (9 States each). The importance of transboundary aquifers should not be forgotten.[3] An estimated 275 transboundary aquifers exist.[4] These aquifers account for more than 100 times the volume of global surface water.[5] Transboundary groundwater is increasingly being seen as an important means of addressing water demand, particularly in water stressed regions of the world.[6]

Across the globe significant pressures on transboundary rivers, lakes and aquifers are becoming increasingly evident and, given the indivisible nature of water, demanding stronger cooperation between States. Population growth, industrialisation and the expansion of irrigated agriculture

[1] Transboundary Freshwater Dispute Database (TFDD) (2014).

[2] UN-Water, 'Transboundary Waters: Sharing Benefits, Sharing Responsibilities' (2008) 1.

[3] TFDD (2014).

[4] United Nations Educational, Scientific and Cultural Organization (UNESCO) (2009) 61.

[5] Ibid.

[6] MacDonald (2012).

have led to a dramatic increase in water demand.[7] Between 1960 and 2000, for instance, world water use doubled from about 1,800 to 3,600 km^3 per year. With world population predicted to grow from 8.3 billion in 2010 to 9.1 billion in 2030 further pressure is likely to be placed on the world's freshwater supplies.[8] Meeting increasing water demands is a major challenge. 41 per cent of the world's population already live in river basins under water stress.[9] A complicating factor is climate change, which is likely to exacerbate water shortages in certain regions, lead to less predictable flows, and increase the likelihood and magnitude of extreme events, that is, floods and droughts.[10]

International law has a long tradition of attempting to manage conflict and build cooperation between States sharing transboundary rivers, lakes and aquifers. It is estimated that over 3,600 transboundary water agreements have been adopted.[11] The majority of agreements relate to navigational uses, which reflected the major use of transboundary waters up until the 20th century.[12] Since then the regime has expanded to include issues such as irrigation for agricultural purposes, energy production techniques, access to safe drinking water, the preservation of natural and cultural heritage and perhaps most importantly, environmental concerns.[13] Only around 400 or so agreements address non-navigational uses of transboundary waters, and many of those agreements are not comprehensive in nature.[14] In surveying the status of international water agreements, UN-Water conclude that:

> Existing agreements are sometimes not sufficiently effective to promote integrated water resources management due to problems at the national and local levels such as inadequate water management structures and weak capacity in countries to implement the agreements as well as shortcomings in the agreements themselves (for example, inadequate integration of aspects such as the environment, the lack of enforcement mechanisms, limited – sectoral – scope and non-inclusion of important riparian States).[15]

---

[7] UNESCO (2009) 168.

[8] United Nations Department of Economic and Social Affairs (UNDESA) (2009).

[9] Revenga et al. (2000) 26.

[10] Bates (eds.) *et al.* (2008).

[11] UNESCO (2009) 6.

[12] Dinar et al. (2007) 58–60.

[13] de Chazournes (2013) 7.

[14] UN World Water Assessment Programme, (2009) 51; Burchi and Mechlem (2005).

[15] UN-Water (2008).

A complicating factor has been the preference of States to enter into bilateral agreements to the exclusion of other riparian States.[16] This trend has led commentators to describe the treaty architecture concerning transboundary water as fragmented; with around 60 per cent of all transboundary rivers, lakes and aquifers lacking any type of cooperative management framework.[17]

Efforts to address this fragmentation are gaining momentum. The International Law Commission (ILC) spent over 20 years on a codification and progressive development effort that ultimately led to the adoption of the Convention on the Law of the Non-navigational Uses of International Watercourses in 1997 (UN Watercourses Convention).[18] While States have been slow to join the UN Watercourses Convention, a recent ratification campaign has meant entry into force is now imminent.[19] As a complement to this global framework instrument, the UN Economic Commission for Europe's Convention on the Protection and Use of Transboundary Watercourses and International Lakes (UNECE Water Convention), will soon be open to membership by all UN Member States.[20] A global regime for transboundary waters is therefore likely to emerge in the foreseeable future; which hopefully will help address fragmentation at the basin level.[21]

A key consideration at this important period in the evolution of international water agreements is to understand what factors influence their implementation, and ultimately their effectiveness. In the last decades, a significant body of research has studied issues around the implementation and effectiveness of treaty arrangements, particularly within the context of multilateral environmental agreements (MEAs).[22] To date there have been limited attempts to examine how this scholarly work could help inform the adoption and implementation of transboundary water agreements. In order to address this gap, this chapter will draw

---

[16] Zawahri and McLaughlin (2011).

[17] Ibid. See also UNESCO (2009) 7.

[18] International Law Commission (ILC) (1994); United Nations, *Convention on the Law of the Non-navigational Uses of International Watercourses* (1997).

[19] United Nations Treaty Division, *Status of Multilateral Treaties Deposited with the Secretary-General* (1997).

[20] The amendment allowing non-UNECE states to join the UNECE Water Convention will become operational once all states parties to the latter instrument as of 2003 have acceded to the amendment. For current status see United Nations Treaty Division, *Convention on the Protection and Use of Transboundary Watercourses and International Lakes* (2012).

[21] Rieu-Clarke and Kinna (2014).

[22] For an overview see Young, King and Schroeder (2008).

upon existing scholarship to examine factors that are likely to affect the implementation of transboundary water agreements; and suggest a number of strategies that may address potential barriers to implementation. However, before examining these factors, it is important to provide some conceptual understanding of key terms.

2. CENTRAL CONCEPTS

Three important aspects of adherence to obligations under international law have been identified in the literature; implementation, compliance and effectiveness.[23]

Implementation of international agreements refers to the actions taken by states, in their domestic sphere, to give the agreement effect. Implementation thus includes the adoption of legislation or regulations, judicial decrees, or other actions. Most treaties require such domestic legislation or executive regulations to become effective law domestically.[24] National implementation has been found to be 'extraordinarily complex' with no single way of putting international agreements into practice within a country. Instead implementation follows different paths in different countries.[25] Implementation strategies also change over time as it is part of a 'perpetual cycle of policy that is driven by new information, experience, and political pressures'.[26]

Compliance means that commitments entered into by a state are fully effectuated in practice.[27] As implementation of the agreement is an important way to reach compliance, implementation is often included in the concept of compliance. This is not necessarily so, however; a state may for example already be in compliance with an agreement when it comes into force, thus not requiring further implementation measures from the state. The understanding of compliance is also generally broader than that of implementation.[28] Besides focusing on whether implementing measures are in operation, compliance also focuses on the degree to

---

23 See Zaelke, Kaniaru and Kružiková (eds) (2005); Weiss and Harold Jakobson (eds) (2000) 4–5.

24 Weiss and Jakobson (2000) 4–5; Weiss (1998–1999).

25 Viktor, Raustiala and Skolnikoff (1998) 3, 5.

26 Ibid, 6.

27 Wolfrum (1998) 29.

28 Weiss (1998–1999).

which the actors addressed by the agreement conform to the implementing measures and obligations.[29] Legal obligations can be either obligations of conduct, for example, to establish a system for allocating water, or obligations of result, for example, to allocate 20 per cent of available water as ecosystem water. The outcome of compliance with the obligations will naturally differ depending on if the obligation is one of conduct or one of result.[30] Compliance can focus on different aspects of conformity, such as procedural compliance, substantive compliance and compliance with the spirit of the agreement.[31] *Procedural compliance* refers to whether states have followed the procedural obligations in the agreement, for example, filed reports or established particular governmental authorities. *Substantive compliance* is compliance with substantive obligations, for example, the obligation not to cause significant harm. A country may comply with its procedural obligations but not with its substantive obligations or vice versa. *Compliance with the spirit of the agreement* is compliance with the main objectives behind the agreement.[32] If, for instance, an agreement requires states to limit their use of certain chemicals that are toxic to aquatic species and a state instead shifts to another chemical not limited by the agreement but equally harmful to aquatic species it would arguably violate the spirit of the instrument.

Effectiveness is arguably the ultimate concern of legal rules and agreements. Three levels of effectiveness are often mentioned in literature; legal effectiveness, behavioural effectiveness and problem-solving effectiveness.[33] Political effectiveness can also be added to this list. In short, *legal effectiveness* focuses on the issue of compliance, whether the outcome conforms to the requirements of the legal rules. This type of effectiveness is fairly easy to measure. However, as Young *et al.* point out, a regime can be legally effective without solving the problem that led to its creation.[34] *Problem-solving effectiveness* focuses on how well the regime works to solve the problem causing the states to enter into the regime in the first place.[35] However, because of the complexity of social and natural systems, it is difficult to ascribe observed changes in them to the operation of the international regime.[36] Young and Levy also point

29 Weiss and Jakobson (2000) 4–5 and Weiss (1998–1999) 1563.
30 Young and Levy (1999) 4.
31 Jacobson and Weiss (1997) 83.
32 Weiss (1998–1999) 1563.
33 See e.g., Bodansky (2010) 253 ff.
34 Young and Levy (1999) 4.
35 Bodansky (2010) 256.
36 Young and Levy (1999) 3.

out that problems that are serious enough to justify the creation of an international regime will lead to actors trying to reach solutions through a variety of initiatives, including some that do not involve the regime directly.[37] Mitchell and Zawahri furthermore, emphasise that a problem-solving understanding of effectiveness might not be appropriate for examining the effectiveness of transboundary watercourses agreements. A problem-solving understanding of effectiveness rests on two assumptions, they argue; one being that there is indeed a solution to the problem that led to the creation of the institution and the second being that there exists a fixed point at which the solution is reached, such as over-harvesting of fish stocks, or protection of endangered species. International river treaties, however, represent a challenge to which there generally is no singular solution.[38] The reason for setting up international river treaties can arguably be generalised as cooperation assistance. The problem here is that riparian states are dependent on other riparian states in the management of the shared resource.

Behavioural effectiveness looks at whether or not the treaty or obligation changes the outcome of the situation, that is, whether the situation is different from what it would have been without the treaty or obligation.[39] As with legal effectiveness, this definition of effectiveness mainly works within the legal system itself, albeit in this latter case, with the need for inputs from social science. Neither of these two definitions of effectiveness is really concerned with acquiring a certain status in the world outside of the legal system. Behavioural effectiveness is instead concerned with the ability of the legal provisions to change people's behaviour. It is the *change* that is in focus here, the aim of the legal provisions is of less concern. Viewing the effectiveness only from a 'before versus after' point of view says very little about whether or not the legal provisions in question really protect the ecosystems or not. Even if an assessment would show that a set of legal provisions were successful in view of both legal and behavioural effectiveness, they might still be ineffective in problem-solving effectiveness, that is, reaching the goals for which they were adopted, if the aim of the provisions had been set too low.

A political approach to effectiveness is similar to problem solving effectiveness in that it focuses on the goals of the regime and how action is spurred towards achieving these objectives. Here specific regulatory

---

37 Ibid.

38 Mitchell and Zawahri (2012) 7.

39 Bodansky (2010) 255.

rules, protocols, and operational targets are seen as means to these ends rather than ends in themselves. This means that activities that move the system towards achieving the objectives of the regime are signs of effectiveness, even if they do not result in full compliance.[40] Mitchell and Zawahri argue that 'an institution is effective when it is able to assist states in managing a problem that has no solution, but rather continuous conflicts of interest'.[41] They refer to this type of institutional effectiveness as 'process management'.

3. FACTORS INFLUENCING TREATY IMPLEMENTATION IN TRANSBOUNDARY WATER SETTINGS

Many theoretical accounts as to why States do or should cooperate over transboundary waters have been put forward. An understanding of these accounts provides an important basis to examine the issues around implementation, compliance and effectiveness highlighted above. Without such an understanding, policy recommendations that seek to improve the design and/or implementation of watercourse treaty arrangements may be misguided.

From a realist perspective, power has been identified as a main driver of cooperation amongst states.[42] According to realist accounts cooperation will be dependent on the will of the most powerful state within a particular region or basin. If the most powerful state is upstream it may have little incentive to cooperate, whereas a downstream hegemon might take the lead in fostering cooperation.[43] A weaker state, according to Lowi, is, 'not in a position to achieve its aims and satisfy its needs in an optimal fashion … In effect, it has little alternative to accept a modus vivendi dictated by the stronger'.[44] In such an interpretation, watercourse treaties would have limited impact. However, others argue that weaker

---

[40] Young and Levy (1999) 3.

[41] Mitchell and Zawahri (2012) 7.

[42] Lowi (1993). Cascao and Zeitoun (2010) 27–42, identify four forms of power, namely: (i) geographic power – riparian position; (ii) material power – economic, military or technological strength, as well as international political and financial support; (iii) bargaining power – the ability to control the rules of the game and to set agendas; and (iv) ideational power – the capacity to impose and legitimize particular ideas and narratives.

[43] Waterbury (1997).

[44] Lowi (n 42) 169.

states are not entirely powerless to influence basin dynamics. Daoudy, for instance, claims that, 'downstream countries can … mobilise structural factors, such as the codification of new legal "rules" on watercourses to bring upstream riparians to cooperate, and therefore acquire structural power'.[45] Similarly, Zeitoun and Jägerskog argue that 'basin bullies can be susceptible to the powers of persuasion, and may be less likely to force an arrangement if they are held accountable to an objective standard, or risk of being "named and shamed"'.[46]

An alternative account of why states cooperate focuses on interest and reciprocity. This account posits that states cooperate when they expect to gain more from collective action than unitary action. An important premise to this account is recognition of water as a 'collective action' problem. This collective action problem is described by Benvenisti as follows, 'each state is interested in getting more out of the resource with minimal costs, and these interests conflict with those of other users. This conflict can lead the parties to a race to the bottom'.[47] However, if states can put in place mechanisms that ensure that a resource is managed in an optimal and sustainable manner, a 'race to the bottom' does not necessarily have to ensue. While the types of mechanisms will be discussed in the next section, it is important to identify here the benefits that might derive from collective action. Sadoff and Grey identify the benefits as being four-fold, namely:

> … environmental benefits to the 'river' (e.g. improved water quality, conserved biodiversity); economic benefits from the 'river' (e.g. increased food and energy production); reduction of costs because of the 'river' (e.g. reduced geo-political tensions, enhanced flood management); and benefits beyond the 'river' catalysing wider cooperation and economic integration.[48]

While, according to Sadoff and Grey, cooperation may lead to a wide-range of benefits to, from, because of, and beyond the river, such cooperation is not immune to power asymmetries. Account must therefore be taken of how benefits are distributed amongst riparian states. As will be discussed below, transboundary treaty regimes have an important role to play in ensuring that benefits are allocated in an equitable and sustainable manner.

---

45 Daoudy (2008).
46 Zeitoun and Jägerskog (2009) 11.
47 Benvenisti (2012) 31. See also Hardin (1968).
48 Sadoff and Grey (2002).

A third account of why states cooperate suggests that inter-state relations are socially constructed, and normative and collective understanding influences the physical and social world.[49] Conca stresses the need to adopt multiple levels of analysis, which link norm development at the global level, to regional, basin-specific, national and local decision-making processes.[50]

All these theoretical accounts of why states cooperate, envisage to a greater or lesser extent a role for transboundary watercourse regimes. Additionally, both internal and external features that influence how and how effectively a watercourse treaty is implemented can be identified either implicitly or explicitly from such accounts. Internal features relate to treaty design; what provisions are included and how they are formulated. External features relate to those factors that influence treaty implementation from outside of the treaty itself. The legal and institutional frameworks, administrative capacity and political system of states are all important external features as are international networks and epistemic communities.

Literature on both international environmental cooperation,[51] and specific studies of international water management,[52] seem to generally agree that the design of international environmental institutions will determine how well they are able to promote cooperation.[53] The most obvious aspect of the design is the actual obligations that are included in the agreement. The substantive obligations to use international watercourses in an equitable and reasonable way and the obligation to not cause significant harm are at the core of the regime of transboundary watercourses. In some form these requirements are included in most river basin agreements. In their basic form they are very general and will often need further specification in relation to the circumstances of the specific watercourse in order to be successfully implemented. A river treaty can give more detailed stipulations as to how the river is to be shared, determine acceptable water withdrawal rates or balance water quality needs, navigation and water levels, thus helping to reduce the stress on the river and its resources and minimise conflict risks.[54] Article 5 of the UN Watercourses Convention requires that in using a watercourse in an

---

49 Dinar (2007) 25. See also Nagtzaam (2009) 50–79.

50 Conca, Wu and Mei (2006).

51 Tir and Stinnett (2012); Haas (1992).

52 Tir and Stinnett (2012) 212; Bernauer (2002); Giordano, Giordano and Wolf (2005).

53 See also Mitchell and Zawahri (2012) 5.

54 Yoffe, Wolf and Giordano (2003) 1124; Tir and Stinnett (2012) 215.

equitable and reasonable manner, the interests of other concerned watercourse states must be taken into account. The assessment of different factors requires, for example, exchange of information and communication among riparian states. Such procedural obligations are often crucial to fulfilling the substantial obligations of equitable utilisation and no significant harm.[55] Therefore, article 6 of the UN Watercourse convention requires that concerned watercourse states 'shall, when the need arises, enter into consultation in a spirit of cooperation'.

The type of commitment involved as well as the depth and stringency of the commitment are highlighted by Bodansky as other factors determining the implementation success of a treaty. The larger the required change from the present, the more probable it is that implementation will be expensive and will conflict with existing interests, and thus be less likely to succeed.[56] More specific obligations, directly under a party's control such as adopting pollution discharge standards are more likely to be successfully implemented than commitments to achieve some general result – including making the nations waters 'fishable' and 'swimmable'. The latter depends on a multitude of factors that may be difficult to change and thus to successfully regulate.[57]

The duty to cooperate and consult with other riparian states is part of an obligation to inform. Leb points to three reasons for providing information in international watercourses; to inform about the general status of the water system; to improve development and management planning capacity and to prevent harm by notifying other states of imminent danger or of planned activities that might negatively impact on the water system or another state's territory.[58] These requirements have crystallised into three categories; regular exchange of data and information; notification of natural emergencies and those caused by human activity; and notification of planned measures.[59] The obligation to carry out an environmental impact assessment (EIA) regarding the effects of projects is closely linked to obligations of information sharing.[60]

---

[55] However, many authors acknowledge that the line dividing substantive and procedural rules is blurred in international water law; Weiss (1998–1999) 207; Okowa (2013) 110.

[56] Bodansky (2010) 207.

[57] Ibid.

[58] Leb (2013) 114.

[59] Ibid.

[60] Ibid.

Several other mechanisms can be included that are generally perceived as facilitators of cooperation, such as establishing river basin organisations, or enabling states to monitor developments within the basin. Mechanisms for conflict resolution, mechanisms to address disputes, enforcement mechanisms to increase the cost of 'cheating', and the exchange of hydrological data to improve the ability to manage a basin are other such mechanisms.[61]

Joint institutions for carrying out the cooperation regarding management of transboundary water resources are highly recommended in order to facilitate cooperation between member states. They provide parties with an opportunity to meet directly and communicate with each other, which in turn is necessary to exchange information, plan and perform maintenance work on the river and so on.[62] Joint institutions can also prevent the emergence of conflicts, or at least aid in dispute settlement.[63] Riparian states sharing a transboundary watercourse with a treaty or a commission are more likely to manage water crises through negotiations than riparians without institutionalised systems.[64] Joint institutions are often responsible for carrying out treaty obligations that work towards improving implementation and effectiveness of the treaty, such as decision-making, monitoring member state behaviour, facilitating enforcement, resolving disagreements over treaty obligations and enhancing the capacity of member countries.[65] The ability to monitor member's activities and the state of the river are important for gathering information and for improving transparency.[66] Exchange of hydrological data is important for developmental purposes (for example, to maximise hydropower effectiveness) and for safety reasons (for example, to provide flood warnings) and the failure to exchange such data can contribute to

---

[61] Mitchell and Zawahri (2012) 3.

[62] Ibid 9.

[63] Tir and Stinnett (2012) 214f.

[64] Mitchell and Zawahri (2012) 2; Hensel, Mitchell and Sowers (2006) 408; Odom and Wolf (2011) 704. See also: Yoffe, Wolf and Giordano (2003); Giordano, Giordano and Wolf (2005); Zawahri (2009).

[65] Although literature is inconclusive as to the relative importance of these factors, there seems to be a general agreement that they are all important, see e.g. Young and Levy (1999); Botcheva and Martin (2002); Mitchell and Zawahri (2012) 4.

[66] Mitchell and Zawahri (2012) 10.

tensions between riparian states.[67] Dispute resolution mechanisms are needed to maintain cooperation through the inevitable disputes that arise over managing the river basin.[68] Mechanisms and provisions that facilitate enforcement can improve the compliance rate by reducing states' incentives to cheat on an agreement or set of rules.[69] Transparency and flexibility to respond to change are other factors that have been brought up by commentators on successful international cooperation.[70] Another value of joint river institutions is their ability to provide an institutionalised mechanism for technical experts, engineers, water resource managers, or an epistemic community to operate within.[71]

However, as implementation is done in a national context, it matters little how good and well designed a specific treaty is if states lack the capacity to implement it into their national settings. Legal and administrative capacities, as well as a political system in which the regime can function are all crucial external features of implementation. Although there is not one correct way to implement international obligations in national legislation, certain factors can be pointed out as important for successful implementation. Generally speaking, a state will need a national legal framework within which the obligations of the international agreement can be made effective. Control over pollution, agricultural irrigation and other uses that are carried out by private actors in a national context need to be enacted in national laws. There also needs to exist an institutional setting to carry out control and enforcement of the obligations. Related to this need is national capacity. Implementation generally requires resources and expertise to draft laws, prepare reports, administer a permitting scheme, monitor behaviour, and bring prosecutions, and so on.[72] This is a matter of knowledge, economic capacity and legal mandate which requires personnel with adequate knowledge and sufficient training with adequate funds and the power to carry out their obligations. To a varying degree industry groups and environmental organisations and other interest groups also participate in implementation.[73] Public participation is increasingly seen as an integral part of the

---

67 Ibid, 14f.

68 Giordano and others (2005); Mitchell and Zawahri (2012) 12.

69 Tir and Stinnett (2012) 216; Mitchell and Zawahri (2012) 13.

70 Mitchell and Zawahri (2012) 5; Chayes and Chayes (1993); Giordano, Giordano and Wolf (2005) 1124; Zawahri (2009) 4.

71 Mitchell and Zawahri (2012) 10.

72 Bodansky (2010) 207.

73 Ibid, 210.

national implementation process.[74] Stakeholders can possess knowledge, influence, funds and so on, making their involvement lead to better-informed decisions and improved implementation.[75] However, the degree to which these groups are able to take part in the process depends, *inter alia*, on the political system. The national political system can determine the level of transparency and the ability of civil society to take part in the decision-making process, leading to greater acceptance of the system. Another external feature of implementation is the impact of international networks and epistemic communities. Epistemic communities are defined as 'a network of professionals with recognised expertise and competence in a particular domain and an authoritative claim to policy-relevant knowledge within that domain or issue-area'.[76] The authoritative claim to knowledge by such a group makes it into a power bloc that policy-makers confer with in order to reduce uncertainty and increase the legitimacy of decisions at the domestic level.[77]

4. CONCLUSIONS

The previous section demonstrated that the factors likely to influence the successful implementation of, compliance with, and effectiveness of transboundary watercourse treaties are manifold. This suggests that designing more effective transboundary watercourse treaties will be contingent upon the specifics of a particular river basin and its riparian states. However, a number of important insights might help shape more effective treaty arrangements. It will be critical to account for the internal and external features noted above that might influence treaty effectiveness as well as those underlying theoretical accounts of why states cooperate. Perhaps the single most important focus in improving the effectiveness of treaty arrangements should be to emphasise the importance of process in the design of treaties. As previously mentioned, there is no 'quick fix solution' to managing the world's transboundary watercourses, so what is required is a mechanism for managing 'continuous conflicts of interest' in a transparent, legitimate and ultimately equitable manner.[78]

---

74 Ibid.
75 Kranz and Mostert (2012) 93.
76 Haas (1992) 3.
77 Ibid, 13.
78 Mitchell and Zawahri (2012) 7.

Such an approach resonates strongly with the traditional theory of compliance espoused by Chayes and Chayes almost 20 years ago.[79] In their seminal work Chayes and Chayes recognised that, 'the principal source of non-compliance is not willful disobedience but the lack of capability or clarity or priority'.[80] Accepting such an interpretation of state behaviour therefore requires a focus on: (i) ensuring transparency in the generation and dissemination of information about the requirements of a treaty and a party's performance thereunder; (ii) an effective mechanism for treaty interpretation and clarification; and (iii) address possible deficits of technical and bureaucratic capability and financial resources through capacity building and technical assistant programmes.[81] These aforementioned elements, which are reflected in the internal and external features noted previously, provide the backbone of compliance mechanisms that are now a common feature in many international environmental agreements.[82]

However, it is a startling fact that very few transboundary watercourse treaties contain compliance mechanisms within their formal design. While it could be maintained that compliance may indirectly feature in the implementation of existing treaty arrangements, it should be remembered that, as noted above, 60 per cent of all transboundary rivers, lakes and aquifers still lack *any* type of cooperative framework, and others are far from being comprehensive.[83] A focus on compliance mechanisms within transboundary watercourse treaties, (which are almost 'a given' for international environmental agreements) could offer one of the most profound approaches to strengthening transboundary water cooperation.

A notable exception to the lack of compliance mechanism, which in itself might offer guidance for states considering strengthening their own transboundary watercourse treaties, is the implementation committee that has recently been established under the UNECE Water Convention.[84] The implementation committee has the role to facilitate, promote and safeguard the implementation and application of, and compliance with, the UNECE Water Convention. It is described as being, 'simple, non-confrontational,

[79] Chayes and Chayes (1994).
[80] Ibid, 22.
[81] Ibid, 22–5.
[82] See Treves *et al.* (eds) (2007).
[83] Zawahri and McLaughlin (2011). See also UNESCO (2009) 7.
[84] UN Doc. ECE/MP.WAT/37/Add.2.

non-adversarial, transparent, supportive and cooperative in nature, building on the distinctive collaborative spirit of the Convention'.[85] The committee is comprised of nine members. They serve in their personal capacity, and are elected by states party to the Convention at the meeting of the parties. A key function of the committee is to provide advice concerning difficulties in the implementation or application of the Convention that have been raised by the parties. The committee may then: (i) suggest or recommend domestic regulatory regimes be set up or strengthened and relevant domestic resources be mobilised as appropriate; (ii) assist in establishing transboundary water cooperation agreements; (iii) facilitate technical and financial assessment, including information and technology transfer, and capacity-building; and (iv) assist in seeking support from specialised agencies and other competent bodies, as appropriate.[86] Additionally, it is envisaged that this implementation committee will be supplemented by a reporting procedure, which is currently under consideration by the meeting of the parties to the UNECE Water Convention.

While the implementation committee under the UNECE Water Convention is at an early stage in its evolution, it is a significant development in the field of transboundary watercourses. More transboundary watercourses agreements, existing or future, would do well to examine the model of the UNECE Water Convention and see how such mechanisms might be incorporated at the basin level – where they are at present significantly lacking. Such non-adversarial, process-based, approaches to compliance may go a long way to addressing the various factors that explain why states should cooperate over water, whilst also clarifying 'internal' features of a treaty regime where appropriate, and responding to the 'external' features that potentially inhibit the implementation of watercourse agreements.

REFERENCES

Bates B.C. *et al.* (eds) (2008), *Climate Change and Water* (Geneva: Intergovernmental Panel on Climate Change).

Benvenisti, E. (2002), *Sharing Transboundary Resources: International Law and Optimal Resource Use* (Cambridge: Cambridge University Press).

Bernauer, T. (2002), 'Explaining Success and Failure in International River Management' 64(1) *Aquatic Sciences* 1.

Bodansky, D., *The Art and Craft of International Environmental Law* (Cambridge, MA: Harvard University Press, 2010).

---

85 Ibid.

86 Ibid.

Botcheva, L. and L. Martin (2002), 'Institutional Effects on State Behavior: Convergence and Divergence' (2002) 45(1) *International Studies Quarterly* 1.

Burchi, S. and K. Mechlem (2005), *Groundwater in International Law* (Rome: FAO).

Cascao, A.E. and M. Zeitoun (2010), 'Power, Hegemony and Critical Hydropolitics' in A. Earle, A. Jägerskog and J. Öjendal (eds) *Transboundary Water Management Principles and Practice* (London: Earthscan)

Chayes, A. and A.H. Chayes (1993), 'On Compliance' 47(2) *International Organization* 175.

Chayes, A. and A.H. Chayes (1994), *The New Sovereignty – Compliance with International Regulatory Agreements* (Cambridge, MA: Harvard University Press).

Conca, K., F. Wu and C. Mei (2006), 'Global Regime Formation or Complex Institution Building? The Principled Content of International River Agreements', 50(2) *International Studies Quarterly* 263.

Daoudy, M. (2008), 'Hydro-Hegemony and International Water Law: Laying Claims to Water Rights' 10 *Water Policy* 89.

de Chazournes, L. (2013), *Fresh Water in International Law* (Oxford: Oxford University Press).

Dinar, A. *et al.* (2007), *Bridges over Water: Understanding Transboundary Water Conflict, Negotiation and Cooperation* (Singapore: World Scientific Publishing Company).

Giordano, M., M. Giordano, and A. Wolf (2005), 'International Resource Conflict and Mitigation' 42(1) *Journal of Peace Research* 47.

Haas, P. (1992), 'Introduction: Epistemic Communities and International Policy Coordination' 46(1) *International Organization* 1.

Hardin, G. (1968), 'The Tragedy of the Commons' 162 *Science* 1243.

Hensel, P., S. Mitchell and T. Sowers (2006), 'Conflict Management of Riparian Disputes' 25 *Political Geography* 383.

International Law Commission (ILC) (1994), 'Draft Articles on the Law of the Non-navigational Uses of International Watercourses' 2(2) *Yearbook of International Law Commission* 89.

Jacobson, H. and E. Weiss (1997), 'Compliance with International Environmental Accords: Achievements and Strategies' in M. Rolén *et al.* (eds) *International Governance on Environmental Issues* (Dordrecht: Kluwer Academic Publishers).

Kranz, N. and E. Mostert (2012), 'Governance in Transboundary Basins – the Roles of Stakeholders; Concepts and Approaches in International River Basins' in A. Earle, A. Jägerskog and J. Öjendal (eds) (2012), *Transboundary Water Management – Principles and Practice* (Abingdon: Earthscan).

Leb, C. (2013), *Cooperation in the Law of Transboundary Water Resources* (Cambridge: Cambridge University Press).

Lowi, M.R. (1993), *Water and Power: The Politics of a Scarce Resource in the Jordan River Basin* (Cambridge: Cambridge University Press).

MacDonald, A. *et al.* (2012), 'Quantitative Maps of Groundwater Resources in Africa' 7 *Environmental Resources Letters* 1.

Mitchell, S. and N. Zawahri (2012), 'The Effectiveness of Treaty Design in Addressing Water Disputes', paper presented at the 2012 International Studies Association Conference, San Diego, CA, accessed 1 April 2015 at http://www.saramitchell.org/mz2013.pdf.

Nagtzaam, G., (2009), *The Making of International Environmental Treaties: Neoliberal and Constructive Analyses of Normative Evolution* (Cheltenham, UK and Northampton, MA, USA: Edward Elgar).

Odom, O. and A. Wolf (2011), 'Institutional resilience and climate variability in international water treaties' 56(4) *Hydrological Sciences Journal* 703.

Okowa, P. (1996), 'Procedural Obligations in International Environmental Agreements' 67 *British Yearbook of International Law* 275.

Revenga, C. et al. (2000), *Pilot Analysis of Global Ecosystems – Freshwater Systems* (Washington, DC: World Resources Institute, 2000).

Rieu-Clarke, A. and R. Kinna (2014), 'Can Two Global UN Water Conventions Effectively Co-exist? Making the Case for a "Package Approach" to Support Institutional Coordination' 23(1) *Review of European Community and International Environmental Law* 15.

Sadoff, C. and D. Grey (2002), 'Beyond the River: The Benefits of Cooperation on International Rivers' 4 *Water Policy* 389.

Tir, J. and D. Stinnett (2012), 'Weathering Climate Change: Can Institutions Mitigate Conflict?' 49(1) *Journal of Peace Research* 211.

Transboundary Freshwater Dispute Database (TFDD) (2014), accessed 1 April 2105 at http://www.transboundarywaters.orst.edu/index.html.

Treves, T. *et al.* (eds) (2007), *Non-Compliance Procedures and Mechanisms and the Effectiveness of International Environmental Agreements* (The Hague: TMC Asser Press, 2007).

United Nations, *Convention on the Law of the Non-navigational Uses of International Watercourses*, (1997) 36 ILM 700.

United Nations Department of Economic and Social Affairs (UNDESA, 2009), 'World Population Prospects: The 2008 Revision', UN Doc. ESA/P/WP.210.

United Nations Educational, Scientific and Cultural Organization (UNESCO, 2009), *Atlas of Transboundary Aquifers* (UNESCO).

United Nations Treaty Division, *Status of Multilateral Treaties Deposited with the Secretary-General*, (Doc. A/51/869, 1997)

United Nations Treaty Division, *Convention on the Protection and Use of Transboundary Watercourses and International Lakes* (Doc. ECE/MP.WAT/14, 2012).

UN World Water Assessment Programme, (2009) 'The United Nations World Water Development Report 3: Water in a Changing World', Paris: UNESCO, and London: Earthscan.

UN-Water, 'Transboundary Waters: Sharing Benefits, Sharing Responsibilities' (2008), accessed 1 April 2015 at www.unwater.org/downloads/UNW_TRANSBOUNDARY.pdf.

Victor, D., K. Raustiala and E. Skolnikoff (1998), 'Introduction and Overview' in Victor, D., K. Raustiala and E. Skolnikoff (eds) *The Implementation and Effectiveness of International Environmental Commitments. Theory and Practice* (Cambridge, MA: International Institute for Applied Systems Analysis/MIT Press).

Waterbury, J. (1997), 'Between Unilateralism and Comprehensive Accords: Modest Steps Toward Cooperation in International River Basins' 13(3) *International Journal of Water Resources Development* 279–90.

Weiss, E. (1998–1999), 'Understanding Compliance with International Environmental Agreements: the Baker's Dozen Myths' 32 U. Rich. L. Rev. 1555.

Weiss, E. and Jakobson, H.K. (eds) (2000), *Engaging Countries: Strengthening Compliance with International Environmental Accords* (Cambridge, MA: MIT Press).

Wolfrum, R. (1998), 'Means of Ensuring Compliance with and Enforcement of International Environmental Law' (1998) 9 *Recueil des Cours* 272.

Yoffe, S., A. Wolf and M. Giordano (2003), 'Conflict and Cooperation over International Freshwater Resources: Indicators of Basins at Risk' 10 *Journal of the American Water Resources Association* 1109.

Young, O., L. King and H. Schroeder (2008), *Institutions and Environmental Change – Principal Findings and Applications, and Research Frontiers* (Cambridge, MA: MIT Press).

Young, O. and M. Levy (1999), 'The Effectiveness of International Environmental Regimes', in O. Young (ed.) *The Effectiveness of International Environmental Regimes: Causal Connections and Behavioral Mechanisms* (Cambridge, MA: MIT Press).

Zaelke, D., D. Kaniaru and E. Kružiková (eds) (2005), *Making Law Work: Environmental Compliance and Sustainable Development* (Folkestone: Cameron May).

Zawahri, N. (2009), 'Mediating International River Disputes: Lessons from the Indus River' 14 *International Negotiation* 281.

Zawahri, N. and S. McLaughlin (2011), 'Fragmented Governance in International Rivers: Negotiating Bilateral Versus Multilateral Treaties' 55 *International Studies Quarterly* 835.

Zeitoun M. and A. Jägerskog (2009) 'Confronting Power in Transboundary Water Interaction' in A. Jägerskog, M. Zeitoun and A. Berntell (eds) *Getting Transboundary Water Right: Theory and Practice for Effective Cooperation* (Stockholm: Stockholm International Water Institute).

8. Fouling Adam's Eden: a legal analysis of the collective action challenge in Lake Victoria

Omondi Robert Owino*

1. INTRODUCTION

> Regrettably, Lake Victoria is today seriously threatened due to receding water levels, soil and waste pollution, over-fishing, and a growing decline in the health of its ecosystems. As a result, the livelihoods and well-being of over 30 million people who live around its basin are at risk. It is imperative that we act urgently and decisively to halt further decline of the lake and the surrounding environment.[1]

Lake Victoria[2] is an indispensable shared resource in the East African Community (EAC)[3] and its basin is one of the most densely populated

* Doctoral Candidate Department of Public Law, International and European Law, Faculty of Law, Bayreuth University (Germany), LL.M (Dar es Salaam), LL.B (Hons) (Moi), Dip (KSL), Advocate of the High Court of Kenya.

[1] Kibaki (2007).

[2] Lake Victoria is the largest lake in Africa by area and also the largest tropical lake in the world. It is also the world's second largest freshwater lake by surface area coming second only to Lake Superior in North America. Lake Victoria boasts a surface area of about 68,000 km² shared by Kenya (6%); Uganda – (45%) and Tanzania (49%) with a shoreline that extends up to about 3,500 km and an average depth of about 40 m and a maximum depth of 80 m. The Lake lies between latitude 0.7°´N – 3°´S and longitude 31.8°´E – 34.8°´E on a catchment area of about 193,000 km² that includes Burundi (7.2%); Kenya (21.5%); Rwanda (11.4%), Tanzania (44.0%) and Uganda (15.9%). Most significantly, the lake is also the source of the White Nile contributing to the Nile River which is the second longest river in the World after Mississippi River and the lifeline of Egypt.

[3] The EAC is an intergovernmental organisation composed of Burundi, Kenya, Rwanda, Tanzania and Uganda located between 5°´30″N 12°´S and

places in the world.[4] The lake's shared nature means that abuse or misuse of the lake by one party sharing the lake affects all other parties. Owing to the shaky structures of cooperation particularly among the littoral states of Kenya, Tanzania and Uganda, the rapidly expanding population that derives its livelihood from the lake, as well as poverty and unrestrained resource exploitation, the lake has become a quintessential case of the Tragedy of the Commons.[5]

The lake's key management challenge can be attributed to a cocktail of factors that include overfishing, introduction of invasive species, industrial pollution, environmental degradation and loss of biodiversity. In addition, conflicts related to decreasing water levels are becoming commonplace in the lake. Schmeier aptly describes these challenges in Lake Victoria as a 'constellation of collective action problems' with a complex 'problem-structure'.[6]

Resolution of these challenges requires joint action through regional cooperation. Unilateral state action has so far continued to exacerbate an already precarious situation in the lake. In the words of Kenneth Waltz: 'collective efforts are needed if common problems are to be solved or somehow managed'.[7] Inquiry into the capacity of extant EAC environmental legal regimes to stimulate cooperation and address these collective action problems is a valid investigation that should form the centerpiece of solutions to these problems. How then is regional environmental law designed to address the collective action problems in Lake Victoria? Or, in an even broader sense, how do the prevailing environmental challenges in the Lake Victoria basin and the accompanying legal, policy and institutional framework reflect similar paradigms among developing countries?

This chapter addresses this question in three sections. The first section traces the legal efforts for realisation of collective action in the lake within a historical context that has been inextricably intertwined with

---

28°′45″E 41°′50″E. The EAC was founded in Arusha (Tanzania) on 30 November 1999 with the signing of the *Treaty for the Establishment of the East African Community* (hereinafter EAC Treaty) between Kenya, Tanzania and Uganda. The EAC Treaty entered into force on 7 July 2000 and was later acceded to by Rwanda and Burundi.

4 Awange and Ong'ang'a (2006) 11.

5 Hardin (1968). Hardin theorised the destruction of a common resource through the action of rational self-interested individuals who at the same time understood the consequences of the action to their group interest.

6 Schmeier (2012) 89.

7 Waltz (1979) 210 quoted in Harris (2007) 199.

fishery resources since the colonial era. The second section contrasts collective action problems with coordination problems and explains why collective action problems in the lake are difficult to resolve. The third section analyses the nature of an appropriate legal framework for regulating collective action problems. It argues that EAC partner states must undertake greater legal commitments to successfully solve transnational collective action problems. This section also critiques the EAC legal framework that regulates environmental concerns in Lake Victoria leading to relevant conclusions.

2. HISTORICAL ORIGINS OF COLLECTIVE ACTION

In the pre-colonial era, Lake Victoria was managed by the local communities' resident around its shore who kept the lake pristine using myths and taboos that prohibited environmental abuse.[8] Even then, technological development was at its nadir and environmental degradation was hardly a point of concern. Colonial rule reassigned management of the lake to the central governments of the larger territories of Kenya, Tanganyika and Uganda in order to facilitate effective resource exploitation and utilisation.[9] The reassignment of power in favour of territorial control disenfranchised the local communities. This created an avenue for populations that previously had no interest in the lake to jump onto the 'gravy train' of economic gain especially by exploiting fishery resources in the lake.

Early co-operation efforts in Lake Victoria crystallised out of the need to prevent overfishing and possible collapse of the lake's fisheries. Fishing in the lake had been principally artisanal and was conducted using local handmade gear such as basket traps, hooks and seine nets. This changed in 1905 when 'efficient flax gillnets' were introduced to the lake.[10] Ohwayo attributes the increase in fishing effort to growing demand for fish in distant markets as well as the growth of urban centres and the completion of the Mombasa-Kisumu Railway in 1908 which facilitated the import of 'modern fishing gear'.[11] Pringle records that due to fears that 'the Africans were overfishing the lake with the aid of imported equipment' in 1921, recommendations were made for a 'closed

[8] Okurut and Othero (2012) 351.
[9] Awange and Ong'ang'a (2006) 19.
[10] Ogutu-Ohwayo (1990) 82.
[11] Ibid.

season' in the lake to local fishermen.[12] The colonial governments lacked a scientific basis to implement such drastic measures and commissioned a study by Michael Graham and Edgar Barton Worthington who came from London in 1927 and spent 1928 undertaking research in the lake.[13]

In 1929 Graham published the outcome of their research in his book *The Victoria Nyanza and its Fisheries.* He confirmed the suspicion of overfishing in the lake and recommended measures which included the use of gillnets of not less than 127 mm mesh size; the establishment of an authority over the entire lake to collect catch statistics, control fishing effort and enforce the mesh size limit; and the establishment of a lake-wide body responsible for biological and ecological research.[14]

These recommendations resulted in the establishment in 1947 of Lake Victoria Fisheries Services (LVFS) with responsibility for administration of fisheries in the lake, including competence to consolidate fisheries development, process and collect catch statistics and enforce fishing regulations and the minimum mesh size limit of 127 mm over the entire lake.[15] The East African Freshwater Fisheries Research Organisation (EAFFRO) was formed in the same year in Jinja, Uganda to 'carry out biological and ecological research on the fishes'.[16] EAFFRO and LVFS subsequently came under the competence of the East African High Commission which was established at the beginning of 1948 as a 'permanent executive authority' for the inter-territorial cooperation between Kenya, Tanganyika and Uganda.[17]

Although efforts under EAFFRO and LVFS were successful, from 1930 to 1940 fishing efforts in the lake escalated while catch rates plummeted from seven to two fishes per net. By 1955 it became unprofitable for the littoral states to maintain the minimum mesh size limit of 127 mm. Due to the restrictive nature of the 127 mm mesh size limit, states sought to defeat it through the illegal use of mesh sizes as small as 114 mm, leading to its repeal in Tanzania and Uganda in 1956 and Kenya in 1961.[18] Repealing the mesh size limit not only signalled the failure of collective action among the littoral states; it was also disastrous for the lake and institutionalised overfishing trends that continue unabated. Ohwayo writes in regard thereto:

---

12 Pringle (2005) 781.
13 Ibid.
14 Ogutu-Ohwayo (1990) 83.
15 Ibid.
16 Twongo, Reynolds and Mewne-Beyanga (1991).
17 Hazlewood (1967) 71.
18 Ogutu-Ohwayo (1990) 84.

> The repeal of this regulation in Uganda and Tanzania in 1956 and in Kenya in 1961 was followed by the collapse of the *0. esculentus* fishery. The recommended mesh of 127 mm caught mature individuals, some of which had bred several times. The 114 mm nets caught some fish before they had matured and still smaller meshes caught predominantly immature individuals … The removal of immature fish reduced subsequent recruitment to the breeding stock. Relaxation of the 127 mm mesh size regulation therefore represented gross mismanagement of the fishery.[19]

This observation provides the clearest evidence that inter-territorial co-operation had served to prevent degradation of the lake's fisheries through establishment of a uniform code of conduct for all littoral states. The bonds of cooperation became weaker among the littoral states with the dawn of independence leading to separate management of the lake by Kenya, Tanzania, and Uganda. The first EAC established in 1967 as a community of these three countries did not have significant legal influence on cooperation in the lake and collapsed 10 years later in 1977.

The second phase of cooperation in the Lake Victoria region that also represents ongoing efforts to realise sustainability in the lake was signalled by the formation of a sub-committee of the FAO Committee for Inland Fisheries of Africa (CIFA) to develop and manage fisheries in Lake Victoria as a collaboration stopgap measure in 1980, following collapse of the first EAC. The lack of strong intergovernmental mechanisms for harmonisation among the lake's littoral states stymied the effectiveness of the CIFA sub-committee and resulted in 'design proposals' for the Lake Victoria Fisheries Organization (LVFO). The Director of the FAO, acting upon the request of Kenya, Tanzania and Uganda submitted a draft Convention for the Establishment of the Lake Victoria Fisheries Organization to the Legal and Technical Consultation Meeting for the Establishment of the Lake Victoria Fisheries Organization held in Dar es Salaam, Tanzania, 12–25 March 1994. The Conference of Plenipotentiaries subsequently adopted the LVFO Convention on 30 June 1994 in Kisumu (Kenya).[20]

The LVFO Convention was adopted against the background of new EAC collaboration efforts that had started with the 1984 mediation agreement between the three East Africa countries to resolve the collapse of the first EAC in 1977. These efforts led to the signing of the Agreement for the Establishment of a Permanent Tripartite Commission for Cooperation between the Republic of Kenya, the United Republic of

---

19 Ibid, 85.

20 East African Community (EAC) (1994) (hereinafter LVFO Convention).

Tanzania and the Republic of Uganda on 30th November 1993 by the Presidents of the three countries.

The littoral states signed the Tripartite Agreement on Lake Victoria Environmental Management Programme (LVEMP-I) in Dar es Salaam on 5 August 1994 recognising that resource use by one Lake Victoria state had impacts on other EAC partner states. The agreement was intended to bring the national jurisdiction of the EAC littoral states within 'a reciprocal co-operative framework backed by a strong political commitment from partner countries'.[21] On 22 October 1998 Kenya, Tanzania and Uganda signed the 'Memorandum of Understanding (MOU) between the Republic of Uganda and the Republic of Kenya and the United Republic of Tanzania for Co-operation on Environment Management'.[22] Under Article 8 of this MOU the littoral states agreed to a process of harmonising their policies, laws and programs for better management of the lake's ecosystem and pollution.

In concert with these efforts the first East Africa Cooperation Development Strategy for the period 1997–2000 was developed by the Secretariat of the Permanent Tripartite Commission for Co-operation of Kenya, Tanzania and Uganda. The Development Strategy designated Lake Victoria an 'Economic Growth Zone' and 'an Area of Common Economic Interest'. The Secretariat also commissioned a study in 1999 to identify a suitable legal and institutional framework for the management of Lake Victoria. The study had two main outcomes. First it recommended establishment of the Lake Victoria Development Program Unit (LVDPU) within the EAC structure as a transitional measure for co-ordinating conservation efforts in the lake that would later develop into a full-fledged and independent organ within the EAC.[23] Secondly the study produced a draft Protocol on Lake Victoria. On 29 November 2003, Kenya, Tanzania and Uganda after much deliberation and negotiation signed the Protocol for Sustainable Development of Lake Victoria Basin and ratified it in December 2004.[24]

The LVFO Convention[25] and the Lake Victoria Basin Protocol which are both anchored in the EAC Treaty, together with the institutions they establish, constitute the major regional legal frameworks that regulate

---

21 UNEP and UNDP (1999) 60.

22 Hereinafter 1998 MOU; Okidi (2006) 175 on background of MOU.

23 EAC (2011) 16.

24 Kisumu (Kenya), 29 November 2003 (EAC (2003); hereinafter Lake Victoria Protocol) concluded pursuant to Art 151 of the EAC Treaty.

25 Kisumu (Kenya) 30 June 1994 (EAC 1994); hereinafter LVFO Convention).

activities within the Lake.[26] The draft EAC Protocol on Environment and Natural Resource Management (which is yet to be ratified) and the EAC Regional Environment Impact Assessment Guidelines for Shared Ecosystems also endorse cooperation in the lake (albeit without giving much detail). In addition to the regional legal framework all Lake Victoria littoral states have enacted national framework legislation and created policies that provide for management of rivers and lakes in almost similar terms.[27] There is also ongoing harmonisation of laws in the EAC with respect to the lake as well as the adoption of further laws such as the Data, Information and Knowledge Sharing Protocol on Lake Victoria to bring into operation the Lake Victoria Basin Protocol. The analysis here is limited to the LVFO Convention and the Lake Victoria Basin Protocol as foundational instruments.

3. NATURE OF COLLECTIVE ACTION PROBLEM

Simply put, a collective action problem between states arises when it is in the common interest of such states to act jointly. However, since individual state interest surpasses the common interest of states, each state chooses unilateral action over joint action, often with negative consequences to the common interest.[28] Collective action theory has been applied to explain global and regional cooperation patterns within shared resources.

A number of international and regional environmental law instruments regulate collective action problems. These include the United Nations Framework Convention on Climate Change (UNFCC) and the Kyoto Protocol (which address climate change); the Convention on International Trade in Endangered Species (CITES); the Montreal Protocol on substances that deplete the ozone layer; the 1994 Danube River Convention; the Mediterranean Action Plan; and regional fisheries Conventions such as the North Pacific Fisheries Convention. Guzman has argued rightly that the ability of international law to establish cooperation in anarchic

---

26 Article 48 of the Lake Victoria Protocol gives the Protocol precedence over any existing framework on the lake while Art 47 incorporates the Protocol as an integral part of the EAC Treaty.

27 Environment Management and Coordination Act 1999 of Kenya, s 42; Environmental Management Act 2004 of Tanzania, ss 54–55 and National Environment Act 1995 of Uganda, ss 34–35.

28 Olson (1971) 2.

situations is what lends value to international law, particularly when cooperation is very difficult to achieve.[29]

Collective action problems can be contrasted with pure coordination problems in which parties inherently desire to cooperate with one another but lack an appropriate framework to coordinate their action.[30] Cooperation is easier to achieve in such cases and the law is much less strenuously involved in creating solutions. Examples of international coordination regimes include the Universal Postal Convention; the International Maritime Organization International Code of Signals for use between merchant and naval vessels; and the Convention for the Unification of Certain Rules Relating to International Carriage by Air (which facilitates global air travel across diverse countries through establishment of uniform standards and eliminates the chaos that would exist in their absence).[31]

The collective action problems in Lake Victoria are succinctly summarised in the following words by Awange and Onga'ng'a:

> Today, the use of Lake Victoria has become a source of great conflicts over the waters, the fish and even the land catchment areas.
>
> …
>
> The present-day conflicts are fueled (sic) by commercial motives backed by technological advancement. In addition, declining economic returns and diminishing natural fish resources contribute to conflicts in fisheries management. The conflicts involve all stakeholders from great men to the ordinary fisherfolk, angler against anglers, and nation against nation.[32]

These problems (unlike coordination problems) are particularly difficult to solve for a number of reasons. First, there is usually asymmetry between individual and collective state interest.[33] In Lake Victoria for example the fish wars and use of inappropriate fishing gear find explanation in the fact that Kenya, Tanzania and Uganda reap larger profits from global Nile perch revenue through unilateral action than they otherwise would through restrictive lake wide regulations. In respect of the lake's water resources, Uganda's hydroelectricity projects on

29 Guzman (2008) 26.
30 Ibid.
31 Ibid.
32 Awange and Ong'ang'a (2006) 64.
33 Bodansky (2010) 263.

Nalubaale, Kiira and Bujagali dams constantly raise concerns of Uganda's unilateral abstraction of waters from Lake Victoria in breach of the extraction curve agreement.[34]

Secondly, solving collective action problems attracts prohibitive costs that states prefer to avoid. A small number of actors facing heavy costs will have greater incentive to frustrate policies aimed at counteracting collective action problems while the benefit that accrues to a majority of beneficiaries may be too meagre to motivate their action.[35] While EAC states all derive an advantage in abating pollution, they only have an incentive to do so to the extent that the costs involved do not outstrip their global benefits.

Thirdly, unlike coordination problems where states have an inherent incentive to cooperate, in collective action problems states have an incentive to cheat or free ride on the efforts of other states.[36] Collectively all the littoral states in Lake Victoria may have an interest in stopping overfishing, falling water levels and pollution of the lake but they also have an incentive to continue polluting and overexploiting the lake if they can externalise costs of their damage to other states.

Finally, collective action problems also affect the competitive position of states in relation to one another. For example in 2003 President Yoweri Kaguta Museveni of Uganda directed the lifting of a fishing ban in Uganda contrary to expert advice after a meeting with Ugandan fish processors and exporters. The fish processors and exporters argued that the imposition of the ban had not only undermined their capacity to compete with Kenya and Tanzania but had also facilitated the smuggling of Ugandan fish to markets in Kenya and Tanzania.[37] Uganda argued that it would only enforce such a ban at a time when the other two littoral states also imposed the ban.

The dichotomy between collective action and coordination problems in the lake is evidenced by the fact that the LVEMP-I succeeded overwhelmingly in fostering effective cooperation among Kenya, Uganda and Tanzania in coordination problems while cooperation proved difficult to achieve in respect of collective action problems. One report observed:

> The LVEMP-I programs have been credited with bringing Kenya, Tanzania, and Uganda together to address challenges that the governments could not effectively manage on their own. The most successful undertakings – water

34 Doya (2009).
35 Bodansky (2010) 144.
36 Guzman (2008) 174.
37 Nakkazi (2003).

> hyacinth control and carrying out fisheries studies – provided quick wins for the partner states, in which they acted on problems that affected large numbers of their populations. The LVEMP framework has demonstrated shortcomings and flaws in the areas where the littoral nations compete or have a strong incentive to mismanage resources. Falling lake levels, which threaten nearly every aspect of lake functioning and livelihood support, and unsustainable rates of fish harvesting, specifically the commercially caught Nile perch, which comprises the backbone of the region's commercial fishing operations, are the most salient examples.[38]

The failure of EAC partner states to effectively manage Lake Victoria under the existing common legal regime has resulted in an open access regime that allows the most aggressive partner state to reap the most benefit. The nature of the legal framework adopted to resolve collective action problems therefore determines to a large extent how successful the EAC states will be in achieving their objective for cooperation. Notwithstanding the fact that proper legal design remains the mainstay of successful cooperation, other extraneous non-legal factors such as politics; state interest; commitment of states; technological and economic capacity also affect resolution of collective action problems.

4. NATURE OF LEGAL FRAMEWORK

The nature of legal agreements that states conclude among themselves to regulate collective action problems is a determinant of costs and benefits that motivate or demotivate states in resolving collective action problems.[39] Bodansky argues that agreements that require very strong and stringent commitment from states will also levy high sovereignty and compliance costs but also confer great benefits to the state parties.[40] 'Strength' and 'stringency' of commitments that states undertake therefore determine depth or shallowness of an agreement. Strength connotes the intensity or the degree to which a commitment limits state sovereignty, while stringency of a commitment is the extent to which a commitment deters states from pursuing a 'business as usual' approach to collective action problems.[41]

---

38 Lubovich (2009).
39 Bodansky (2010) 161.
40 Ibid.
41 Ibid.

Stringency escalates the projected 'costs of compliance' while strength amplifies the 'potential costs of non-compliance'.[42] This means that as stringency increases, greater behavioural change will be expected and compliance costs will appreciate. On the other hand the more intense the commitment, the more limited state sovereignty will be and the greater the costs of non-compliance will be to a state. This implies that states will be more comfortable in concluding shallow agreements which exert less demand on their sovereignty.[43] It will also be easier for states to opt out of their commitments if these agreements do not work; additionally the benefits to be realised in deep agreements may be too remote and such agreements will not necessarily guarantee reciprocity to warrant investment of costly action by states.

The nature or design of an agreement will therefore impact the strength and stringency of agreements and will influence states 'cost benefit calculations' in deciding which agreements they conclude.[44] For example, non-binding agreements will be less stringent and weaker compared to binding agreements; enforcement procedures are superfluous in non-binding agreements and compliance costs will be very low. Binding instruments will, however, possess degrees of stringency and strength along a spectrum ranging from agreements with very deep commitments to those with very shallow commitments. Less stringent agreements will be more flexible, meaning that they will also possess lower sovereignty and compliance costs. Strong agreements will evince more precision, thereby creating less room for undesirable conduct. For example, when a fisheries treaty lays down strict total allowable catch limits, a violation will be easy to discern compared to when the treaty restricts state conduct that exceeds unspecified 'sustainable fishing limits'. These factors will often determine the effectiveness of an agreement.

In terms of function, international environmental law agreements may either be constitutive or regulatory.[45] Constitutive agreements establish a system of governance or institutions for a particular subject matter while regulatory agreements prescribe rules of conduct that govern specific areas (for example rules under MARPOL for building oil tankers). Bodansky argues that 'constitutive agreements are by their nature shallow; they aim to establish a general system of governance and impose

42 Ibid.

43 Downs, Rocke and Barsoom (1996).

44 Bodansky (2010) 178; Sandler (2004) 12 observes that 'a proactive design of the rules may foster cooperation without the need for costly government intervention or structures'.

45 Bodansky (2010) 158.

few, if any, requirements. In contrast, regulatory agreements vary widely in their stringency'.[46] Proceeding from these theoretical suppositions, the Lake Victoria Basin Protocol and the LVFO Convention can be analysed in order to draw conclusions on their strength and stringency.

4.1 Lake Victoria Basin Protocol

The Lake Victoria Basin Protocol is fundamentally a constitutive agreement which establishes the Lake Victoria Basin Commission (LVBC) through the EAC Council of Ministers[47] as the principal institution with broad competence to: 'promote, facilitate and coordinate activities of different actors towards sustainable development and poverty eradication of the Lake Victoria Basin …' through, *inter alia*, harmonisation of policies, laws, regulations and standards.[48]

The Protocol clothes the LVBC with only enough power to coordinate partner states' activities but significantly shies away from creating a common regulatory regime. This is evident in many provisions of the Protocol which vest main decisions over the Lake and its basin exclusively in partner states.[49] A common regulatory regime would require the EAC partner states to surrender greater powers to the LVBC, thereby incurring greater compliance and sovereignty costs. To highlight the lack of gravitas in the Lake Victoria Basin protocol, the LVBC can be contrasted with the International Joint Commission (IJC) established under the 1909 Boundary Waters Treaty,[50] which is comparatively vested with a greater mandate by the contracting parties (for example, to adjudicate disputes between contracting parties relating to their rights, obligations, or interests of their inhabitants along the common frontier; the finding of the IJC guides the contracting parties).[51]

Due to its fundamentally constitutive design, the Lake Victoria Basin Protocol has failed to achieve even what would be termed as its marginal regulatory role of harmonising policies, laws, regulations and standards

---

[46] Ibid, 177.

[47] The Council of Ministers is established under Art 9 of the EAC Treaty and is the policy-making organ of the EAC as stipulated under Art 14 of the EAC Treaty.

[48] Lake Victoria Protocol, Art 33(3)(a).

[49] Ibid, Arts 4–8, 12.

[50] Treaty Relating to the Boundary Waters and Questions Arising along the Boundary between the United States and Canada, (Washington) 11 January 1909, accessed 2 April 2015 at http://www.ijc.org.

[51] Ibid, Art IX.

in the Lake Basin.[52] The 4th EAC Development Strategy for the period 2011–2016 highlighted the major challenge of the LVBC thus: 'the mandate of promoting sustainable utilization and management of the natural resources and protection of environment within Lake Victoria Basin is being constrained by incomplete harmonization of policies, laws and standards, weak governance and institutional structures'.[53] The EAC partner states have essentially settled for a shallow agreement that demands less commitment to solve complex collective action problems.

4.2 Lake Victoria Fisheries Organization Convention

The LVFO convention was a forerunner of cooperation efforts between Kenya, Tanzania and Uganda in recognition of the need for joint action among these three countries in managing threats posed to the lake through overfishing, pollution, hyacinth blooms and eutrophication. The Convention established the LVFO as an international regional Organization to advance cooperation between the three countries; harmonise national measures in respect of living resources in the lake and to promote conservation and management of the lake by adopting appropriate measures.[54]

The Convention established the Council of Ministers responsible for fisheries of the contracting parties as the supreme, as well as the policy-making, organ of the LVFO.[55] The influence of the council's authority over the LVFO is so far reaching that it permeates every sphere of its operation. For instance the Council sets up committees or subsidiary bodies as it may deem fit to discharge functions of the LVFO;[56] it sets the general standards and guidelines for managing the LVFO;[57] appoints the executive director of LVFO;[58] considers any proposal for amendment of the Convention and is also responsible for adopting such amendments;[59] and also establishes staff positions and determines the working conditions of LVFO staff and is responsible for adopting or amending Staff Regulations of the LVFO.[60]

---

52 Ibid, Art 33(3)(a).
53 EAC (2011) 49.
54 LVFO Convention, Art II(2).
55 Ibid, Arts V(1) and VI(1)(a).
56 Ibid, Art IV(2).
57 Ibid, Art VI(1)(c).
58 Ibid, Art VI(1)(g).
59 Ibid, Art XX(2) and Art VI(1)(h).
60 Ibid, Art VI(1)(l).

The overall effect of the Council's involvement means that the LVFO can make few decisions that are not influenced by politics and competing state interests. This is because the Council reports directly to the summit made up of the presidents of the three countries under the EAC Treaty. The Council enjoys veto power over any decision taken by the LVFO with the effect that the contracting parties incur very minimal sovereignty or compliance costs. The Council as constituted plays a door-keeping role and safeguards against grave infringement of state interests by the LVFO. The LVFO Convention also adopts consensus as a mode of decision making by the Council. This creates an obstacle to negotiation and makes the parties settle for the 'lowest common denominator' policy options.[61]

That the LVFO Convention has been designed for shallow commitments is evident in its flexible amendment procedures as well as the ease of terminating or withdrawing from the Convention. The sovereignty costs of withdrawal are very low and contracting parties only need to issue a notice of withdrawal to the depository after the expiry of two years from the date of signing the Convention.[62] The Convention also utilises imprecise language, for example, the need to develop uniform management measures among contracting parties 'to the extent *appropriate*'.[63] In terms of stringency, the LVFO Convention falls woefully short in altering behaviour in the Lake Victoria region. The number of fishers in the Lake escalated by 58 per cent from 129,305 in 2000 to 205,249 in 2012;[64] use of illegal gear such as gillnets with less than 5 inch (127 mm) mesh size increased by 77 per cent from 113,177 in 2000 to 200,689 in 2012;[65] while intensification of fishing effort was reflected by the lake-wide increase in the number of outboard engines by 392 per cent from 4,108 in 2000 to 20,217 in 2012.[66]

5. CONCLUSION

The legal instruments so far adopted by the EAC partner states to regulate resource exploitation in Lake Victoria can be termed cosmetic *vis à vis* the collective action challenges they ought to address. They are

---

61 Palmer (1992) 264.
62 LVFO Convention, Art XXII(2).
63 Ibid, Preamble.
64 EAC and LVFO (2013) 13.
65 Ibid, 31.
66 Ibid, 18.

merely constitutive instruments that are acutely shallow in depth since they attract only the weakest of commitments from partner states and they fail to engender behavioural change in the Lake Victoria Basin.[67] It follows, therefore, that national implementation of regional laws, even if it were perfect, remains only as good as the quality of regional laws that EAC partner states adopt in respect of Lake Victoria and its basin.

Cooperation in managing the Lake requires that EAC partner states establish regional institutions with regulatory competence whose decisions can bind partner states. Only such an avenue will effectively address the collective action problems that are apparent in Lake Victoria. For this option to succeed the establishment of a well-crafted incentive system that countermands unilateral state interest will be critical. This is because regulatory instruments invite EAC partner states to incur greater sovereignty and compliance costs that are likely to hinder political will.

EAC partner states must reckon with the reality that application of state sovereignty as the predominant paradigm of shared resource regulation has been considerably reconfigured due to its inadequacy in addressing complex and emerging shared resource problems, which are highly incompatible with Westphalian notions of territorial sovereignty.[68] The choice therefore lies between pursuit of short term national interests that portend long term regional doom and taking decisive regional regulatory action to abate the rapidly unfolding tragedy of the commons in the Lake Victoria.

Most importantly, however, this case study of the Lake Victoria basin constitutes the starting point for critically interrogating similar transboundary collective action paradigms among developing countries. This exercise is important in finding out how the asymmetry between the nature of collective action challenges on one side and the legal, policy and institutional frameworks adopted to address these challenges on the other, actually exacerbate the said challenges.

REFERENCES

Awange, J. and O. Ong'ang'a (2006), *Lake Victoria: Ecology, Resources, Environment* (Berlin: Springer).

Bodansky. D. (2010), *The Art and Craft of International Environmental Law* (Cambridge, MA: Harvard University Press).

Downs, G., D. Rocke and P. Barsoom (1996), 'Is the Good News about Compliance Good News about Cooperation?' 50 *International Organization* 379.

---

67 Victor, Raustiala and Skolnikoff (1998) 4.

68 Friedmann (1964) 60–7; Gillespie (2001) 140.

Doya, M. (2009), 'Lake Victoria Meeting Fails to Address Key Resource Concerns' (*The East African,* 30 November), accessed 2 April 2015 at http://www.theeastafrican.co.ke/news/-/2558/814246/-/py9aqxz/-/index.html.

East African Community (1994), *Convention for the Establishment of the Lake Victoria Fisheries Organization.*

East African Community (1998), *Memorandum of Understanding between the Republic of Uganda and the Republic of Kenya and the United Republic of Tanzania for Co-operation on Environment Management.*

East African Community (1999), *Treaty for the Establishment of the East African Community.*

East African Community (2003), *Protocol for Sustainable Development of Lake Victoria Basin.*

East African Community (2011), *Development Strategy (2006–2010).*

East African Community (2011), *Development Strategy (2011–2016).*

East African Community and Lake Victoria Fisheries Organization (2013), *Regional Status Report on Lake Victoria Bi-ennial Frame Surveys between 2000 and 2012* (February).

Friedmann, W. (1964), *The Changing Structure of International Law* (New York: Columbia University Press).

Gillespie, A. (2001), *The Illusion of Progress: Unsustainable Development in International Law and Policy* (Abingdon: Earthscan Publications).

Guzman, A. (2008), *How International Law Works: A Rational Choice Theory* (Oxford: Oxford University Press).

Hardin, G. (1968), 'The Tragedy of the Commons' 162 *Science* 1243.

Harris, P. (2007), 'Collective Action on Climate Change: The Logic of Regime Failure' 47 *Natural Resources Journal* 196.

Hazlewood, A. (1967), *Economic Integration in East Africa* (Oxford: Oxford University Press).

Mwai Kibaki (2007), former President of Kenya at the inauguration of the Lake Victoria Basin Commission in Kisumu, 11 June, accessed 10 April 2015 at http://www.vub.ac.be/klimostoolkit/sites/default/files/documents/env_policy_brief_lake_victoria.pdf.

Lubovich, K. (2009), 'Cooperation and Competition: Managing Transboundary Water Resources', (*Foundation for Environmental Security and Sustainability,* Working Paper), accessed 2 April 2015 at http://www.fess-global.org/WorkingPapers/Lake_Victoria_Working_Paper.pdf.

Nakkazi, E. (2003), 'Experts Protest as Uganda Lifts Fishing Ban' (*The East African,* 27 October), accessed 2 April 2015 at http://www.theeastafrican.co.ke/business/-/2560/241576/-/7ohgqhz/-/index.htm.

Ogutu-Ohwayo, R. (1990), 'The Decline of the Native Fishes of Lakes Victoria and Kyoga (East Africa) and the Impact of Introduced Species especially the Nile Perch, Lates Niloticus, and the N. Tilapia, Oreochromis Niloticus' 27 *Environmental Biology of Fishes* 81.

Okidi, C. (2006), 'Legal and Institutional Aspects of Management of the Environment in Lake Victoria Basin' in E. Odada, D. Olago and W. Ochola (eds), *Environment for Development: An Ecosystems Assessment of Lake Victoria Basin Environmental and Socio-Economic Status, Trends and Human Vulnerabilities* (UNEP and PASS (Pan Africa START Secretariat)).

Okurut, T. and D. Othero (2012), 'A Holistic Approach to Natural Resource Management: A Case of Lake Victoria Basin' in V. Grover and G. Krantzberg (eds), *Great Lakes: Lessons in Participatory Governance* (Boca Raton, FL: CRC Press).

Olson, M. (1971), *The Logic of Collective Action: Public Goods and the Theory of Groups* (Cambridge, MA: Harvard University Press).

Palmer, G. (1992), 'New Ways to Make International Environmental Law' 86 *American Journal of International Law* 259.

Pringle, R. (2005), 'The Origins of the Nile Perch in Lake Victoria' 55 *BioScience* 780.

Sandler, T. (2004), *Global Collective Action* (Cambridge: Cambridge University Press).

Schmeier, S. (2012), 'Governing International Watercourses: River Basin Organizations and the Sustainable Governance of Internationally Shared Rivers and Lakes' (PhD Thesis, Berlin Graduate School for Transnational Studies).

Twongo, T., J. Reynolds and P. Mewne-Beyanga (1991), 'Management Issues, Options and Strategies for Lake Victoria Fisheries' (*FAO Corporate Document Repository*), accessed 2 April 2015 at http://www.fao.org/docrep/006/AD147E/AD147E05.htm.

UNEP and UNDP, *Report on the Legal and Institutional Issues in the Lake Victoria* (UNEP and UNDP, 1999).

Victor, D., K. Raustiala and E. Skolnikoff (1998), 'Introduction and Overview' in D. Victor, K. Raustiala and E. Skolnikoff (eds), *The Implementation and Effectiveness of International Environmental Commitments: Theory and Practice* (Cambridge, MA: International Institute for Applied Systems Analysis/MIT Press).

Waltz, K.N. (1979), *Theory of International Politics* (Boston, MA: McGraw Hill) 210, quoted in Paul G. Harris, 'Collective Action on Climate Change: The Logic of Regime Failure' (2007) 47 *Natural Resources Journal* 196, 199.

9. Marine protection treaties in Antarctic Waters: fragmentation or coordination in international treaty implementation

Gregory Rose

Awareness of the need for cross-sectoral coordination in marine management emerged in the middle of the last quarter of the twentieth century.[1] Marine management fragmentation occurring at the national level is mirrored at the international level, where improved coordination in the implementation of multilateral environmental agreements (MEAs) is needed. This chapter considers international environmental coordination using a case study of Antarctic marine governance.

1. CONCEPTS

The terminology used here reflects usage in the United Nations Environment Programme's (UNEP's) *Guidelines on Compliance with and Enforcement of Multilateral Environmental Agreements* (UNEP Guidelines).[2]

A State is said to 'implement' an international norm at the domestic level when it adopts appropriate domestic measures to meet its obligations. Implementation measures might include legislation, policies or

[1] Underdahl (1980) . Convention on the Law of the Sea (UNCLOS), preamble. Chapter 17 of Agenda 21 (United Nations, 1992), and UN Open-Ended Informal Consultative Process on Oceans and Law of the Sea, held annually. See http://www.un.org/Depts/los/consultative_process/consultative_process.htm, accessed 2 April 2015.

[2] The UNEP Guidelines are in two parts: Part I – *Guidelines for Enhancing Compliance with Multilateral Environmental Agreements* and Part II – *Guidelines for National Enforcement, and International Cooperation in Combating Violations of Laws Implementing Multilateral Environmental Agreements.*

allocation of resources.[3] Legal implementation occurs in three phases: adopting national legal measures; enforcing them; and reporting on the implementation measures.[4]

MEA 'enforcement' is the process of ensuring domestic conformity with national laws that implement MEAs.[5] This typically involves coercive apparatus, such as inspectors, police, courts and tribunals. There is no MEA addressing international enforcement.

International compliance mechanisms seek to ensure national implementation of MEAs.[6] Part I of the UNEP Guidelines defines compliance as:

> the fulfilment by the contracting Parties of their obligations under a multilateral environmental agreement and any amendments to the multilateral environmental agreement.[7]

Reporting is often an obligation within an MEA's compliance mechanism.[8] It is helpful to report on obligations under particular treaty provisions, rather than for a treaty overall.[9] That an implementation measure is taken neither indicates that it is adequate nor that the State is compliant as implementation may be partial.[10]

---

[3] The UNEP Guidelines Part I define implementation as 'inter alia, all relevant laws, regulations, policies, and other measures and initiatives that contracting Parties take or adopt and/or take to meet their obligations under a multilateral environmental agreement and its amendments, if any' (sic). UNEP (2001) Part I, p 2.

[4] Sands (2003) 174.

[5] Part II of the UNEP Guidelines define enforcement as 'the range of procedures and actions employed by a State, its competent authorities and agencies to ensure that organisations or persons, potentially failing to comply with environmental laws or regulations implementing multilateral environmental agreements, can be brought or returned into compliance and/or punished through civil administrative or criminal action'. UNEP Guidelines, Part I, p 9.

[6] Mitchell (1998) 24.

[7] UNEP Guidelines, Part I, p 2. The UNEP Guidelines Part II define compliance from a domestic perspective as 'the state of conformity with obligations, imposed by a state, its competent authorities and agencies on the regulated community, whether directly or indirectly through conditions and requirements, licences and authorisations, in implementing multilateral environmental agreements' (p 8).

[8] A major study of implementation, including reporting, is Victor, Raustiala, and Skolnikoff (1998).

[9] Mitchell (1998) 5–6.

[10] Chayes and Chayes (1995).

An environmental audit may be undertaken to assess compliance or to evaluate due diligence in risk management or to measure environmental performance. The International Standards Organisation defines an environmental audit as:

> a systematic, documented verification process of objectively obtaining and evaluating evidence to determine whether specific environmental activities, events, conditions, management systems, or information about these matters conform with audit criteria, and communicating the results of this process to the client.[11]

The International Organization of Supreme Audit Institutions (INTOSAI) established a Working Group on Environmental Auditing (WGEA) in 1992[12] to assist national government auditors and Supreme Audit Institutions (SAIs). The WGEA has encouraged MEA audits to assist governments to improve policies and practices and to provide secretariats with information to assist State parties.[13] Between 2003 and 2011, 80 such audits were conducted.[14] Over 50 multinational cooperative audits have been conducted since 1995 to address specific issues across a region.[15]

Different meanings of 'effectiveness' relate to disparate goals, including environmental quality, economic efficiency and political process.[16] In this chapter, effectiveness concerns progress towards environmental quality goals specified in the MEA.[17]

The MEAs surveyed here are global and regional. There is substantial overlap among parties to multiple global MEAs, which are often widely ratified. Their overlapping parties provide opportunities for cross-institutional MEA coordination. The parties to regional environmental treaties are more diverse than for global MEAs. Nevertheless, they are typically also parties to other treaties with similar regional structures,

---

[11] ISO 14010, s 3.9. The International Chamber of Commerce definition of environmental auditing addresses essentially private sector activity and is less suited to public sector auditing. Geldard (1995) 1.

[12] Van Leeuwen (2004).

[13] UNEP (2010) 37.

[14] International Organisation of Supreme Audit Institutions (INTOSAI) (2012) 6.

[15] Ibid, 12.

[16] Young and Levy (1999) 3–6.

[17] A statement of effectiveness involves a causal link from the MEA to the measured change and assessment of success in solving the targeted problem. Objective evaluation is possible where the objectives of the MEA define quantifiable outcomes and impacts. Mitchell (1998).

resources and challenges. The same secretariats may even serve several regional treaties, generating opportunities to coordinate between them.

However, divergences between subject matters and identities of States for global and regional regimes can inhibit coordination across them. Poor coordination concerns in Antarctic waters are identified here as treaty norms that require incompatible management practices or that enable inconsistent practices by failing to specify regime relationships.

2. METHOD

Doctrinal analysis is used here to examine the extent to which MEA instruments overlap, and whether their norms require or permit conflicting approaches. The next step is a survey of implementation by international institutions[18] to see whether, where there are conflicting treaty norms, cross-institutional coordination might avoid conflicting implementation. The third step is to examine coordination across MEA systems to promote efficiency.

Legal frameworks for Antarctic waters have developed in ad hoc response to political management concerns, generating regime complexity. Primary within the Antarctic Treaty System (ATS) is the Antarctic Treaty, covering the area south of 60° South latitude.[19] The most relevant ATS instruments for management of Antarctic marine living resources are the Convention for the Conservation of Antarctic Marine Living Resources (CCAMLR) and the Madrid Protocol. These instruments apply in the same area as the Antarctic Treaty, though the CCAMLR extends beyond to a line approximating the Antarctic 'convergence'.[20] The CCAMLR establishes a framework for marine living resources exploitation within the ATS. The Madrid Protocol establishes stringent environmental protection within the Antarctic Treaty area.[21] Its annexes create obligations to limit environmental impacts, conduct prior assessment of

---

[18] Tanaka (2008) 20.

[19] Article VI of the Antarctic Treaty provides that 'The provisions of the present Treaty shall apply to the area south of 60° South Latitude, including all ice shelves, but nothing in the present Treaty shall prejudice or in any way affect the rights, or the exercise of the rights, of any State under international law with regard to the high seas within that area'. As of 27 April 2014, 50 countries are party to the Antarctic Treaty. See http://www.ats.aq/devAS/ats_parties.aspx?lang=e, accessed 2 April 2015.

[20] Where Antarctic surface waters moving northward sink below sub-Antarctic waters. Moore, Abbott and Richman (1999).

[21] Redgwell (1994); Joyner (1996).

possible environmental impacts, and to undertake monitoring.[22] The regional treaties of the ATS intersect with five other sets of global norms:

(1) fisheries exploitation norms, comprising conservation, optimal utilisation, and maximum sustainable yield;
(2) wildlife conservation and habitat protection norms, addressing ecosystem-based management, the precautionary approach, and environmental impact assessment;
(3) marine pollution controls, comprising movement or discharges of wastes and toxic substances;
(4) compliance and enforcement norms, comprising flag, coastal, port, and joint implementation measures; and
(5) dispute settlement norms, comprising compulsory and non-compulsory procedures.

The Treaties referred to in this chapter are listed in the Table of Treaties at Section 13, below.

3. FISHERIES EXPLOITATION NORMS

Fisheries standards are found predominantly, but not exclusively, in fisheries laws. Standards from the ATS and wildlife treaties also apply. These three sets of standards are not well integrated and exhibit minor inconsistencies.[23] Concerning harvest targets, for example, regimes are designed to achieve 'optimal utilisation,' 'maximum sustainable yield,' as well as the 'conservation' of the stock of fish. The CCAMLR, the Convention on Biological Diversity (CBD), and Convention on International Trade in Endangered Species (CITES) endorse marine living resources (MLR) utilisation, with the qualifiers that it must be 'sustainable,' as compared to 'optimal' as used in the fisheries instruments.[24]

Concerning standards for conservation, there is potential inconsistency between a strictly protective standard in the MEAs, as compared to

---

[22] Principles are set out in Art 3 of the Madrid Protocol. In relation to environmental impact assessment (EIA), see Art 8. EIA procedures were updated in 2005: Resolution 4 (2005), ATCM XXVIII, CEP VIII, Stockholm (Updating of Guidelines for Environmental Impact Assessment in Antarctica).

[23] Rose and Milligan (2011).

[24] The CCAMLR, Art 3(c), does not refer to 'sustainable' utilisation of MLR but requires that such utilisation be consistent with the 'sustained conservation of Antarctic marine living resources'.

fisheries treaties and the CCAMLR.[25] The fisheries treaties defer to the stricter conservation standards that States might choose to apply to marine mammals, such as the Convention for the Regulation of Whaling (ICRW), which has established a whale protection century in the Southern Ocean.[26] However, conflict could arise between the conservation standards of the CCAMLR and those under CITES. CITES Article XV, paragraph 2, provides that, upon receiving the text of a proposed amendment to Appendices I and II involving marine species, the Secretariat of CITES is obliged to 'consult' the relevant 'inter-governmental bodies having a function in relation to those species … with a view to ensuring coordination with any conservation measures enforced by such bodies'.[27] To date, normative conflicts have been avoided.

4. WILDLIFE CONSERVATION AND HABITAT PROTECTION NORMS

The norms for ecosystem-based management (EBM),[28] environmental impact assessment (EIA),[29] and the precautionary approach[30] form the foci of analysis here of the interaction between standards relating to wildlife species conservation and habitat protection.

The CCAMLR defers, in relation to whales, to the ICRW.[31] The application of Annex II of the Madrid Protocol restricts human interactions with marine mammals, subject to the requirement that 'nothing in the Annex shall derogate from the rights and obligations of Parties under

---

25 Regarding maximum sustainable yield, see Maunder (2008).

26 ICRW, Schedule 7(b).

27 COP-11 to CITES has recommended that parties to the convention agree to not issue trade permits in relation to species protected from commercial whaling under the ICRW. CITES COP-11, 10–20 April 2000, Conf. no. 11.4 (Rev. COP-12).

28 Kappel and Martone (2006); Hemphill and Shillinger (2006); Fabra and Gascon (2008).

29 Okowa (1996); Sands (2003) 799–825. See also Principle 17 of the Rio Declaration (UNCED 1992).

30 Freestone (1996); Trouwborst (2002) 62; and Marr (2003). Also Principle 15 of the Rio Declaration (UNCED 1992).

31 CCAMLR, Art VI, provides that '[n]othing in this Convention shall derogate from the rights and obligations of Contracting Parties under the International Convention for the Regulation of Whaling and the Convention for the Conservation of Antarctic Seals'.

the [ICRW]'.[32] Also within the ATS, the Madrid Protocol's strict conservation standards are suspended in deference to the standards of other ATS instruments, including the CCAMLR, to ensure that the ATS instruments are consistent.[33]

In 2014, the International Court of Justice found Japan to be in breach of its ICRW obligations by reason of its lethal capture of fin whales under the Japanese Whale Research Program under Special Permit in the Antarctic (JARPA II).[34] Australia had argued that developments within general international environmental law had led to a new objective for the ICRW, that is, the 'conservation of whales as an end itself'.[35] Support for this position was mixed among the majority decision of the 16 member Court.[36]

Some judges seemed willing to impose MEA consistency upon the ICRW. Voting with the majority, in a separate declaration Judge Keith stated that the broader context of the ICRW needs to be considered by the Court. Judge Trindade voted with the majority but took Judge Keith's view further. Judge Trindade argued that treaties other than the ICRW that have established frameworks for conservation and management of MLR, such as the CBD, are evidence of *res juris communis*, that is, collective legal opinion.[37] In his view, that collective legal opinion forms the 'juridical conscience of what is necessary' in international law, generating customary norms for the interpretation of treaty systems.[38] Accordingly, treaties such as the ICRW must be re-interpreted in the context of the practice of other marine conservation and management MEAs. The approaches of Judges Keith and Trindade were implicitly rejected by Judge Greenwood in his separate and legally orthodox opinion that it is the relevant body of practice of the ICRW Parties in implementing the ICRW (to the extent that this practice reflects an agreement among the Parties) that offers guidance for the Court's

---

[32] Madrid Protocol, Art 7.

[33] Madrid Protocol, Art 4.

[34] Judgement of the Court 31 March 2014, *Whaling in the Antarctic (Australia v Japan: New Zealand Intervening)*.

[35] Memorial of Australia, *Whaling in the Antarctic (Australia v Japan; New Zealand intervening)*, International Court of Justice, General List No. 148, 31 March 2014, para 2.98.

[36] By 12 votes to 4, ibid, paras 228–223.

[37] Ibid, paras 38–39.

[38] Ibid, paras 89–90.

interpretation.[39] Although Judge Trindade's assumptions and juridical reasoning are dubious for their radical departure from treaty law,[40] they could indicate a trend in doctrine concerning subordinate policy under treaties, requiring consistency in implementation policies across treaty systems.

In relation to MLR other than whales, exploitation standards in the ATS and the Convention on the Law of the Sea (LOSC) generate other potential normative inconsistencies. The CCAMLR refers to 'conservation' including 'rational use',[41] rather than to optimum utilisation including 'maximum sustainable yield',[42] which could give rise to inconsistent standards for harvest targets.

Such inconsistencies are also present between the MEAs and the ATS and international fisheries treaties concerning norms for ecosystem-based management and environmental impact assessment. This poses challenges to integrated governance in Antarctic waters and necessitates caution to avoid conflicts between applied standards.

5. MARINE POLLUTION CONTROL NORMS

The most significant introduction of oil pollution into the Antarctic region has been from ships,[43] including significant oil spills from the MV Explorer in 2007 and the Endless Sea in 2012. An amendment to Annex I of the Convention on Pollution from Ships (MARPOL) focusing on the Antarctic entered into force in August 2011 to prohibit crude oil of particular densities for ships within the Antarctic area.[44]

The Antarctic Treaty Consultative Parties adopted norms governing marine pollution in the Madrid Protocol. Potential conflicts between the Madrid Protocol and the MARPOL Convention are addressed by deference to the MARPOL Convention, under Annex IV of the Madrid

---

[39] Judge Greenwood's position reflects the established principle in international law; see ibid, para 6.

[40] The persuasive power of Judge Trindade's separate opinion is diminished by its capricious departure from principles of customary international law (dismissing the role of state practice in the formation of international custom) and assertion of the primacy of juridical conscience above the will of states; cf: ibid, paras 89–90,.

[41] CCAMLR, Art II.1-2.

[42] UNCLOS, Arts 61.3 and 62.1.

[43] Secretariat of the Antarctic Treaty (1979)X-7' (1979).

[44] IMO 2011 (MARPOL Amendments).

Protocol.[45] Movements of hazardous wastes in the region under the Basel Convention on Transboundary Movement of Hazardous Wastes are provided for within Annex III of the Madrid Protocol, which provides that '[i]n the elaboration of a waste classification system ... care should be taken to avoid inconsistences with classifications employed in other relevant international agreements'.[46] The Basel Convention itself prohibits all parties from allowing hazardous waste to be exported 'within the area south of 60[47] South latitude'[48] but itself defers to MARPOL by excluding wastes derived 'from the normal operation of a ship'.[49] This deference demonstrates successful avoidance of the risk of duplication and inconsistencies.

6. COMPLIANCE AND ENFORCEMENT NORMS

Efforts to manage fisheries south of the Antarctic convergence are confronted by significant challenges because Antarctic waters are remote from centres of administration, subject to extreme weather, and extend over a vast area. Much commercial fishing remains illegal or unreported. During the 1996–97 fishing season, for example, the estimated total catch of Patagonian toothfish (*dissostichus eleginoides*) in Antarctic waters greatly exceeded the total allowable catch.[50]

It is encouraging then that compliance and enforcement measures for vessel licensing, observation and inspection, and international cooperation, demonstrate little normative conflict. For example, vessel monitoring data under the CCAMLR and the Convention for the Conservation of Southern Bluefin Tuna (CCSBT) for southern bluefin tuna in Antarctic waters are compatible. Although the dominant instrument is the CCAMLR, it conforms to the enforcement framework in UNCLOS and its supplementary instruments.[51] The same is true of the CCSBT, the Agreement to Promote Compliance with International Conservation and Management Measures by Fishing Vessels (Compliance Agreement) and

---

45 See Wood (2003).
46 Antarctic Treaty.
47 Ibid, Art 4(6).
48 Ibid, Art 1(4).
49 Agnew (2000).
50 See, e.g., Rayfuse (1998); Bialek (2000); Kaye (2007).
51 Under UNCLOS the risk of fragmentation was noted long ago. Boyle (1997).

the Agreement on Port State Measures to Prevent, Deter and Eliminate Illegal Unreported and Unregulated Fishing (PSM Convention).

Normative inconsistencies arise only where subordinate measures are adopted. Concerning catch documentation, for example, CITES requirements for permits for the transfer of listed endangered species are not compatible with catch documentation requirements under the CCAMLR or CCSBT.

7. DISPUTE SETTLEMENT

A consequence of overlaps is that a dispute concerning Antarctic waters may engage dispute settlement mechanisms from several instruments with potential inconsistencies between them.[52] The different mechanisms are compared in the following list related to harvesting of living resources:

- non-compulsory procedures, Article XXV of the CCAMLR;
- compulsory binding procedures, Part XV, section 2, of UNCLOS, subject to Part XV, section 1;
- non-compulsory procedures, Article 16 of the CCSBT, relating to southern bluefin tuna; and
- non-compulsory procedures, Article XVIII of CITES, for species included in Annex 1 of CITES.

In relation to protection of the marine environment there are also inconsistencies between dispute settlement mechanisms:

- compulsory arbitration in the circumstances referred to in Article 20 of the Madrid Protocol, or consent-based procedures, where the dispute falls within the spatial jurisdiction;
- compulsory binding procedures, Part XV, section 2 of UNCLOS, subject to Part XV, section 1, and in accordance with Article 297(1)(c);
- compulsory non-binding conciliation, Article 27 of the CBD, subject to Article 22(1);

---

52 Australia and New Zealand applied to the International Tribunal (ITLOS) for provisional measures prior to an arbitral tribunal constituted under Article 287 and Annex VII. *Southern Bluefin Tuna Cases (New Zealand v Japan; Australia v. Japan)* (Provisional Measures) (Order of 27 August 1999), [28], [29], 38 I.L.M. 1624 (1999) (*Southern Bluefin Tuna* cases). See also Bialek (2000).

- compulsory binding arbitration, Article 10 of the MARPOL Convention, where the dispute relates to vessel source pollution; and
- non-compulsory procedures, Article XVIII of CITES, where the dispute relates to international trade in endangered species.

Concerning fish harvesting on the high seas, the potential for conflicts among dispute procedures might be partly resolved by Article 281 of UNCLOS. This prevents recourse to UNCLOS dispute settlement procedures where another agreement between the parties excludes any further procedure. The scope of Article 281 of UNCLOS was a central issue in *Southern Bluefin Tuna Cases (New Zealand v Japan; Australia v Japan),* concerning a unilateral decision by Japan to exceed national catch limits under the CCSBT.[53] A central question was the interaction between compulsory procedures in UNCLOS and the consent-based dispute settlement mechanisms in Article 16 of the CCSBT.[54] The arbitral tribunal rejected Japan's argument that the CCSBT functioned as a *lex specialis,* excluding the application of UNCLOS.[55]

Conflicts could also arise between the compulsory procedures in UNCLOS and those in the Madrid Protocol, the CBD and the MARPOL Convention. Article 282 of UNCLOS provides that other international agreements can apply if those procedures are compulsory and binding.[56] Therefore, consistency might be promoted by the adoption of common arbitration mechanisms. Nevertheless, Article 22 of the CBD, compelling implementation in accordance with the law of the sea, is likely to work

---

[53] ITLOS considered that an Annex VII general arbitral tribunal would have *prima facie* jurisdiction and prescribed provisional measures. *Southern Bluefin Tuna* cases, *Provisional Measures* at 62. For a comprehensive discussion see Brunne and Hay (1999).

[54] It noted that: 'it is a commonplace of international law and State practice for more than one treaty to bear upon a particular dispute. There is no reason why a given act of a State may not violate its obligations under more than one treaty. There is frequently a parallelism of treaties, both in their substantive content and in their provisions for settlement of disputes arising thereunder'. *Southern Bluefin Tuna Cases (Australia and New Zealand v Japan) (Jurisdiction and Admissibility)* (Award of 4 August 2000) [52], 119 I.L.M. 508, 548. Compare the approach adopted in the *Mox Plant Case (Ireland v United Kingdom)* (Provisional Measures) (Order of 31 December 2001) 49–52, 41 I.L.M. 405 (2002). See also Oxman (2001); Kwiatowska (2003).

[55] Concerning the meaning of Art 282, see Kwiatowska (2003) 376–77; Oxman (2001) 253; and Forster (2003) 616–17.

[56] Coordination is characterised as taking place through hierarchical, market, or network structures. See Pierre and Peters (2000) 15–21; Bevir (2009) 56.

against an interpretation of the CBD procedures as constituting 'an agreement to exclude any further [LOSC] procedure' under Article 281 of UNCLOS.

8. POLICY AND ADMINISTRATION COORDINATION SURVEY: ANTARCTIC

If inter-governmental institutions that manage Antarctic waters are to implement integrated marine governance, they need to coordinate administration.[57] Although disparate treaties may permit incompatible management practices, parties to Antarctic waters administrations do seek consistency to integrate decision-making despite fragmented law.

This healing tendency towards integrated governance is strongest among treaties in the same subject matter grouping. Decision-making within the bodies of the ATS is well integrated, compared to decision-making across the ATS and wildlife protection and nature conservation treaties.

Wastes, hazardous chemicals and pollution at sea are regulated through different international organisations, including the International Maritime Organisation (IMO), UNEP, and the Food and Agriculture Organisation of the United Nations (FAO). Although the ATS Consultative Parties maintain consultations in relation to shipping standards of the IMO, patterns of cross-reference with other institutions are uneven.[58] Environmental governance requires management that methodically crosses inter-governmental institutional boundaries, utilizing cooperation between them and also networks between them, national governments and industry and civil society actors.[59]

The judgement by the International Court of Justice on the Japanese scientific whaling program indicates the potential for cross-influences on the soft law made under treaties, by shaping decisions by treaty conferences of parties and sub-committees.

---

57 Scott (2010) 43.

58 Haward and Vince (2008) 13; Stewart and Jones (2003).

59 Secretariat of the Antarctic Treaty. See http://www.ats.aq/e/about.htm, accessed 2 April 2015.

9. JOINT SECRETARIAT FUNCTIONS

Due to conflicting territorial claims, the Antarctic Treaty had no secretariat for almost half a century and conferences were organised by parties on a rotating basis. On 1 September 2004, a permanent secretariat was established in Buenos Aires.[60] However, the Antarctic Secretariat does not service the whole ATS. The CCAMLR Secretariat, for example, is served by a secretariat established in 1983 in Australia.[61] Other Southern Ocean regional MEAs also have separate secretariats.[62]

There are obvious advantages from the co-location or sharing of functions. Beginning in 2005, Parties to the Basel Convention, Rotterdam Convention on the Prior Informed Consent Procedure for Chemicals in International Trade (PIC Convention) and Stockholm Convention on Persistent Organic Pollutants (POPS Convention) initiated a process to enhance synergies in their implementation. While the legal autonomy of the conventions was maintained, the Conferences of the Parties to the conventions commenced the synergies process through an extraordinary common meeting of the Parties in Bali in February 2010, followed by one in 2013. The Parties agreed to implement joint activities, joint managerial functions and joint audits.[63] An Executive Secretary is intended to ensure optimal use of resources.[64] The savings have been invested in a technical assistance programme for developing nations and countries with economies in transition.[65] The Executive Secretary will also propose an integrated organisational structure.[66]

Inter-secretariat MoUs have also been established across biodiversity MEAs. Similarly, regional fisheries management organisation Secretariats are extending coordination through MoUs. CCAMLR has adopted two MoUs relating to adjacent and overlapping fisheries, with the Western

---

60 Commission for the Conservation of Antarctic Marine Living Resources. See https://www.ccamlr.org/en/organisation/secretariat, accessed 2 April 2015.

61 The Secretariat for the 2001 Agreement on Albatross and Petrels, also based in Hobart, covers much of the Southern Ocean; Agreement on Albatross and Petrel 2001.The Convention for the Conservation of Antarctic Seals 1972 is served by a secretariat based in the British Foreign and Commonwealth Office.

62 Decisions BC.Ex-1/1, RC.Ex-1/1, SC.Ex-1/1.

63 UNEP World Conservation Monitoring Centre (2012), 6.

64 Food and Agricultural Organisation of the United Nations (2013).

65 Executive Secretary, Proposal for the organisation of the secretariats of the three conventions. See http://synergies.pops.int/SynergiesProcess/JointManagerialFunctions/JointManagerialFunctionsProposal/tabid/2619/language/en-US/Default.aspx, accessed 2 April 2015.

66 Scott (2010) 192–7.

and Central Pacific Fisheries Commission and the Agreement for the Conservation of Albatross and Petrel (ACAP).

The Antarctic Treaty Secretariat, however, remains relatively insular.[67] There are as yet no joint secretariat functions shared between it and other MEAS or regional treaties.

10. COORDINATED IMPLEMENTATION ASSISTANCE

Where a lack of environmental capacity is the cause of national non-compliance, coordination of treaty implementation assistance, such as information, technical support and financial assistance, would be more effective than piecemeal efforts. Non-compliance assistance measures could be easier to coordinate than general implementation assistance as they are nominated as implementation priorities and are fewer than general requests for assistance. In an extraordinary case involving five overlapping MEAs, Ukraine's proposal to construct a Danube-Black Sea Shipping Canal in the Bystroe estuary of the Danube Delta, demonstrated the potential for coordinated MEA non-compliance mechanisms.[68] This has not yet occurred in the Antarctic context.

11. PERFORMANCE AUDITING OF IMPLEMENTATION

Many treaties require Parties to exchange information. They might be required to provide information on proposed environmentally sensitive trade or industrial developments, on ambient environmental conditions or on environmental technologies. For example, CITES requires Parties to submit annual import/export statistics,[69] while the UN Fish Stocks Agreement and the ICRW require Parties to submit annual catch/permit reports.[70] This transactional data is operational information, to be distinguished from MEA performance information. Nevertheless, operational and performance information are often inter-related.[71]

---

[67] Ibid, 208.

[68] CITES, Art VI.6.

[69] Fish Stocks Agreement, Art 5(j); Whaling Convention, Art VIII.1.

[70] Rose (2006).

[71] E.g. CBD, Art 26 ; CMS, Arts V.5 and VII.5; Vienna Convention, Art 5. The Ramsar Convention text does not refer to reporting requirements. Recommendation 2.1 of the Conference of the Contracting Parties (1984) urged parties

Most MEAs refer to reporting requirements generally, which are elaborated by the Parties.[72] Some oblige their Parties to provide the secretariat with annual implementation reports.[73] These may involve details of national programs, policies and measures.[74] Instructions on national performance reports are available from the Secretariat and the majority of MEA websites have guidelines.[75] For example, the World Heritage Convention has guidelines that specify the purpose, format and general requirements of periodic reports.[76] Some MEA websites provide templates.[77]

Concerning performance review information applicable to Antarctic waters, Article 17 of the Madrid Protocol requires Parties to report annually on steps to implement the Protocol. A reporting template was adopted in 2001.[78] This requires States to outline their compliance with

---

to submit detailed reports six months before each ordinary meeting of the Conference see http://www.ramsar.org/sites/default/files/documents/library/key_rec_2.01e.pdf (accessed 10 April 2015).

72 See e.g., Basel Convention, Art 13 and Montreal Protocol, Art 7. Biosafety Protocol, Art 33 requires reports every four years.

73 UNCCD, Art 9.1; POP Convention, Art 7(1). See also POP website, at http://www.pops.int/documents/implementation/nips/, accessed 2 April 2015.

74 Relevant websites (all accessed 2 April 2015): CMS: http://www.cms.int/sites/default/files/document/CP7CF7_06_2_national_report_0.pdf; World Heritage http://whc.unesco.org/reporting/prexpl.htm; Ramsar Convention:http://www.ramsar.org/sites/default/files/documents/library/key_rec_2.01e.pdf (accessed 10 April 2015); CBD: https://www.cbd.int/reports/guidelines/default.shtml; Biosafety Protocol: http://www.biodiv.org/biosafety/cop-mop/result.aspx?id=8291; POPs: http://www.pops.int/documents/guidance/; PIC: http://www.pic.int/Implementation/ResourceKit/tabid/1064/language/en-US/Default.aspx; Vienna Convention: http://ozone.unep.org/new_site/en/ozone_data_tools.php; Montreal Protocol: http://ozone.unep.org/Data_Reporting/Data_Reporting_Tools/data-reporting-handbook.e.pdf; UNFCCC: http://unfccc.int/national_reports/items/1408.php; and Kyoto: http://unfccc.int/national_reports/accounting_reporting_and_review_under_the_kyoto_protocol/items/1029.php.

75 World Heritage Convention website, http://whc.unesco.org/reporting/prexpl.htm; also POPs http://www.pops.int/documents/guidance/ (both accessed 2 April 2015).

76 See e.g., CBD, CITES, Ramsar Convention, and Basel Convention.

77 Secretariat of the Antarctic Treaty (2011), Art 17.

78 Appendix 4 of the XXIV ATCM Final Report, paras 2.4.1–2.5, available 2 April 2015 at http://www.ats.aq/documents/recatt/Att315_e.pdf.

the Protocol and national legislation, and to provide scientific and operational information.[79]

Some MEAs have verification requirements that test the accuracy of performance information, usually through on-site inspections. For example, the UNFCCC/Kyoto Secretariats conduct on-site verifications.[80] The CITES Secretariat conducts *ad hoc* verification of compliance.[81]

Failure to comply with performance review obligations is increasingly treated as substantive national non-compliance, generating an international response, as with CITES and the Kyoto Protocol. Under CITES, Parties are recommended not to trade with a Party that has failed to report for three consecutive years.[82] Alternatively, further performance information obligations may be required of the defaulting Party. The Cartagena Protocol on Biosafety and Kyoto Protocol require that the defaulting Party submit a compliance plan.[83]

For Antarctic waters, the CCAMLR established a Standing Committee on Implementation and Compliance in 2001 to 'review and analyse information pertaining to activities of Contracting Parties and non-Contracting Parties which undermine the provisions of the Convention, including in particular IUU fishing, and recommend actions to be taken'.[84] The 33rd Antarctic Treaty Consultative Meeting, in 2010 noted that '[t]he Committee agreed that there is an urgent need to ensure that all Parties are fulfilling all information exchange requirements of the Treaty and Article 17 of the Environmental Protocol'.[85] Further developments on a non-compliance response under the Environment Protocol

---

79 E.g. The Basel Convention 'Verification' provision (Art 19) addresses a trigger mechanism for the NCP. The Fish Stocks Agreement includes an obligation to develop national verification procedures (Art 18.3).

80 Reeve (2002) 75.

81 Resolution Conf. 11.17 (Rev. CoP16), available 2 April 2015 at http://www.cites.org/eng/res/11/11-17R16.php.

82 Kyoto website http://unfccc.int/kyoto_mechanisms/compliance/items/3024.php and Biosafety website, http://www.biodiv.org/biosafety/issues/compliance2.aspx (both accessed 2 April 2015).

83 CCAMLR (2001).

84 CEP XXIII Report, para 14.

85 The primary multi-sectoral UN organisations promoting linkages are UNEP, the UN Development Programme (UNDP), and the UN University (UNU). In 1997, the UNDP convened an *Expert Meeting on Synergies in National Implementation between the Rio Agreements* to pursue synergies at the national level of, inter alia, the CBD, UNFCCC and UNCCD. See Lasén Diaz (2002), 49–50.

could be considered in the future. However, treaties specific to Antarctic waters still lack verification procedures and systems for non-compliance response.

Synergies in national performance review information across treaties occur already between the biodiversity-related MEAs.[86] Biannual meetings are held for the five biodiversity-related MEAS (CBD, CMS, CITES, World Heritage and Ramsar Conventions) within the Biodiversity Liaison Group.[87] In 1997, the World Conservation Monitoring Centre (WCMC) produced a *Feasibility Study for the Information Management Infrastructure* for biodiversity-related MEAs, commissioned by UNEP and the Secretariats of the CBD, CITES, CMS, the Ramsar and the World Heritage Conventions.[88] However, progress towards harmonisation of national reporting, including performance reporting, and other forms of implementation coordination, has been lacklustre. Greater progress might be expected in future in the cluster of MEAs on chemicals regulation. For Antarctic waters, there is as yet little synergy in performance information reporting, auditing or verification.

Potential linkages in performance review information will arise where treaties regulate overlapping sites, species, substances or emissions. Performance review information will be most useful when review requires statistical, transactional or other quantifiable data, rather than descriptive evaluations which typically address policy measures customised to particular MEAs, and may be less factually objective.

12. CONCLUSION

The fact that it is feasible to compare norms across treaties demonstrates parallelism in legal developments. The congruence between applicable standards indicates policy transfer or diffusion, even where coordination is not explicit.[89] This suggests that congruence is developing as cross-institutional communication improves.

---

[86] Joint website of the Biodiversity Related Conventions Biodiversity Liaison Group http://www.biodiv.org/cooperation/related-conventions/blg.shtml (accessed 2 April 2015).

[87] Lasén Diaz (n 85) 50–52.

[88] Levi-Faur and Vigoda-Gadot (2004) 1–9.

[89] OECD website, at http://www.oecd.org/topic/0,2686,en_2649_34307_1_1_1_1_37465,00.html

In Antarctic waters, treaty conflicts have usually been avoided by hierarchies or qualifications, which provide that one instrument does not derogate from another. Hierarchies enable internal consistency within the ATS and the fisheries clusters of instruments, but there is ambiguity. The MEAs evidence no basic pattern of ordering relationships between themselves or with other fisheries or ATS instruments. An additional layer of complexity emerges concerning the legal status of subordinate institutional decisions. Although the CBD ostensibly overrides other international instruments where serious damage to biodiversity is likely, derogation would be qualified according to the legal status of the decisions under the CBD. For example, a CBD party's decision to protect biodiversity might be considered to derogate from a CCAMLR decision but not from an amendment to the CCAMLR itself.

Implementation of MEAs regulating Antarctic waters using subordinate policy and management measures indicates awareness of the potential for conflicting decision-making by responsible governing bodies across treaty regimes, and that the bodies have opted for consistency, rather than conflict. This seems to be largely a function of mutual awareness, which is strongest within common subject area treaties, but not top the degree of joint secretariat functions and coordination of implementation assistance.

To address these shortcomings, a stronger structure of networks between the institutions that govern Antarctic waters is needed. For instance, it would be helpful to expand deliberate dialogue between the ATS bodies and other MEA governing bodies, including workshops to identify situations where normative inconsistencies have practical implications and to identify pragmatic solutions.

Coordination to improve implementation assistance delivery to countries that are systemically non-compliant could prioritise shared subject matters under inter-related treaties. Also, protocols for coordination of performance information between secretariats would enhance their capacities to trigger non-compliance investigations. An analogy can be made with the peer reviews conducted by the Secretariat of the Organisation for Economic Cooperation and Development (OECD) on progress in its member countries and three non-member countries.[90] These reviews are

[90] Antarctic Treaty, adopted 1 December 1959, in force 23 June 1961, 402 U.N.T.S. 71, accessed 2 April 2015 at http://www.ats.aq/documents/keydocs/vol_1/vol1_2_AT_Antarctic_Treaty_e.pdf.

conducted cyclically to assess whether the country is meeting its domestic and international environmental obligations. Similarly, multi-tasking a monitoring or verification mission across Antarctic MEA Secretariats could be done by a team of experts for different MEAs administered by one organisation.

Resolving normative inconsistencies is an essential first step to meet the neglected challenge of integrated governance in Antarctic waters. To improve the implementation of environmental norms in the region, it should be followed by the introduction of internationally coordinated performance audits and verification for conservation and management of Antarctic waters.

13. TABLE OF TREATIES

Table 9.1 Antarctic Treaty System (ATS)

- Antarctic Treaty[91]
- Convention for the Conservation of Antarctic Marine Living Resources (CCAMLR)[92]
- Protocol on Environmental Protection to the Antarctic Treaty (Madrid Protocol)[93]

[91] Convention for the Conservation of Antarctic Marine Living Resources, adopted 20 May 1980, in force on 7 April 1982, 1329 U.N.T.S. 47 (CCAMLR), accessed 2 April 2015 at https://www.ccamlr.org/en/system/files/e-pt1.pdf. The Convention for the Conservation of Antarctic Seals is not active in the absence of commercial sealing.

[92] Protocol on Environmental Protection to the Antarctic Treaty, adopted 4 October 1991, in force 14 January 1998, 30 I.L.M. 1455 (Madrid Protocol) accessed 2 April 2015 at http://www.ats.aq/documents/recatt/Att006_e.pdf.

[93] United Nations Convention of the Law of the Sea, adopted 10 December 1982, in force 16 November 1994, 1833 U.N.T.S. 397 (UNCLOS), accessed 2 April 2015 at http://www.un.org/depts/los/convention_agreements/texts/unclos/unclos_e.pdf.

Table 9.2 Fisheries

• United Nations Convention of the Law of the Sea (UNCLOS)[94]
• Agreement for the Implementation of the Provisions of the United Nations Convention on the Law of the Sea Relating to the Conservation and Management of Straddling Fish Stocks and Highly Migratory Fish Stocks (Fish Stocks Agreement)[95]
• Convention for the Conservation of Southern Bluefin Tuna (CCSBT)[96]
• Agreement to Promote Compliance with International Conservation and Management Measures by Fishing Vessels (Compliance Agreement)[97]
• Agreement on Port State Measures to Prevent, Deter and Eliminate Illegal Unreported and Unregulated Fishing (Port State Measures Convention) (developed under the auspices of the Food and Agricultural Organization of the United Nations (PSM Agreement)[98]

[94] Agreement for the Implementation of the Provisions of the United Nations Convention on the Law of the Sea Relating to the Conservation and Management of Straddling Fish Stocks and Highly Migratory Fish Stocks, adopted 4 August 1995, in force 11 December 2001, 2167 U.N.T.S. 3 (Fish Stocks Agreement), accessed 2 April 2015 at http://www.un.org/depts/los/convention_agreements/texts/fish_stocks_agreement/CONF164_37.htm.

[95] Convention for the Conservation of Southern Bluefin Tuna, adopted 10 May 1993, in force 20 May 1994, 1819 U.N.T.S. 359 (CCBST), accessed 2 April 2015 at www.pca-cpa.org/showfile.asp?fil_id=1591.

[96] Agreement to Promote Compliance with International Conservation and Management Measures by Fishing Vessels, adopted at the twenty-seventh Conference of the Parties to the Food and Agriculture Organization (November 1993), in force 24 April 2003 (Compliance Agreement).

[97] Agreement on Port State Measures to Prevent, Deter and Eliminate Illegal Unreported and Unregulated Fishing, adopted at the 137th Session of the FAO Council (November 2009), not yet in force.

[98] International Convention for the Regulation of Whaling, adopted 2 December 1946, in force 10 November 1948, 161 U.N.T.S. 72 (ICRW), accessed 2 April 2015 at https://archive.iwc.int/pages/view.php?ref=3607&k=.

Table 9.3 Wildlife conservation

- International Convention for the Regulation of Whaling (ICRW)[99]
- Convention on International Trade in Endangered Species of Wild Fauna and Flora, signed March 3, 1973 (CITES)[100]
- Agreement for the Conservation of Albatrosses and Petrels, 2001 (ACAP)[101]
- Convention on the Conservation of Migratory Species of Wild Animals, opened for signature 23 June 1979 (CMS)[102]
- Convention on Biological Diversity, opened for signature 5 June 1992 (CBD)[103]

Table 9.4 Waste and hazardous materials

- International Convention for the Prevention of Pollution from Ships as modified by the protocol of 1978 (MARPOL Convention)[104]
- Convention on the Prevention of Marine Pollution by Dumping of Wastes and Other Matter
  opened for signature 29 December 1972 (London Convention)[105]
- Basel Convention on the Control of Transboundary Movements of Hazardous Wastes and their Disposal
  opened for signature 22 March 1989 (Basel Convention)[106]

[99] Convention on the International Trade in Endangered Species of Wild Fauna and Flora, adopted 3 March 1973, in force 1 July 1975, 993 U.N.T.S. 243 (CITES).

[100] Agreement on the Conservation of Albatrosses and Petrels, adopted 19 June 2011, in force 1 February 2004, 2258 U.N.T.S 257 (ACAP).

[101] Convention on the Conservation of Migratory Species of Wild Animals, adopted 23 June 1979, in force 1 November 1983, 1651 U.N.T.S. 28395 (CMS).

[102] Convention on Biological Diversity, adopted 5 June 1992, in force 29 December 1993, 1760 U.N.T.S. 79 (CBD).

[103] International Convention for the Prevention of Pollution from Ships, adopted in London, 2 November 1973 and 17 February 1978, respectively, reprinted in International Maritime Organization, MARPOL 73/78 Consolidated Edition (2006) (MARPOL Convention).

[104] Convention on the Prevention of Marine Pollution by Dumping of Wastes and Other Matter, adopted 13 November 1972, in force 30 August 1975, 1046 U.N.T.S. 120 (London Convention).

[105] Basel Convention on the Control of Transboundary Movements of Hazardous Wastes and their Disposal, adopted 22 March 1989, in force 5 May 1992,

Table 9.4 (continued)

- Rotterdam Convention on the Prior Informed Consent Procedure for Certain Hazardous Chemicals and Pesticides in International Trade opened for signature 10 September 1998 (PIC Convention)[106]
- Cartagena Protocol on Biosafety to the Convention on Biological Diversity of 5 June 1992 adopted 29 January 2000 (Biosafety Protocol)[107]
- Stockholm Convention on Persistent Organic Pollutants opened for signature 22 May 2001 (POPs Convention)[108]

Table 9.5 Atmospheric pollution

- Vienna Convention for the Protection of the Ozone Layer opened for signature 22 March 1985 (Vienna Convention)[109]
- Montreal Protocol on Substances that Deplete the Ozone Layer opened for signature 24 September 1987 (Montreal Protocol)[110]
- United Nations Framework Convention on Climate Change opened for signature 9 May 1992 (UNFCCC)[111]
- Kyoto Protocol to the United Nations Framework Convention on Climate Change opened for signature 11 December 1997 (Kyoto Protocol)

1637 U.N.T.S. 57 (Basel Convention), accessed 2 April 2015 at http://www.un.org/documents/ga/conf151/aconf15126-1annex1.htm.

106 Cartagena Protocol on Biosafety to the Convention on Biological Diversity, adopted 29 January 2000, in force 11 September 2003, 2226 U.N.T.S 208 (Biosafety Protocol).

107 Stockholm Convention on Persistent Organic Pollutants, adopted 22 May 2001, in force 17 May 2004, 40 I.L.M. 532 (POPs Convention).

108 Vienna Convention for the Protection of the Ozone Layer, adopted 22 March 1985, in force 22 September 1988, 26 I.L.M. 1529 (Vienna Convention).

109 Montreal Protocol on Substances that Deplete the Ozone Layer, adopted 16 September 1987, in force 1 January 1989, 26 I.L.M 1550 (Montreal Protocol).

110 United Nations Framework Convention on Climate Change, adopted 9 May 1992, in force 21 March 1994, 31 I.L.M. 849 (UNFCCC).

111 Kyoto Protocol to the United Nations Framework Convention on Climate Change, adopted 11 December 1997, in force 16 February 2005, 37 I.L.M. 22 [Kyoto Protocol].

REFERENCES

Agnew, D. (2000), 'The Illegal and Unregulated Fishery for Toothfish in the Southern Ocean and the CCAMLR Catch Documentation Scheme' 24 *Marine Policy* 361.

Bevir, M. (2009), *Key Concepts in Governance* (London: SAGE Publications Ltd).

Bialek, D. (2000), 'Australia and New Zealand v Japan: Southern Bluefin Tuna Case' 1 *Melbourne J. Int'l L.* 8.

Boyle, A. (1997), 'Dispute Settlement and the Law of the Sea Convention: Problems of Fragmentation and Jurisdiction' 46 *Int'l & Comparative L. Q.* 37.

Brunne, J. and E. Hay (1999), 'Symposium: Southern Bluefin Tuna Cases Preliminary Measures' 10 *Yearbook of Int'l Environmental L.* 3.

Chayes, A. and A. Chayes (1995), *The New Sovereignty: Compliance with International Regulatory Agreements* (Cambridge, MA: Harvard University Press).

Fabra, A. and V. Gascon (2008), 'The Convention on the Conservation of Antarctic Marine Living Resources (CCAMLR) and the Ecosystem Approach' (2008) 23 *Int'l J. Marine & Coastal Law* 567.

Food and Agriculture Organisation of the United Nations (1995), *Agreement to Promote Compliance with International Conservation and Management Measures by Fishing Vessels*, accessed 2 April 2015 at http://www.fao.org/docrep/MEETING/003/X3130m/X3130E00.HTM.

Food and Agriculture Organisation of the United Nations (2009) *Agreement on Port State Measures to Prevent, Deter and Eliminate Illegal Unreported and Unregulated Fishing*, accessed 2 April 2015 at http://www.fao.org/fileadmin/user_upload/legal/docs/2_037t-e.pdf.

Food and Agriculture Organisation of the United Nations (2013), 'Extraordinary UN conference takes historic strides to strengthen chemical safety globally', accessed 2 April 2015 at http://www.fao.org/news/story/en/item/175896/icode/.

Forster, M. (2003), 'The Mox Plant Case: Provisional Measures in the International Tribunal for the Law of the Sea' 16 *Leiden J. Int'l Law* 611.

Freestone, D. (1996), *The Precautionary Principle and International Law: the Challenge of Implementation* (The Hague: Kluwer Law International).

Geldard, R. (1995), *Environmental Auditing in Victoria: Private enterprise and public sector examples* (Monash University LLM thesis).

Haward, M. and J. Vince (2008), *Oceans Governance in the Twenty-first Century: Managing the Blue Planet* (Cheltenham, UK and Northampton, MA, USA: Edward Elgar).

Hemphill, A. and G. Shillinger (2006), 'Casting the Net Broadly: Ecosystem-Based Management beyond National Jurisdiction' 7 *Sustainable Dev. L. & Pol'y* 56.

International Maritime Organisation (2011), 'Antarctic fuel ban and North American ECA MARPOL amendments enter into force on 1 August 2011', (Press Briefing 44, 29 July), accessed 2 April 2015 at http://www.imo.org/mediacentre/press briefings/pages/44-marpol-amends.aspx.

International Organisation of Supreme Audit Institutions (INTOSAI) Working Group on Environmental Auditing (2012), *Improving National Performance: Environmental Auditing Supports Better Governance and Management*, accessed 2 April 2015 at http://www.environmental-auditing.org/LinkClick.aspx?fileticket=zo0Jfb JMX2E %3d&tabid=261.

International Whaling Commission (2006), *Annual Report of the International Whaling Commission: Chair's Report of the 58th Annual Meeting*, accessed 2 April 2015 at https://archive.iwc.int/pages/view.php?ref=1572&search=%21collection49&order_by=relevance&sort=DESC&offset=0&archive=0&k=.

Joyner, C. (1996), 'The 1991 Madrid Environmental Protection Protocol: Contributions to Marine Pollution Law' 20 *Marine Policy* 183.

Kappel, C. and R. Martone (2006), 'Ecosystem-based Management' in E. Duffy and C. Cleveland (eds), *Encyclopedia of Earth*, accessed 2 April 2015 at http://www.eoearth.org/article/Ecosystem-based_management.

Kaye, S. (2007), 'IUU Fishing in the Southern Ocean: Challenge and Response', in G. Triggs and A. Riddell (eds), *Antarctica: Legal and Environmental Challenges for the Future* (London: British Institute of International and Comparative Law).

Kwiatowska, B. (2003), 'Ireland v. United Kingdom Mox Plant Case: Applying the Doctrine of Treaty Parallelism' 18 *Int'l J. Marine & Coastal Law* 1.

Lasén Diaz, C. (2002), *Legislative Complimentarity and Harmonization of Biodiversity-Related Multilateral Environmental Agreements*, available 2 April 2015 at https://www.cbd.int/doc/nbsap/legislation/LegalDiscussion.pdf.

Levi-Faur, D. and E. Vigoda-Gadot (2004), 'The International Transfer and Diffusion of Policy and Management Innovations: Some Characteristics of a New Order in the Making', in E. Vigoda-Gadot and D. Levi-Faur (eds), *International Public Policy and Management: Policy Learning beyond Regional, Cultural and Political Boundaries* (Hamilton: Dekker Publishers).

Marr, S. (2003), *The Precautionary Principle in the Law of the Sea: Modern Decision-Making in International Law* (The Hague: Martinus Nijhoff Publishers).

Maunder, M. (2008), 'Maximum Sustainable Yield', in S. Jorgensen and B. Faith (eds), *Encyclopaedia of Ecology* (Amsterdam: Elsevier, 2008).

Mitchell, R. (1998), 'Sources of Transparency: Information Systems in International Regimes' 42(1) *Int'l L. Stud. Q.* 109.

Moore, K., M. Abbott and J. Richman (1999), 'Location and Dynamics of the Antarctic Polar Front from Satellite Sea Surface Temperature Data' 104 *J. Geophysical Research* 3059.

Mox Plant Case (Ireland v United Kingdom) (Provisional Measures) (Order of 31 December 2001) 49–52, 41 I.L.M. 405 (2002).

Okowa, P. (1996), 'Procedural Obligations in International Environmental Agreements' 67(1) *British Yearbook of International Law* 275.

Oxman, B. (2001), 'Complementary Agreements and Compulsory Jurisdiction' 95 *American J. Int'l Law* 227.

Pierre, J. and G. Peters (2000), *Governance, Politics and the State* (Basingstoke: Macmillan Publishers Limited).

Rayfuse, R. (1998), 'Enforcement of High Seas Fisheries Agreements: Observation and Inspection under the Convention on the Conservation of Antarctic Living Marine Resources' 13 *Int'l J. Marine & Coastal Law* 579.

Redgwell, C. (1994), 'Environmental Protection in Antarctica: The 1991 Protocol' 43 *International Comp. L. Q.* 599.

Reeve, R. (2002), *Policing International Trade in Endangered Species: The CITES Treaty and Compliance* (Abingdon: Earthscan).

Rose, G. (2006), *Comparative Analysis of Compliance Mechanisms under Selected Multilateral Environmental Agreements* (United Nations Environment Program).

Rose, G. and B. Milligan (2011), 'Law for the Management of Antarctic Marine Living Resources: From Normative Conflicts Towards Integrated Governance?' 20(1) *Yearbook of International Environmental Law* 41.

Sands, P. (2003), *Principles of International Environmental Law* (2nd edn, Cambridge: Cambridge University Press).

Scott, K. (2010), 'Safety of Shipping in the Southern Ocean' 16 *Journal of Int'l Maritime Law* 21.

Secretariat of the Antarctic Treaty, 'Recommendation ATCM X-7' (1979), accessed 2 April 2015 at http://www.ats.aq/devAS/info_measures_listitem.aspx?lang=e&id=129.

Secretariat of the Antarctic Treaty, *Review of the Implementation of the Madrid Protocol: Annual report by Parties* (2011), accessed 2 April 2015 at http://www.asoc.org/storage/documents/Meetings/ATCM/XXXIV/review_of_the_madrid_protocol. pdf.

Southern Bluefin Tuna Cases (New Zealand v Japan; Australia v Japan) (Provisional Measures) (Order of 27 August 1999), [28], [29], 38 I.L.M. 1624 (1999).

Southern Bluefin Tuna Cases (Australia and New Zealand v Japan) (Jurisdiction and Admissibility) (Award of 4 August 2000) [52], 119 I.L.M. 508.

Stewart, J. and G. Jones (2003), *Renegotiating the Environment: The Power of Politics* (Sydney: Federation Press).

Tanaka, Y. (2008), *A Dual Approach to Ocean Governance: The Cases of Zonal and Integrated Management in International Law of the Sea* (Farnham: Ashgate).

Trouwborst, A. (2002), *Evolution and Status of the Precautionary Principle in International Law* (The Hague: Kluwer Law International).

Underdahl A. 'Integrated Marine Policy: What? Why? How?' (1980) 4 *Marine Policy* 159.

United Nations (1992) *Agenda 21: Programme of Action for Sustainable Development*, UN Doc. A/CONF.151/26.

United Nations Environment Program (UNEP 2001), *Guidelines on Compliance With and Enforcement Of Multilateral Environmental Agreements*, accessed 2 April 2015 at http://www.unep.org/delc/Portals/119/UNEP.Guidelines.on.Compliance.MEA.pdf.

United Nations Environment Program (UNEP 2010), Auditing the Implementation of Multilateral Environmental Agreements (MEAs): A Primer for Auditors (2010) 37, accessed 10 April 2015 at http://www.environmental-auditing.org/LinkClick.aspx?fileticket=NrVuKEhCRq8%3d&tabid=128&mid=568.

United Nations Environment Program World Conservation Monitoring Centre (2012), *Promoting synergies within the cluster of biodiversity-related multilateral environmental agreements: Summary report*, accessed 2 April 2015 at http://www.unep-wcmc.org/system/dataset_file_fields/files/000/000/046/original/Promoting_synergies_summary_report.pdf?1395761916.

Van Leeuwen, S. (2004), 'Auditing International Environmental Agreements: The Role of Supreme Audit Institutions' 24 *The Environmentalist* 93.

Victor, D., K. Raustiala and E. Skolnikoff (1998), 'Introduction and Overview', in D. Victor, K. Raustiala and E. Skolnikoff (eds), *The Implementation and Effectiveness of International Environmental Commitments: Theory and Practice* (Cambridge, MA: International Institute for Applied Systems Analysis/MIT Press).

Young, O. and M. Levy (1999), 'The Effectiveness of International Environmental Regimes', in O. Young (ed.), *The Effectiveness of International Environmental Regimes: causal connections and behavioural mechanisms* (Cambridge, MA: MIT Press).

Wood, K. (2003), 'The Uncertain Fate of the Madrid Protocol to the Antarctic Treaty in the Maritime Area' 34 *Ocean Development & Int'l Law* 139.

10. The effectiveness of instrument mixes in environmental law: insights from ship-source pollution

Javier de Cendra

1. INTRODUCTION

This book addresses the implementation of environmental laws. This chapter shall explore a specific instance of this challenge, the impact that the choice of environmental policy instruments has on the effectiveness of environmental laws through which those instruments are adopted.[1] That is: how does the choice of a specific instrument, or a combination of instruments, affect the effectiveness of the law through which they become part of the body of environmental legislation? New instruments to deal with a specific environmental problem never exist in a vacuum, but rather are part of a complex regulatory and economic framework that is embedded in cultural and social practices, which may need to change for the environmental problem to be addressed. It is obvious that cultures and social practices must impact on the effectiveness of environmental instruments, and thus the design of instrumental strategies needs to take into account sociocultural realities underpinning the practices that they intend to change. This suggests that the effectiveness of one instrument can seldom be analysed in isolation from pre-existing instruments, nor from the society within which they are expected to work. These issues will be explored in this chapter using a case-study of a specific environmental problem, ship-source pollution in the European Union,

[1] This chapter is based in work carried out in the context of the following project: Milieu Ltd, Evaluation study on the Implementation of Directive 2009/123/EC on amending Directive 2005/35/EC on ship-source pollution and on the introduction of penalties for infringements, European Commission Study Contract N° JUST/2011/JPEN/PR/1028/A4. I would like to gratefully acknowledge Milieu and the Commission for their permission to draw from that work in this chapter.

particularly in Spain. This is a serious environmental problem, so much so that the legislator has resorted to a combination of strict standards (the prohibition of discharges) combined with administrative and criminal sanctions and charges for waste treatment in an effort to ensure the effectiveness of prohibitions and hence protection of the sea.

This case-study will discuss socio-economic and cultural factors that may impact upon the effectiveness of environmental instruments. While some of those factors bear upon the regulator and enforcement agencies, others bear upon the regulated. Factors affecting the former include, for example: (1) the capacity and willingness of agents, the judiciary and lawyers to implement and enforce standards and sanctions; (2) the willingness and degree to which ex-post assessments of effectiveness are carried out and changes made to the framework if necessary. The regulated are affected by issues such as: (1) their perception of ethical duties towards society and the environment; (2) the degree to which they believe that sanctions imposed by law are dissuasive; and (3) a calculation of the benefits and costs of (not) complying with legal obligations.

The discussion will be carried out in the light of an analysis of the relevant legal materials and interviews with key agents.

The next section of the chapter will discuss theoretical aspects of instrument choice for effective environmental protection, and will provide definitions of key terms. Section 3 introduces the problem of ship source pollution and the legal regime within the European Union and Spain to address it. Section 4 asks whether the instrument mix is effective. Section 5 questions why the mix seems to be (in)effective, and Section 6 provides concluding remarks.

2. INSTRUMENT CHOICE, INSTRUMENT MIX, AND EFFECTIVENESS

A basic starting point is to consider that environmental law needs to answer three key questions: (1) should a human activity be restricted for the sake the environment?; (2) if so, by how much?; and (3) what is the best way to achieve that goal? Responding to these questions requires taking into account insights from a number of disciplines, mixed with political and socio-cultural realities.

This chapter leaves aside the first two questions and focuses on the relatively technical issue of choosing the right (mix of) policy instruments to achieve the goal. The threshold question is which instruments are available, and how to choose among them? In response to the first question the (broad) categories include: (1) prescriptive regulation ('command and control'); (2) property rights ('market mechanisms'); (3) prices ('market mechanisms'); (4) financial payments ('subsidies' and 'incentives'), and; (5) persuasion or educational instruments ('information').[2] Not all instruments are appropriate for all environmental problems, and all have pros and cons.[3] However, it is accepted that most of the time a mix of instruments is necessary to deal with any particular environmental issue.[4] The question of how to choose among (combinations of) instruments is usually answered by evaluating such combinations against four categories of criteria: effectiveness, efficiency, political feasibility and fairness. These are often considered ex ante, in the absence of empirical evidence.[5] Whilst all those criteria are important, the central one is effectiveness, that is, the degree to which the intended or expected results are achieved, (or for environmental policy whether a policy achieves its

---

[2] Command and control instruments provide clear instructions to the regulatees, and should offer certainty. Certainty requires that a regulatory response follow from violations.

The effectiveness of command and control instruments reflects two assumptions: (i) that the regulator can set the standard at an adequate level, and that (ii) the regulator can monitor compliance. A third assumption is that the regulator is able and willing to impose a penalty. Property rights-based approaches are often applied to problems of the commons, where some pollution or environmental damage is acceptable. The claimed advantage is cost-efficiency and effectiveness. They have disadvantages: they rely upon private monitoring of rights, do not effectively value non-market uses of environmental goods, raise issues of distributive justice, and generally depend partly upon regulatory frameworks. Price-based instruments (e.g. taxation) can offer cost-effectiveness and efficiency, but are argued not to be as effective as property rights-based instruments, and are often politically contested. Financial incentives can encourage with economic benefits desired behaviours, but have disadvantages including regulatory capture, perversity incentives, economic distortion, and they may encourage damaging activities, or reduce desirable incentives. Information instruments can be useful either stand-alone or in combination with other approaches. However, they risk ineffectiveness, particularly if the culture is hostile to environment protection. There is no perfect instrument. It is often considered that combinations of instruments are necessary to ensure an effective response to an environmental challenge. The right combination of instruments will depend on the specific case, requiring careful analysis of the socioeconomic context.

[3] There is an established literature on instrument choice in environmental law. See Salzman (2013). On the effectiveness of combinations of instruments, see Faure (2012) 293–336.

[4] Dovers (2005).

[5] Holder and McGillivray (2007) 127.

purpose in improved environmental status).[6] While several disciplines offer evaluation tools, including policy evaluation, evaluation theory and logic modelling, the evaluation of environmental policy effectiveness is challenging because of the difficulties in establishing a causal link between policies and effects, gaps in data, and because of the unavoidable political dimension of the exercise.

As important as asking whether an instrument is effective, is the question about why it is (not) effective. Already some time ago, Allot[7] suggested that the effectiveness of law depends on its capacity to persuade society to comply, rather than on its binding nature or the enforcement mechanisms utilized. He argues that people comply for reasons including: (1) a sense of (moral or ethical) duty; (2) a feeling that there is no alternative to compliance; and (3) risk-weighted cost-benefit analysis. He then suggests possible reasons for the lack of effectiveness of law: (1) inability of the law to convey persuasive messages and the limited effort in monitoring and evaluation; (2) conflict between the aims of the legislator and of society (for instance where the legislator does not act upon the motivations of citizens); (3) the volume of laws, which affects the capacity of society to understand and act upon them; and (4) the lack of proper monitoring of compliance, perhaps due to lack of resources and/or of willingness. These reasons may lead citizens to conclude that laws have no ethical or moral force and/or cannot be enforced, and/or not present credible threats.

A further element in explaining the (lack of) effectiveness has to do with the issue of the scale of the environmental problem and of the societal change that is needed to deal with it. When the scale is huge and/or social behaviours are entrenched, social transformations are needed, which, according to Allot, are better achieved through 'model' laws rather than through 'programmatic' laws. Model laws offer good reasons for behavioural changes, while programmatic laws seek change by a 'vision' to be achieved through law.

Thus, the effectiveness of environmental instruments mixes adopted through legislation arguably depends – from the perspective of those affected by it – on: (1) the conviction of their ethical and moral worth; (2) conviction about the inevitability of compliance; and (3) the perception of a net benefit (economic, reputational or otherwise). The three justifications can and often will occur jointly. While one may be enough

---

[6] This is indeed the definition adopted in the Millenium Ecosystem Assessments. See United Nations Environment Programme (2005).

[7] Allot (1981) 229–42.

to tilt the balance, compliance will always be more compelling when the three are combined.

With this conceptual framework I now turn to the issue of ship-source pollution control in Spain, and whether it can be considered to be effective.

3. THE PROBLEM

Maritime pollution is an important problem particularly in areas with high concentrations of population and economy activity, such as seas adjacent to the European Union. According to the European Commission, marine ecosystems face increasing pressure from human activities both on land and at sea. Forty-one per cent of the European population live in coastal regions and economic activities depending on the marine environment are growing.[8] Member States confirm that European Seas do not enjoy good environmental status. One reason is pollution. While pollution in the marine environment has decreased in some places, levels of nutrients and certain hazardous substances are overall still above acceptable limits. Oxygen depletion is particularly serious in the Baltic and Black seas. Marine litter, mostly plastic, is a growing issue. For instance, in the North Sea over 90 per cent of Fulmar sea birds have plastic in their stomach. On average 712 items of litter are found on a 100m stretch of beach on the Atlantic Coast. The Commission concludes that more efforts need to be made to meet the 2020 objective of reaching good environmental status. One source is pollution from ships. While the sinking of the *Prestige* in November 2002, and of the *Erika* in December 1999 are dramatic examples demonstrating the need for more effective control of ship-source pollution, accidents are not the main source of pollution. Rather, the key sources are, among others, shipping, port activities, aquaculture and offshore oil exploration.[9] The EU has in the last few years incorporated into domestic law the relevant international law.[10]

---

[8] European Commission (2014).

[9] European Environment Agency (2014) 16.

[10] These rules incorporate into Community law the 1973 International Convention on the Prevention of Pollution from Ships and its 1978 Protocol (Marpol Convention 73/78). This will make it possible to harmonise application of this convention.

3.1 The Instrumental Framework for Ship-source Pollution in the European Union

Given the slow progress in curbing environmental pollution in general and ship-source pollution in particular, as well as the perceived lack of effectiveness of prohibitions on discharges and administrative sanctions, the EU has recently added criminal sanctions for environmental damage, including ship-source pollution, to the instrument mix. Two important directives on environmental criminal law (Directive 2008/99/EC)[11] and on ship source pollution (Directive 2005/35/EC),[12] have been adopted by member states. The premise of this legislation is that sometimes criminal sanctions are more effective than administrative sanctions.

Directive 2009/123/EC[13] was adopted on 21 October 2009 to strengthen the criminal law under Directive 2005/35/EC on ship source pollution and penalties for infringements. Directive 2009/123/EC amended Directive 2005/35/EC, obliging member states to provide that certain ship-source discharges of polluting substances into specific areas are to be considered criminal offences if committed with 'intent, recklessly or with serious negligence and result in serious deterioration of the quality of the water'. The Directive considers that repeated minor cases that collectively result in the deterioration of the quality of water must be regarded as criminal offences if committed with intent, recklessly or with serious negligence. Criminal sanctions can be imposed both on natural and legal persons.[14] The Directive makes it clear that inciting or aiding and abetting such criminal offences may also be punishable as a criminal offence. It also widened Directive 2005/35/EC by obliging member states

---

[11] Directive 2008/99/EC of the European Parliament and of the Council of 19 November 2008 on the protection of the environment through criminal law, [2008] OJ L 328.

[12] Directive 2005/35/EC of the European Parliament and of the Council of 7 September 2005 on ship-source pollution and on the introduction of penalties for infringements, [2005] OJ L 255.

[13] Directive 2009/123/EC of the European Parliament and of the Council of 21 October 2009 amending Directive 2005/35/EC on ship-source pollution and on the introduction of penalties for infringements, [2009] OJ L 280/52.

[14] Pursuant to Article 8(b) of Directive 2005/35/EC amended by Directive 2009/123/EC, member states are required to take measures to ensure that legal persons can be liable for criminal offences committed for their benefit by any natural person either individually or as part of an organ of the legal person, who has authority within the structure of the legal person. Each member state must ensure that a legal person can be held liable where lack of supervision or control by a natural person enables a criminal offence. Liability will not exclude criminal

to introduce 'effective, proportionate and dissuasive sanctions for criminal offences related to ship-source pollution.[15]

3.2 The Legal Framework in Spain

Spain is a decentralised state, composed of 17 Autonomous Regions. The division of powers between the federal level and the regions is determined in Articles 148 and 149 of the Constitution, though ambiguities remain. Concerning maritime pollution, the capacity of the Autonomous Regions is limited. Under Article 114 of the Coastal Act (Law 22/1998, of 28 July), their competence is circumscribed to the territorial ambit, excluding the territorial sea and internal waters. They can regulate maritime transport within the Autonomous Region, the implementation of national law regarding safety and rescue at sea, and the legislation regarding non-commercial ports and ports not of national interest. Autonomous regions, if they have developed these competences in their Statutes of Autonomy, are able to exercise powers in relation to pollution control. They must cooperate with the Maritime Authorities and the Directorate General for Merchant Shipping (DGMS).

The transposition of Directive 2005/35/EC did not require extensive developments to Spanish domestic law, aside from changes to the Spanish Criminal Code through Organic Law 5/2010, and the adoption of Royal Decree (RD) 394/2007 to transpose Articles 3 and 7 of Directive 2005/35/EC.[16]

---

proceedings against perpetrators, inciters or accessories. Article 8 requires member states to ensure that effective, proportionate and dissuasive sanctions are applied.

[15] The deadline for implementation of the Directive was 16 November 2010.

[16] The other elements of Directive 2005/35/EC were accounted for in national legislation by provisions of domestic law and international law.

> Royal Legislative Decree 2/2011, of 5 September, approving the consolidated version of the Law of State ports and the Merchant Navy, Official Journal N.253 of 20 October 2011 (RDL 2/2011); Royal Decree 1737/2010, of 23 December, adopting the regulation that deals with the inspections of foreign ships in Spanish ports, Official Journal N.317 of 30 December 2010 (RD 1737/2010); Organic Law 5/2010, of 22 June, amending Organic Law 10/1995, of 23 November, (the Spanish Criminal Code) (SCC); Royal Decree 394/2007, of 31 March, on measures dealing with ships in transit that perform polluting discharges in Spanish waters, Official Journal N.81, of 4 April 2007 (RD 394/2007); Royal Decree 1398/1993, of 4 August, adopting the regulation on the procedure to exercise sanctioning powers, Official Journal N.189 of 09/08/1993 (RD 1398/1993); Law 30/1992, of 26 November, on the legal regime of the public administration and the common administrative procedure

For the Criminal Code the transposition of Directive 2009/123/EC[17] only required a small amendment to Article 325 – which contains the basic provision on environmental crimes – making an explicit reference to criminal acts committed on the high seas. Article 325 SCC establishes as criminal activities actions that 'cause or directly or indirectly perform emissions, discharges, radiations, extractions or excavations, landfills, noise, vibration, injection, deposit, in the atmosphere, soil, subsoil or ground water, ground or sea, including the sea, with incidence even in border areas and water catchments that might seriously impair the balance of natural systems'.

RDL 2/2011 confers powers over merchant shipping (including navigational and human safety in the sea and pollution prevention and control) to the Ministry of Public Infrastructure. Article 263 provides a role for the Ministry in fighting pollution, conducted through the DGMS and a Public Company, SASEMAR (Society for Sea Rescue and Maritime Security). Article 267 RDL 2/2011 grants SASEMAR authority over search and rescue, controlling and aiding shipping and environmental protection. Article 264 RDL 2/2011 requires that public authorities must collaborate. Maritime Authorities have been created for each port with responsibility for maritime protection.

(LAPPAC); Ratification instrument of 22 June 184, of 1978 Protocol relative to the International Convention for the Prevention of Ship Pollution 1973, signed in London on 17 February 1978 (Official Journal N.249 of 17 October 1984 (MARPOL73/78 Ratification Instrument); 2004 Amendments to the Ratification Instrument of 22 June 1984 (MARPOL 73/78), adopted on 15 October 2004, through Resolution MEPC 117(52), Official Journal No. 38, 13 February 2007; 2004 Amendments to the Ratification Instrument of 22 June 1984 (MARPOL73/78), adopted on 15 October 2004, through Resolution MEPC 118(52), Official Journal No.38 of 13 February 2007 (The latest amendments to MARPOL73/78 published in the Official Journal are from 26 March 2010); and Spanish Civil Code, Official Journal N.206 of 25 July 1889, last amended on 22 July 2011.

Directive 2009/123/EC was transposed by Organic Law 5/2010, published before the deadline for transposition of the directive. Full implementation took place 36 days after the deadline. The following bodies are involved in ship-source pollution: Directorate General for Merchant Shipping (Dirección General de la Marina Mercante), DGMS; Society for Sea Rescue and Maritime Security (Sociedad de Salvamento y Seguridad Marítima), SASEMAR; (Maritime Authorities (Capitanías Marítimas; Guardia Civil (a military body; The National Commission of Sea Rescue (Comisión Nacional de Salvamento Marítimo).

[17] Ministry of Justice through Organic Law 5/2010 amending the SCC.

SASEMAR monitors the territorial waters of Spain through means including planes, for polluting activities. Once a potential instance is detected, SASEMAR will inform the Maritime Authority of the nearest port. The Maritime Authority is empowered to decide whether to request the ship to enter into port for inspections. If sufficient evidence is gathered, SASEMAR will inform the Directorate General of Merchant Shipping, which may decide on administrative proceedings. If the DGMS considers that the pollution may constitute an environmental crime, it will inform the State prosecutor (Ministerio Fiscal). As noted in section 3, the instrument mix for ship-source contains four instruments: (1) a prohibition to discharge pollution; (2) criminal sanctions; (3) administrative sanctions; (4) a pollution treatment charge.

3.3 Sanctions

Directive 2005/35 Article 3 prohibits pollutant discharges in certain areas if committed with intent, recklessly or with serious negligence. Under some conditions they are to be regarded as criminal offences.

Criminal sanctions for environmental crimes are considerable in Spain. Article 325 of the SCC establishes a penalty of imprisonment for a period from two to five years, as well as fines. Fines can be very high. To illustrate, the minimum sanction applicable is €480 and the maximum €288,000. The minimum wage in Spain is €641.40 per month, so even the lowest possible fine alone almost equals the minimum wage. On top of that, there is the option of imposing a prohibition to carry out a profession or occupation for between one to three years for a variety of acts that may seriously impair natural systems. The higher the risk of serious damage to people, the longer the length of imprisonment. The penalties can be modulated taking into account aggravating (Articles 326 and 330 SCC) or mitigating factors (Article 331 SCC).

Article 312 RDL 2/2011 deals with administrative sanctions upon natural or legal persons. For serious violation, the penalty is a fine up to €601,000 for marine pollution. For a very serious offence, the penalty is a fine up to €3,005,000. In the event of offences from the accumulation of misdemeanours, prior to the deadline for prescription, the fine shall be the sum of the fines for each. For very serious infringements the authorities can detain the vessel or impede its entry or loading and unloading operations in addition to the applicable sanction.

Last but not least, ports impose a MARPOL charge on ships to treat their waste. Under section 5 RDL 2/2011 (Article 132) this is based on the size of the ship, and is payable regardless of whether a ship discharges, the number of times it does so or volume of waste.

4. THE EFFECTIVENESS OF THE MIX: INITIAL CONSIDERATIONS

As suggested above, the effectiveness of instrument mixes depends on a number of factors. This section will start with a legal appraisal of effectiveness, while the next one will make several fact-based considerations.

4.1 Criminal Sanctions

In theory, the effectiveness of sanctions depends on their ability to dissuade potential tortfeasors. That partly depends on the one hand on the probability of detection and conviction and on the size of the penalty (including its capacity to reflect the damage to society and the benefits achieved by the author, and on the other on the proportionality between the penalty and the severity of the breach.

The sanctions by the SCC are widely perceived to be high, more so after the transposition of the Directive. Imprisonment is always contemplated. Fines can be very high, and are coupled with a prohibition to carry out a profession. Moreover, the principle of proportionality seems to have been adequately taken into account by the SCC. Distinctions are made between endangerment, harm, and damage; between intent and recklessness, and mitigating and aggravating circumstances. Proportionality is ensured by a gradation of the sanction on the basis of the degree of endangerment and by the possibility to attenuate through voluntary reparation. The SCC makes it clear that whenever the act results in the loss of human life, the sanctions for environmental harm will be applied without prejudice to the sanctions applicable to the human impacts. Loss of human life as a result of environmental crime is considered to be death by serious negligence, and incurs imprisonment of between one and four years (Article 142 SCC). From this description it follows that the remaining issue to appraise the effectiveness of sanctions has to do with the probability of detection. This issue will be discussed in section 8 below.

4.2 Administrative Sanctions

As with criminal law, the effectiveness of administrative penalties relies on their ability to dissuade tortfeasors, which depends on the same factors applying to criminal sanctions. Article 312 RDL 2/2011 deals with administrative sanctions, applicable to natural and legal persons.

With serious violations the fine can reach a maximum of 600,001 euros, and for very serious offences 3 million euros. For serious or very serious offences caused by repeated misdemeanours, the fine is calculated by adding up the individual fines. Moreover, and in case of very serious offences, the authorities can decide either to detain the vessel or impede its entry into port or its loading and unloading operations, on top of the applicable sanction. In conclusion, while administrative sanctions are high and yet respect the principle of proportionality, the key missing element is the degree of their enforcement, which will be discussed in section 5.

4.3 Charges

A charge will be effective if it changes the incentives that operators have to discharge waste into the sea. If operators prefer to pay the charge rather than throw the waste overboard, then the charge can be considered to be effective. Effectiveness depends thus on a rational cost-benefit analysis that compares the expected damage arising from the sanction (calculated as the probability of detection multiplied by the penalty) with the savings accrued if the waste is discharged overboard. So it is not possible to say much from a theoretical perspective in the absence of some empirical evidence.

5. EFFECTIVENESS OF THE INSTRUMENT MIX: EMPIRICAL ISSUES

Of course, it is one thing to discuss the effectiveness of the law on the books and quite another to examine its effectiveness on the ground. To recap, the degree of effectiveness of law depends on a number of issues, including the capacity and willingness to enforce it, the capacity and willingness to assess its effectiveness and to make changes if necessary, the moral and ethical views of the regulated, the perception they have about the effectiveness of the law, and the outcome of a rational cost-benefit analysis confronting costs of compliance vis-à-vis benefits of non-compliance. This section will examine some evidence in order to cast light on the effectiveness of the current legal framework for ship-source pollution. It will start by looking at the issue from the perspective of the regulators and enforcement authorities (5.1) and then will look at it from the perspective of the regulated.

5.1 Effectiveness from the Perspective of Regulators and Enforcement Authorities

5.1.1 The capacity to investigate and enforce

As mentioned, RDL 2/2011 confers competence for merchant shipping (on the Ministry of Public Works working through the DGMS and SASEMAR. Under Directive 2009/123/EC (Article 268 RDL 2/2011) SASEMAR is to monitor polluting activities within the territorial waters of Spain. It has 11 helicopters and five planes[18] placed on the Spanish coast. The staff is supported by the Centre for Maritime Safety *Jovellanos*, with technical education. Aerial surveillance is interrelated with CleanSeaNet and SafeSeaNet from EMSA, and the monitoring service LRIT (long-range identification tracking).

Article 264 RDL 2/2011 requires that all the competent public authorities with competence to deliver these tasks must, in accordance with the principle of cooperation, do so through the corresponding plans and programmes. SASEMAR is supported by authorities with capacity to monitor spills in the sea. Agreements have been signed with national public authorities such as the police, the *Guardia Civil*, fishing authorities, customs authorities, and with neighbouring countries, EMSA and other international fora (REMPEC, IMO, etc). In addition, Article 264 RDL 2/2011 established the National Commission of Sea Rescue, regulated through RD 1217/2002 as amended by RD 765/2010, to facilitate cooperation of public authorities.

Article 266 RD 2/2011 establishes the Maritime Authorities (*Capitanías Marítimas*) for each port that has a certain intensity of navigational load, or for reasons of shipping traffic, safety, or maritime protection. Each Authority has authority within the port, including authorisations to ships to enter into the port, where anchoring is permitted, prohibition to sail through or anchor in certain areas, *inter alia*, for environmental reasons, the inspection of Spanish ships, and foreign ships where this is authorised by conventions, and all functions necessary for its tasks, including controlling environmental pollution.

Article 265 establishes the Permanent Commission for the investigation of maritime incidents and accidents within the Ministry of Public Infrastructure. It is authorised to inspect the technical aspects of incidents and accidents (excluding the allocation of responsibility or fault). It is

[18] For more details, see the Plan Nacional de Seguridad y Salvamento Marítimo 2010/2018, 32.

independent from the Maritime and any other authority where conflicts of interest may arise.

In addition to setting up the institutional and governance architecture, Article 264.2 RDL 2/2011 creates the National Plan on addressing the safety of human life in the sea and maritime pollution. The plan has the following basic objectives:

- to coordinate the activities of all the different actors that are capable of contributing to the goals of the plan, whether they are of a public or private nature;
- to implement a system to serve maritime shipping that covers the entire coast of Spain;
- to further develop the existing means for rescue operations and environmental protection;
- to establish a capacity building plan for all the human resources engaged in the tasks enumerated in the plan.

The latest plan, valid to 2018, aims to strengthen preventive strategies, particularly in the most sensitive areas. It focuses on reinforcing aerial inspections, the use of the criminal procedures to sanction discharges, engaging with European and international monitoring and reporting systems, inspection of ships, fostering cooperation between relevant authorities and implementation of innovative technologies. The plan has four programmes: (1) preventive systems, which focuses, for example, on interlinkages between EMSA (CleanSeaNet), aerial surveillance, cooperation amongst authorities with aerial surveillance capacity, and criteria for the evaluation of risks; (2) response mechanisms, reinforcing the institutional structure to respond to accidents and incidents in the sea, and which involves the DGMS, SASEMAR, Maritime Authorities and coordination rescue centres (*Centros de Coordinación y Salvamento Marítimo*) across the Spanish coast; (3) cooperation among national and international authorities; and (4) research and innovation.

5.1.2 The practice of investigations and inspections

There are three ways in which potentially criminal conduct can come before the court: (1) a declaration by the police; (2) a complaint, named or anonymous; (3) pressing of charges. Articles 303 and 308 the Royal Decree of 14 September 1883, *Ley de Enjuiciamiento Criminal* (LPC) indicate other avenues through which the State Attorney and the judge may become aware of the criminal conduct (the press, private denouncement, anonymous communication, and so on). When the State Prosecutor has evidence to conclude that actions may be criminal, it is obliged to request the competent judge to start criminal proceedings. The law gives the right to the victim and anyone willing to do so (*action popularis*), to initiate criminal proceedings.

Once potential pollution is detected via surveillance or a complaint, SASEMAR informs the Maritime Authority of the nearest port, which then informs the DGMS. The DGMS can order inspection of the ship under Article 297 RDL 2/2011. RD 1737/2012, which regulates the inspections of foreign vessels is relevant here. Article 18 deals with denunciations of ships. DGMS decides whether a denunciation is well-founded. It can decide to order the ship's master to bring the ship into port, for more detailed inspections. If the evidence is not inadequate, or exclusively from aerial surveillance, the decision usually is not to force the ship to enter into port. Aerial inspections cannot establish with certainty the nature of the spill, nor prove a causal link with a specific ship. According to interviewees at DGMS, if evidence comes also from samples taken from the seawater, the DGMS will remain sceptical, and only if there is reasonable evidence about the existence of a causal link, shall the order to enter into port be given.

In order to gather sufficient evidence it is necessary to combine aerial surveillance with evidence from the sea (of requisite quality) and from the ship. There are discharges that are authorised by MARPOL, hence it is necessary to prove that the discharge is illegal. To prove that a certain discharge comes from a specific ship is difficult, due to the structure of ships, the number of tanks (which can run into the hundreds), and the many plausible explanations.

An important practice is that judges tend to accept plausible explanations to discard criminal proceedings. According to one interviewee, in over 90 per cent of cases it is not possible to prove a causal link. In Spain, judges and courts will not initiate criminal proceedings without the three types of evidence. For criminal proceedings it is necessary to send the evidence to the prosecutor, thus the ship has to wait in the port. Given the economic costs to the operator, prosecutors are reluctant to initiate the process. There are problems with the legal validity of evidence, because the plane pilots are not civil servants, and their testimony has less value than otherwise. There are also issues of non-standardisation of instrumentation, due to lack of EU-wide standards. As a result, defence lawyers routinely challenge the evidence, including in administrative proceedings. Another reason not to pursue sufficient evidence of the causal link is the economic cost of testing samples from the seawater and the ship. According to one interviewee, the cost of testing one sample by the laboratories of CEDEX/CESIC is around €100/hour, with each test lasting around five to six hours.

Depending on the number of samples the total costs could be significant. As a result, only the larger spills are sampled and tested.

Once the DGMM becomes aware of a discharge by a ship outside territorial waters, if the ship is due to enter a port of another EU member state, the DGMS is obliged under RD 394/2007 to cooperate with the competent Maritime Authority of that member state, in relation to inspections and enforcement. When the ship is sailing towards a port outside the EU, the DGMS must request the port to adopt the measures to deal with the discharge. If a discharge has taken place on the high seas and the ship enters a Spanish port, the DGMS is competent to inspect the ship and to decide whether to initiate administrative or criminal proceedings.

Provided that there is sufficient evidence of the causal link, then the DGMS will order the ship into port, and subject it to inspection, pursuant to Article 12 RD 1737/2012 and Annex I, Part II, sections 2A and 2B. It may decide to retain the ship in the port and start administrative proceedings. The DGMS is obliged to inform the State Prosecutor whenever there is evidence of a crime.

An illegal activity might also constitute an infringement of administrative law. To decide a breach of administrative environmental law or of criminal law, a key issue is the gravity of the danger to people and the environment.[19] According to the Supreme Court (Judgment of 1 April 2003), this is a normative issue for the judge, based on the composition, volume and duration of the polluting discharge on a given medium (water, air, or soil), the conditions of the medium receiving the discharge, and the potential impacts.

As a result of this vague criterion the DGMS and the State Prosecutor have an agreement on how to determine whether a specific case should be prosecuted initially through the administrative or through the criminal procedure. The key criteria must be as objective as possible, to simplify and accelerate the adoption of the decision. The criteria used are quantitative. Spills in the Mediterranean Sea located closer to 12 miles from the coast, of 2 km^2 or more, must be notified to the State Prosecutor. Spills further than 12 miles from the coast, must have a surface equal or larger than 3 km^2. For spills in the Atlantic Ocean, the State Prosecutor will be informed when the spill has a surface of at least 5 km^2 – if located closer than 12 miles from the coast – and at least 10 km^2 if located further than 12 miles from the coast. The rationale is

[19] Supreme Court of Spain, Judgment of 30 September 1998.

that spills above a certain size have the potential to cause serious environmental damage.

DGMS must inform the State prosecutor if a spill exceeds the threshold criteria on penalty of criminal sanctions (Article 408 SCC) but rarely do discharges lead to criminal proceedings. Administrative proceedings are the norm because these are more straightforward as proof that the causal link is not required. Once in port, the ship is subject to inspection (pursuant to RD 1737/2012). If irregularities are found (for example, in the oil log book, the navigation diary, or other documentation) or if there are discrepancies between registries a sanction is imposed automatically. The interviewees insisted that the DGMS's role is not to sanction, but to help ships comply. If plausible explanations are furnished, and if there is no gross negligence, administrative proceedings are generally not pursued.

According to Article 25 RD 1737/2010 the Ministry of Public Works must ensure that the arrival and departure of any ship at Spanish ports is notified quickly to the inspections database of the European Commission through 'SafeSeaNet' under Article 3 letter s) of Directive 2002/59/EC. Once that information is transferred the DGMS is exempt from supplying information under paragraph 1.2 and 2, letters a) and b) of Annex XV of DR 1737/2010.

Article 26 requires mechanisms for cooperation between the DGMS port authorities, the autonomous administration and any other agencies and companies involved, to ensure that the DGMS obtains:

(a) information notified in accordance with the arrival of ships into Spanish ports;
(b) information on ships that have not sent all the data required, Royal Decree 1381/2002 of 20 December on port reception facilities for ship-generated waste and cargo residues in Royal Decree 210/2004, of February 6, and Regulation (EC) no. 725/2004, where applicable;
(c) information on the ships which have proceeded to sea without complying with the provisions of Article 7 or 10 of Royal Decree 1381/2002 of 20 December;
(d) information concerning ships which have been denied access to the port or have been expelled for maritime security reasons;
(e) information on deficiencies in application of Article 24 dealing with reports by the inspectors of the Maritime Authorities.

Under Article 23 of RD 1737/2010, inspections must be carried out by qualified inspectors who have been approved by the Ministry of Public

Works. The 2010–2018 National Plan for Safety and Maritime Rescue establishes a plan to improve the technical capacity of inspectors. The Permanent Commission for the investigation of maritime incidents and accidents has a preventive and analytical role, determining the reasons for incidents and accidents and providing recommendations.

5.1.3 Willingness to enforce?

Surprisingly there have been no cases when a person, legal or natural, has been criminally penalised for maritime pollution. Thus it is difficult to assess empirically the performance of the penalties. According to a Spanish prosecutor interviewed, there have been, in the last ten years, four cases criminally prosecuted in relation to spills. One was closed by the prosecutor, while the other three are *sub-iudice* so information is not available. The reasons for a low level of prosecutions appear to be: (1) the culture in the Spanish legal system, where criminal proceedings in relation to environmental damage are used only in extraordinary circumstances; (2) the sceptical approach of the competent authorities (DGMS) towards the potential criminal nature of discharges; and (3) historically the State Prosecutor has been more focused on pursuing environmental crimes on land rather than on the sea.[20]

An important variable is the cooperation between the public authorities with knowledge of the potential criminal activity and the state attorney. The public authorities might be at the level of the autonomous regions, local authorities, the ombudsman, and the police forces. The annual report of the Prosecutor suggests that cooperation varies significantly across both the level of authority and issues. The report suggests that a closer cooperation between the state prosecutor and the competent authorities (in this case the maritime port authorities) would increase the dissuasive effect of criminal law. More cooperation would help detect possible crimes, which would facilitate the criminal proceedings and reduce feelings of impunity. The same prosecutor suggests that the transposition of the Directive will have the eventual effect of increasing criminal prosecutions. A recent agreement between the State prosecutor and the DGMM may lead to increased criminal proceedings.

In Spain, criminal law is a measure of last resort. The social impact of a conviction is considerable, and the mere fact of charges impacts on social status. This affects the willingness of prosecutors to press charges. There is also a widespread impression that some persons prefer to be

[20] Interviews with a member of DGMM and with a member of the office of the State Attorney.

charged under criminal rather than administrative provisions, with low changes of conviction due to stringent evidentiary requirements.[21]

One interviewee considered that the sanctions can be high whenever negligence is involved. Representatives in relevant authorities have indicated that whilst they possess statistical data regarding spills, administrative proceedings and penalties data are very poor – though improving – and only for use within public authorities. They expect that the quality of statistics will improve and it will ultimately be possible to share it more widely. Analysis of administrative sanctions and circumstantial evidence from the interviews suggest that administrative sanctions are indeed effective, proportionate and dissuasive. In spite of the lack of statistics, a sign of dissuasiveness and effectiveness is that the quality of the water within ports has improved steadily with declining spills. An interviewee suggests that it is rare that a ship that has made a serious discharge will avoid a sanction. This is because the Maritime Authorities start administrative proceedings as soon as they detect an irregularity, and are thorough in the MARPOL inspections. It is suggested that when the discharge is large, the operator usually pays the fine, as long as this is not too high. The interviewee suggests two main reasons: (1) the desire to avoid negative publicity; (2) conscience. If the fine is very substantial, potentially impacting the economic health of the operator, a challenge will probably follow. The higher administrative organ will review the administrative procedure. If it finds irregularities it will reverse the sanction. The tentative conclusion is that lower sanctions for serious offences are dissuasive. An interviewee suggested as additional evidence that in very few instances has the same operator/ship been sanctioned twice.

As mentioned above, the instrument mix also includes a charge. Interviewees suggested an element that has been effective is the MARPOL charge imposed on all ships to treat their waste. This charge, regulated in section 5 RDL 2/2011 (Article 132), is a fixed charge based on the size of the ship. It is payable regardless of whether a ship discharges, how often or the volume it discharges. Thus the incentive to discharge illegally in the seas has almost disappeared. From an economic perspective the charge might be criticised because it is not linked to economic capacity, activity or the risk, (and might be regarded as a subsidy to the largest polluters); however, it has had the virtue of effectively removing incentives for dumping, particularly for the most active operators.

---

21 Primo de Rivera (2007).

5.2 Effectiveness from the Perspective of the Regulated

Recalling the conceptual framework proposed above, there are three general reasons why actors comply with law: (1) (moral or ethical) duty; (2) rational calculation; (3) because there is no other identified alternative.

The limited evidence gathered in the preparation of this work and alluded to in the previous section supports the conclusion that the instrument mix is moderately effective. The reasons seem to match the theory put forward by Allot. First, actors that have been detected and sanctioned pay out the fines (as long they are not too high) partly out of a sense of having breached an ethical or moral duty. They only decide to challenge the sanction when it is so high that it threatens their viability. This suggests that they perceive the penalty as disproportionate – hence lacking moral force.

Second, actors that pay the charge and comply with the law prohibiting discharges do apply a rational calculation of costs and benefits. It makes economic sense to pay the (unavoidable) MARPOL charge and discharge pollution in the port.

Third, actors usually do not get sanctioned a second time. This might be a sign of an understanding of the harm done by their actions and of ethical aspects, and of acknowledgment that in most cases there is no other choice but to comply.

In sum, it would seem that law is moderately effective because it comports with a relatively widespread acceptance of the unethical nature of ship-source pollution, it is enforceable – at least through administrative sanctions – and provides an economic incentive to 'do the right thing'.

6. CONCLUDING REMARKS

Ship-source pollution is a serious problem that has merited the adoption, through law, of a mix of environmental policy instruments – a prohibition to discharge pollution into the sea, administrative and criminal sanctions, and a charge. The foregoing analysis has suggested that while the combination of instruments seems to be moderately effective (judged by the general improvement in the quality of water mainly at ports) environmental policy instruments working in isolation are less effective than when combined. For instance, while criminal sanctions should in theory be effective, in practice their impact seems to be limited. Not a single criminal case has ended in a sanction. This does not mean that criminal sanctions are not having a deterrent effect *ex ante*, which would be a sign of effectiveness. The interviews indicate that criminal law in Spain does have a real *ex ante* deterrence effect because of negative social consequences from criminal prosecution and conviction. There seems to be agreement amongst the interviewees that the transposition of Directive 2009/123/EC may over time lead to more criminal proceedings. But at the same time, it seems clear that the effectiveness of criminal sanctions on the whole might be limited because of the socio-cultural and economic setting in which they are being introduced. Criminal sanctioning is seen in Spain as a measure of last resort, mainly due to the crippling effects it may have on business activities. In addition, the costs of the proceedings can become prohibitive. Inspectors understand their work as supportive and educational, rather than punitive. Last but not least, administrative sanctions are easier to enforce because they are based on objective infringements rather than on proof of fault and causation. For all these reasons, criminal sanctions remain only a complement to administrative sanctions.

Since administrative sanctions are substantial and relatively easy to impose, they are rather effective. One interviewee affirmed that operators that discharge pollution and are caught will almost always pay the penalty as long as it is not too large, for two reasons: (i) the risk of negative publicity; and (ii) conscience. This double rationale suggests that persuasion is potentially a more effective instrument – in many cases – than criminal sanctions. However even administrative sanctions are not enough in themselves to reduce pollution, particularly because sanctions are an *ex-post* instrument. They require monitoring and enforcement with attendant costs, and can end up in tangled judicial cases particularly for serious offences. Given political, economic and cultural realities, other instruments are also needed. The MARPOL charge provides a direct incentive to ship operators to discharge their waste in port. While this might be considered as a subsidy for active operators, it has the highest potential for reducing illegal discharges. Even for the smaller operators the costs of discharging waste in the harbour are lower than the costs of discharging at sea if they are caught, providing a strong incentive not to discharge at sea.

Thus, at least for the case examined, an instrument mix that combines in the right proportion strict standards, financial incentives, persuasion and criminal sanctions can offer a very high level of effectiveness, even in the absence of perfect information and with high administrative costs. Such an instrument mix taps into the three issues that are required to ensure effectiveness of environmental law: (1) consistency with the perceived ethical or moral duties of the majority of actors; (2) the perception that in most cases compliance is unavoidable (because detection is easy and sanctioning automatic; (3) an economic incentive.

We return to the question posed in the introduction about the impact that the choice of environmental policy has on the effectiveness of environmental laws through which those instruments are implemented. The impact appears to be substantial, and much hinges on how the mix of instruments fits with prevailing ethical standards, while trying to modify them through persuasion, economic incentives, and for blatant violations, administrative and criminal sanctions. The precise right mix in all its technical details will depend on factors of an economic, social and cultural nature. Interventions should be designed with an eye to potential causes of ineffectiveness, including excessive complexity, detachment from the specific concerns of firms and citizens, and a mismatch between the obligations and the enforcement resources.

REFERENCES

Allot, A. (1981), 'The Effectiveness of Laws' 15(2) *Valparaiso University Law Review* 229–42.

Dovers, S. (2005), *Environment and Sustainability Policy: Creation, Implementation, Evaluation* (Sydney: Federation Press).

European Commission (2014), 'The first phase of implementation of the Marine Strategy Framework Directive (2008/56/EC) The European Commission's assessment and guidance', COM/2014/097 Final.

European Environment Agency (2014), *Our Seas, Our Future – moving towards a new understanding* (Luxembourg: Publications Office of the European Union) 16.

Faure, M. (2012), 'Effectiveness of Environmental Law: What does the evidence tell us?' 36(2) *William & Mary Environmental Law and Policy Review* 293–336.

Holder, J. and D. McGillivray (2007), *Taking Stock of Environmental Assessment: Law, Policy and Practice* (Abingdon: Routledge Cavendish) 127.

Primo de Rivera, B.L. (2007), 'La gran línea divisoria entre las sanciones administrativas y el delito ecológico', Noticias Jurídicas, accessed 2 April 2015 at http://noticias.juridicas.com/articulos/30-Derecho-Medioambiental/200702-22357 1214523365586.html.

Salzman, J. (2013), 'Teaching Policy Instrument Choice in Environmental Law: The Five "P's"' XXIII *Duke Environmental Law & Policy Forum* 363.

United Nations Environment Programme (2005), Millenium Ecosystem Assessment Full Report, Vol. 3: Policy Responses (Washington, DC: Island Press).

11. Implementing environmental law and collaborative governance

Cameron Holley and Andrew Lawson

1. INTRODUCTION

Traditionally, statutory regulation was viewed as the primary mechanism for achieving environmental and social change. Its uniform system and top down implementation was expected to engineer social and environmental change at every location.[1] However, this vision never constituted an entirely satisfactory empirical account of the realities of environmental governance, and there is significant variance in how communities and governments seek to resolve environmental challenges.[2] The last four decades have seen an expansion in environmental governance by non-state actors,[3] often in response to the perceived inefficiencies and limits of traditional legal regulation (that is, hierarchical government control, detailed and rigid state rules and judicial enforcement). While legal regulation has had some success in curbing point source pollution, it has fallen far short in addressing complex challenges such as biodiversity, water extraction and diffuse pollution from agriculture. To tackle these 'wicked problems', business, civil society and governments have developed a range of tools such as market instruments, voluntarism, self-regulation and (importantly for this chapter), collaboration.

While collaboration has a long history, only in the last two decades have collaborative natural resource approaches become an important instrument in the regulatory tool kit. Recognising that complex socio-ecological systems cannot be readily governed by a single actor (government), collaborative approaches to governance are distinctively

---

[1] Galanter (2011); von Benda-Beckmann (1989), 130–31.

[2] Galanter (2011).

[3] Braithwaite (2008), *Regulatory Capitalism: How It Works, Ideas for Making It Work Better* (Edward Elgar, 2008); Braithwaite (2005).

polycentric – the state no longer plays the central role in governance.[4] Non-state actors assume administrative, regulatory and implementing functions previously undertaken by the state. In its pure form (for example, self-governing communities) the state may not be explicitly involved at all.[5] Under such arrangements power is diffuse, and sanctions, in the absence of state or other regulatory mechanisms, involve shaming and other forms of informal social control.[6]

Although there is no single collaborative governance model, this approach is identified by a number of characteristics: cooperation, integration, participation, adaptation and often non-binding (or soft law) guidelines and agreements.[7] Examples of this approach are increasing across the globe, including Regional Natural Resource Management (RNRM) in Australia, the Delta Plan process in California, Audited Self Management (ASM) in New Zealand, and the Water Framework Directive in the European Union.

These and other collaborative governance (CG) 'experiments' have given rise to a range of important, but under-examined, regulatory design and implementation challenges. Despite a growing literature examining CG,[8] there is a lack of empirical evidence to connect governance theory with grounded practice to identify what works, when and how. This chapter draws on a comparative empirical examination of CG to provide insights on two implementation questions: What forms of government intervention and institutional design produce successful collaborative processes? And should we blend collaborative elements with traditional legal approaches, to better govern human impacts on the environment?

This chapter commences by canvassing the theoretical rationale and challenges of collaboration as an innovation in governance in Section 2. Section 3 then evaluates the implementation of two distinct collaborative natural resource governance programs developed in New Zealand and Australia, drawing on approximately 80 interviews. Section 4 identifies some conditions under which successful collaboration is likely. Section 5 concludes by identifying some important issues for future research.

---

4 Gunningham (2008) 12.

5 Ibid. Although note that the State may recognise the self-determination of the self-governing communities themselves. Ostrom (2010) 643.

6 Gunningham (2008) 12.

7 Holley, Gunningham and Shearing (2011); Lobel (2004) 343.

8 For example, see: Tan, Bowmer and Baldwin (2012); Holley (2012); McKay (2011).

2. COLLABORATIVE GOVERNANCE – RATIONALE, BENEFITS AND CHALLENGES

2.1 Rationale and Benefits – Heterogeneity, Place and Stewardship

Collaboration (like notions of partnerships and networks)[9] is a broad term defined in this chapter as a 'consensus' process, involving two or more parties reaching agreement to share power and pool knowledge and resources (for example, information, money, labour) to solve shared problems.[10]

Compared to traditional governance, collaborative approaches are arguably better suited to landscape heterogeneity. The 'environment' is a web of numerous interrelated landscape processes that vary spatially and temporally – some are micro-level, some operate far beyond a landholder's boundaries, some are relatively fast (plant growth or animal movement), and some are slow (soil organic matter accumulation, or population dynamics). Diverse landholders, on properties that differ in size and land use, manage a large collection of landscape elements – including soils, fields, trees and watercourses.[11] Traditional legal approaches are undiscriminating in the face of such heterogeneity and specificity:

> It is almost inconceivable that a rule prescribed in Washington [or Canberra, Brussels, Beijing, etc.] could have identified the precise mix of restoration measures that would provide the greatest conservation benefits on that particular patch of habitat, much less one that would simultaneously be economically feasible for the landowner.[12]

Accounting for a heterogeneous landscape and diverse land managers requires a governance system that adopts institutional solutions at the scale at which natural resource problems manifest themselves.[13] Such an approach is embraced by CG, which features a place-based focus (for

---

9 Axelrod (2007).
10 Karkkainen (2003); Gray (1989); Head (2005) 146.
11 Stobbelaar *et al.* (2009).
12 Karkkainen (2003) 977.
13 Stobbelaar *et al.* (2009) S176; Karkkainen (2004) 76; Arnold and Gunderson (2013).

example, region or catchment) and a problem-solving orientation involving broad participation of land managers and other relevant stakeholders, to develop and implement solutions cooperatively.[14]

In addition to CG's capacity to account for heterogeneity, it also has the ability to develop stewardship norms of sustainable behaviour.

In the academic literature on regulating behaviour, self-regulation by individuals is thought to be highly effective, sustaining behaviours over the long-term even in the face of adversity. External regulation (such as by governments using the threat of prosecution) can be powerful, but can also produce confounding motivations, such as resentment and evasion. Where external incentives are applied, those that *reinforce* intrinsic standards and internalised social norms are often considered more effective than those that *replace* internal motivations.[15]

Traditional sanctions have been demonstrated in laboratory and field experiments to sometimes 'crowd-out'[16] intrinsic motivation and trust.[17] The result theoretically is an unhealthy positive-feedback loop – the more externally directed drivers such as law that you have, the more you need, because intrinsic motivations are crowded-out further and further.

'Hard' law has been successful in controlling some socially unacceptable behaviours but these are only a small part of the behaviours that degrade natural resources.[18] Damage to natural resources is often the result of common, socially acceptable behaviours that give rise to perverse environmental outcomes. Over-consumption of natural resources is in part a response to marketing, and practices historically promoted by governments (for example, over-allocation of water). This context requires a change of the social norms of ordinary citizens, which regulation focused on deterrence is unlikely to achieve. Many citizens are predisposed to do what is right, but limited in their knowledge or economic capacity to do so, or labour under peer group pressure.[19]

CG approaches are thought to be more adept at changing behaviour by focusing on internalised norms, developed from social context and shared values. CG activates these norms by engaging landholders directly in decision-making and implementation of natural resource management, in partnership with government, scientists, NGOs and others. Through

---

[14] Freeman (1997) 22.

[15] Gardner and Stern (1996); McKenzie-Mohr (2011).

[16] Reeson and Tisdell (2008); Sidman (1989).

[17] Berg *et al.* (1995); Frey (1997); Gneezy and Rustichini (2000); Frey and Oberholzer-Gee (1997); Frey and Goette (1999).

[18] Martin and Gunningham (2011) 143.

[19] Ibid, 143.

collaborative decision-making and dialogue, a shared understanding of environmentally important norms can emerge. Furthermore, by engaging individual resource users in direct decision-making and implementation, CG helps to promote the sense of control essential for *self-efficacy* (an individual's belief that he or she can achieve certain goals). Self-efficacious individuals invest more effort in achieving goals (buy-in) and are less inclined to be waylaid by adversity.[20]

2.2 Challenges – Incentives, Transaction Costs and Relationships with other Policies

The success of a CG arrangement can be constrained by a range of challenges, including incentive structures, transaction costs and counter-productive relationships between CG and other policies.

CG arrangements are dependent on land managers having an incentive to participate. If the incentive does not inherently and patently emerge in the relationship (for example, through a significant market advantage for good land management), then it must be engineered into the design of the arrangement.[21] Policymakers have an important role in helping create adequate incentives.[22] Incentives for motivating behaviour have been categorised as positive and negative.[23] Positive incentives allocate exclusive benefits to participants, such as exemptions from statutory processes; recognition in the marketplace; technical assistance and financial incentives. Negative incentives include the threat of government intervention, adverse publicity, consumer pressure, and legal liability. Which of these incentives are effective and in what context remains an ongoing issue for policy-makers.

The transaction costs of collaboration – that is, the personal time, resources, and travel expenses associated with participating in the interactive process – can stymie efforts to cooperate to capture mutual gains.[24] While scholars have suggested various ways to offset transaction costs (for example, nested structures, funding) it is still unclear when and in what ways these approaches are effective in supporting collaboration in water and natural resource contexts.[25]

---

20 Bandura (1997) 483.
21 Morgenstern and Pizer (2007).
22 Gunningham and Sinclair (2002).
23 Moffet and Bregha (1998).
24 Margerum (2007).
25 Holley (2010).

The hard work of negotiating and co-creating well-designed collaborations can likewise be undone by governments incidentally devising other policies and funding programs that compete with CG. Duplication in governance obligations adds additional layers of complexity and counterproductive conflict or competition.[26] Given these concerns, scholars have begun to identify possible relationships between CG and traditional regulatory approaches, including positive ones such as 'default hybridity' (where both systems remain independent but interact in mutually supporting ways), and negative ones such as 'gap theory' (where the gap between law and collaboration inhibits mutual success).[27]

We return to consider these challenges, and whether CG delivers on purported benefits below by exploring case studies from New Zealand and Australia.[28]

---

[26] Rose (2011) 9.

[27] Trubek and Trubek (2006); Alexander (2009) 179–180.

[28] The chapter's research was partially funded by an Australian Research Council Discovery Early Career Researcher Award (DE140101216), a UNSW Law Research and Development Support Scheme, and a UNSW Faculty Research Grant Program. The chapter's findings are drawn from qualitative interviews conducted across Audited Self-Management (ASM) in New Zealand and Regional Natural Resource Management (RNRM) in Queensland. Some elements of these findings were developed and appeared in Holley (2012) and Holley (2015). ASM and RNRM were studied as a part of two broad research agendas: an ongoing study into collaborative approaches to water governance; and a study into collaborative natural resource management that spanned two research projects from 2005–2012. As with most social research, ethical and confidentiality requirements require the chapter to preserve the anonymity of specific interviewees, save for a general description of their stakeholder category. Interviewees were selected to capture some of the main forms of diversity across the types of stakeholders involved in the case studies (e.g. farmers, citizens, national, state, regional and local governments and non-government organisations). Twenty-eight interviews were conducted in the ASM cases during 2011–2012. The ASM cases were selected because, *inter alia*, they were some of the most 'information rich' examples of ASM in practice (that is, the more advanced pilots at the time of research). In RNRM, 57 interviewees were drawn from two regional bodies in Queensland. Both of these case studies were selected because they were information rich (e.g. groups that had substantially implemented their plan of action and faced some of the most difficult natural resource problems in the State, including rural, coastal and highly urbanised areas).

3. FINDINGS

3.1 Audited Self Management

In the Canterbury region of New Zealand the local government is known as Environment Canterbury (ECan) and has a long history of experimenting with CG approaches as a complement to its traditional regulatory role under the Resource Management Act 1991 (RMA).[29] In addition to the RMA, the Local Government Act 2002 (LGA) provides ECan with a direct mandate for CG experimentation, requiring ECan to achieve sustainable development (as defined by community outcomes) through government, industry and community collaboration. These can be used in tandem with the provisions for regulating sustainable management under the RMA.[30]

ASM involves farmers voluntarily coming together to form a collaborative group (typically a formal legal entity such as an irrigation collective) that self-manages its water use and environmental effects on the local water system.[31] Through this group, responsibilities for day-to-day water management and compliance are transferred to farmers under conditions agreed with ECan. These conditions include collaboratively setting water quantity and quality goals (in cooperation with NGOs) for their shared aquifer or catchment; real time telemetered data monitoring; management rules; third party audits of compliance; continuous monitoring, reflection and improvement; and reporting of performance to the regulator. Instead of traditional individual licence requirements and state monitoring of individual farmers, collaborative groups self-regulate their members and monitor activities themselves (self-management aspect), and report to the independent third party and the regulator (audit aspect).[32]

At the time of research a number of pilots of ASM were underway in Canterbury. Two of the more advanced sites were the focus of this study: ASM1, a small, local aquifer scale collaboration involving 12 farmers; and ASM2, with 200 irrigators and multiple surface and groundwater consents within a river catchment.

The fundamental challenge for these two cases was engaging with otherwise reluctant water users (who either do not accept that there is a

---

[29] Memon and Gleeson (1995); Gunningham (2002) 22.
[30] Local Government Act 2002, ss 10, 14, 76–81, 91, 92; Palmer (2004) 752–6; Jenkins (2007) 2.
[31] Irrigation NZ (2011) 3–4.
[32] Curtis and Heiler (2010).

need to improve water management or who viewed the effort involved as costly and antithetical to their economic self-interest). Two strategies were successfully employed by ECan to ensure that farmers agreed to cooperate in the two pilots.

The first was ECan's promotion of potential economic benefits that could arise from ASM, including bulk technology purchases by the group (providing savings to members) and greater flexibility to informally trade water amongst members (rather than through the cumbersome alternative approval process). While these benefits were important and welcomed by farmers, they were not sufficient on their own to motivate all relevant landholders to participate. In this case, ECan had recourse to a second tool, namely regulation. Most respondents suggested farmers engaged in ASM's to 'stave off regulation'[33] and avoid the procedures and potential penalties associated with the RMA.[34] As one farmer put it: 'we wanted to stop compliance officers coming in and trying to make an example of us'.[35]

Together, these incentives were sufficient to bring core groups of landholders to the table to negotiate a self-management scheme. As both pilots were based around existing irrigation schemes, participants also had a base level of pre-existing trust that made it easier to negotiate and collaborate.

Even so, progress toward an agreement was substantially slower in ASM2 than ASM1. The small scale and limited number of water users in ASM1 kept transaction costs low, resulting in a detailed agreement in less than a year. This was relatively quick compared to ASM2 where the challenge of 200-odd farming interests reaching agreement was greater. Even with in-kind support from ECan officers (for example, information provision and assistance with negotiation), it took over two years for ASM2 to reach even a loose, incomplete agreement, and no implementation has occurred to date.

One of the main implementation successes reported by ASM1 respondents was that farmers had genuinely collaborated to implement the agreement and manage the water amongst them. A key to this success

---

33 Interview NZ1, Government.

34 One particular benefit of ASM in the case study was the review and amalgamation of consent conditions applying to the scheme that farmers believed would ultimately reduce the costs and complexity of complying with the RMA. Other procedures/penalties under the RMA included ECan imposing monitoring obligations on consent holders and substantially increased penalties for breaches. See: Resource Management Act 1991, s 108(3)–(5).

35 Interview NZ8, Farmer.

was that the collaborative approach and its real time database leveraged peer pressure amongst the collective's water users to encourage compliance. As one farmer explained:

> Every member can go in and see what their neighbours are doing and if they go over their entitlements we get very angry … its absolute transparency. The system takes away the risk of abuse.[36]

However, the findings suggested that there were limits to ASM's collaborative norms and informal means of social control. Farmers reported that while they were not afraid to have 'hard' conversations with their neighbours, when it came to truly recalcitrant individuals,[37] they felt their control was limited: 'we aren't policeman, so we don't want to act too aggressively'.[38]

While these limits may undo a purely community driven scheme, the availability of threats of enforcement and loss of water consents under the RMA acted as a powerful incentive to ensure potentially recalcitrant farmers 'toed' the ASM line. As one government respondent explained:

> The RMA is regulating in the background, and while people are being cooperative and as helping as they can be, we have that ability to say 'okay we don't want to be your friend now'.[39]

After a year, the results of ASM1 seemed very promising. Government respondents reported substantial reductions in their monitoring and compliance costs:

> If we [the regulator] had gone and done the work of monitoring it would have cost 1000 hours of our time. Now with the collective group providing the data via telemetry it might only cost 50 hours.[40]

These savings reportedly enabled them to shift scarce resources to other pressing water issues.

---

[36] Interview NZ2, Farmer.

[37] Respondents suggested that such recalcitrant behaviour was likely to be a problem because: 'some farmers are rogues, if there's half a chance to get away with it they will try – my mate is rogue, he would get up in the middle of the night to open his gate and let the water flow' Interview NZ2, Farmer.

[38] Interview NZ3, Farmer.

[39] Interview NZ4, Government.

[40] Interview NZ1, Government.

While it is still too early to say whether ASM effected water efficiency or quality improvements, respondents reported greater buy-in into water management and stronger stewardships ethics. As one farmer explained:

> It's shifting minds away from complying with licenses or consents to encouraging ownership of the water, so it's no longer the government's water but it's our water, our group owns it and if an individual takes water he is taking our water.[41]

The findings suggest that ASM can foster successful collaborative approaches by engaging relevant stakeholders. This success was attributable to a number of key conditions, including ECan's in-kind support, the small scale and small population involved in ASM1, peer pressure, and the hybrid relationship between traditional regulation and ASM. However cooperation barriers posed by the larger and more complex ASM2 limited the success of ASM and appear to reduce its utility (at least in its current form) as a feasible solution applicable to a wide range of water problems.

3.2 Regional Natural Resource Management

The second and far more complex CG case study is concerned with a large scale RNRM program in Australia, which commenced in 2000, when the Australian Government, in partnership with the states, developed a regional and more strategic approach to natural resource management (NRM).[42] Almost $7 billion of investment has been delivered via 56 collaborative regional bodies across Australia, including 14 in Queensland, the focus of this chapter.[43]

In Queensland, regional bodies were initiated as community-based, incorporated, not-for-profit organisations, required to consult and work in partnership with their regional community, including community representative and local governments, to develop and implement RNRM

---

[41] Interview NZ7, Farmer.

[42] Over the last decade and half, this involved a number of key programs, including the National Action Plan for Salinity and Water Quality (NAP) in 2000/01, the Natural Heritage Trust program (NHT) in 2001/02, the Caring for Our Country in 2008 and the National Landcare Programme in 2014. See, for example: Commonwealth of Australia (2008); Natural Resource Management Ministerial Council (2002); and http://www.nrm.gov.au (accessed 3 April 2015).

[43] Robins and Dovers (2007).

planning documents with targets and actions, subject to government approval and accountability requirements.[44]

Compared to the ASM, RNRM seeks a far more ambitious approach to CG that includes: (i) Federal and State governments negotiating bilateral agreements that set policies and rules for regionally focused governance; (ii) State government agencies collaborating to support regional delivery and pursue a 'whole of government approach'[45] and (iii) local and regional government and non-government stakeholders negotiating and implementing actions to achieve regional and national priorities.[46]

The initial challenges and successes of RNRM bodies forming and developing regional plans have been documented in detail elsewhere.[47] Concern about natural resource management and the availability of monetary incentives led regional non-government stakeholders to successfully form regional bodies across most regions. Using government funding, these bodies spent thousands of hours consulting with local communities to develop a plan that set regionally tailored targets and actions (aligned with national priorities). These repeated interactions and consensus orientated negotiations – while not conflict free – helped build relationships, reduce mistrust and ensure buy-in on regional plans.

Building on this trust, the bodies used public funding to leverage contributions from farmers and other stakeholders in the delivery of education programs, on the ground actions (for example, re-vegetation) and monitoring. These actions have reportedly led to significant outcomes including important (albeit limited) rehabilitation of riparian zones and remnant vegetation.[48] Further, the data revealed significant behavioural change, including improved awareness and attitudes regarding natural resource management.[49] One respondent explained:

> When you talk to farmers now the difference in attitude compared with say 10 years ago, where you had the industry in total denial of any environmental

---

44 See for example: Commonwealth of Australia and State of Queensland (2001); Commonwealth of Australia and the State of Queensland (2004).

45 Interview 334, Regional Body Staff. See also https://www.dnrm.qld.gov.au/land/accessing-using-land/natural-resource-management/nrm-investment-program (accessed 10 April 2015).

46 Head (2005) 144.

47 For further see: Lane, Taylor and Robinson (2009); Robins and Kanowski (2011).

48 Interview 438, Regional Body.

49 Interview 434, Regional Body noting: 'I think they've raised the profile of environmental issues. I do think they've achieved that, which is great'.

> impact and now it's just completely the opposite, where they want to be part of the solution. So I think that's probably our main achievement.[50]

While these are positive achievements, collaborative implementation was limited in ways that constrained the success of RNRM and its achievement of significant improvements to natural resource conditions. Many challenges have been documented elsewhere,[51] but here we focus on three issues from the empirical research.

First was a lack of cooperation between State and Federal Governments. This arose in part from a lack of trust:[52]

> [the State] continues to blame the Federal Government and the Federal Government continues to blame the State Government.[53]

Compounding this challenge was the Federal Government's failure to include adequate financial incentives to encourage the State to meaningfully cooperate and share its power and resources with the Federal Government. As one respondent put it:

> [the Federal Government] think they've so much money to run this that the State will click and dance. Well it started to click and dance and then it decided well no, get nicked … there's not enough money … so you had a failed system to start off with.[54]

Second, respondents reported that lack of government investment was the main reason RNRM: (i) had failed to fully engage with farmers and key stakeholders in the regions (for example, due to a lack of funding to cover high transaction costs of collaborating across very large regions, some of which were over 100,000 square kilometres); and (ii) had yet to achieve any major improvements in natural resource conditions, due to underinvestment relative to the complexity of the challenges. As one RNRM stakeholder pointed out:

> I mean look on a comparative basis $200 million for saving the reef … the Queensland government spends that on one piece of road infrastructure when it's upgraded … so you just, you can't help but think that we still have a well, a fair path to travel.[55]

---

50 Interview 4312, Regional Body.
51 See for example: Lane, Taylor and Robinson (2009).
52 Interview 334, Regional Body.
53 Interview 442, Peak Industry Body.
54 Interview 3210, Science; Interview 323, Government Agency.
55 Interview 411, Government Agency.

Third and finally, the relationship between RNRM and traditional regulation was fragmented and there was a lack of integration between targets and actions contained in regional plans and the more conventional regulatory tools under State legislation (for example, the Vegetation Management Act 1999 (Qld)). The findings suggested State statutory instruments remained on parallel rather than integrated paths with RNRM.[56] As one respondent explained:

> The tension lies in this issue of statutory delivery tools that government has their hands on and the outcome that the community through the regional bodies want to achieve. That's where the jury is out in lots of ways and the partnership, the alliance, if you like, between regions and government legislation – they haven't achieved it yet.[57]

As other interviewees portrayed it, there was a disconnect between the State departments and their statutes, on the one hand, and the regions and their non-statutory plans on the other:

> There's no translation process of regional plans into the state-wide legislative program and in the end the governments are spending a lot of money on regional arrangements and if they aren't using the regional programs to actually guide government programs and activities, then there's a disconnect that is unhealthy … because public money … has been not efficiently utilised.[58]

This tendency for agencies to overlook RNRM plans appeared to stem from a perceived lack of legitimacy in the eyes of State agencies.[59] According to some State agency respondents, regional bodies were the 'poor cousins' of government and had dubious authority and weak capacities.[60] Although this view was not held by all State agencies, it was sufficiently widespread that one respondent suggested regional bodies 'almost existed in spite of Queensland agencies'.[61] This enmity and lack

---

[56] It is important to note that regional bodies were required to ensure the targets and actions within the regional plans were consistent with existing statutory processes. Even so, active State support in delivering on these targets still appeared to be lacking.

[57] Interview 323, Government Agency.

[58] Interview 421, Government Agency.

[59] Interview 421, Government Agency. Interview 411, Government Agency. See also Department of Natural Resource Management (2005) 7.

[60] Interview 323, Government Agency.

[61] Interview 421, Government Agency.

of State agency support for integration was confirmed by regional bodies: 'I've got a very low opinion on State Government involvement'.[62]

The fissure between RNRM and traditional statutory programs combined with the lack of funding and effective Federal-State cooperation, conspired against major improvements in natural resource conditions. One respondent bluntly summed up:

> I'd be hard pressed to say 'here's something that the regional body did that's really good, that's made a real positive difference to the environment'.[63]

4. DISCUSSION

The findings from ASM and RNRM confirm that collaboration can deliver some of its purported benefits. For example, ASM1 was successful in enabling ECan and land managers to come together at a local scale to foster strong self-regulatory norms, stewardship and buy-in to water management. Similarly RNRM facilitated a new web of regional cooperation[64] that promoted stewardship norms and delivered some regionally tailored solutions.

Nevertheless, achieving *successful* collaboration was far from easy. Realising collaboration is time and resource intensive, particularly for larger scales and numerous stakeholders. The success of RNRM was also qualified by difficulties in securing government cooperation, funding deficiencies, and fissures between its collaborative approach and traditional statutory programs.

What broader lessons can be gleaned? While there are inherent dangers in generalising from this type of research,[65] the findings suggest conditions may enhance the effectiveness of CG, including trust-building via negotiated decision-making; incentives to engender interest from stakeholders; sufficient government funding or in-kind support to offset transaction and implementation costs; and a commitment to achieving complementarity of approaches.

---

62 Interview 437, Regional Body.

63 Interview 421, Government Agency.

64 Karkkainen (2004).

65 In particular, the findings offer only a snapshot of these evolving processes. Time is, in fact, a vital issue from the perspective of successful collaborative approaches as many of the impacts of governance efforts are only experienced over the longer term. Sabel and Simon (2006); Holley and Gunningham (2011).

4.1 Building Trust

Building trust makes it easier for stakeholders to collaborate.[66] Trust-building through regular negotiations and consensus-oriented decision-making were vital to facilitate working relationships among non-government actors engaged in ASM and RNRM. Certainly, building trust will not always be easy.

Building trust is time consuming particularly in settings involving numerous individuals (as in ASM2) and it may be difficult where there is entrenched mistrust, as was the case between Federal and State governments in Australia. In such instances, other tools, such as incentives, may be needed to enhance a party's motivation to work cooperatively.

4.2 Incentives

The ASM case revealed that economic benefits are important to successful collaboration (as it was for encouraging farmers in ASM to engage in actions). Another significant incentive may be harnessing peer pressure, as the findings in ASM also confirmed.[67] However, even in small close-knit communities where such pressures may be expected to work most effectively, there were limits to the ability of stakeholders to convince recalcitrant peers to take action.

In such cases, government-backed incentives are likely to be needed. As in RNRM, these can take the form of federal funding programs. Such funding can be vital to engaging not only non-government actors, but also government actors (like State governments).[68] Yet, it is clear from the experience of State and Federal relations in RNRM that when incentives are used, they will need to be tailored to offer sufficient inducement.

In addition to positive incentives, negative incentives can also be employed to induce cooperation. This was evident in the form of the RMA, which was necessary to induce cooperation from a number of farmers in ASM. Such pressure (and the threat of legal action) seems to be an essential underpinning to 'softer' inducements: 'bargaining in the shadow of the law' is fundamentally important in many CG initiatives to induce reluctant stakeholders to collaborate.[69]

---

66 Stewart and Jones (2003).
67 Schlager (2004) 154–5.
68 Wondolleck and Yaffee (2000) 224.
69 Karkkainen (2004).

4.3 Funding Commensurate to Transaction Costs/Responsibilities

Many authors have suggested that sufficient support for collaborators to enable them to offset transaction costs and take meaningful action is vital to collaboration.[70] The findings support these claims. In both ASM2 and RNRM the costs of CG were high across the large number of interests and larger regional scales respectively. Such high costs slowed agreement, undermined successful engagement and constrained improvements to environmental conditions on the ground.[71] While government support and funding was provided, it was insufficient. The funding and in-kind support needed to be commensurate with the collaborative process and implementation tasks.

4.4 Fostering Complementarity

Returning to the 'gap' and 'default hybridity' concepts mentioned above, at a descriptive level, the ASM program appeared to best approximate 'default hybridity', relying heavily on the RMA's regulatory framework to induce farmers to take on the monitoring and management of their water use. Respondents reported that the RMA was sufficiently harsh to compel otherwise recalcitrant stakeholders to abide by ASM's collaborative rules, thus increasing the likelihood of environmental improvements.

To many, this finding and the success of hybrids will appear obvious, and in very broad terms, consistent with underlying principles of 'shadow of the law' and the regulatory pyramid.[72] However, such conclusions on the benefits that arise from hybridity (and how best to achieve them) remain important within the legal literature where CG is often seen as alternative rather than supplement to legal regulation.[73]

Unlike ASM there was little evidence of constructive hybridity in the RNRM. In Queensland, RNRM illustrated the gap thesis, which attests to the imperviousness of traditional legal rules, and to the existence of a gap between formal law and new collaborative forms of governing.[74] This gap stemmed from a lack of a 'whole of government' approach at the

---

70 For example: John (2005) 230–42.
71 Bonnell and Koontz (2007).
72 Ayres and Braithwaite (1992); Mnookin and Kornhauser (1979).
73 Blomgren-Bingham (2010); Holley and Gunningham (2011).
74 De Búrca and Scott (2006).

State level, and an enmity held by many State agencies towards community based regional arrangements. In the eyes of these State government actors, regional bodies lacked the skills, authority and legitimacy otherwise bestowed on agencies and legal regulation.

How to close this gap? One option may be to imbue cooperative approaches with legal backing to ensure a level of formal statutory legitimacy, and enhance the likelihood of regulatory agencies supporting such processes.[75]

Legal backing can, however, undo the benefits that collaborative community structures are meant to provide, namely flexibility and legitimacy with the community. Given this, an alternative may be to overcome agency resistance by using law to influence agency culture. As law and control remain the language of regulators, changing their culture may require governments to specifically legislate that each agency must collaborate.[76] This could also involve setting performance goals for regulators that are most likely to be achieved by facilitating CG. ECan embraced collaborative approaches, in part because it had a legislative foundation for CG under the LGA. Legislatures could also look to use the law to impose other incentives or default punishments such as reduction of funds, if regulators fail to engage constructively with CG.

5. CONCLUSION

It is increasingly important for environmental law scholars to account for the growing plurality of approaches to implementing legal and policy norms. Traditionally, lawyers have focused on direct regulation and the courts. However, this approach takes a restrictive view of actors, institutions and approaches in the environmental law sphere.[77] A robust understanding of environmental law will necessitate a broader view of how law and innovative forms of governance are implemented together in the same policy sphere.

This chapter has sought to contribute to these ends through an analysis of local ASM cases studies in New Zealand and more complex regional collaborative processes in Australia with insights into the successful implementation of collaborative approaches, namely the need for building trust, utilising regulatory and other incentives to motivate action,

---

75 Moore and Rockloff (2006).

76 Haines and Gurney (2003).

77 Wilkinson (2010) 715; Braithwaite (2005).

providing sufficient resourcing, and ensuring complementary relationships are developed between law and CG.

While the chapter has provided insights, it has also raised issues that require further inquiry. These include both descriptive and normative work on the implementation of CG with other forms of governance. This includes exploring default hybridity and CG's relationship with traditional hierarchical law.[78] For example, are there settings where default rules are politically or legally unfeasible?[79] If so, what other forms of social pressures can secure sustainable behaviours?[80] And moving beyond traditional law, when and how can CG productively interact with market-based instruments, which are increasingly used in natural resource and water contexts? To what extent do hybrid (collaboration, hierarchy and market) approaches to governance hold out the best hope for implementation? Or should hybrid solutions be abandoned in favour of other innovations that ensure democratic input and accountability?[81] Moreover, scholars could examine additional institutional examples of CG in practice to understand both the constructive and destructive roles that legal regulation may play in different contexts.[82]

REFERENCES

Alexander, L. (2009), 'Stakeholder Participation In New Governance: Lessons From Chicago's Public Housing Reform Experiment' 16 *Georgetown Journal on Poverty Law & Policy* 117.

Alexander, L. (2010), 'Reflections On Success And Failure In New Governance And The Role Of The Lawyer' *Wisconsin Law Review* 737.

Arnold, C. and L. Gunderson (2013), 'Adaptive Law and Resilience' (2013) 43 *Environmental Law Reporter* 10426.

Axelrod, R. (1984), *The Evolution of Cooperation* (New York: Basic Books 1984).

Ayres, I. and J. Braithwaite (1992), *Responsive Regulation: Transcending the Deregulation Debate* (Oxford: Oxford University Press).

Bandura, A. (1997), *Self-efficacy: The Exercise of Control* (London: WH Freeman and Company).

Berg, J. *et al.* (1995), 'Trust, Reciprocity, and Social History' 10 *Games and Economic Behavior* 122.

---

[78] Trubek and Trubek (2006).

[79] Lobel (2006) 269.

[80] Wilkinson (2010); Alexander (2010) 745–6; Gunningham, Kagan and Thornton (2003).

[81] Sabel and Simon (2006); Trubek and Trubek (2010).

[82] Trubek and Trubek (2006) 564; De Búrca and Scott (2006) 6–9.

Blomgren-Bingham, L. (2010), 'The Next Generation of Administrative Law: Building the Legal Infrastructure for Collaborative Governance' *Wisconsin Law Review* 297.

Bonnell, J. and T. Koontz (2007), 'Stumbling Forward: The Organizational Challenges of Building and Sustaining Collaborative Watershed Management' 20 *Society and Natural Resources* 153.

Braithwaite, J. (2005), 'Neoliberalism or Regulatory Capitalism' (2005) Occ. Paper 5 *Regulatory Institutions Network* 34.

Braithwaite, J. (2008), *Regulatory Capitalism: How It Works, Ideas for Making It Work Better* (Cheltenham, UK and Northampton, MA, USA: Edward Elgar).

Commonwealth of Australia (2008), *Our Vital Resources: A National Action Plan for Salinity and Water Quality* (Australian Government).

Commonwealth of Australia and State of Queensland (2001), *An Agreement between the Commonwealth of Australia and the State of Queensland for the Implementation of the Intergovernmental Agreement on a National Action Plan for Salinity and Water Quality.*

Commonwealth of Australia and the State of Queensland (2004), *Bilateral Agreement between the Commonwealth of Australia and the State of Queensland to Deliver the Natural Heritage Trust.*

Curtis, A. and T. Heiler (2010), 'Developing Audited Self-Management Systems' NZARM Conference, Christchurch.

De Búrca, G. and J. Scott (2006), 'Introduction: New Governance, Law and Constitutionalism' in G. De Búrca and J. Scott (eds), *Law and New Governance in the EU and the US* (Oxford: Hart Publishing).

Department of Natural Resource Management (2005), *Options for Future Community Engagement in Regional Natural Resource Management* (Queensland State Government).

Freeman, J. (1997), 'Collaborative Governance in the Administrative State' 45(1) (Oct) *UCLA Law Review* 1.

Frey, B. (1997), *Not Just for the Money: An Economic Theory of Personal Motivation* (Cheltenham, UK and Northampton, MA, /USA: Edward Elgar).

Frey, B. and L. Goette (1999), 'Does Pay Motivate Volunteers?' (1999) Institute for Empirical Research in Economics, Working Paper 7.

Frey, B. and Oberholzer-Gee, F. (1997), 'The Cost of Price Incentives: An Empirical Analysis of Motivation Crowding-out' 87 *American Economic Review* 746.

Galanter, M. (2011), 'Varieties of Variance in India's Legal System: Fractures and Fissures in the Great Pyramid' (Workshop on 'Legal Pluralism and Democracy: When Does Legal Pluralism enhance, when does it erode Legitimacy of and Trust in Democratic Institutions' at the International Institute for the Sociology of Law, Onati, 9–11 June).

Gardner, G. and P. Stern (1996), *Environmental Problems and Human Behavior* (Boston: Allyn and Bacon).

Gneezy, U. and A. Rustichini (2000), 'A Fine is a Price' 24 *Journal of Legal Studies* 1.

Gray, B. (1989), *Collaborating: Finding Common Ground for Multiparty Problems* (San Francisico: Jossey-Bass).

Gunningham, N. (2008), 'Innovative Governance and Regulatory Design: Managing Water Resources' (Landcare Research).

Gunningham, N., R. Kagan and D. Thornton (2003), *Shades of Green: Business, Regulation and Environment* (Redwood, CA: Stanford University Press).

Gunningham, N. and D. Sinclair (2002), 'Environmental Partnerships: Combining sustainability and commercial advantage in the agriculture sector' (*RIRDC*), accessed 3 April 2015 at https://rirdc.infoservices.com.au/items/02-004

Haines, F. and D. Gurney (2003), 'The Shadows of the Law: Contemporary Approaches to Regulation and the Problem Of Regulatory Conflict' 25(4) *Law & Policy* 353.

Head, B. (2005), 'Participation or Co-Governance? Challenges for Regional Natural Resource Management' in R. Eversole and J. Martin (eds), *Participation and Governance in Regional Development* (Farnham: Ashgate).

Holley, C. (2010), 'Removing the Thorn from New Governance's Side: Examining the Emergence of Collaboration in Practice & the Roles for Law, Nested Institutions & Trust' 40(7) *Environmental Law Reporter* 10656.

Holley, C., N. Gunningham and C. Shearing (2011), *The New Environmental Governance* (Abingdon: Earthscan).

Holley, C. and N. Gunningham (2011), 'Natural Resources, New Governance and Legal, Regulation: When Does Collaboration Work?' 24 *New Zealand Universities Law Review* 309.

Holley, C. (2012), 'Transboundary Environmental Governance, Collaboration and the Law: Empirical Insights from Water and Natural Resource Management in Inland Queensland, Australia', in R. Warner and S. Marsden (eds) *Transboundary Environmental Governance: Inland, Marine and Coastal Areas* (Farnham: Ashgate Publishing).

Holley, C. (2015), 'Crafting Collaborative Governance: Water Resources, The Delta Plan and Audited Self-Management' 45 *Environmental Law Reporter* 10324.

Irrigation NZ (2011), *Workshop Report Building Knowledge and Understanding of Audited Self-Management*, accessed 3 April 2015 at http://www.irrigationnz.co.nz/assets/Uploads/001-INZ-Audited-Self-Management-14-8-11.pdf.

Jenkins, B. (2007), 'Canterbury Strategic Water Study: Briefing Document to Canterbury Mayoral Forum' (ECan).

John, D. (2005), 'Civic Environmentalism' in R. Durant, D. Fiorino and R. O'Leary (eds) *Environmental Governance Reconsidered* (Cambridge, MA: MIT Press).

Karkkainen, B. (2003), 'Adaptive Ecosystem Management and Regulatory Penalty Defaults: Toward a Bounded Pragmatism' 87 *Minnesota Law Review* 943.

Karkkainen, B. (2004), 'Post Sovereign Environmental Governance' 4(1) *Global Environmental Politics* 72.

Lane, M., B. Taylor and C. Robinson (2009), 'Introduction: Contested Country – Regional Natural Resource Management in Australia' in M. Lane, C. Robinson and B. Taylor (eds), *Contested Country: Local and Regional Natural Resources Management in Australia* (Collingwood, Vic: CSIRO).

Lobel, O. (2004), 'The Renew Deal: The Fall of Regulation and the Rise of Governance in Contemporary Legal Thought' 89 *Minnesota Law Review* 342.

Lobel, O. (2006), 'Governing Occupational Safety in the United States' in G. De Búrca and J. Scott (eds), *Law and New Governance in the EU and the US* (Oxford: Hart Publishing).

Margerum, R. (2007), 'Overcoming Locally Based Collaboration Constraints', 20(2) *Society & Natural Resources* 135.

Martin, P. and N. Gunningham (2011), 'Leading Reform of Natural Resource Management Law: Core Principles' 28 *Environmental and Planning Law Journal* 137.

McKay, J. (2011), 'Australian Water Allocation Plans and the Sustainability Objective' 56(4) *Hydrological Sciences Journal* 615.

McKenzie-Mohr, D. (2011), *Fostering Sustainable Behavior: An Introduction to Community-Based Social Marketing* (Gabriola Island, BC: New Society Publishers).

Memon, P. and B. Gleeson (1995), 'Towards a New Planning Paradigm? Reflections on New Zealand's Resource Management Act' 22(1) *Environment and Planning B: Planning and Design* 109.

Mnookin, R. and L. Kornhauser (1979), 'Bargaining in the Shadow of the Law: The Case of Divorce' 88(5) *Yale Law Journal* 950.

Moffet, J. and F. Bregha (1998), 'An Overview of Issues with respect to Voluntary Environmental Agreements' 8(1) *Journal of Environmental Law and Practice* 63.

Moore, S.A. and S. Rockloff (2006), 'Organizing Regionally for Natural Resource Management in Australia: Reflections on Agency and Government' 8 *Journal of Environmental Policy and Planning* 259.

Morgenstern, R. and W. Pizer (2007), 'Concluding Observations: What Can We Learn from the Case Studies' in R. Morgenstern and W. Pizer (eds), *Reality Check – The Nature and Performance of Voluntary Environmental Programs in the United States, Europe, and Japan* (Washington, DC: Resources for the Future).

Natural Resource Management Ministerial Council (2002), *Framework for the Extension of the Natural Heritage Trust* (Australian Government).

Ostrom, E. (2010), 'Beyond Markets and States: Polycentric Governance of Complex Economic Systems' 100 *American Economic Review* 641.

Palmer, K. (2004), 'Local Government Law and Resource Management' *NZ Law Review* 751.

Reeson, A. and J. Tisdell (2008), 'Institutions, Motivations and Public Goods: An Experimental Test of Motivational Crowding' 68 *Journal of Economic Behavior & Organization* 273.

Rhodes, R. (2007), 'Understanding Governance: Ten Years On' 28 *Organization Studies* 1243.

Robins, L. and S. Dovers (2007), 'Community-based NRM Boards of Management: Are they up to the Task?' 14 *Australasian Journal of Environmental Management* 111.

Robins, L. and P. Kanowski (2011), '"Crying for our Country": Eight Ways in Which "Caring for our Country" has Undermined Australia's Regional Model for Natural Resource Management' 18(2) *Australasian Journal of Environmental Management* 88.

Rose, G. (2011), *Gaps in the Implementation of Environmental Law at the National, Regional and Global Level* (First Preparatory Meeting of the World Congress on Justice, Governance and Law for Environmental Sustainability, 12–13 October, UNEP).

Sabel, C. and W. Simon (2006), 'Accountability without Sovereignty' in G. De Búrca and J. Scott (eds), *Law and New Governance in the EU and the US* (Oxford: Hart Publishing).

Schlager, E. (2004), 'Common Pool Resource Theory' in R. Durant, D. Fiorino and R. O'Leary (eds), *Environmental Governance Reconsidered* (Cambridge, MA: MIT Press).

Sidman, M. (1989), *Coercion and its Fallout* (Authors Cooperative Inc).

Stewart, J. and G. Jones (2003), *Renegotiating the Environment: The Power of Politics* (Sydney: Federation Press).

Stobbelaar, D.J. *et al.* (2009), 'Internalization of Agri-environmental Policies and the Role of Institutions' 90 *Journal of Environmental Management* S175.
Tan, P., K. Bowmer and C. Baldwin (2012), 'Continued Challenges in the Policy and Legal Framework for Collaborative Water Planning' 474 *Journal of Hydrology* 84.
Trubek, D. and L. Trubek (2006), 'New Governance and Legal Regulation: Complementarity, Rivalry, and Transformation' 13 *Columbia Journal of European Law* 540.
Trubek, D. and L. Trubek (2010), 'The World Turned Upside Down: Reflections on New Governance and the Transformation of Law' Wis L Rev 719.
von Benda-Beckmann, F. (1989), 'Scape Goat and Magic Charm: Law in Development Theory and Practice' 28 *Journal of Legal Pluralism* 129.
Wilkinson, M. (2010), 'Three Conceptions Of Law: Towards A Jurisprudence Of Democratic Experimentalism' *Wisconsin Law Review* 673.
Wondolleck, J. and S. Yaffee (2000), *Making Collaboration Work: Lessons From Innovation in Natural Resource Management* (Washington, DC: Island Press).

12. Private environmental enforcement: using supply chain requirements to achieve better environmental outcomes

LeRoy Paddock and Molly Masterton[1]

1. INTRODUCTION

Complex, multi-level international supply chains are now an integral part of the world economy. For example, large retailers may purchase many of their products from companies in China, India or other countries where the cost of manufacturing is lower than in the retailer's home country. Similarly, automobile manufacturers today source parts from many countries rather than manufacturing the parts themselves or buying them from local parts manufacturers. As companies, especially in the United States and the European Union, have increasingly outsourced manufacturing or moved manufacturing offshore, these operations have become for the most part beyond the reach of national environmental laws.[2] The facilities may be located in countries that have either weak environmental laws or weak enforcement of environmental laws. National governments typically have little leverage over the extra-territorial operations of multinational companies.[3] Further, aspects of product manufacturing, including greenhouse gas emissions, energy use, and reuse or recycling design requirements, remain outside the regulatory system even in countries with sophisticated programs. Thus, as nations increasingly

---

[1] Portions of this chapter are derived from Paddock (2008) and Paddock (2012).

[2] Sutherland (2010) 302–3.

[3] Council Directive 2002/95/EC of 27 January 2003 on the restriction of the use of certain hazardous substances in electrical and electronic equipment [2003] OJ L 37/19 (commonly referred to as the Restriction of Hazardous Substances Directive or RoHS). See also, e.g., Minn. Stat. §§ 115A.1310–1330 (2012).

focus on sustainability as a societal goal, achieving better environmental outcomes is more and more dependent upon private regulatory and enforcement mechanisms to drive environmental conduct.

As products or parts are sourced from often distant locations, companies find that they need to focus on management of their supply chain to assure product quality and protect their reputation, among other concerns. These supply chain concerns also extend to environmental attributes of products or parts. Companies both local and multinational have used environmental supply chain requirements, also known as 'green' supply chain management (GSCM), for a number of reasons important to their economic decision making. GSCM can be considered a convergence of traditional supply chain management, defined broadly as the oversight of product life cycles throughout the supply chain from manufacturing and transport to use and end life, and newer developing systems for environmental management.[4] Not all environmental supply regimes, however, are the same. Some touch only 'first tier' suppliers while others go much deeper into the supply chain; some involve single companies and single products while others involve large collaborative efforts among industry groups; and some employ much more in-depth oversight mechanisms than others. It is therefore important to look beyond the fact that a company imposes supply chain environmental requirements to examine the nature and extent of those requirements.

This chapter explores this relatively new form of private environmental governance, which is likely to become a central element of international environmental regulation over the next several years. It first lays out some of the key governance concepts that demonstrate why private environmental supply chain requirements are so important in achieving sustainability-based outcomes. The chapter then turns to a description of the various types of supply chain management mechanisms, seen through the lens of several business models. These mechanisms rely heavily on traditional contract law but also incorporate familiar environmental management tools such as training, inspection and auditing to assure compliance with the supply chain requirements. Ultimately, the authors deduce that expanded use of green supply chain strategies will be best promoted if private actions are coordinated with actions taken by government entitites, using a hybrid approach that draws upon a number of traditional legal structures, including government compliance and

[4] For a general overview of green supply chain management and its origins, see Srivastava (2007) 53–4.

enforcement programs, use of transparent regulatory agendas and government procurement regulations. The chapter concludes by noting the need for additional research that will provide a more sophisticated understanding of which supply chain mechanisms can most effectively serve as private regulatory and enforcement mechanisms, complementing more traditional modes of environmental controls.

2. THE ROLE OF INTERNAL ECONOMIC DRIVERS AND SOCIETAL VALUES

In today's globalised economy, achieving the goal of sustainable development[5] requires new governance mechanisms that incorporate, but also reach well beyond, traditional regulatory programs. Several factors make new forms of environmental governance a necessity. These include: globalisation of the economy; outsourcing and offshoring of manufacturing; difficulty in regulating diffuse, smaller (but still significant) sources of pollution and environmental harm; and the political stalemate in the United States (at the federal level) and in other countries, which hampers the enactment of new environmental legislation. These new forms of governance cannot simply rely on regulation to drive behavior; instead they must incorporate economic and social behavioural drivers.[6]

Supply chain management implicates both internal corporate economic drivers and social norms. When a company makes a decision to exceed baseline environmental regulatory requirements or to incorporate sustainability into their planning, the decision might be viewed as resulting from organisational values or corporate social responsibility (CSR). While organisational values can have an impact on environmental behaviour, especially as manifested through senior managers who are committed to environmental performance or to the concept of sustainability, more often

---

[5] Bosselmann and Grinlinton (2002) viii, 2 observe:

> The notion of 'sustainability' is more than a catchy phrase for an improved environmental protection strategy. Many commentators have linked sustainability to fundamental concepts such as freedom, justice and equity. There is a widespread perception today that sustainability must inform future development of society in much the same way as freedom and equity informed its present development. Only a sustainable society, capable of working with nature, not against it, will have a chance of survival.

[6] For a more detailed discussion of economic and values-based environmental behavioral drivers see LeRoy Paddock (2008).

CSR is based upon underlying economic considerations that have changed significantly over the last decade.

These 'internal' economic drivers include: reputation; customer desires or requirements; investor pressure; operational risk; liability mitigation; the ability to attract and retain employees; insurance cost and availability; community license to operate; lender concerns or requirements; government and public relations; the ability to plan operations and anticipate or even shape future regulatory standards; access to markets; product differentiation; green procurement standards; industry codes of conduct; international environmental standards such as ISO 14000; and operational efficiency.[7] Internal economic drivers such as reputation and consumer demands are, of course, linked to societal values.[8] From an operational perspective, research has suggested that improved environmental practices may help a company to gain competitive advantage by reducing production inefficiencies, increasing brand loyalty, or even creating new markets with potential for significant revenue growth.[9]

Reputational value is a good illustration of the importance of these internal economic factors. Reputation, estimated to now account for 30 to 70 percent of a company's value, is one of the key drivers of environmental performance.[10] Environmental behaviour or misbehaviour can have a significant impact on reputation. For example, the BP Horizon oil spill and BP's earlier refinery explosion significantly eroded the firm's reputation[11] and even led to a boycott of its retail outlets.[12] Such an impact can occur as a result of environmental problems that occur along a firm's supply chain, leading companies to pay increasing attention to their supply chain as an aspect of reputation management. Studies have indicated that it can take four years for a company to recover its reputation following a reputation-damaging crisis.[13] Although not as tangible as a patent or a trademark, corporate reputation can create direct financial benefits, including enhanced brand value and better access to

---

7 See Paddock (2012) 10624–5.

8 Ibid.

9 Esty and Winston (2006) 13–14. GE provides the best example of this last reason. It launched 'Ecoimagination,' which among other things includes putting new green products on the market that are expected to generate $20 billion in revenues by 2010. See Eisner (2007) 574–5.

10 Burke, Martin and Cooper (2011).

11 See Mouawad and Schwartz (2010).

12 See Malik (2010).

13 Burke, Martin, and Cooper (2011) 4.

capital markets.[14] Thus, building a good reputation is an aspect of competitive advantage. As Esty and Winston observed, '[t]he logic of corporate environmental stewardship need not stem from a personal belief that caring for the natural world is the right thing to do. If critical stakeholders believe the environment matters, then it's the right thing to do *for your business*.'[15]

Community and customer concerns are also an important force to be reckoned with. In their research on the pulp and paper industry, Gunningham, Kagan and Thornton found firms were motivated to go beyond compliance because of pressures related to their 'social license to operate'.[16] Firms are so motivated because the social license can be enforced in very real ways such as enhancing or destroying a firm's reputation, putting pressure on regulators to more vigilantly enforce existing regulations, filing of citizen suits, lobbying for tighter regulations, and market pressures through, for example, boycotts.[17] The authors found that pulp and paper mill firms were generally highly motivated to stay ahead of environmental regulations so that they could remain in the public's good graces.[18]

Investor pressure can also play an important role in the way companies approach environmental issues. The engagement of the Nathan Cummings Foundation is a good example of this dynamic. The Nathan Cummings Foundation, which has supported environmental causes, in 2003 held 32,000 shares in Smithfield Foods.[19] Smithfield had been criticised for some of its agriculture and animal protection practices. The Foundation decided to exercise its proxy rights in an effort to encourage changes in some of these practices. Even though the resulting shareholder resolution filed by the Foundation did not come close to attracting a majority of votes, filing of the resolution led the company to negotiate with the Nathan Cummings Foundation about improvements that could be made in Smithfield's environmental performance.[20] Among the motivations for Smithfield to enter into the negotiations was maintaining its reputation among its key customers including McDonalds and Wal-Mart.[21] Supply chain requirements are a major issue for Smithfield in

14 See generally Black, Richardson and Carnes (2000).
15 Esty and Winston (2006) 13–14.
16 Gunningham, Kagan and Thornton (2004).
17 Ibid, 319–20.
18 Ibid.
19 Paddock (2009) 103.
20 Ibid, 104.
21 Ibid.

that all of its top twenty customers imposed some form of supply chain requirements.

The need and the ability to leverage economic and value-based motivations for environmental improvement as part of a governance system fundamentally alters the role of government and the private sector in environmental protection. As Marc Allen Eisner has noted:

> Future gains in environmental quality may be impossible without a fundamental reconsideration of regulatory design. This reconsideration must take the form of incorporating advances in corporate self-regulation, associational regulation, and standards into the regulatory system and thinking creatively about how public policies can be used to reinforce incentives or compensate for their absence.[22]

3. DEVELOPMENTS IN GREEN SUPPLY CHAIN MANAGEMENT

One of the critical economics-based environmental behavioural drivers today involves corporate management of business supply chains. While a given product's materials may have several intrinsic environmental impacts, the supply chain that brings the materials together to make up products creates further complexities, and it is more often than not responsible for the majority of negative externalities affecting the environment. The complex and indirect nature of these issues is what has led organisations such as Business for Social Responsibility to call upon companies to integrate sustainable practices into every aspect of their operations, creating 'a comprehensive set of policies, practices and programs that are integrated into business operations, supply chains and decision-making processes throughout the company.'[23]

Supply chain requirements are derived from a number of sources. They may include adoption of pre-existing certification programs such as the Forest Stewardship Council's Sustainable Forestry Initiative program,[24] the Marine Stewardship Council certification for sustainable fisheries,[25] or the German government Blue Angel program.[26] They may also be based on contract specifications or codes of conduct developed by an

---

22 Eisner (2007) 282.

23 Benoit and Vickery-Niederman (2011) 2.

24 See Sustainable Forestry Initiative, 'Getting Certified'.

25 See Marine Stewardship Council, 'MSC Standards and Certification Requirements'.

26 See Ecolabel Index, 'Blue Angel'.

individual company, by industry associations such as the Electronic Industry Citizenship Coalition (EICC)[27] or the Consumer Goods Forum,[28] or by international organisations such as the United Nations' Food and Agriculture Organization Code of Conduct for Responsible Fisheries.[29] Finally, supply chain requirements may be developed by individual companies or commercial sectors to address particular supply chain issues, or to address a broad set of environmental issues important to the company's bottom line.

A key study conducted by Professor Michael Vandenbergh found that:

> In some cases this new form of private governance transfers pressures created by public entities, but in many cases it bypasses public entities altogether, transferring demands for social amenities directly from the citizens of one country to the firms operating in another. This private governance exists as a network of private standards and agreements that influence the behavior of firms on issues sovereign states are unwilling or unable to address.[30]

Professor Vandenbergh then observed that:

> Of the seventy-four firms included in the study [of private supply chain contracting] across all eight sectors … 53 percent impose environmental supply-chain requirements. The extent of supply-chain contracting is even more impressive when examined from the perspective of total sales. Of the $2.8 trillion in total sales represented by the seventy-four firms in the study, firms that impose environmental supply-chain requirements account for $2.2 trillion, or more than 78 percent of the total.[31]

This chapter examines a particular strand of supply chain management, 'green supply chain management' or 'GSCM'. Samir Srivastava defines GSCM as 'integrating environmental thinking into supply chain management, including product design, material sourcing and selection, manufacturing the final product to the consumers, and end life'.[32] There exists no internationally accepted framework for measuring the environmental footprint of the supply chain, and GSCM can take many different forms and occur at various levels within the supply chain.

---

27 See Electronic Industry Citizenship Coalition, 'Code of Conduct'.

28 See Consumer Goods Forum, 'Sustainability'.

29 See Food and Agriculture Organisation of the United Nations, *Code of Conduct for Responsible Fisheries*.

30 Vandenbergh (2007).

31 Ibid, 926–36.

32 Srivastava (2007) 53.

A given supply chain may have six or more levels (with multiple corporate participants at all levels), including raw material, suppliers, manufacturers, retail and distribution, consumer use and waste[33] (as represented in Figure 12.1). Each of the links in the supply chain may present a different concern in the form of natural resources impacts, emissions, energy consumption, waste management, or other environmental issues. The essence of a GSCM approach is to identify the various 'links' in the chain where environmental issues arise, whether at the sourcing or manufacturing phases, during product use, or in the waste phase. Corresponding initiatives may include methods for placing pressure on suppliers and manufacturers and control systems for monitoring compliance throughout the supply chain.[34]

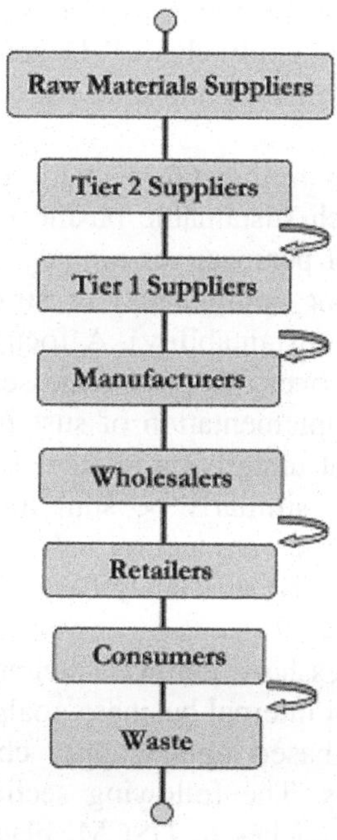

Figure 12.1 Levels of a supply chain

Figure 12.1 is a conceptualisation of a supply chain for consumer goods. Those approaches that focus on one 'level' of the chain, such as one tier

33 See Ho *et al.* (2009).
34 MVO Platform (2008) 2.

of suppliers, may be described as horizontal in nature, whereas approaches that seek to address externalities up and down the chain are vertical.

4. DEFINING STRATEGIES IN GREEN SUPPLY CHAIN MANAGEMENT

GSCM schemes may be thought of as a continuum which on one end relies primarily on third-party certification of environmental practices and environmental management systems, with deep engagement by a company with various tiers of suppliers at the other end. Businesses may fall within various places on global value chains, which can vary greatly in structure, pathways from raw material to consumer use, and coordination between members of the supply chain.[35] Depending on what a business's supply chain looks like from the outset, some goals may be more achievable than others.

According to the environmental mediation organisation RESOLVE, companies may approach sustainable business measures such as certification from a number of perspectives ranging from tactical risk management (aiming mostly for compliance) to strategic opportunity (driven more toward long-term sustainability). A focus on risk may evolve to a more strategic approach over time, as businesses realise tangible competitive advantages from implementation of sustainability measures.[36] Other experts have posited that underlying strategies of businesses that engage in GSCM practices can similarly be split into four categories, among which businesses combine strategies and evolve from one phase to another: (A) risk-based, (B) efficiency-based, (C) innovation-based and (D) closed loop strategies.[37]

Although some studies have defined categories of green supply chain management based upon internal business goals,[38] fewer have categorised management practices based upon supply chain structure and use of compliance mechanisms. The following section offers an overview of presently observed approaches to GSCM, placing them into a typology of GSCM systems. They represent approaches that are both vertical (focusing up and down the supply chain from raw materials to post

---

35 Gereffi, Humphrey and Sturgeon (2005).

36 RESOLVE and Steering Committee of the State-of-Knowledge Assessment of Standards and Certification (2012) 43.

37 Simpson and Samson (2008) 13–14.

38 RESOLVE (2012).

consumer disposal) and horizontal (focusing on only one level of the supply chain such as first tier suppliers or a particular resource), and range from approaches that are primarily based on contract specifications, to those that involve long-term working relationships with suppliers and approaches that employ a range of compliance mechanisms. Although a typology may imply a hierarchy of approaches, these approaches are better thought of as complementary. Businesses may move from one approach to another, or the approaches may be used in combination to create an integrated strategy for environmental management.

5. RELIANCE ON CERTIFICATION AND AUDITING

By providing a mechanism for evaluation and monitoring of the production process, certification systems can aid businesses in management and improvement of their global supply chain. Perhaps most attractive to businesses because of the clarity of objectives they provide, most certification systems involve: (1) substantive standards for businesses – that is, a set of standards to which a business can certify and show that its practices are environmentally appropriate – or (2) procedural standards, such as ISO 14001, that require business to adopt environmental management systems ('EMS') with a particular structure for operations, monitoring, and enforcement.[39]

Natural resource extraction and subsequent commoditisation is a common context for environmental certification. The Forest Stewardship Council (FSC), for instance, was founded in 1993 as one of the first collaborative efforts to bring together NGOs, retailers and manufacturers to agree upon a set of internationally-applicable forest management criteria.[40] FSC certification requires wood to be traced from origin to manufacturing, creating a 'paper trail' and placing additional pressure upon various levels in the supply chain. Wood harvested according to

---

[39] Meidinger (2001). ISO 14001 is an environmental management standard developed by the International Standards Organization that, if adopted by a company, requires the company to assess its environmental attributes, create a plan for reducing adverse impacts caused by the company, periodically audit its facility to determine whether environmental goals are being achieved, inform management of the results of the audits and make adjustments needed to assure that goals are achieved. See International Standards Organization, 'ISO 14000 – Environmental Management'.

[40] RESOLVE (2012) 6–7.

FSC standards can be identified by a label indicating that the wood was grown and harvested in a sustainable manner. The Home Depot became the first major retailer to sell FSC-certified wood in 1994, and since then has played a central role in creating a market for sustainably grown and harvested lumber.[41] Interestingly, part of the impetus for change within Home Depot resulted from NGO concerns and the possibility of public campaigns or other actions highlighting what they perceived as unsustainable forestry practices by the company.[42]

In addition to prompting change of market structure and promoting transparent, chain-of-custody-based management, certification programs may also trigger more formal adoption of legal reforms. The ISO 14001 Standard, for instance, has been adopted as a national standard by China.[43] The same phenomenon can occur at the local government level; in 2006, the District of Columbia adopted green building requirements mirroring the Leadership in Energy and Environmental Design (LEED) voluntary rating system as part of its city code.[44] Indeed, because of their formal and institutionalised nature, certification programs are often discussed as a target for incorporation into legal systems.[45]

6. CONTRACTING WITH SUPPLY CHAIN PARTICIPANTS

As a result of challenges presented by global supply chains and insufficient international regulation, many businesses seeking to build or protect social or environmental value in their supply chains have turned to their contracts to drive change. As a mechanism for quality control, ensuring specific forms of environmental compliance, and increasing supply chain security, contracts can play an important role and benefit both retailers and consumers.[46] In addition to allowing businesses to improve their own performance, GSCM contracting may also trigger a 'transplanting effect' in which contractual standards may become the norm in other jurisdictions, thus benefiting both the business and the residents of nations with historically fewer regulatory standards or weaker enforcement.[47]

---

41 Home Depot, *2013 Sustainability Report* 14, (2012) 14.
42 See Krill (2001).
43 Lin (2009).
44 D.C. Code § 6-1451.01 et seq. (2012).
45 Meidinger (2001) 10176.
46 Roberts (2010) 87–8.
47 Ibid; Lin (2009) 714–16.

Nike, which contracts with over 900 factories globally, sets contractual standards for both environmental and labour practices.[48] The company's supply chain practices have understandably increased in the wake of a public backlash against the labour practices of independent contract manufacturers. During the 1990s, the company defended itself against negative publicity by claiming it had no control over its overseas manufacturers.[49] Today, however, Nike maintains a vigorous code of conduct and deploys auditing systems through the vehicle of its contracts.[50] In 2010, Nike issued a set of performance standards including a goal of 20 per cent reduction in CO^2 emissions per pair of running shoes between 2011 and 2015, an increase in water efficiency by 15 per cent, and a 10 per cent reduction from manufacturing waste.[51] Its progress on the CO^2 reductions target is not regularly published, but between 2009 and 2011, the company achieved a total reduction of 2.8 per cent. One of its newer products, the Flyknit Lunar shoe line, also takes upstream waste into account and reduces waste by an average of 80 per cent when compared to typical Nike running footwear.[52] By shrinking the distance between its corporate headquarters and suppliers, Nike has been able to improve product design and system performance. As the company noted in a recent performance report: 'We know better the factories we work with, and they know better what we expect of them.'[53]

7. SUPPLY CHAIN TRANSPARENCY AND CLOSED LOOP SYSTEMS

In light of the resource-heavy nature of certain supply chain management practices, many businesses have opted for transparency and disclosure of supply chain activities as an initial practice that may become the foundation for broader sustainability initiatives. One area ripe for study of supply chain transparency is mineral extraction, an industry that has been disproportionately associated with conflict areas, human rights abuses, and environmental degradation.[54] In particular, the prevalence of

---

[48] Nike Inc, *Sustainable Business Performance Summary* (2011) 10.

[49] Spar and Burns (2002).

[50] Nike Inc, *Sustainable Business Performance Summary* (2011) 41–2.

[51] Carus (2013). See also Nike Inc., 'The Future: Closed-Loop Business Model'.

[52] Carus (2013).

[53] See Nike Inc., 'How We Do Business: Manufacturing'.

[54] See generally RESOLVE, *Tracing a Path Forward* (2010).

rare earth minerals in the global electronic industry presents some unique challenges to supply chain transparency. Although there is a demand for responsibly produced minerals in the electronics market,[55] certification at the retail end presents a challenge. Electronics such a cellular phones are composed of many metals and other minerals, each of which typically make up a small percentage of the components in each product.[56] These conditions can be easily distinguished from other retail products, such as lumber, where the end product is composed of one or a few main materials of concern. This fact has allowed physical tracking of wood materials through the supply chain using, for example, radio-frequency identification (RFID) tags, a feat difficult to imagine – though perhaps not impossible – for minerals used in electronics.[57]

Attempting to tackle the minerals tracing problem head-on is the Electronics Industry Citizenship Coalition (EICC), a global partnership that includes the world's major electronics manufacturers, software firms, IT firms and manufacturing service providers.[58] EICC members agree to audit and enforce full traceability measures as well as due diligence standards for a variety of metals, including tin, tantalum, tungsten and gold. One notable EICC member, Apple, Inc., has targeted use of PCB in its products by requiring suppliers upstream to undergo audits and produce action plans.[59] Although current systems are typically inadequate to track materials flow with confidence in these supply chains, future strategies such as multi-sector partnerships with the formal mining sector may alleviate these challenges.[60]

8. DEEP SUPPLY CHAIN ENGAGEMENT

Still other initiatives may consider the full product life cycle, including 'all stages of a product system, from raw material acquisition or natural resource production to the disposal of the product at the end of its life, including extracting and processing of raw materials, manufacturing,

55 See, e.g. United Nations G8 Summit Declaration, *Growth and Sustainability in the World Economy* (2007). See also Welle (2013).

56 RESOLVE, *Tracing a Path Forward* (2010) 23.

57 Timpe (2005).

58 See generally Electronic Industry Citizenship Coalition and Global e-Sustainability Initiative (2008).

59 Friends of Nature *et al.* (2013) 3.

60 RESOLVE, *Tracing a Path Forward* (2010) 30–32.

distribution, use, re-use, maintenance, recycling and final disposal'.[61] By looking at the entire life cycle of a product, a business can avoid shifting externalities from one stage of the product's life cycle to another.

Emblematic of this 'deep' green supply chain management approach, Michigan-based furniture manufacturer Herman Miller has been a leader in embedding environmental concerns in its corporate culture. Using what they have termed a 'cradle to cradle' system, Herman Miller designs products for environmental quality throughout the supply chain.[62] This approach epitomises vertical supply chain management.

Herman Miller assesses all of its furniture for recyclability and disassembly. The measurement system uses a scale of orange, red, yellow and green for materials and a target to completely disassemble the product in thirty minutes or less using one person and standard tools. Using the McDonough Braungart Design Chemistry (MBDC) system, the company categorises material by the type of impact it creates – recyclability, human health risk, and so on – and by the magnitude of that impact. MBDC also provides measures and targets that allow companies to track progress of green programs, while clearly communicating priorities to employees and supply chain partners.

Largely collaborative in nature, Herman Miller's approach to working with suppliers and manufacturers relies heavily on metrics and targets in order to communicate priorities and promote acceptance among partners. The company also maintains a technical assistance capability at its headquarters to assist suppliers in meeting company standards and to help maintain long-term relationships with the suppliers. Value is created in this sort of system by sharing of intelligence and know-how regarding environmental performance, emerging technologies and emerging regulatory issues.

9. A NOTE ON COMPLIANCE MECHANISMS

Private enforcement tools such as those described herein can be successful only if there is some form of internal compliance mechanism. In addition to guidelines and frameworks, sustainability tool kits should also have internal mechanisms that guide the process of compliance and provide sanctions – direct or indirect – for noncompliance. Some

---

[61] United Nations Environment Programme *et al.* (2009), *Guidelines for Social Life Cycle Assessment of Products* 33.

[62] Wilkerson, 'Following Products through the Green Supply Chain'.

examples of GSCM-specific compliance strategies include supplier auditing, direct sourcing, life cycle monitoring systems and cradle-to-grave or zero-waste systems.[63] Although these strategies may have different names, commonalities among top performing companies include regularly tracking performance, utilising technology solutions to enable improvements and track results, and having a designated executive leader for their green supply chain initiatives.[64]

A useful distinction for such mechanisms is whether the company uses a coercive or a collaborative approach to greening its supply chain. Fully coercive approaches pass responsibility upstream by introducing contractual clauses for suppliers or requiring suppliers to independently meet standards. Collaborative approaches, by contrast, take advantage of existing relationships and social capital to not only assist with the process, but to guide it throughout the supply chain to achieve mutually agreed-upon goals.[65] Collaboration on environmental performance issues tends to increase the range and complexity of possible outcomes, but requires a far greater level of involvement for customers and suppliers.

10. PROMOTING EXPANDED USE OF EFFECTIVE GREEN SUPPLY CHAIN REGULATION AND ENFORCEMENT

This chapter has noted how evolving internal economic drivers, globalisation of the economy, and outsourcing of manufacturing and the changing nature of societal values have stimulated a wide variety of green supply chain mechanisms. While the specific impacts of private supply chain requirements are not as predictable as the results of well-enforced government regulation, they nevertheless have the potential for producing environmental outcomes that are essential to sustainability. One course of action would be to leave to the market place the continued evolution of green supply chain requirements; in fact, much of this development likely will remain in the private sector with varying degrees of public transparency. However, there is a role that governments can play in promoting green supply chain management. The following discussion explores ways that government may direct this movement

63 Ibid 2.

64 Aberdeen Group 3. According to this study, 97% of the top GSCM performers track energy usage and logistics and transportation costs.

65 Simpson and Samson (2008) 13.

towards the use of stronger tools that are both enforced and more transparent to the public.

Michael Vandenbergh has noted that 'a policymaker not only has traditional regulatory and economic tools at her disposal, she also can seek to stimulate private environmental contracting in supply-chain, credit, corporate asset, insurance, and other markets'.[66] This facilitative role may include collection and dissemination of information regarding private standards or creating settings conducive to business collaboration.[67] Additionally, government could promote green supply chain management by supporting research that would provide better information about how well various supply chain models function in producing better environmental results, and on the effectiveness of different supply chain compliance and enforcement mechanisms.

Coordinating government green supply chain contracting with private green supply chain activities could also magnify the efforts of some private supply chains by adding the purchasing power of the federal government. The U.S. government has focused on environmentally preferred purchasing since 1993 with the promulgation of Executive Order 12873, focusing on federal acquisition, recycling and waste prevention.[68] In 2002, the Organization for Economic Cooperation and Development (OECD) Environment Ministers approved its OECD Council Recommendation on Improving the Environmental Performance of Public Procurement.[69] The Bush Administration continued the support for environmentally preferred purchasing through Executive Order 13423, entitled 'Strengthening Federal Environmental, Energy, and Transportation Management'.[70] The emphasis on green procurement accelerated under President Obama, who in 2009 issued Executive Order 13514, focusing on 'Federal Leadership in Environmental, Energy and Economic Performance.'[71] The green procurement movement in the United States is reflected in other green procurement efforts in other parts of the world such as the work of the Nordic Council of Ministers.[72]

---

66 Vandenbergh (2007) 968.

67 Ibid.

68 Executive Order No. 12,873, 58 Fed Reg 54911 (20 October 1993).

69 Organisation for Economic Co-operation and Development (2002) 3.

70 Executive Order 13,514, 3 CFR 13514 (24 January 2007), accessed 3 April 2015 at http://www.gpo.gov/fdsys/pkg/FR-2007-01-26/pdf/07-374.pdf.

71 Ibid.

72 Nordic Council of Ministers, *Green Procurement Makes a Difference!* (2009).

A new organisation promises the ability to leverage government, university-based, and private procurement standards to green the supply chain. The Sustainable Purchasing Leadership Council is a non-profit organisation formed in 2013 whose mission is to support and recognise purchasing leadership that accelerates the transition to a prosperous and sustainable future.[73] The Council includes two federal agencies, several state agencies, a number of universities, and several private businesses who are product providers. Government compliance and enforcement programs could also better support and leverage supply chain management.[74] Enforcement programs have, for some time, encouraged company voluntary efforts that are designed to prevent pollution (such as EPA's WasteWise program),[75] deploy better environmental management systems (such as ISO 14001), and promote environmental auditing,[76] all of which can have an impact on internal economics and on values. But enforcement officials typically have not assessed the extent to which their programs can and should strategically take into account internal economics and societal values in general, and supply chain regulation and enforcement specifically, as part of the larger effort of environmental agencies to achieve sustainable outcomes.[77] Just as they have done with other pollution prevention and compliance assistance efforts, compliance and enforcement officials should find ways to encourage GSCM by developing and disseminating information on the most successful approaches to supply change management. Enforcement officials could also encourage GSCM practices through settlement agreements similar to the approach enforcement officials have taken in cases where part of an enforcement settlement includes a requirement to develop an effective environmental management system.

Further, governments can stimulate greener supply chains by making clear issues that are of concern but that are not yet regulated. Creating a transparent 'regulatory agenda' would allow companies to build these issues into their supply chain requirements before regulatory action

---

[73] See Sustainable Purchasing Leadership Council, http://www.purchasingcouncil.org/ accessed 3 April 2015.

[74] The Green Suppliers Network, a collaborative effort between the U.S. Environmental Protection Agency and the U.S. Department of Commerce, also provides a forum for environmentally-driven suppliers to work closely with regulators. Green Suppliers Network, 'Manufacturing a Sustainable Future'.

[75] *See* United States Environmental Protection Agency, 'Conserving Resources, Preventing Waste'.

[76] United States Environmental Protection Agency, 'EPA's Audit Policy'.

[77] Paddock (2008) 10628.

occurs, resulting in earlier environmental improvements and perhaps helping companies to shape the nature of the government activity or regulation. The use of hydro fluorocarbon (HFC) refrigerants provides an interesting example. HFCs replaced CFCs as a refrigerant because of the dramatic, adverse effect CFCs had on stratospheric ozone depletion. However, HFCs have a greenhouse gas potential that is 1,400 times higher than carbon dioxide and make up 1.5 per cent of total global warming potential.[78] Recognising that HFCs were likely to eventually be subject to regulation, the Consumer Goods Forum (made up of several of the World's largest consumer goods companies including Pepsico, Nestle, Coca-Cola, Tesco, Wal-Mart, Unilever and Heineken), through the organisation's sustainability initiative, established in 2011 a goal to begin phasing out HFCs by 2015.[79] These companies are a major user of refrigerants around the world.

This foresight involved in the HFC phase-out initiative is underscored by the fact that the United States and China announced in early September 2013 that they would seek to end the use of HFCs using the Montreal Protocol as a vehicle.[80] The anticipatory move made by the Consumer Goods Forum will give the participating companies some advantage in making the move to a new generation of refrigerants by having more time to find alternatives.

As discussed earlier, for many companies, reputation is one of the most important drivers of environmental behaviour. Government agencies may be able to leverage this fact in the context of green supply chain management by recognising companies that demonstrate leadership in GSCM. Governments have for some time experimented with ways to recognise superior environmental performance through voluntary programs, leadership initiatives, and rating systems. In the United States, this effort began in earnest in the early 1990s with a voluntary toxics reduction program known as '33/50', which challenged companies to reduce the use of 33 of the most toxic chemicals by 50 per cent within a period of a few years.[81] EPA began its most ambitious effort to recognise and support superior performance near the end of the 1990s with the 'Performance Track Program'.[82] EPA designed a Performance Track to recognise facilities (and later companies) that exceeded environmental

---

78 See Consumer Goods Forum, 'Refrigeration'.

79 Ibid.

80 See Eilperin (2013) A3.

81 United States Environmental Protection Agency, *33/50 Program: The Final Record.*

82 See United States Environmental Protection Agency, 'Performance Track'.

requirements in a variety of areas. Participants were expected to use an environmental management system to assess their environmental impacts, set 'stretch goals' to reduce several of the impacts, and report regularly on the results they achieved. Performance Track companies were expected to have a good compliance record. This EPA recognition helped enhance the reputation of participant companies.

Although the Obama Administration terminated Performance Track, the idea of recognising superior performance, such as through supply chain management, remains important. The Rand Corporation study of the Performance Track program and other voluntary environmental programs concluded that voluntary programs 'can complement regulatory approaches to accelerate environmental improvement'.[83] The report also concluded that members of the program displayed 'increased consideration of environmental issues in formal decision-making processes'.[84] Thus, recognising leadership in GSCM could be an important way of encouraging companies to adopt GSCM programs or enhance existing GSCM regulatory and enforcement programs.

11. CONCLUSION

It is clear that green supply chain management is a growing part of business and equally clear that these private environmental regulatory mechanisms are an essential element of any effort to achieve sustainable development. Supply chain approaches, however, vary greatly from one company to another and from one material to another. As we expect that green supply chain management is likely here to stay, it is important that companies, NGOs and regulators better understand the various forms of GSCM and that the impact of these variations on the ability to assure GSCM requirements can produce actual environmental results. This will require more in-depth understanding of the actual contractual language imposing the requirements, non-contractual arrangements that impact supply chains, the arrangements between companies and their suppliers to provide suppliers with the support needed to meet the requirements, and the oversight mechanisms that are used to assure compliance with the supply chain requirements. In the interim and as more information becomes available on the efficacy of supply chain interventions, governments can play an important role in encouraging the adoption of strong

[83] Hassell (2010) xiii.
[84] Ibid, 88.

and enforceable supply chain requirements that can augment government regulatory efforts.

REFERENCES

Aberdeen Group, *Building a Green Supply Chain: Social Responsibility for Fun and Profit* (2008).

Benoit, C. and G. Vickery-Niederman (2011), 'The Sustainability Consortium' in *Social Sustainability Assessment Literature Review* (White Paper, no. 102, Sustainability Consortium).

Black, E., V. Richardson and T. Carnes (2000), 'The Market Valuation of Corporate Reputation' 3 *Corporate Reputation Review* 31.

Bosselmann, K. and G. Grinlinton (eds) (2002), *Environmental Law for A Sustainable Society* (New Zealand Centre For Environmental Law).

Burke, R., G. Martin and C. Cooper (2011), *Corporate Reputation: Managing Opportunities and Threats* (Farnham: Gower Publishing, 2011).

Carus, F. (2013), 'Will Nike Deliver on its 2015 Performance Standards?' (*The Guardian,* 15 February), accessed 3 April 2015 at http://www.theguardian.com/sustainable-business/blog/nike-deliver-2015-performance-innovation.

Consumer Goods Forum, 'Refrigeration', accessed 3 April 2015 at http://www.theconsumergoodsforum.com/sustainability-strategic-focus/climate-change/refrigeration.

Consumer Goods Forum, 'Sustainability', accessed 3 April 2015 at http://www.theconsumergoodsforum.com/sustainability.aspx.

Ecolabel Index, 'Blue Angel', accessed 3 April 2015 at http://www.ecolabelindex.com/ecolabel/blue-angel.

Eilperin, J. (2013), 'U.S., China Agree on Cutting Potent Greenhouse Gases' (*The Washington Post,* 7 September).

Eisner, M. (2007), *Governing the Environment: The Transformation of Environmental Regulation* (Boulder, CO: Lynne Rienner).

Electronic Industry Citizenship Coalition, 'Code of Conduct', accessed 3 April 2015 at http://www.eicc.info/eicc_code.shtml.

Electronic Industry Citizenship Coalition and Global e-Sustainability Initiative (2008), *Social and Environmental Responsibility in Metals Supply to the Electronic Industry.*

Esty, D. and A. Winston (2006), *Green to Gold: How Smart Companies Use Environmental Strategy to Innovate, Create Value, and Build Competitive Advantage* (New Haven, CT: Yale University Press, 2006).

Food and Agriculture Organisation of the United Nations, *Code of Conduct for Responsible Fisheries*, accessed 3 April 2015 at http://www.fao.org/docrep/005/v9878e/v9878e00.HTM.

Friends of Nature *et al.* (2013), *Apple Opens Up: IT Industry Supply Chain Investigative Report – Phase VI.*

Gereffi, G., J. Humphrey and T. Sturgeon (2005), 'The Governance of Global Value Chains' 12 *Review of International Political Economy* 78–104.

Green Suppliers Network, 'Manufacturing a Sustainable Future', accessed 3 April 2015 at http://gsn.nist.gov/industry.html.

Gunningham, N., R. Kagan and D. Thornton (2004), 'Social License and Environmental Protection: Why Businesses Go Beyond Compliance' 29 *Law and Social Inquiry* 307.

Hassell S. and others, *An Assessment of the U.S. Environmental Protection Agency's National Environmental Performance Track Program* (RAND Corporation, 2010).

Ho, J. *et al.* (2009), 'Opportunities in Green Supply Chain Management' 8 *Coastal Business Journal* 18.

Home Depot (2012), *2013 Sustainability Report 14*, accessed 3 April 2015 at https://corporate.homedepot.com/CorporateResponsibility/Environment/Documents/Sustainability__Brochure_pages.pdf.

International Standards Organization, 'ISO 14000 – Environmental Management', accessed 3 April 2015 at http://www.iso.org/iso/home/standards/management-standards/iso14000.htm.

Krill, J. (2001), 'Felling the Lumber Giants' 22 Multinational Monitor, accessed 3 April 2015 at http://multinationalmonitor.org/mm2001/01jan-feb/corp5.html.

Lin, L. (2009), 'Legal Transplants Through Private Contracting: Codes of Vendor Conduct in Global Supply Chains as an Example' 57 *American Journal of Comparative Law* 711.

Malik, N. (2010), 'BP Protests Threaten Independent Dealers' (*The Wall Street Journal*, 16 June 2010), accessed 10 april 2015 at http://www.wsj.com/articles/SB10001424052748703280004575308973098327064.

Marine Stewardship Council, 'MSC Standards and Certification Requirements', accessed 3 April 2015 at http://www.msc.org/about-us/standards.

Meidinger, E. (2001), 'Environmental Certification Programs and U.S. Environmental Law: Closer Than You May Think' 31 *Environmental Law Review* 10162.

Mouawad, J. and J. Schwartz (2010), 'Cleanup Costs and Lawsuits Rattle BP's Investors' (*The New York Times,* 1 June), accessed 3 April 2015 at http://www.nytimes.com/2010/06/02/us/02liability.html?_r=1&.

MVO Platform(2008), *View on Supply Chain Responsibility*, accessed 10 April 2015 at http://mvoplatform.nl/publications-en/Publication_2774.

Nike Inc., 'The Future: Closed-Loop Business Model', accessed 3 April 2015 at http://www.nikebiz.com/crreport/content/strategy/2-1-3-the-future-closed-loop-business-model.php?cat=cr-strategy.

Nike Inc., 'How We Do Business: Manufacturing', accessed 3 April 2015 at http://www.nikeresponsibility.com/report/content/chapter/manufacturing#topic-destination-a-truly-sustainable-supply-chain.

Nike Inc., *Sustainable Business Performance Summary* (2011), accessed 3 April 2015 at http://www.nikeresponsibility.com/report/files/report/NIKE_SUSTAINABLE_BUSINESS_REPORT__FY10-11_FINAL.pdf.

Nordic Council of Ministers, Green Procurement Makes a Difference! (Denmark 2009).

Organisation for Economic Co-operation and Development *Recommendation of the Council on Improving the Environmental Performance of Public Procurement* (2002).

Paddock, L. (2008), 'Green Governance: Building the Competencies Necessary for Effective Environmental Management' 38 *Environmental Law Review* 1060.

Paddock, L. (2009), 'The Farm to Fork Initiative: A Shareholder and Management Partnership,' in National Research Council (ed.) *Enhancing the Effectiveness of Sustainability Partnerships* (Washington, DC: The National Academies Press).

Paddock, L. (2012), 'Beyond Deterrence: Enforcement and Compliance in the Context of Sustainable Development' 42 *Environmental Law Review* 10622.

RESOLVE and Steering Committee of the State-of-Knowledge Assessment of Standards and Certification, *Towards Sustainability: The Roles and Limitations of Certification* (2012).

RESOLVE, *Tracing a Path Forward: A Study of the Challenges of the Supply Chain for Target Metals Used in Electronics* (2010).

Roberts, T. (2010), 'Innovations in Governance: A Functional Typology of Private Governance Institutions' 22 *Duke Environmental Law & Policy Forum* 67.

Simpson, D. and D. Samson (2008), 'Developing Strategies for Green Supply Chain Management' *Decision Line* 12.

Spar, D. and J. Burns (2002), 'Hitting the Wall: Nike and International Labor Practices' 9 *Harvard Business Review* 700.

Sutherland, P. (2010), 'Globalization and Corporate Law' in M. Faure and A. van der Walt (eds), *Globalization and Private Law* (Cheltenham, UK and Northampton, MA, USA: Edward Elgar).

Srivastava, S. (2007), 'Green Supply-Chain Management: A State-of-the-Art Literature Review' 9 *International Journal of Management Reviews* 53.

Sustainable Forestry Initiative, 'Getting Certified', accessed 3 April 2015 at http://www.sfiprogram.org/getting-certified/.

Timpe, D. (2005), *Barcode and RFID Technologies: Alternatives to Log Stamping for Wood Identification in Forestry?* (Sweden: Fibre Science and Communication Network).

Sustainable Purchasing Leadership Council, accessed 3 April 2015 at http://www.purchasingcouncil.org/.

United Nations Environment Programme *et al.* (2009), *Guidelines for Social Life Cycle Assessment of Products* (C. Benoit and B. Mazjin (eds)).

United Nations G8 Summit Declaration, *Growth and Sustainability in the World Economy* (2007).

United States Environmental Protection Agency (US EPA 1999), *33/50 Program: The Final Record* (EPA-745-R-99-004).

United States Environmental Protection Agency, 'Conserving Resources, Preventing Waste', accessed 3 April 2015 at http://www.epa.gov/epawaste/conserve/smm/wastewise/index.htm.

United States Environmental Protection Agency, 'EPA's Audit Policy', accessed 10 April 2015 at http://www.epa.gov/compliance/incentives/auditing/auditpolicy.html.

United States Environmental Protection Agency, 'Performance Track', accessed 3 April 2015 at http://www.epa.gov/performancetrack/.

Vandenbergh, M. (2007), 'The New Wal-Mart Effect: The Role of Private Contracting in Global Governance' 54 *ULCA Law Review* 913.

Welle, D. (2013), 'The Campaign for Clean Mobile Phones', accessed 3 April 2015 at http://www.dw.de/the-campaign-for-clean-mobile-phones/a-15982934 (21 September).

Wilkerson, T., 'Following Products through the Green Supply Chain' (*Awareness Into Action*), accessed 3 April 2015 at http://www.awarenessintoaction.com/whitepapers/green-supply-chain-sustainable-programs.html.

13. Hybrid governance and 'wicked' natural resource risks

Paul Martin and Peter Noble[1]

This chapter focuses on the changing nature of natural resource sustainability issues, the ability of traditional legal arrangements to cope, and the necessity for a transition to a new form of hybrid governance.[2] *Natural resource governance* is the system through which an organisation (a society, country, culture, corporation) governs (controls, manages, directs, shapes) how natural resources are used or protected, to avoid abuses of power or opportunity and to ensure that the collective interest is protected.[3] The IUCN defines governance as 'interactions among structures, processes and traditions that determine how power and responsibilities are exercised, how decisions are taken, and how citizens or other stakeholders have their say in the management of natural resources – including biodiversity conservation' (IUCN WCC Resolution 3.012).

Environmental law academics often focus on command and control regulation by government. This under-emphasises the systemic functions of law, and overstates the role of government. Relevant legal arrangements also include laws necessary for market instruments (such as property law) and private action (such as actions for environmental nuisance), administrative law (such as controls over government decisions or abuses of process), corporations' law (including directors' and

---

[1] The continuing support of TAL Life Limited (Australia) and Dai-Ichi Life (Japan) and the research assistance of Dr. Elodie LeGal, are gratefully acknowledged. The support of the Australian Research Council for the 'Next Generation Landscape Governance' research project is thankfully acknowledged.

[2] Hybrid natural resource governance involves government, NGO and/or commerce or industry. It is different to 'co-regulation' or 'collaborative governance' (or similar terms), connoting a strategic partnership reflecting an alignment of aims, and significant and perhaps irreversible investments of resources.

[3] *Natural resources law* connotes legal arrangements governing use and conservation of natural resources.

officers' duties), planning law, and many other legal instruments and institutions. Whilst the governance actions of public authorities (viz. regulation, government extension and communications, subsidization) are important, private actors have fundamental roles. These span: resource stewardship by businesses, industry natural resource governance (viz. corporate internal standards, strategies and investment, industry-wide standards, and industry public-good leadership actions); community or Non-Government Organisation (NGOs) activities (viz. 'green' consumerism and related marketplace standards, political activism, philanthropy and voluntarism); and personal actions (viz. implementation of self-standards, consumer, political or volunteer actions, and stewardship actions motivated by the public good or private interests).

We trace the evolution of natural resource governance in common law countries over the last three centuries,[4] noting that radical changes have occurred in response to changes to issues and political institutions for managing the competing interests in society.[5] We discuss complex, systemic environmental risks, policy failure, and the economic, intellectual, jurisdictional or other legal limits to the capacity of government to cope with these issues.

We then consider developments in private-sector natural resource governance, and the potential for a new strategic partnership in natural resource governance. The private sector (business and civil society) commands a lion's share of financial and natural resources, has political power, and significantly determines the extent to which ecological sustainability is achievable. This suggests that NGOs and business must be involved. But to what degree can the stereotypical antagonistic relationship between business, government and civil society organisations over environmental issues be made more constructive? Other authors have considered the phenomenon of co-regulatory instruments and arguments for government/industry partnership on environmental issues.[6] Our contribution is to consider the same issues from a strategic policy perspective.

---

[4] For further historical details see Robert V. Percival *History of Environmental Law (1) and (2)*, accessed 3 April 2015 at http://www.iucnael.org/essentials-readings-in-environmental-law-topics.

[5] The complex interaction between environmental law, conflict and broader social institutions is examined in Becker and Martin (2011).

[6] See Holley and Lawson, Ch 11, and Paddock and Masterton, Ch 12, also Richardson (2005); Benjamin Richardson (2011).

1. THE DIALECTIC OF RESOURCE GOVERNANCE

In the common law countries early legal natural resource governance including rules of trespass, or criminal laws against poaching, supported private exploitation. With increased competition for resources (particularly with industrialisation) came torts associated with land and natural resources. These were mainly managing competition rather than for protection of the environment. Managing water used for milling and mining, for example, triggered riparian rights and new uses of the laws of nuisance.

During the late 18th and the 19th centuries three things changed. Human population approximately doubled in the 200 years before 1850.[7] Notably in the U.K., and then the U.S.A., the Scientific Enlightenment fuelled the industrial revolution, scientific farming, and changes to man's relationships with nature. Enclosure laws and farming technology contributed to dispossession and urbanisation. Technological invention and the ideas of Locke[8] promoted a belief that the owner had absolute dominion including the freedom to destroy nature.

Rousseau and Darwin[9] opened up a different perspective on nature. Privilege allowed the study of nature as science, landscape or natural art and visits to the country or walking as recreational activities; the nature poetry of Byron, Coleridge or Wordsworth,[10] the romantic art of the Pre-Raphaelite Brotherhood,[11] and the writings of Henry David Thoreau in America,[12] gave the intellectual impetus to a romantic movement for nature. Ideas sympathetic with stewardship arose alongside the economic philosophies of rampant industrialisation.

Over two centuries in cities, the living conditions of the poor became inhumane. Overcrowding; dumping of excreta into streets, cesspits or rivers; disease and crime prevailed in many cities. In the 19th century, industrialisation meant coal-dust and coal-smoke, industrial effluent emitted to the rivers or dumped on land, and scarring of the landscape.

---

7 For example Worldometers, 'Word Population: Past, Present and Future'.

8 Locke (1689).

9 Rousseau (1754) 151; Darwin (1859).

10 George Gordon Byron (1788-1824); viz. Childe Harold Canto, 'There is pleasure in the pathless woods' iv, Verse 178; Samuel Taylor Coleridge, (1772–1834); William Wordsworth, 'To the Cuckoo' (Poetry Foundation, 1770–1850) http://www.poetryfoundation.org/poem/174831 accessed 8 August 2014; William Wordsworth 'I Wandered Lonely as a Cloud'.

11 From 1848.

12 Thoreau, 'Walden' (*Thoreau Reader,* 1854).

Frustration with the resulting harms triggered political demands to regulate industry. In the 12th century the first rules against air pollution from coal had been briefly in place.[13] The late 1800s saw more serious attempts to govern environmental public health. The strengthening of democracy lent importance to the interests of the populace. The British Alkali Acts of 1863 targeted industrial emissions, introducing State legal controls over industrial processes for public good purposes.[14]

In response to romantic and scientific appreciation of landscapes (catalyzed partly by photography[15]), a movement for government protection of aesthetic and cultural values emerged. Private conservation (hunting and forestry) reserves had long existed but the new movement combined democratic activism with popular environmental aesthetics and philosophy. The first national parks were created in the U.S.A. in 1872 (Yosemite National Park) and in Australia in 1879 (The Royal National Park).[16] In England, national parks did not emerge till the following century, as traditional rights of traverse across private lands allowed nature lovers to ramble, and landscaped gardens satisfied the needs of aesthetes.

Political antagonism between industrial and environmental interests was entrenched along with political environmentalism and the role of government as an arbiter of conflict over nature. These were the foundations for political contests and the role of government in natural resource governance during the 20th century.

2. 'VICIOUS' GOVERNANCE CHALLENGES

Early natural resource governance addressed harms where cause and effect relationships were linear and within a single jurisdiction (such as deforestation, hunting, emission of effluent or clearing of land). By 1901 the earth's population was around 1.6 billion. By the end of the century, 6 billion people needed to be fed, housed and clothed and increasingly

---

[13] Jacobson (2012) 74.

[14] See Miller, Vandome and McBrewster (eds) (2011). Also the 5th Annual Report of Proceedings by the Inspector (under the Alkali Act) 1869, (available online through Google Books), with its emphasis upon scientific assessment of cause and impact, and graduated control.

[15] Photographs by William Henry Jackson apparently being pivotal in creating awareness of the magnificent areas that became Yellowstone National Park.

[16] Established in 1879 as 'The National Park', renamed Royal National Park in 1955.

demanded products and services requiring greater and more technologically complex demands upon natural resources, particularly associated with industrial chemistry. For industry, water and air increasingly acquired economic value as pollution sinks; with urbanisation the concentration of pollutants became significant to human welfare.

There are fundamental differences between controlling (for example) local tree removal or waste dumps, and (for example) bio-accumulation of poisons in pelagic fish or raptors, acid rain damage to the Black Forest, ozone-depleting substances or atmospheric carbon. These issues exhibit unexpected dynamics, due to complex industrial ecologies and eco-social systems. Causes and effects cross jurisdictional boundaries through non-localised production and consumption chains,[17] compounded by auto-poetic effects of chemical and other physical interactions. We will term risks with such 'wicked'[18] systemic characteristics *complex*.

The agricultural revolution made it possible to feed an exploding population. It also generated complex risks as agricultural chemicals had unanticipated impacts on soil structure that did not become apparent for decades; dams led to salinity; and removal of forests led to erosion and siltation and even to changes in weather.[19] Industrial chemistry and engineering allowed farming that created unanticipated consequences, which lagged the benefits by decades as the result of unanticipated system relationships. Multinational business models and trade meant that decisions, actions and effects took place in different jurisdictions. Unforeseen effects were spatially or temporally remote from their causes, or arose from apparently unrelated causes. Growing sophistication in business (including international trade) made control of commerce difficult for governments.[20]

The dust storms that swept the prairies of the U.S.A. and Canada between 1934 and 1937 were a shocking illustration of the effects of mechanised ploughing for intensive grain production. In Australia, salinisation caused by land clearing was first noted in 1924.[21] Realisation of

---

[17] Manyika *et al.* (2014).

[18] An ill-defined problem involving complex cause and effect relationships, where there is no objective solution and/or any solution is likely to give rise to new, probably intractable, problems. Ten characteristics are discussed in Rittel and Webber (1973).

[19] For details see Natural Resources Management and Environment Department, 'Floods and Droughts'.

[20] Manyika *et al.* (2014).

[21] Wood (1924).

the significance of the problem and its systemic causes took decades.[22] Later in the 20th century, Rachel Carson's 'Silent Spring' highlighted the accumulating effects of pesticides (DDT). Bio-accumulation became a concern in terrestrial and marine systems. In urban settings, waste, asbestosis, 'sick-building syndrome', and emission impacts upon climate all highlight risks where impacts are remote in space and time from their causes.

The changing challenge of governing is illustrated by the biofuel industry.[23] Towards the end of the 20th century, mandates and subsidies were created to support the biofuel industry[24] triggering rapid growth, with the United Nations Food and Agriculture Organization (FAO) estimating an approximately eightfold increase between 1988 and projections to 2018.[25] Biofuel plantations were established by clearing native forests or by displacing local people.[26] Economic distortions arose. Pro-biofuel public policy became an impediment to carbon emissions control and biodiversity protection. Because key knowledge assets of the industry are intellectual property or commercial secrets, and the value chain is often controlled by multinational corporations, it is difficult for national governments to govern the industry. Laws protecting private interests, competition and free trade restrict intervention. Government interventions have become part of the governance problem.[27] What has resulted is the proliferation of competing government, community-based and industry initiatives.[28]

This history highlights complex interactions between consumer demand, politics, entrepreneurship, technologies and social/environmental impacts. It demonstrates the limits of governments in the face of complex transnational commercial arrangements. The biofuels challenge is still developing, with projected increases in production, advanced technologies and commercial models pursued by powerful multinational corporations, with public and private sector bodies pursuing

---

[22] Pannell (2002).

[23] For a history, and a discussion of the emergence of forms of hybrid governance, see Bailis and Baka (2011). Martin and Legal (forthcoming, 2015).

[24] For analysis of biofuel subsidies in a number of countries see http://www.iisd.org/gsi/biofuel-subsidies/biofuels-what-cost (accessed 3 April 2015).

[25] World Food and Agriculture to 2030/50 Ch 9 Biofuels p. 16.

[26] Ibid. Also Mol (2010).

[27] Martin and LeGal (2015). Risks associated with risk management interventions are termed 'risk/risk'. For example, the availability of insurance may lead to under-management or moral risk.

[28] Englund and Berndes (forthcoming 2015).

competing governance proposals. Many natural resource governance problems have similar risk characteristics: climate and air pollution, biodiversity, forest clearing and alternative energy policies all involve complex issues where governance is far from completely within the power of government. The limits to government are becoming apparent under the influence of world demographics, interconnectivity, technological and commercial innovation and changes to political contexts. We cannot turn the clock back to a simpler time, nor expect that governance instruments will always work as they used to.

3. LIMITS TO GOVERNANCE

The role of government has changed over the last 50 years. Popular environmentalism became politically significant in the latter 20th century. This generated a 'sustainable consumption' agenda. Because of political pressures and because of environmental and social justice ills, the middle part of the 20th century witnessed an explosion in environmental regulation. The Ecolex database combines information on legal instruments from FAO, the International Union for Conservation of Nature (IUCN) and the United Nations Environment Programme (UNEP). By 2013 it had referenced 2,070 environmental agreements, of which 670 were multilateral; 110,000 national laws and regulations; 33,700 legal and policy literature records; and 1,100 court decisions.

From the 1970s there were increases in non-government investments, including environmental philanthropy and voluntary arrangements.[29] Environmental market instruments and market-like arrangements (such as auctions and tenders for the allocation of public funds) emerged as alternatives or complements to state-based regulation or state support for conservation. Market and quasi-market arrangements are now used from local through to international public and private governance. The contemporary mix of public sector instruments includes policed regulation, environmental incentive and subsidy systems, environmental taxation, ecology and pollution reporting, expanded civil and administrative rights and liabilities, environmental purchasing, resource management research and development, environmental extension and engagement, institutional supports for voluntarism and responsible consumption (such as controls over 'greenwash' and environmental deception), directors' and officers'

[29] We lack 'hard data' about the amount of investment in natural resource conservation and restoration, and the sources of this investment. There is data about the number of programs and it would be possible to trace their histories.

duties, corporate reporting (for example, emissions and compliance), development controls and public participation requirements. Also relevant are environmental conditions on exploitation of public resources, subsidies and incentives, land-use approvals, industry development programmes (including tax and regulatory concessions), and some industry research and development. Private arrangements are just as diverse.

Critics of government actions complain that environmental regulation ('green tape') has excessive economic costs. Such critiques rarely consider the public good effectiveness of environmental governance, but there is ample evidence that many interventions deliver far less than ideal benefit/cost performance.[30] Environmental commentators are also concerned about the insufficient effectiveness of natural resource governance, more than its economic cost.[31] These concerns are reflected in Clause 19 of the Rio+20 document 'The Future We Want':[32]

> We recognize that the 20 years since the United Nations Conference on Environment and Development in 1992 have seen uneven progress, including in sustainable development and poverty eradication. We emphasize the need to make progress in implementing previous commitments. We also recognize the need to accelerate progress in closing development gaps between developed and developing countries, and to seize and create opportunities to achieve sustainable development through economic growth and diversification, social development and environmental protection. To this end, we underscore the continued need for an enabling environment at the national and international levels, as well as continued and strengthened international cooperation, particularly in the areas of finance, debt, trade and technology transfer, as mutually agreed, and innovation, entrepreneurship, capacity-building, transparency and accountability. We recognize the diversification of actors and stakeholders engaged in the pursuit of sustainable development. In this context, we affirm the continued need for the full and effective participation of all countries, in particular developing countries, in global decision-making.

The IUCN has initiated a 'Natural Resource Governance Framework' project, to provide an independent method to determine the strengths and

---

30 Notwithstanding criticisms of regulatory efficiency, and a seemingly general belief that market instruments are far more efficient, we have not found reliable *ex post* data to demonstrate that market instruments or other interventions perform consistently better. Bartel *et al.* (2007) 3–9.

31 See for example Lazarus (2008). From a more abstract perspective, developments in 'earth jurisprudence' and associated fields See for example, Tolan (2008); Voigt (ed.) (2013).

32 UN General Assembly Resolution 66/288.

weaknesses of natural resource decision-making and implementation. It will help decision-makers, whether citizens, economic institutions or political authorities to make better and fairer decisions that will underpin the sustainable management of natural resources and improve existing governance arrangements.[33] That project incorporates an evaluation being conducted between the IUCN World Commission on Environmental Law and the IUCN Environmental Law Centre. UNEP has also initiated implementation audits of international environmental agreements.[34]

Whilst we cannot measure the ecological benefits from environmental governance we assume a positive impact, but the underlying problems of resource depletion continue at an alarming rate. Other chapters in this book provide examples where the implementation of natural resource governance partly or completely failed and generated unexpected impacts. Policy-making and implementation is intrinsically risky. The nature of contemporary challenges is increasing this riskiness.

Reflecting the 'vicious' nature of the problems being addressed, governance interventions demonstrate three types of possible failure: political, instrumental or 'spill overs'.[35] For example political activism has often distorted biofuels policy and restricted government capacity to govern the risks, control mechanisms have fallen short, and policies have triggered undesirable spill overs.

Policy risk in natural resource governance will become more complex. The use of market-based instruments involves sophisticated arrangements[36] and calls on knowledge and institutions beyond traditional governance. Environmental property rights now exist to address air quality, water quality, biodiversity and aesthetics, and many others. International market-based approaches exist for carbon, air quality, or fisheries, and the risks of market instruments are compounded by the complexities of international governance. Whilst there have been notable successes, some market and market-like interventions have failed, and the risks of perverse effects from market instruments are insufficiently

---

[33] IUCN Natural Resource Governance Framework, (2013).

[34] Memorandum of Understanding between UNEP and the International Organization of Supreme Audit Institutions (INTOSAI – Working Group on Environmental Auditing, WGEA). See *Auditing the Implementation of Multilateral Environmental Agreements (MEAs): A Primer for Auditors* (UNEP FI Asset Management Working Group 2010a).

[35] Martin and Williams (2010).

[36] The searchable OECD *Database on instruments used for environmental policy* provides details of the many different instruments used in different countries, accessed 3 April 2015 at http://www2.oecd.org/ecoinst/queries.

acknowledged. The collapse of the European carbon market illustrates the vulnerability of market-based policies and limits to the governance capacity of governments and environmental NGO sectors. The risks of failure with any innovation are higher in its early stages, before experience and specialisation increase reliability. There is no reason to believe that novel market instruments will be immune from this characteristic.[37]

The risks of novel market instruments are illustrated by the REDD+ scheme.[38] Harnessing the international carbon-credits market, REDD+ aims to provide an economic incentive for the preservation of native forests, and protection of traditional users. Accredited REDD+units are to be supported by supply conditions and state arrangements to advance biodiversity and social justice. REDD+ is vulnerable to many risks.[39] Because the social justice and biodiversity values are supply conditions (costs) rather than priced attributes (revenue), the incentive is to minimise investment.[40] A failure by some REDD+ suppliers to meet the stewardship conditions could undermine the credibility of all REDD+ units from all suppliers, even those with effective governance. Risks like this are complex, and effective governance will require efficient public and private performance and integrity.

4. EVOLVING TOWARDS HYBRIDITY

By the start of the 21st century the environment was a contested political space. Issues are argued in the media and within communities, generating political turbulence. The simple 'economic production vs. environment protection' stereotype, whilst relevant, no longer adequately describes political alignments.[41] Governments have sought to refine their response to this political turbulence, whilst NGOs and industry have made strong

---

37 Teece (1986).

38 For a detailed discussion of REDD+ in the Asian context see International Journal of Rural Law & Policy 2013 Special Edition, 'REDD+ and legal regimes of mangroves, peatlands and other wetlands: ASEAN and the world', accessed 3 April 2015 at http://epress.lib.uts.edu.au/journals/index.php/ijrlp/issue/view/271. For discussion of risk issues see Larson and Petkova (2011); Martin (2013); Angelsen *et al.* (eds) (2012) 31–48; Gupta (2012).

39 Phelps, Webb and Koh (2011); Martin (2013).

40 Martin (2013).

41 Illustrative examples include farming and environmental alignments in opposition to mining and urbanisation of farmland; the role of retail in the competition between traditional and organic or humane farming; or the advocacy of the insurance industry for more effective climate action.

leadership claims in governance. All sectors have new strategies and new institutions to advance aspects of natural resources governance. The assumption that government will lead, and be the most powerful actor supporting the public interest is no longer universally valid.

Whilst this chapter concentrates upon governance roles for commerce and industry the NGO (or civil society) sector is pivotal. Civil strategies can be categorised as:

(1) Political activism, through formal channels (viz. parliamentary process, lobbying, 'green' political parties), communications (viz. media activism, education), and direct action (viz. demonstrations, blockades, riots, civil disobedience);
(2) Legal activism at a local or international level, relying upon legal arrangements such as administrative law, criminal law, civil rights, treaties and conventions, as well as environmental laws;
(3) Consumer or citizen activism (viz. consumer education, responsible consumption brands and product standards, consumer activism with supply and waste chains, advocating environmental disclosure, and 'green entrepreneurship' such as establishing new products or suppliers, or conservation);
(4) Voluntary investment of labour or funds, through philanthropy or on-ground voluntary conservation, and voluntary market schemes, such as carbon offset or biodiversity protection independent of government programs.

The number of environmental NGO's is uncountable.[42] They exist at local community, state and national and international jurisdictional levels. Many involve only a few people, are localised and exist for a short time for a specific issue such as a local development or a short-term campaign. Some have become powerful on the national and international stage. NGOs are often creative and energetic and can be politically powerful. NGO organisations will be important to future hybrid models of governance. Analysis of their future role justifies a dedicated study, but is not the focus of this chapter.

---

[42] Wikipedia lists 175 NGOs, of which 68 are designated as 'international', under its list of environmental organisations, accessed 3 April 2015 at http://en.wikipedia.org/wiki/List_of_environmental_organizations This generally excludes 'green' political parties (see http://en.wikipedia.org/wiki/List_of_green_parties (accessed 3 April 2015)), international environmental and social justice bodies, industry natural resource governance organisations, (which we will discuss later) and thousands of local or ephemeral bodies.

Corporate responses range from non-recognition of environmental sustainability as a management issue, through shallow-commitment (for example, a media release about the firm's commitment, or simple actions to reduce input costs of water, energy or other resources) to deep commitments where the firm focuses strategically upon improving its own environmental stewardship and stewardship by others. Overlaid on firm-specific responses are sector- or industry-wide responses to natural resource governance. These we will consider a little later, as a collective reaction to changing strategic imperatives.

Sustainability is defined to suit particular situations. For the purpose of this chapter we refer to its use in environmental policy, and in corporate strategy where the focus is 'sustainable competitive advantage'. The intersection of these is where strategic support for investment of corporate resources into natural resource governance is most likely.

The Bruntland Report defined Sustainable Development as 'development that meets the needs of the present without compromising the ability of future generations to meet their own needs'.[43] In corporate strategy 'sustainable competitive advantage'[44] reflects that corporations aim to optimise their mix of value delivery and costs, and be resilient to changes in context and competitive pressures.[45] Both involve decisions and allocations of resources to protect or restore the means to deliver human values.[46] They share a focus upon environment (or context) and resources, though in different ways. In business, the scarce resources include wealth, natural resources, human capital and market franchises.

Using a value chain for a hypothetical manufacturing enterprise (Figure 13.1), we illustrate how diverse might be the resource stewardship demands upon the firm.[47] (The numbering refers to numbering of the activity where these management issues might arise).

---

[43] Brundtland (1987) defined sustainability as 'forms of progress that meet the needs of the present without compromising the ability of future generations to meet their needs.' See also Bosselmann (2013) 9–42.

[44] Porter (2008).

[45] Extended to the comparative and competitive advantages of nations (and later into considering the way in which environmental regulation can drive competitive advantage). See Porter (1998).

[46] This is contrasted with the 'deep ecology' philosophy, where the focus is less upon continuation of human uses of the earth, than it is upon constraining human uses to protect the health of the earth and all species on the earth *per se*. See for example Devall and Sessions (1985).

[47] 'Stewardship' referring to the corporation's care in the use and conservation of natural resources under its control and 'governance' referring to participation in natural resource governance more broadly.

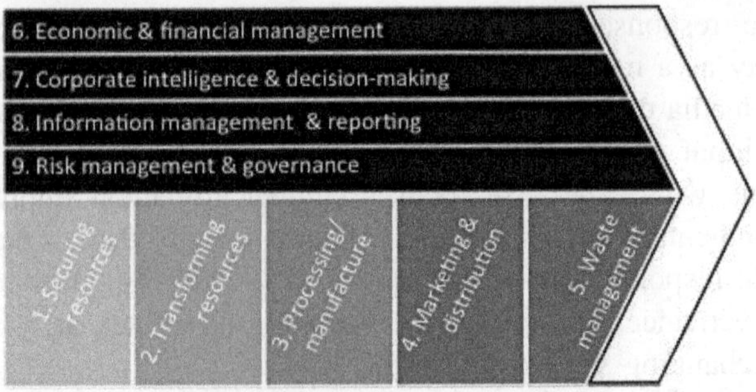

Figure 13.1 Value chain activities

(1) Resource access (for example, protection of the firm's social license, environmental impact assessment, ensuring resource availability, and controlling costs). Environmental issues in infrastructure design and construction or procurement (for example, EIA,[48] environmental standards), process environmental engineering or product design for sustainability. Environmental requirements of design and purchasing standards can add to demands upon management.

(2) Impact of environmental issues on processing costs, environmental controls, waste-management, effects upon general costs (for eample, transport, labour, energy, and so on). Managing waste and emissions including regulatory and administrative controls, emissions reporting, permits and trading of emission units.

(3) Production standards (regulatory, consumer and purchaser, lifecycle analysis and reporting where used), waste and by-product management, industry and host-community stewardship standards. Management of facilities, including reducing energy and water use.

(4) Consumer or buyer-chain standards, ecological ('green') branding or positioning as responsible stewards and management of reputational risks (for example, claims of irresponsibility or 'greenwash'). Environmental 'corporate citizenship' self-standards or industry standards.

(5) Extended responsibility requirements (for example, packaging waste), emission standards and controls. Managing waste costs or disposal.

---

48 Environmental Impact Assessment for projects and processes.

(6) Administrative, regulatory and other reporting. Environmental stewardship impacts on financing (for example, investor reputation, funder environment requirements, ethical status of investment).
(7) Monitoring evolving legal or social expectations, resource costs and related intelligence. Monitoring effects of environmental policy such as environmental taxation and pricing. Corporate environmental strategy and public positioning, and operational or economic issues such as resource cost and availability.
(8) Sometimes complex reporting, including emissions reporting, incident reporting, and perhaps data gathering, analysis and reporting of life-cycle or environmental benchmarks data.
(9) Risks including corporate or community disasters including reputational risk, potential increased costs or non-availability of resources. Personal civil or criminal penalty risks of the corporation or its executives from environmental or health laws. Director's political or reputational risk for failures to deal effectively with issues.[49]

This is far from an exhaustive list. It suggests that sustainability concerns for the corporation are shifting from being episodic and narrow to being systemic and strategic.

We have identified drivers for corporate engagement with environmental sustainability. These are relevant to different functional departments and corporate specialists, and require different strategic responses. Corporate motivations are moving beyond a 'feel good' or 'public relations' rationale to involve 'hard headed' economics, accounting, information systems, strategy, and the personal interests of executives.

- *Driver A: Environmental performance and brand value.* The task of ensuring a positive image has an 'attack' and 'defence' dimension. Managers want to create a positive image on selected attributes, and to avoid being poorly perceived on all others that are relevant.
- *Driver B: Natural resource supply and costs.* This driver is obvious for primary-sector enterprises (for example, farming, mining and fisheries) and for some manufacturing industries. Even for service enterprises the costs of inputs like water, power and transport are relevant.

[49] There is a burgeoning literature on environmentally related risks for corporations. Some examples are Aalders (2002); Ernst and Young (2003); Ernst & Young (2011). Krechowicz (2009); Wellington and Sauer (2005).

- *Driver C: Sustainability risk-management.* Risk issues can be categorised under six headings:
  (a) the availability or cost of resources – impacting upon product and process design and engineering, purchasing and logistics;
  (b) operations – impacting upon process management and engineering, logistics and facilities management;
  (c) capital assets – impacting upon capital allocation and operations, insurance and risk management;
  (d) the product or corporate reputation – affecting market positioning, political support, or community engagement;
  (e) from resource related policy decisions, which can affect almost any aspect of the business;
  (f) the personal welfare of executives and directors, from criminal or civil liability, or reputational harm.
- *Driver D: Sustainability and corporate citizenship.* A less tangible but real driver is the desire of executives and stakeholders to be good citizens.

The chief accountant will respond to different drivers than the public relations manager. Senior executives will have different concerns to operational managers and workers. How they interpret phenomena, and the strategies and tactics they use, will also differ. When the strategic rationale is unclear the default is to treat the issue as 'corporate social responsibility' or 'good corporate citizenship', rather than as strategic or economic.

The global strategy consultancy McKinsey highlights that a collision is shaping up among the rising demand for resources, constrained supplies, and changing social attitudes toward environmental protection.[50] They estimate that demand for oil, coal, iron ore and other natural resources will rise by at least a third, that the supply of natural resources will be constrained, and that increased regulatory and social scrutiny will compound the cost pressures. Many studies point to increased risk potentials of climate change, including on insurance costs and the availability of some insurance products. Services from the environment are often under-priced, such as water, or the use of rivers and air as emissions 'sinks'. A shift towards environmentally rational economic policy is

---

[50] Bisson, Stephenson and Viguerie (2010). McKinsey has focused upon sustainability issues as a key strategic concern.

occurring through Pigouvian pricing, consumption taxes, emissions taxes or quasi-market instruments, with variable success.[51]

5. THE BUSINESS RATIONALE

Until recently natural resource governance implied an antagonistic political relationship between business and environmental interests, because wealth production often depended upon use or destruction of natural resources. Agriculture and extractive industries together now represent less than 6 per cent of world GDP, manufacturing around 30 per cent, with services constituting the balance (2012 estimate).[52] A majority of corporations have no intrinsic economic motivation for antagonism to conservation, and most have reasons for wanting environmental governance to be more efficient. Many firms (including those dependent upon resource extraction and processing) have reasons to be seen as good environmental stewards. Even if an industry depends on resource extraction and processing, many firms realise that resource availability and price, and their social license to continue to use resources, are reasons to engage with sustainability. Business engagement with sustainability has two dimensions: individual firm action (stewardship engagement) and collective action by business (governance engagement). The crossover between these two forms is found in activities like environmental philanthropy, industry natural resource governance initiatives and environmental citizenship actions not specifically linked to the corporation's value chain. We will now consider a strategic rationale for corporate involvement in collective action to improve natural resource governance, and the potential for business to contribute to a more effective and more efficient hybrid governance model.

Business could bring much more to the natural resource governance table. What business does well includes:

(1) Large-scale behaviour change, including shaping norms of resource consumption.
(2) Converting resources into revenue, including pricing (otherwise) unpriced or under-priced goods and services and generating income by intangible value.
(3) Efficient administration and logistics.
(4) Securing and managing funds and other resources.

---

51 OECD (2006).
52 Index Mundi Factbook (2014), 'World GDP – composition by sector'.

(5) Translating inefficiencies (such as risk or transaction costs) into opportunities (viz. insurance and risk-management, and transaction services).[53]

More effective governance is more likely if industry invests their specialised knowledge, resources and political power to this end. Three practical criteria provide a basis for identifying where and how value to the firm and public benefit might be jointly optimised.

- Criterion 1: The public good will also provide economic and strategic benefits to the firm or its stakeholders. Activities that produce multiple benefits for the four drivers (A to D) particularly advantages that are not readily duplicated, are more valuable.[54]
- Criterion 2: Investment will produce a disproportionate leverage. This is more likely if the investment: (a) involves little cost beyond what the firm would otherwise spend; and/or (b) where the firm can, because of unique resources and expertise, produce a disproportionate benefit.[55] The first leg suggests the value of a strategic, rationale for voluntary reporting or corporate philanthropy.[56] The second aspect suggests a strategy that leverages specialist competences and resources, to support public benefit.
- Criterion 3: The Board can demonstrate to stakeholders (particularly shareholders and policy-holders) the rationale for its public good activities, and can point to tangible benefits.

Whilst ancient antagonisms and inadequate institutional arrangements impede hybrid natural resource governance that can harness these competences there are moves towards convergence of public and private interests in natural resource governance, identified by commentators and astute executives. In a recent interview US President Obama suggested that there is a distinction between the political stance of executives, and the *realpolitik* of climate change risk.

---

[53] Leibenstein (1966).

[54] Generally reflecting 'strategic option' theories in business.

[55] This criterion mirrors the concept of resource structure as the source of competitive advantage and explanation of strategic success. Barney and Clark (2007).

[56] See, e.g under the Global Reporting Initiative, (The 'GRI') or other voluntary social and environmental reporting schemes.

> President Obama: There's a huge gap between the professed values and visions of corporate CEOs and how their lobbyists operate in Washington. And I've said this to various CEOs. ... I think goes for a whole range of other issues like climate change, for example. There aren't any corporate CEOs that you talk to at least outside of maybe – no, I will include CEOs of the fossil fuel industries – who are still denying that climate change is a factor. What they want is some certainty around the regulations so that they can start planning. Given the capital investments that they have to make, they're looking at 20, 30 year investments. They've got to know now are we pricing carbon? Are we serious about this? But none of them are engaging in some of the nonsense that you're hearing out of the climate change denialists.[57]

Given the strategic drivers, engaging in sustainability does not necessarily require that business abandon a 'hard headed' economic and strategic logic. In particular, resource-related risk is a key intersection between resource governance, corporate strategy and corporate economic stewardship.

6. EVOLVING PRIVATE SECTOR ENGAGEMENT

The extent of private enterprise engagement in environment governance initiatives can easily be understated, because these are fragmented. Eight types of natural resource governance initiatives are undertaken by industry bodies, beyond the stewardship within the firm. These are:

(1) Environmental value chain management, particularly by firms whose stewardship credentials depend upon a chain of suppliers.[58]
(2) Carbon pollution and climate change initiatives, including financing and risk management.
(3) Industry research on sustainability, including product and service design, and industrial ecologies.
(4) Co-regulation linking government regulation and industry 'voluntary' codes and standards.[59]

---

[57] *The Economist* (2014), 'Barack Obama talks to *The Economist:* An interview with the president'.

[58] For a description see Martin and Verbeek (1998). Hagelaar, van der Vorst and Marcelis (2004); and Chiabotti (2004).

[59] See Chapter 5 (Doelle) and Chapter 13 (Holley and Lawson).

(5) Voluntary environmental performance standards, including industry programs,[60] the Global Reporting Initiative (GRI) and Socially Responsible Investment (SRI).[61]
(6) Strategic partnerships, particularly with NGOs, around environmental certification and branding, and joint civic action on environmental issues.
(7) International initiatives, such as by the World Business Council for Sustainable Development,[62] the World Bank and the United Nations.[63]

Industry sustainability initiatives are numerous and diverse. Impediments to the collaboration needed to make the total (public and private) resource governance system more efficient, effective and fair are weakening. However, we would not yet discount their significance and the need for institutional and interpersonal initiatives if effective hybrid governance is to emerge. Neither would we give a Panglossian view of the effectiveness of private sector initiatives. For almost every industry sustainability initiative there are critics who suggest cynical motivations, ineffectiveness or perverse effects. However, government and civil society initiatives also share the problem of unreliability. It is not possible to say whether industry-based initiatives are more or less effective overall than government or civil society action. Our hypothesis is that a combination of capabilities and initiatives is more likely to be effective than competing approaches, and hybridity should lead to vigour. Regardless of the source of initiatives, integrity and effectiveness are the central concerns.

Because complex risk issues, including climate change, are the major challenge to governance efforts, it is worth considering the potential for a deep collaboration between the public and private sector on these issues.

---

[60] There is a dazzling array of industry sustainability initiatives. Wikipedia provides a summary of sustainability initiatives from very many industries, from agriculture, forestry, fisheries, mining, manufacturing, public utilities, construction, transport, and others.

[61] The Global Reporting Initiative provides a widely used voluntary sustainability reporting framework. The Sustainability Disclosure database currently references and benchmarks the voluntary reports of 6,547 corporations around the world. Among the initiatives advancing sustainability reporting is the Global Initiative for Sustainability Ratings.

[62] The increased interest of business towards the framing of natural resources governance policy is articulated in Fussler (2012).

[63] Particularly through the United Nations Environment Program (Fussler 2012).

Industry is increasingly aware that they not only face challenges because of their impacts upon the environment, but also because of the impact of the environment upon them.

Financiers and insurers have few reasons to be deluded about the impact of environmental issues upon the businesses and those they ensure. It is in their interests that the risk effects of environmental issues are managed, and that volatility is controlled. It is not surprising that the finance and insurance sectors lead industry in addressing environmental risk issues in their own operations, in the operations of their clients and customers, and in developing a collective stance on natural resource governance risk issues.

The United Nations has sought to engage the finance and insurance industries. Particularly through the UNEP Finance Initiative, strategies to involve the finance sector as leaders in sustainability have been implemented. A number of publications set the scene for collaboration with the finance industry[64] through the UNEP Sustainable Finance Initiative, involving more than 200 banks, insurers and fund managers.[65] The development of the Principles for Sustainable Investment is significant.[66] The role of risk and insurance was given specific attention with a number of reports,[67] and then with the four Principles for Sustainable Insurance in 2012:[68]

1. We will embed in our decision-making environmental, social and governance issues relevant to our insurance business.
2. We will work together with our clients and business partners to raise awareness of environmental, social and governance issues, manage risk and develop solutions.
3. We will work together with governments, regulators and other key stakeholders to promote widespread action across society on environmental, social and governance issues.
4. We will demonstrate accountability and transparency in regularly disclosing publicly our progress in implementing the Principles.

---

64 Freshfields Bruckhaus Deringer (2005); UNEP FI Asset Management Working Group (2005); UNEP FI Asset Management Working Group (2007); UNEP Finance Initiative (2009a); UNEP FI Asset Management Working Group (2009); UNEP FI Asset Management Working Group (2010b).

65 UNEP Finance Initiative (2014).

66 Principles for Responsible Investment, (*PRI Association,* 2014). A number of research reports and other documents expand upon these principles and their path towards implementation.

67 UNEP Finance Initiative (2007); UNEP Finance Initiative (2009b).

68 UNEP Finance Initiative (2012).

Of particular note is Principle 3. At the Rio+20 summit the business sector signalled a new activism in resource governance. The World Business Council for Sustainable Development has given a clear signal of policy direction that business would wish to see pursued, and the finance and insurance sectors have aligned themselves with the idea that business does need to engage with the development of public policy in a new way.

7. QUO VADIS?

Driven by community pressures, concepts of good corporate governance, and economic self-interests (that admittedly do include defence against legal and political pressures), the private sector is strengthening its natural resource governance arrangements. Unconstrained by nation-state jurisdictional and constitutional limits, and with significant economic and political power, emerging arrangements have the potential to be synergistic with the actions of government, or to overtake or perhaps undermine government.

Businesses' increased concern is apparent in the increase of private sector sustainability initiatives. History, however, suggests that it will be difficult to move from an antagonistic and distrustful governance paradigm to a collaborative governance relationship.[69] That history also suggests that whilst we may try many models, many are likely to fail.[70] As yet there has been no effective dialogue about what a natural resource governance paradigm involving industry leadership as well as leadership by non-government sustainability advocates, and government authorities, might look like.

Environmental governance in practice is already significantly different to the 20th century archetype. Private governance arrangements from both business and civil society are already very powerful shapers of resource stewardship, and already have in place often powerful resource governance mechanisms. In many situations these are, in practice, more effective in shaping resource use and conservation than are traditional regulation or even formal market instruments. Over time it should be expected that effective governance will require efficient integration of public, business and civil initiatives.

As complex environmental risk has emerged as the most intractable challenge of sustainability, the skills and market power of industry have

---

69 Reflecting the logic of institutional path dependence. Liebowitz and Margolis (1995).

70 See Teece (1986).

become far more necessary to the design and implementation of effective public governance. The industry has signalled its interest in such an involvement but as yet the traditional divide has not been broached.

It is important for legal scholars and policy-makers to focus greater (and creative) attention on the hybrid model of natural resource governance that is evolving. The non-government aspects of the future hybrid model are developing with little attention to the value of synergy in systems of governance, and without serious attention to the need for strong integrity mechanisms[71] for these to be optimally effective. The voices of naysayers and sceptics should be heard, but the alternative to an effective hybrid is an increasing inability to effectively govern for sustainability. From this, everyone will lose.

REFERENCES

Aalders, M. (2002) *Drivers and Drawbacks: Regulation and Environmental Risk Management Systems* (CARR Discussion Papers, DP 10, Centre for Analysis of Risk and Regulation).

Angelsen, A. *et al.* (eds) (2012), '*The Evolution of REDD+*' in *Analysing REDD+: Challenges and Choices* (Barat: Cifor).

Bailis, R. and J. Baka (2011), 'Constructing Sustainable Biofuels: Governance of the Emerging Biofuel Economy' 101(4) *Annals of the Association of American Geographers* 827.

Barney, J. and D. Clark (2007), *Resource-based Theory: Creating and Sustaining Competitive Advantage* (Oxford: Oxford University Press).

Bartel, R. et al. (2007), *Developing a Good Regulatory Practice Model for Environmental Regulations Impacting on Farmers* (Surry Hills, NSW: Australian Farm Institute)

Becker, J. and P. Martin (2011), 'A Tale of Two Systems: Conflict, Law and the Development of Water Allocation in Two Common Law Jurisdictions' (2011) *International Journal of Rural Law and Policy* 1-19.

Bisson, P., E. Stephenson and S.P. Viguerie (2010), 'Pricing the Planet' (*McKinsey and Company – Insights and Publications,* June), accessed 3 April 2015 at http://www.mckinsey.com/insights/sustainability/pricing_the_planet.

Bosselmann, K. (2013), *The Principle of Sustainability: Transforming Law and Governance* (Farnham: Ashgate Publishing).

Brundtland, G.H. (1987), *'Our Common Future', World Commission on Environment and Development* (United Nations).

Byron, Lord, 'Childe Harold Canto': 'There is pleasure in the pathless woods' iv, Verse 178, accessed 3 April 2015 at https://archive.org/stream/childeharold spil05131gut/chpl10.txt.

[71] Governance mechanisms for arrangements, to ensure the reliability of their performance, particularly the absence of known governance failings such as agency capture, inefficiency and fraud.

Chiabotti, T. (2004), 'Evaluating corporate environmental strategy: a case study of six multinational companies' (PhD thesis, University of Florida).

Darwin, C. (1859), 'On the Origin of Species by Means of Natural Selection' (London: Murray).

Devall, B. and G. Sessions (1985), *Deep Ecology: Living as if Nature Mattered* (Layton, UT: Gibbs Smith).

Economist, The (2014) 'Barack Obama talks to *The Economist:* An interview with the president', accessed 3 April 2015 at, http://www.economist.com/blogs/democracyinamerica/2014/08/barack-obama-talks-economist.

Englund, O. and G. Berndes (forthcoming 2015), 'The Roles of Public and Private Governance in Promoting Sustainable Bioenergy' in Y. Le Bouthillier, H. McLeod-Kilmurray, P. Martin, and A. Cowie (eds), *The Law and Policy of Biofuels* (Cheltenham, UK and Northampton, MA, USA: Edward Elgar).

Ernst and Young (2003), *Responding to a Black Swan – Principles and Protocols or Responding to Unexpected Catastrophic Event* (Ernst & Young).

Ernst and Young (2011) *The Materiality of Environmental Risk to Australia's Finance Sector* (Ernst & Young).

Freshfields Bruckhaus Deringer (2005), *A Legal Framework for the Integration of Environmental, Social and Governance Issues into Institutional Investment* (UNEP Finance Initiative).

Fussler, C. (2012), *Changing Pace: Policy Options to Scale and Accelerate Business Action Towards Vision 2050*, (WBCSD).

Global Initiative for Sustainability Ratings, accessed 3 April 2015 at http://ratesustainability.org.

Global Reporting Initiative, The, accessed 3 April 2015 at https://www.globalreporting.org.

Gupta, J. (2012), 'Local Forests and REDD+ Governance: Win-win or Lose-lose?' 4(6) *Current Opinion in Environmental Sustainability* 620–27.

Hagelaar, G., J. van der Vorst and W. Marcelis (2004), 'Organising Life-cycles in Supply Chains' 45 *Greener Management International* 27–42.

Index Mundi Factbook (2014), 'World GDP – composition by sector', accessed 3 April 2015 at http://www.indexmundi.com/world/gdp_composition_by_sector.html.

IUCN Natural Resource Governance Framework (10 January 2013), accessed 3 April 2015 at http://www.iucn.org/knowledge/focus/ipbes_focus/iucn_natural_resource_governance_framework.

Jacobson, M.Z. (2012), *Air Pollution and Global Warming: History, Science, and Solutions* (2nd edn, Cambridge: Cambridge University Press).

Krechowicz, D. (2009), *Emerging Risk – Impacts of Key Environmental Trends in Emerging Asia* (Washington, DC: World Resources Institute).

Larson, A., and E. Petkova (2011), 'An Introduction to Forest Governance, People and REDD+ in Latin America: Obstacles and Opportunities' 2(1) *Forests* 86–111.

Lazarus, R. (2008), *The Making of Environmental Law* (Chicago: University of Chicago Press).

Leibenstein, H. (1966), 'Allocative Efficiency vs. "X-Efficiency"' (1966) 56(3) *The American Economic Review* 392–415.

Liebowitz, S. and S. Margolis (1995), 'Path Dependence, Lock-in, and History' 11 *Journal of Law, Economics & Organization* 205–26.

Locke, J. (1689), 'Second Treatise of Government' (*Awnsham Churchill*), accessed 3 April 2015 at http://www.earlymoderntexts.com/pdfs/locke1689a.pdf.

Manyika J. *et al.* (2014), 'Global flows in a digital age: How trade, finance, people, and data connect the world economy' McKinsey Report.

Martin, P., 'The Risks of Using REDD+ to Manage Rich Socio-ecological Systems' (2013) *International Journal Of Rural Law And Policy*, accessed 3 April 2015 at http://epress.lib.uts.edu.au/journals/index.php/ijrlp/article/view/3352 2014.

Martin, P. and E. Legal (forthcoming 2015), 'Biofuels: Why Should We Be Cautious About Policy?' in Y. Le Bouthillier, H. McLeod-Kilmurray, P. Martin, and A. Cowie (eds), *The Law and Policy of Biofuels* (Cheltenham, UK and Northampton, MA, USA: Edward Elgar).

Martin, P. and M. Verbeek (1998), *A National Materials Accounting Strategy: A Path to Competitive Advantage for Australian Industry* (Armidale, NSW: Profit Foundation Pty Limited).

Martin, P. and J. Williams (2010), *Policy Risk Assessment* (CRC for Irrigation Futures Technical Report Series No. 03/10. March).

Miller, F., A. Vandome and J. McBrewster (eds) (2011) *Alkali Act 1863* (International Book Marketing Service Limited).

Mol, A. (2010), 'Environmental Authorities and Biofuel Controversies' 19(1) *Environmental Politics* 61–79.

Natural Resources Management and Environment Department, 'Floods and Droughts', (*FAO Corporate Document Repository*), accessed 3 April 2015 at http://www.fao.org/docrep/005/y3918e/y3918e06.htm.

OECD (2006), *The Political Economy of Environmentally Related Taxes* (Paris: OECD), accessed 3 April 2015 at http://browse.oecdbookshop.org/oecd/pdfs/product/9706081e.pdf.

Pannell, D. (2002), 'Dryland Salinity: Economic, Scientific, Social and Policy Dimensions' (2002) 45(4) *Australian Journal of Agricultural and Resource Economics* 517–46.

Phelps, J., E.L. Webb and L.P. Koh (2011), 'Risky Business: An Uncertain Future for Biodiversity Conservation Finance Through REDD+' 4(2) *Conservation Letters* 88–94.

Porter, M. (1998), *The Competitive Advantage of Nations* (Basingstoke: Palgrave MacMillan).

Porter, M. (2008), *Competitive Advantage: Creating and Sustaining Superior Performance* (New York: Simon and Schuster).

Principles for Responsible Investment, (*PRI Association,* 2014), accessed 3 April 2015 at http://www.unpri.org.

Richardson, B. (2011), 'Sovereign Wealth Funds and the Quest for Sustainability: Insights from Norway and New Zealand' 2 *Nordic Journal of Commercial Law* 1–27.

Richardson, B. (2005), 'The Equator Principles: The Voluntary Approach to Environmentally Sustainable Finance' 14(11) *European Environmental Law Review* 280–90.

Rittel, H. and M. Webber (1973), 'Dilemmas in a General Theory of Planning' 4 *Policy Sciences* 155–69.

Rousseau, J. (1754), 'Discourse on the Origin and Basis of Inequality among Men' (1754) Public domain translation by Ian Johnston of Malaspina University-College, Nanaimo, British Columbia, accessed 10 April 2015 at https://www.oneeyedman.net/school-archive/classes/fulltext/www.mala.bc.ca/~johnstoi/rousseau/seconddiscourse.htm

Sustainability Disclosure database, accessed 3 April 2015 at https://www.globalreporting.org/reporting/report-services/sustainability-disclosure-database/Pages/default.aspx.

Teece, D. (1986), 'Profiting from Technological Innovation: Implications for Integration, Collaboration, Licensing and Public Policy' 15(6) *Research Policy* 285–305.

Thoreau H.D., 'Walden' (*Thoreau Reader,* 1854), accessed 3 April 2015 at http://thoreau.eserver.org/walden00.html.

Tolan, P. (2008), 'Ecocentric Perspectives on Global Warming: Toward an Earth Jurisprudence' (2008) 1(4) *Global Studies Journal* 39.

UNEP Finance Initiative (2007), *Insuring for Sustainability – Why and how the leaders are doing it* (UNEP Finance Initiative, 2007).

UNEP FI Asset Management Working Group (2005), *Show Me the Money: Linking Environmental, Social and Governance Issues to Company Value* (UNEP Finance-Asset Management Working Group of the United Nations Environment Programme Finance Initiative, 2005).

UNEP FI Asset Management Working Group (2007), *Demystifying Responsible Investment Performance: A Review of Key Academic and Broker Research on ESG Factors* (UNEP Finance Initiative).

UNEP FI Asset Management Working Group (2009) *The Materiality of Climate Change: How Finance Copes with the Ticking Clock* (UNEP Finance Initiative).

UNEP FI Asset Management Working Group (2010a) *Auditing the Implementation of Multilateral Environmental Agreements (MEAs): A Primer for Auditors* (UNEP), accessed 3 April 2015 at http://www.unep.org/delc/Portals/119/audingmeas.pdf.

UNEP FI Asset Management Working Group (2010b), *Translating ESG into Sustainable Business Value – Key Insights for Companies and Investors* (UNEP Finance Initiative).

UNEP Finance Initiative (2009a), *Fiduciary Responsibility – Legal and Practical Aspects of Integrating Environmental, Social and Governance Issues into Institutional Investment* (UNEP Finance Initiative).

UNEP Finance Initiative (2009b) *The Global State of Sustainable Insurance – Understanding and Integrating Environmental, Social and Governance Factors in Insurance.* (UNEP Finance Initiative).

UNEP Finance Initiative (2012) *PSI – Principles for Sustainable Insurance*, (UNEP Finance Initiative, 2012) United Nations PSI Principles of Sustainable Insurance, accessed 3 April 2015 at http://www.unepfi.org/fileadmin/documents/PSI_document-en.pdf.

UNEP Finance Initiative (2014), 'What we do' accessed 3 April 2015 at www.unepfi.org.

UN General Assembly Resolution 66/288, adopted by the General Assembly on 27 July 2012, accessed 3 April 2015 at http://sustainabledevelopment.un.org/futurewewant.html.

Voigt, C. (ed.) (2013), *Rule of Law for Nature: New Dimensions and Ideas in Environmental Law* (Cambridge: Cambridge University Press).

Wellington, F. and A. Sauer (2005), *Framing Climate Risk in Portfolio Management* (Washington, DC: Ceres, World Resources Institute).

Wood, W. (1924), 'Increase in Salt in Soil and Streams Following the Destruction of Native Vegetation' 10(7) *Journal of the Royal Society of Western Australia* 35–47.

Wordsworth, W., 'To the Cuckoo' (*Poetry* Foundation, 1770–1850), accessed 3 April 2015 at http://www.poetryfoundation.org/poem/174831.

Wordsworth, W., 'I Wandered Lonely as a Cloud' (*Poetry Foundation*), accessed 3 April 2015 at http://www.poetryfoundation.org/poem/174790.
Worldometers, 'Word Population: Past, Present and Future', accessed 3 April 2015 at http://www.worldometers.info/world-population/#pastfuture.

14. Regulators networks: collaborative agency approaches to the implementation and enforcement of environmental law

Grant Pink and Robyn Bartel

1. INTRODUCTION

Regulators, irrespective of geographic location, the entities and sectors they regulate and the nature of the commodities regulated, face a common challenge of maintaining institutional capacity for undertaking effective regulatory activities. This chapter considers how agencies engaged in environmental regulation and enforcement use network learning to close this capacity gap. The chapter consists of five sections. Section 1 consists of a brief introduction, providing some context around environmental regulation, environmental regulatory tools and regulator networks. Section 2 profiles several networks designed to aid environmental regulation and enforcement. Section 3 explores some benefits and functions of networks including learning and capacity-building. Section 4 explores how network efficacy may be evaluated. Section 5, the conclusion, includes a research agenda to advance the utility of networks as a tool for implementing environmental law.

1.1 Environmental Regulation

Environmental regulation and enforcement involves distinct challenges when compared to mainstream law enforcement, including complexity and culture.[1] Complexity arises due to regulatory schemes which have been designed to serve differing and sometimes poorly enunciated goals, developed over relatively short periods of time. Most environmental

[1] Clifford and Edwards (2012); White (2008); Wijbenga *et al.* (2008).

legislation has evolved over recent decades and includes relatively novel components.[2] Consequently these regimes lack an extensive body of case law[3] or common law[4] considered critical enablers to effective regulation and enforcement. A volatile policy context is ensured by rapidly advancing scientific understanding of environmental harms, shifting popular and political responses, and a dynamic biophysical environment. The cultural challenges relate to tensions between different expectations of the role and function of environmental agencies. Bricknell observes that 'agencies who only recently adopted the mantle of regulator are still negotiating the regulatory culture'.[5]

1.2 Traditional Regulatory Tools

Regulation is about the use of power, persuasion or influence by one party against another to do something that they otherwise would not have done.[6] Freiberg suggests that (governmental) regulators have access to six forms of power: economic, transactional, authorisational, structural, informational and legal.[7] These powers are used singularly or in combination to produce behavioural change to achieve the desired regulatory outcome. In terms of environmental regulation it is the *authorisational* and *legal* powers that are used most frequently. They contain traditional regulatory tools such as; licensing, registration, permission, certification, accreditation and litigation; and primary, delegated and quasi-legislation respectively.[8]

1.3 Enforcement Networks: A Non-traditional Regulatory Tool

Matching regulatory tools (whether traditional or non-traditional) to policy problems and desired outcomes is difficult.[9] The use of regulatory tools is dependent on contextual factors such as: jurisdiction, the nature of the problem and social, economic and environmental aspects. When considering the use of 'tools' or 'instruments' by government Salamon suggests that 'tools' can be defined broadly to include 'an identifiable

---

2 Du Rées (2009).
3 Reeve (2002).
4 Bates (2006).
5 Bricknell (2010) 114.
6 See Freiberg (1987) 226.
7 Freiberg (2010) 84.
8 Ibid, 85.
9 Ibid, 87.

method through which collective action is structured to address a public problem'.[10] Similarly regarding 'instruments', Gunningham and Grabosky consider them to be 'the tools employed by institutions to do what they wish to do'.[11]

Due to the complicated nature of environmental regulation, and the small pool of specialist knowledge from which to draw, agencies often look to their peers for assistance. Over time these peer relationships have formed into networks. These have been employed as a form of 'collective action'; a 'tool employed by institutions'. Over the last 20 years there has been a proliferation of environmental enforcement networks (EENs) and enforcement networks,[12] with the latter focusing to a greater or lesser extent on environmental issues.[13] For the purpose of this chapter we adopt Provan *et al.*'s definition of a network as 'a group of three or more organisations connected in ways that facilitate achievement of a common goal'. They describe the relationships between network members as 'primarily nonhierarchical, and participants often have substantial operating autonomy'.[14] In this chapter enforcement networks and regulator networks are used interchangeably, except where specifically indicated otherwise.

2. ENVIRONMENTAL ENFORCEMENT NETWORKS

A range of network types are identified in the literature:

- Slaughter identifies three types of networks: information networks, enforcement networks and harmonisation networks;[15]
- Milward and Provan suggest networks form around: service implementation, information diffusion, problem-solving and community capacity-building;[16]

---

[10] Salamon (2002) 19.

[11] Gunningham and Grabosky (1998) 37.

[12] Pink (2010); Pink (2011). For example INTERPOL's Environment Crime Programme and the World Customs Organizations Regional Intelligence Liaison Officers and/or Project Skyhole Patching which focused on ozone depleting substances.

[13] See Pink (2010); Pink (2015); Pink and Lehane (2012).

[14] Provan, Fish and Sydow (2007) 482.

[15] Slaughter (2004) 52–61.

[16] Milward and Provan (2006).

- Isett *et al.* suggest a typology of: policy networks, collaborative networks and governance networks;[17]
- Popp *et al.* refer to networks that are mandated and formal and/or informal and emergent.[18]

In this chapter, in respect to environmental regulation and enforcement, and to identify the different learning and capacity building needs, we consider three main forms: geographically-based networks, discipline-based networks and commodity-based networks. There are also hybrid forms of networks which exhibit features of the other three.

2.1 Commodity-based Networks

Examples of commodity-based networks are the Wildlife Enforcement Networks described by their capabilities in Table 14.1. Although having wildlife in common, enforcement in this area is multifaceted. It is concerned with the treatment, trade and movement of wildlife and wildlife products within jurisdictions, across regions and internationally.

Wildlife Enforcement Networks are prolific. This is probably due to the fact that the 1975 Convention on International Trade in Endangered Species of Wild Fauna and Flora (CITES) is the longest standing multilateral environmental agreement (MEA) and mega fauna has and continues to receive significant media attention.[19] INTERPOL-WCWG is very operationally focused, initiating and leading projects and global enforcement operations[20] to combat the poaching, trafficking or possession of legally protected flora and fauna. INTERPOL's-WCWG operates regionally or nationally through the coordinated efforts of its member countries. Although ASEAN-WEN operates as a regional

---

[17] Isett *et al.* (2011).

[18] Popp *et al.* (2013).

[19] In February 2014 the British Royal Family held a high level meeting in London involving 46 countries focusing on Illegal Wildlife Trade. See http://www.cites.org/eng/news/pr/2014/london-conference-20140214.php (accessed 3 April 2015). In the United States of America, President Barack Obama released a National Strategy for Combating Wildlife Trafficking. In part, the strategy seeks to develop effective worldwide Wildlife Enforcement Networks (WENs). See http://www.whitehouse.gov/sites/default/files/docs/nationalstrategywildlifetrafficking.pdf (accessed 3 April 2015).

[20] For more information on the nature and scale of these operations refer to the Operations RAMP (reptiles and amphibians) and TRAM (traditional Asian medicines) at http://www.interpol.int/Crime-areas/Environmental-crime/Operations (accessed 3 April 2015).

Table 14.1 Wildlife Enforcement (Commodity-based) Networks

EEN	Level	Est.	Focus*	Activity**	Formality
Australian Wildlife Enforcement Network[21]	Regional	1994	Commodity (Wildlife)	Operations	Semi-formal
National Inter-Agency CITES Enforcement Collaboration Group (NICECG)[22]	National	2011	Commodity (Wildlife)	Policy/ Project	Formal
Association of Southeast Asian Nations' Wildlife Network (ASEAN-WEN)[23]	Regional	2005	Commodity (Wildlife)	Operations	Formal
South Asia Wildlife Enforcement Network (SAWEN)[24]	Regional	2005	Commodity (Wildlife)	Operations	Formal
INTERPOL Wildlife Crime Working Group (INTERPOL-WCWG)[25]	Global	1994	Commodity (Wildlife)	Operations	Semi-formal

Notes: *(Commodity, Discipline, Geographic or Hybrid); **(Operations, Policy/Project or Hybrid).

[21] This network saw senior wildlife enforcement officers gather and operate for a decade before its activities were largely incorporated into the Australasian Law Enforcement and Regulators Network (AELERT) when it formed in 2004. Many of the activities of this network were subsequently progressed by the then AELERT Wildlife Crime Working Group and later AELERT Operations Cluster.

[22] See http://www.cites.org/eng/news/pr/2012/20120509_certificate_cn.php (accessed 3 April 2015).

[23] See http://www.asean-wen.org/index.php/about-us/what-is-asean-wen (accessed 3 April 2015).

[24] See http://www.sawen.org/ (accessed 3 April 2015).

[25] See http://www.interpol.int/Crime-areas/Environmental-crime/Environmental-Compliance-and-Enforcement-Committee/Wildlife-Crime-Working-Group (accessed 3 April 2015).

'intergovernmental law-enforcement network'[26] it is the world's largest wildlife law enforcement network. It involves police, customs and environmental agencies of all ten ASEAN countries. ASEAN-WEN facilitates increased capacity and better coordination and collaboration of law enforcement agencies between Southeast Asian countries, regionally and globally.[27] ASEAN-WEN SAWEN, also operating regionally, seeks to 'strengthen, promote and co-ordinate regional co-operation for curbing illegal wildlife trade'.[28] It 'helps foster broader awareness on the issues and implications of wildlife trade across countries by sharing information on common problems and developing response strategies; building capacity of enforcement staff and sharing information and experiences'.[29] NICECG is unusual in its primarily project and policy activity-based focus. It was established in China '... to facilitate the collection and exchange of intelligence, enhance capacity building, and coordinate joint enforcement activities'.[30]

2.2 Geographic-based Networks

The International Network of Environmental Compliance and Enforcement – Seaports Enforcement Security Network (INECE-SESN) is an example of a geographic network (Table 14.2). Participation in this network is open to governments, organisations, and individuals with responsibility for controlling shipments of hazardous waste through seaports.

Table 14.2 Seaport (Geographic-based) Network

EEN	Level	Est.	Focus*	Activity**	Formality
INECE-SESN[31]	Global	2008	Commodity (Hazardous Waste)	Operations	Semi-formal

Notes: *(Commodity, Discipline, Geographic or Hybrid); **(Operations, Policy/Project or Hybrid).

[26] See http://www.asean-wen.org/index.php/about-us/what-is-asean-wen (accessed 3 April 2015).

[27] Ibid.

[28] See http://www.sawen.org/mission/ and http://www.sawen.org/specific-objectives/ (both accessed 3 April 2015).

[29] See http://www.sawen.org/establishment-of-sawen/ (accessed 3 April 2015).

[30] See http://www.cites.org/eng/news/pr/2012/20120509_certificate_cn.php (accessed 3 April 2015).

[31] International Network of Environmental Compliance and Enforcement (INECE) (2011).

The INECE-SESN has worked closely with various national, regional and international partners including the:

- Secretariat of the Basel Convention;
- European Union Network for Implementation and Enforcement of Environmental Law Transfrontier Shipments of Waste (IMPEL-TFS);
- Asian Network for Prevention of Illegal Transboundary Movement of Hazardous Wastes;
- United Nations Environment Programme (UNEP);
- United Nations Office of Drugs and Crime (UNODC); and
- World Customs Organization (WCO).

The INECE-SESN has an operational focus. Its core membership is regulatory (practitioners and managers) professionals involved in inspection and monitoring of transboundary movements of hazardous waste through seaports.[32] Together, members build capacity, raise awareness, and facilitate enforcement collaboration to detect and control illegal and dangerous transboundary shipments of environmentally-regulated goods through seaports.[33] INECE-SESN has identified gaps in inspections and enforcement programs and responded by developing tools and resources.[34] It has also been effective in sharing expertise and promoting cooperation and collaboration. This has led to the development and delivery of training material and sessions and inspector/officer exchanges.

2.3 Discipline-based Networks

Prosecution and Investigation Networks are examples of discipline-based networks (Table 14.3). Prosecution networks are concerned with the discipline (or professional stream) and practice and procedure associated with prosecution and litigation of breaches of environmental laws. As the work of prosecutors is defined by the laws within jurisdictions (i.e. national, regional and international) these networks have a membership which reflects such a spread.

---

32 Heiss et al. (2011).
33 Ibid.
34 See INECE (2011); INECE (2012a); INECE (2012b).

Table 14.3 Prosecution and Investigation (Discipline-based) Networks

EEN	Level	Est.	Focus*	Activity**	Formality
European Network of Prosecutors for the Environment (ENPE)[35]	Regional	2012	Discipline (Prosecution)	Operations	Informal
Latin American Environmental Prosecutors Network (LAEPN)[36]	Regional	2008	Discipline (Prosecution)	Operations	Informal
Global Network of Prosecutors and General Attorneys (GNoPG)[37]	Global	2011	Discipline (Prosecution)	Hybrid	Semi-formal
Natural Resource Investigation Group (NRIG)[38]	Sub-national	2001	Discipline (Investigation)	Operations	Informal

Notes: *(Commodity, Discipline, Geographic or Hybrid); **(Operations, Policy/Project or Hybrid).

Prosecution Networks are a relatively recent phenomenon. None of the networks in Table 14.3 existed prior to 2008. These networks provide opportunities for knowledge exchange and transfer on routine and bespoke issues. The aims of LAEPN are 'to facilitate the communication and the exchange of experiences among the Prosecutors members to

[35] See http://www.basel.int/Default.aspx?tabid=2940 (accessed 3 April 2015).

[36] See http://www.mpambiental.org/?acao=quemsomos (accessed 3 April 2015).

[37] See http://inece.org/2013/01/31/innovative-activities/ and http://inece.org/topics/good-governance/prosecutors-network/ (both accessed 3 April 2015).

[38] The NRIG operated in South Australia, one of Australia's provinces, from 2001 and was instrumental in shaping AELERT mentioned above.

strength[en] the fight against crimes and to enforce the law'.[39] LAEPN members exchange and share '... information, to research environmental law, jurisprudence, texts and examples of actions (models to legal actions)'.[40] GNoPG was launched by INECE and the International Union for the Conservation of Nature (IUCN) to '... provide prosecutors and attorneys general that are educated on environmental compliance and enforcement issues and possess the skills and tools, relative to their legal system and culture, to successfully prosecute environmental crimes'.[41] GNoPG connects prosecutors and general attorneys and links them with existing geographic-based, discipline-based or commodity-based networks.[42] ENPE was established as an informal network between prosecutors in EU member countries 'to help practitioners connect; to share experiences and data on environmental crime; and to look at crucial issues linked to the environment'.[43] ENPE confine their activities to 'criminal prosecution of any environmental crime'.[44] The Prosecution Networks hold meetings, workshops and training sessions, and produce a range of material. The Natural Resource Investigation Group (NRIG) brings investigation officers together from four agencies[45] in the environmental portfolio at least twice a year to share experiences, lessons learned and advances in investigation methods.

2.4 Hybrid Networks

Table 14.4 presents capability profiles for some of the major hybrid networks from across the world.

---

39 See http://www.mpambiental.org/?acao=quemsomos (accessed 3 April 2015).

40 Ibid.

41 See https://www.iucn.org/news_homepage/news_by_date/?7962/LAUNCHING-OF-THE-GLOBAL-NETWORK-OF-PROSECUTORS-AND-GENERAL-ATTORNEYS (accessed 3 April 2015).

42 Ibid.

43 See http://www.basel.int/Default.aspx?tabid=2940 (accessed 3 April 2015).

44 Ibid.

45 The agencies are the environmental protection agency, fisheries department, water resources department and national parks and wildlife service located in South Australia, one of Australia's provinces.

Table 14.4 Environmental Enforcement (Hybrid) Networks

EEN	Level	Est.	Focus*	Activity**	Formality
Australasian Environmental Law Enforcement and Regulators neTwork (AELERT)[46]	Regional	2004	Hybrid	Hybrid	Semi-formal
Asian Environmental Compliance and Enforcement Network (AECEN)[47]	Regional	2005	Hybrid	Hybrid	Formal
Commission for Environmental Cooperation (CEC)[48]	Regional	1994	Hybrid	Hybrid	Formal
East African Network for Environmental Compliance and Enforcement (EANECE)[49]	Regional	2010	Hybrid	Hybrid	Semi-formal
European Union Network for the Implementation and Enforcement of Environmental Law (IMPEL)[50]	Regional	1992	Hybrid	Hybrid	Formal
International Network for Environmental Compliances and Enforcement (INECE)[51]	Global	1990	Hybrid	Policy/ Project	Semi-formal

46 See http://www.aelert.net (accessed 3 April 2015).
47 See http://www.aecen.org (accessed 3 April 2015).
48 See http://www.cec.org (accessed 3 April 2015).
49 See http://www.eanece.org/eanece/ (accessed 3 April 2015).
50 See http://www.impel.eu (accessed 3 April 2015).
51 See http://www.inece.org (accessed 3 April 2015).

Table 14.4 (continued)

EEN	Level	Est.	Focus*	Activity**	Formality
INTERPOL Wildlife Crime Working Group (INTERPOL-WCWG)[52]	Global	1992	Hybrid	Operations	Formal
Jordan Network for Environmental Compliance and Enforcement (JNECE)[53]	Regional	2013	Hybrid	Hybrid	Semi-formal
Network for Ireland's Environmental Compliance and Enforcement (NIECE)[54]	Regional	2004	Hybrid	Hybrid	Semi-formal
West African Network for Environmental Compliance and Enforcement (WAECEN)[55]	Regional	2013	Hybrid	Hybrid	Semi-formal

Notes: *(Commodity, Discipline, Geographic or Hybrid); **(Operations, Policy/Project or Hybrid).

As previously mentioned, hybrid networks are established when the main forms of networks (geographically-based, disciplined-based and commodity-based) combine either bilaterally or multilaterally. AELERT and IMPEL are two hybrid networks which have various Clusters[56] that generate benefits to member agencies of a tactical, operational and strategic nature. These benefits include project and policy initiatives. They can involve numerous permutations arising from overlapping commodities, sectors, regulatory regimes and disciplines. For example AELERT's Operations Cluster has established a National Waste Operations Group. This group with representatives from each jurisdiction

52 http://www.interpol.int/Crime-areas/Environmental-crime/Environmental-Compliance-and-Enforcement-Committee/Wildlife-Crime-Working-Group (accessed 3 April 2015).

53 See http://www.inece.org/resources/jnece (accessed 3 April 2015).

54 See http://www.epa.ie/enforcement/pa/network/ (accessed 3 April 2015).

55 See http://www.inece.org/2013/11/12/wanece (accessed 3 April 2015).

56 For AELERT Clusters see https://aelert.net/cluster-working-groups/; for IMPEL clusters see http://impel.eu/about/clusters/ (both accessed 3 April 2015).

provides an avenue for national coordination of waste regulatory strategies and operational activities through the sharing of best practice materials, and operational and intelligence activities.[57] IMPEL's *Recommended Minimum Criteria for Environmental Inspections* (or RMCEI) is an attempt to achieve operational standardisation in spite of legal and political differences.[58]

3. NETWORKING LEARNING AND CAPACITY BUILDING

Improved knowledge flow and enhanced learning are the chief benefits for which networks exist and these areas are essential for improving their efficacy.[59] This language may be overtly, and overly, instrumentalist. However the learning is not for learning's sake – it is task-oriented – specifically for solving environmental and social ills and achieving public policy goals. Particularly if we have regard to the complex environmental and public policy problems that agencies are tasked with solving, and the deficiencies in resources and capacity within the public sector, this language is helpful in focusing our attention on utility and efficacy. As Popp *et al.* observe:

> Some argue that inter-organisational networks exist because of a moral imperative. That is, the important issues facing society (e.g., poverty, crime, health promotion, economic development, the environment, natural disasters, education, healthcare reform) must be addressed, yet clearly cannot be tackled by single organisations working on their own.[60]

Such networks therefore, whether formal, informal, mandated or emergent, are goal-oriented. They exist because it is believed that outcomes can be achieved together which may not be attained by one member alone, that is, they have a collective action function to create public

---

[57] See https://aelert.net/national-waste-operations-group/ (accessed 3 April 2015).

[58] For more detailed information on the RMCEI see European Union Implementation and Enforcement of Environmental Law (IMPEL) (n.d.); Liebregts and Kramers (2008).

[59] See discussion in Provan and Lemaire (2012).

[60] Popp *et al.* (2013) 7.

value.[61] Learning is undertaken to achieve improvements in network outcomes. Popp *et al.* describe three dimensions to learning in networks: information diffusion and knowledge exchange, network learning and innovation.[62] A fourth dimension is capacity-building.[63]

3.1 Information Diffusion and Knowledge Exchange

Information and knowledge are necessary components in learning.[64] Learning within regulator networks may pertain to explicit, formal elements of a single agency's, or a single practitioner's, remit, as well as to specific intervention approaches or regulatory tools. Learning may also relate to internal processes as well as capacity building such as professional development and training. Tacit and situated knowledge may also be shared, as well as the unique learning related to social capital. Social capital 'is based on attributes of the relationship between individuals' rather than knowledge and information, which is classified as human capital.[65] This can be significant for networks:

> By working together, organizations in a community learn to understand and trust one another, as well as learn whom not to trust. This learning can be extremely important, not just for the production of current services, but also for the joint production of services to be performed in the future, particularly in other service domains.[66]

Learning within networks may occur informally as well as formally. Formal learning may be facilitated through conferences, staff exchanges and twinning initiatives,[67] collaborative training and joint exercises,[68] project work (collaborative and co-design) resulting in generic training

---

[61] Agranoff and McGuire (2001) 296; Bryson, Crosby and Stone (2006); Isett et al. (2011); Provan and Milward (2001) 415; Provan *et al.* (2007) 482; Provan and Lemaire (2012).

[62] Popp *et al.* (2013) 8. See also Podolny and Page (1998); Powell (1990); Thorelli (1986).

[63] Pink (2010).

[64] Hartley and Benington (2006) 102.

[65] Provan and Lemaire (2012) 639. See also Agranoff and McGuire (2001) 302.

[66] Provan and Milward (2001) 417.

[67] Asian Environmental Compliance and Enforcement Network (AECEN) (2010). Australasian Environmental Law Enforcement and Regulators neTwork (AELERT) (2011).

[68] Heiss *et al.* (2011).

material and other documentation[69] and national, regional and global enforcement activities. Informal learning may occur through the experience of cultures and paradigms – which may be significant in accelerating learning, including embedding reflective practice. Emulation and imitation may also occur formally or informally. For example a network may officially adopt the practice of one agency member, or a practitioner within an agency may learn of the practice of another, comprising dissemination through word-of-mouth.

Agranoff and McGuire have highlighted the impact of networks on learning in their observation that 'knowledge creation and learning occur best when people are reacting to someone else's thinking'.[70] Mere exposure to or sharing of information does not result in learning or guarantee adoption and improved results. Knowledge exchange is not a simple linear process:

> Instead, knowledge is continuously reviewed, recreated or re-appreciated as it is taken into different settings or is rediscovered in relation to new purposes or alongside existing 'old' knowledge.[71]

Learning may occur at the individual or group level. There is also a significant body of literature related to organisational learning.[72] Learning may also occur at the network level itself.

3.2 Network Learning

Networks may draw knowledge from outside and from their member agencies, but also generate new learning.[73] Knight differentiates between learning achieved *within* networks (including cognitive learning and behavioural change by individuals)[74] and learning achieved *by* networks.[75] Knight and Pye go further to state that in the absence of changes

---

69 For more information on the project relating to the Recommended Minimum Criteria for Environmental Inspections (or RMCEI) see http://impel.eu/projects/doing-the-right-things-ii-step-by-step-guidance-book-for-planning-of-environmental-inspections/ (accessed 3 April 2015); Liebregts and Kramers (2008).

70 Agranoff and McGuire (2001) 296.

71 Hartley and Benington (2006) 104.

72 See for example Garvin, Edmondson and Gino (2008); Senge and Sterman (1992).

73 Capaldo (2014); Phelps, Heidl and Wadhwa (2012).

74 Knight (2002).

75 Knight and Pye (2005); Schulz and Geithner (2010) 69.

to network-level properties, there is no network learning. They differentiate this from inter-organisational learning, which occurs at the level of the individual, group or organisation.[76] Provan *et al.* agree that although learning at lower levels may also occur outcomes must be evident at the network level.[77] Therefore, while network learning can also result in behavioural and cognitive outcomes, at the network level it may result in social, political, situated and practice oriented development of network practices, interpretations and structures, and may include innovations.[78] Ameli and Kayes observe that learning outcomes should also include changes within the member agencies.[79]

Network learning is therefore a multi-level process. Within the public sector it often, also necessarily (and increasingly under new collaborative governance models), involves social and societal learning encompassing the community and non-government sector.[80] There have been limitations identified with simpler learning cycles, and even social (also known as double-loop) learning. These learning cycles may only address the proximate causes of problems and ignore fundamental structural, systemic and philosophical issues.[81] For initiating innovative insights and approaches, triple-loop learning, also known as transformative learning (also epistemic learning)[82] has been developed. Pahl-Wostl considers that formal networks may be limited to single-loop learning.[83] However transformative learning and formal networks may not be mutually exclusive.[84] Pahl-Wostl also observes that where networks are at least partially informal (in the sense of not being rule and outcome-bound), issue-specific and comprising a community of practice they can support innovation and the more advanced social and societal learning and

---

[76] Knight and Pye (2005) 371.
[77] Provan, Fish and Sydow (2007) 506.
[78] Knight and Pye (2005) 384–5.
[79] Ameli and Kayes (2011). The RMCEI mentioned previously is a prime example.
[80] Armitage *et al.* (2011); Berkes (2009); Pahl-Wostl (2009); Pahl-Wostl et al. (2007); Waddell (2002); Kate Wilner *et al.* on behalf of the Coastal CURA Team (2012).
[81] Pahl-Wostl (2009); Waddell (2002).
[82] See Sterling (2011).
[83] Pahl-Wostl (2009) 361.
[84] See for example Bulkeley (2005); Wright and Pandey (2010).

critical reflection necessary for transformation.[85] Linkages to formal policy processes may enhance efficacy.[86]

3.3 Innovation

Networks create innovation and are themselves examples of innovative governance. Pahl-Wostl defines a network as a mode of governance distinct from bureaucracies and markets.[87] Public sector networks are increasingly oriented towards civil society: incorporating the non-state actors under wider notions of enfranchisement and governance.[88] Their cooperative spirit is opposed to the competitive ethos dominant elsewhere.[89] Such innovations are essential to avoid perpetuating the failures of inappropriately technocratic, bureaucratic and anthropocentric paradigms to solving environmental and related social problems, and to escape also the lock-in and path dependency of existing approaches.[90] It has also been observed that the 'new public management'[91] paradigm and ideological preference for business processes and market solutions is ill-suited to solving wicked problems such as those faced by environmental agencies.[92] Networks are thus a means for solving regulatory and market failure[93] and perhaps bureaucratic failure.

Within networks, Thorgren *et al.* have identified that both bottom-up and top-down strengths can foster innovation. Bottom-up (or grass-roots) generation and maintenance of a network is necessary for member commitment, motivation and social capital. Top-down support is necessary for fostering cooperation, communication and transparency among network members; coordinating activities; analysing network strengths and weaknesses; and motivating prospective network members to be

---

85 Pahl-Wostl (2009) 361. See also Armitage, Marschke and Plummer (2008); Huntjens et al. (2011); Wilner *et al.* (2012).

86 Pahl-Wostl (2009) 362.

87 Pahl-Wostl (2009) 356. See also Podolny and Page (1998); Powell (1990).

88 See for example Ansell and Gash (2008); Bartel (2013); Bryson *et al.* (2006); Pahl-Wostl (2009); and Holley and Lawson (Chapter 11 herein).

89 Provan and Milward (2001) 415.

90 See for example Holling and Meffe (1996); Pahl-Wostl (2009); Stanley (1995) 255-62; Westley *et al.* (2011); Wilner *et al.* (2012); Woodhill and Röling (1998).

91 See for example Pfiffner (2004) .

92 Isett *et al.* (2011) and see discussion in Agranoff and McGuire (2001) 319ff; Provan and Lemaire (2012) and Australian Public Service Commission (2007).

93 Isett et al. (2011) 159.

engaged in setting the agenda for the network.[94] At the same time control should not be heavy-handed since this may threaten flexibility and stifle creativity.[95]

One way through which innovation can be supported within and by networks is by bringing together more voices and perspectives to policy questions.[96] Different views need to be 'crowded in' rather than 'crowded out'. However local and vernacular knowledge is often under-utilised since scientific and bureaucratic knowledge is seen as more valid.[97] Many voices may also bring conflict and disagreement – but this may be exactly what is required to generate innovation.[98] For this approach to flourish there needs to be trust and respect for diversity.[99]

It must be recognised that networks do not exist in a political or ideological vacuum. While it is too early to declare the end of hierarchical command-and-control or of traditional government bureaucracy[100] one of the reasons for which networks may exist is the growing need for external sources of 'value-adding' skillsets and knowledge required to function effectively in an increasingly complex environment. This context comprises of contradictory elements, including demands for 'small' government but with increasing 'client' focus, and demands for productivity and efficiency gains, in conditions of overwhelming information, as well as deregulation and regression of environmental protections.[101] Popp *et al.* note that networks need to be proactive as well as reactive, forming 'in advance recognition of the complexity of the issue at hand and with a realistic view of the benefits to be gained through an inter-organisational network approach'.[102] This goes against the predominant crisis-driven and reactive problem-response of public policy more generally.

---

94 Thorgren, Wincent and Örtqvist (2009) cited in Popp *et al.* (2013) 35.

95 See for example Agranoff and McGuire (2001) 310.

96 See discussion in Agranoff and McGuire (2001) 321 re collaborative networks.

97 See for example Armitage *et al.* (2011); Bartel, McFarland and Hearfield (2014). Holling and Meffe (1996); Marshall (2013); Ostrom (2000); Claudia Pahl-Wostl *et al.* (2011); Wilner *et al.* (2012); van Tol Smit, de Loë and Plummer (2015).

98 Popp *et al.* (2013) 35.

99 Hartley and Benington (2006).

100 McGuire and Agranoff (2011).

101 Hartley and Benington (2006); McGuire and Agranoff (2011); Prieur (2012).

102 Popp et al. (2013) 23.

3.4 Capacity Building

Capacity building activities of networks, reflecting the demands placed upon them, generally include:

- Building relationships and strengthening capacity across jurisdictions;
- Sharing information and experiences;
- Raising awareness and improving environmental compliance and environment efforts; and
- Developing standardised practices and procedures to support enforcement.[103]

Most environmental regulatory agencies, even longstanding and traditional environment protection agencies,[104] undergo internal cultural realignment. The most substantial of these may become necessary when the activities and focus of the agency move from what was a policy, program and environmental stewardship centric focus, to one that is more adversarial in nature with an amplified focus on regulatory, compliance and enforcement.[105] Internal cultural realignment results in agencies having specific short, medium, long term and ongoing needs to build and maintain capacity. Short-term (and immediate) capacity is often required initially to carry out basic regulatory functions – whereas ongoing needs tend to form part of continuous improvement practices. Capacity is often sought in areas such as:

- Staff recruitment, training and retention;
- Development and maintenance of policies;
- Development and maintenance of procedures;
- Selection and reporting against key performance indicators;
- Identification and selection of and monitoring and reporting against priorities; and

---

[103] Pink (2010) 7.

[104] Such as the Swedish Environmental Protection Agency, United States Environment Protection Agency, and the Victorian Environment Protection Agency established in 1967, 1970, and 1971 respectively.

[105] Pink (2008).

- Establishing partnerships with co-regulators,[106] allied agencies[107] and academic and research institutions.[108]

One tangible example of capacity building requirements is the training of regulatory and enforcement staff. Training has multiple dimensions including: individual competence, group and executive competence, organisational competence and long-term capacity building.[109]

Capacity-building needs to concentrate on what is required to support higher level learning, including seeing knowledge as a co-production – an 'emergent, relational dynamic of social interactions'[110] – rather than relying on external sources.[111] As Armitage *et al.* conclude:

> Capacity-building efforts should create enabling conditions for learning which will inevitably involve a concern with issues of power, culture, institutions, worldviews and values.[112]

Such approaches may challenge traditional government styles (as well as traditional government itself) and their utilisation may be resisted by '… the inertia of institutions, resistance to changes in power structures and costs (perceived) to be associated with a transformation'.[113] Resistance to change may be high, especially as transformative change is expected of everyone, including the self, not just others.[114] Here there are also growing expectations placed on managers to support learning workplaces within their own agencies and wider network.[115] As Provan and Lemaire observe 'public managers must now confront the challenge of managing not only within but also across organisations and institutions

---

[106] Co-regulators here would typically include other environmental regulators from within the same level of government and jurisdiction and those in different levels.

[107] Allied agencies here, depending on the specific case and commodity, could include; police agencies, customs and port authorities, taxation agencies, immigration agencies and intelligence agencies.

[108] Academic and research institutions here, would typically include universities and governmental and non-governmental research institutes and think tanks.

[109] Pink (2008) 228.

[110] Ison, Blackmore and Iaquinto (2013) 35.

[111] Wilner *et al.* (2012).

[112] Armitage *et al.* (2008) 96.

[113] Pahl-Wostl (2009) 363.

[114] Taylor (2008).

[115] See for example discussion in Choy (2009).

through network arrangements'.[116] Leadership of networks demands, and appears to exhibit, different skillsets than that of agency-level leadership.[117]

4. NETWORK EVALUATION AND EFFICACY

Popp *et al.* have defined network effectiveness 'as the achievement of positive network level outcomes that cannot be attained by individual organisational participants acting alone'.[118] Since all regulator networks are goal-oriented it is vital that progress is evaluated. Ideally evaluation is integrated in the learning cycle, learning evaluation or development evaluation.[119] As Provan *et al.* have observed:

> Effectiveness is ... related to the concept of network learning ... the organisation learns from those organisations around them, and as they evolve, the network is more likely to evolve in ways that lead to network effectiveness. Without learning and evolution, the network may fail.[120]

4.1 Assessment and Appraisal of Network Effectiveness

Provan and Lemaire consider there to be five characteristics of effective networks:[121]

(1) *Involvement at multiple levels* – multiplex ties at all hierarchical levels are stronger than if network ties rely on only a few individuals (this also supports adaptive capacity and resilience).[122]
(2) *Network design* – integration must be selective and appropriate. Too much integration leads to moribund embeddedness; too little and there is insufficient coordination and collaboration and the network fails to exist. A combination of strong and weak ties is also appropriate.[123]

---

[116] Provan and Lemaire (2012) 638, 642, 643. See also Milward and Provan (2006); Moynihan *et al.* (2011).
[117] Agranoff and McGuire (2001) 296; Silvia and McGuire (2010).
[118] Popp *et al.* (2013) 10.
[119] See for example Patton (2011); Patton (2006).
[120] Provan *et al.* (2007) 506.
[121] Provan and Lemaire (2012) 643.
[122] See discussion in Pahl-Wostl (2009) 357.
[123] See also discussion of overprocessing by McGuire and Agranoff (2011).

(3) *Appropriate governance* – Provan and Lemaire differentiate the following types which may be suitable in different contexts: shared governance; lead organisation; and network administration organisation. They observe that trust is essential for the successful operation of any of these forms.[124]
(4) *Building and maintaining legitimacy* – both internal and external legitimacy is essential.
(5) *Stability* – here there may be trade-offs with flexibility, another desirable network feature.[125]

Further work is required in evaluating network effectiveness.[126] Interorganisational networks especially are under-researched, particularly at the whole network level.[127] There is a gap between research and practice[128] and the field is complicated by inconsistent terminology and indeterminacy around the unit of study and analysis.[129] Evaluation is a difficult art, and not just because of causality and confounding factors (that is, were outcomes achieved because of the network or some other factor?). There are many other questions. For example: Is efficacy to be measured only against aims that the network itself sets? Against what baselines should achievements be assessed?[130] According to McGuire and Agranoff '[e]ffectiveness can be measured by the extent to which a network achieves its goals, whatever the goal is and however it has been formulated'.[131] However, network aims may or may not be formalised to a measurable degree. Evaluation needs to take into account equity, as well as cost-effectiveness and efficiency, and what alternative approaches may have been available. Essentially, networks are about delivering better public policy outcomes at the same or reduced cost, although the financial imperative may be less pertinent for the public sector than it is for the private.[132]

---

[124] Provan and Lemaire (2011).
[125] See also Agranoff and McGuire (2001) 305.
[126] Provan and Milward (2001); Provan and Lemaire (2012); and see also Newig and Fritsch (2009).
[127] Isett *et al.* (2011); Provan *et al.* (2007); Provan and Lemaire (2012).
[128] Isett *et al.* (2011).
[129] Dawes (2012); Hartley and Benington (2006); Isett *et al.* (2011); Knight (n 74); McGuire and Agranoff (2011); Popp *et al.* (2013); Provan et al. (2007); Provan and Lemaire (2012) 639; Sanderson (2002) and see also Shipan and Volden (2012); Stone (1999).
[130] Agranoff and McGuire (2001) 311.
[131] McGuire and Agranoff (2011) 272.
[132] Provan and Milward (2001) 417, 422.

Popp *et al.*[133] suggest the following evaluation questions:

(1) Does the network have a clear vision and goals that are understood and supported by all members?
(2) Is the governance structure a good fit for this network?
(3) Is the network appropriately resourced to do its work?
(4) Does the leadership style fit with what we know about effective network leadership?
(5) Are important management tasks being attended to, and is the management focus evolving appropriately over time?
(6) Is attention being paid to both the management of the network, and management in the network?
(7) Does the network have both the internal and the external legitimacy it requires?
(8) Is the network/relationship structure evolving as expected and contributing positively to the work of the network?
(9) Is there an optimal mix of strong and weak ties among network members?
(10) Are the linkages targeted and appropriate?
(11) Is there trust among network members?
(12) Are power differentials being recognised and addressed as appropriate?
(13) Are there multiple levels of involvement?
(14) Is there a balance of stability and flexibility?

For environmental enforcement networks (EENs) specifically, there are no real evaluation practices other than internal and basic project management and standard committee/governance style reporting. Given the dearth of evaluation practices specifically designed for EENs, in 2011 Pink and Lehane developed a Network Evaluation Matrix (NEM) for EENs. The NEM drew upon Pink's 2010 study which sought to identify strategies that agencies might use to gain greater benefit from their association with networks.[134] The study identified 12 strategies, since referred to by the International Network of Environmental Compliance and Enforcement as the 'Pink Principles of Networks'.[135]

In Provan and Milward's 2001 treatment of network evaluation they concluded that evaluation cannot be limited to the network level, it also needs to be conducted at staff level and community and customer/client/

[133] Popp *et al.* (2013) 68.
[134] Pink (2010).
[135] INECE (2011) 136.

citizen level as well as integrated assessment across all levels.[136] While Provan and Milward were concentrating on public health provision, their observations are pertinent. For example, with regards to efficacy at the client level environmental agencies must satisfy people's expectations but also concerns about the environment. Provan and Milward's evaluation criteria included reduced incidence of the problem, as well as public perception of the problem having been solved. For environmental agencies, this may include meeting the expectations of international and national environmental interest groups as well as citizens and residents within any one agency's jurisdiction. As Provan and Milward observe, satisfaction of expectations may be problematic, since different groups may have different (and dynamic) views on a desirable, or achieved, outcome.[137] The same applies within networks.[138] For Provan and Milward, evaluation criteria at the agency level include client outcomes, resource acquisition, and costs. These are related: for example, network affiliation enables access to resources that may achieve better outcomes at reduced cost. Generally speaking this is also the criterion for an integrated assessment: 'the network is considered successful if the community in general, and clients in particular, are better served by an integrated network of providers'. For public sector groups '[s]takeholders tend to evaluate, reward, or punish individual agencies, regardless of the network's role in enhancing or limiting client outcomes'.[139]

4.2 Network Commitment

At the network level Provan and Milward recommend the following evaluation criteria:

- Membership growth;
- Network governance arrangements and cost of network maintenance;
- Range of services provided;
- Integration/coordination of services and absence of service duplication; and
- Member commitment to network goals.[140]

---

136 See also McGuire and Agranoff (2011) 274.
137 Provan and Milward (2001) 421.
138 See also Davidson-Hunt (2006).
139 Provan and Milward (2001) 422.
140 Ibid.

Such commitment at a member agency level is essential for the network to survive and is significant at the staff level. To be achieved, collective network goals need to be shared by individual participants. As ultimately it is their participation and motivation which is key to success it is essential that personal incentive systems are supportive.[141] It appears that at both individual and agency level self-interest is key: the relevant question according to Provan and Milward is: 'how can network involvement benefit me/my agency?'.[142] For some agencies there may be essential knowledge or economies of scale provided by a network, for other agencies it may be more a question of public relations or need for legitimacy or credibility to join a network.[143] Provan and Lemaire note that '[w]hile public sector (and non-profit) organisations are certainly not immune to self-interest, collective action is an important consideration'.[144] Provan and Milward recognise that this aspect may be significant for public sector networks:

> The advantage of public-sector networks is that many of the individuals who are employed by network organizations are professionals, with values and commitment to clients and the public good that often outweigh their commitment to specific programs or organizations.[145]

5. CONCLUSION

5.1 Improving Network Effectiveness

Regulatory failures in the environmental sphere are ubiquitous. It is imperative that new methods are deployed for better environmental, and inter-related, social outcomes.[146] Networks are one mode of public sector collaborative governance which have emerged recently to tackle the immense challenges and wicked problems of a human-dominant but approach-deficient Anthropocene.[147]

Regulator Networks are changing the way in which environmental regulation is undertaken. Networks do this by breaking down traditional barriers, including the borders of jurisdictions and government portfolios,

---

141 Isett et al. (2011) 164.
142 Provan and Milward (2001) 420; See also Pink (2015).
143 See also Podolny and Page (1998).
144 Provan and Lemaire (2012) 639.
145 Provan and Milward (2001) 423.
146 See for example Pahl-Wostl (2009).
147 See for example Westley *et al.* (2011) 762–80.

as well as building approaches that are co-operative, collaborative, iterative and adaptive rather than merely command and control.[148] Engagement with environmental enforcement networks has been found to be a key factor in organisational success[149] which is leading to additional demands being placed on environmental enforcement networks.

5.2 A Research Agenda

In addition to the need for general research into network effectiveness, a specific research agenda to identify the most effective means of capacity building within environmental regulatory agencies is required. To improve implementation of environmental law, five areas for possible exploration are *staffing*, *organisational culture*, *organisational structure*, *change* and *capacity building typologies*. More specifically:

- *Staffing* – How and to what extent is the recruitment, training and continuing professional development of staff factored into capacity building within environmental regulatory agencies?
- *Organisational Culture* – What influence does organisational culture play in capacity building and is there an optimal form or type of organisational culture conducive to capacity building?
- *Organisational Structure* – Do certain organisational structures (or aspects of) facilitate or inhibit capacity building efforts?
- *Change* – How do environmental regulatory agencies deal with change: reactively, pro-actively or hybrid and how does this influence capacity building?
- *Capacity Building Typologies* – Do the various capacity building arrangements and efforts share common traits such that different capacity building typologies exist?

This chapter has highlighted the enabling roles that regulator networks, learning, capacity-building and evaluation have and might play in assisting environmental regulatory agencies to perform their activities. It is likely that environmental regulatory agencies will continue to learn and collaborate in such a way that transformational change and learning becomes an increasingly core capability. Further research into networks and learning and capacity-building will improve implementation and enforcement of environmental law.

---

148 Pahl-Wostl (2009) 355.

149 See O'Leary and Lynott (2011); Nicholson (2011); Pink and Lehane (2011); Stas (2011).

REFERENCES

Agranoff, R. and M. McGuire (2001), 'Big Questions in Public Management Research' 11(3) *Journal of Public Administration Research and Theory* 295.

Ameli, P. and D. Kayes (2011), 'Triple-loop Learning in a Cross-sector Partnership: The DC Central Kitchen Partnership' 18(3) *The Learning Organization* 175.

Ansell, C. and A. Gash (2008), 'Collaborative Governance in Theory and Practice' 18(4) *Journal of Public Administration Research and Theory* 543.

Armitage, D. *et al.* (2011), 'Co-management and the Co-production of Knowledge: Learning to Adapt in Canada's Arctic' 21(3) *Global Environmental Change* 995.

Armitage, D., M. Marschke and R. Plummer (2008), 'Adaptive Co-management and the Paradox of Learning' 18 *Global Environmental Change* 86.

Asian Environmental Compliance and Enforcement Network (AECEN) (2010), *Nepal and Malaysia Finalize Twinning Partnership Work Program.* (News release, 5 May), accessed 3 April 2015 at http://www.aecen.org/nepal-and-malaysia-finalize-twinning-partnership-work-program.

Australasian Environmental Law Enforcement and Regulators neTwork (AELERT) (2011) *Australian-Vietnamese Twinning Program – Phase 2* (News Release 24 March), accessed 3 April 2015 at http://www.aelert.com.au/?p=1274.

Australian Public Service Commission (2007), *Tackling Wicked Problems – A Policy Perspective* (Commonwealth of Australia).

Bartel, R. (2013), 'Vernacular Knowledge and Environmental Law: Cause and Cure for Regulatory Failure' 19(8) *Local Environment* 1.

Bartel, R., P. McFarland and C. Hearfield (2014), 'Taking a De-Binarized Envirosocial Approach to Reconciling the Environment vs Economy Debate: Lessons from Climate Change Litigation for Planning in NSW, Australia' 85(1) *Town Planning Review* 67.

Bates, G. (2006), *Environmental Law in Australia* (6th edn, Sydney: LexisNexis Butterworths).

Berkes, F. (2009), 'Evolution of Co-management: Role of Knowledge Generation, Bridging Organizations and Social Learning' 90 *Journal of Environmental Management* 1692.

Bricknell, S. (2010), 'Environmental Crime in Australia' *AIC Reports: Research and public policy series 109* (Canberra: Australian Institute of Criminology).

Bryson, J., B. Crosby and M. Stone (2006), 'The Design and Implementation of Cross-sector Collaborations: Propositions from the Literature' 66(S1) *Public Administration Review* 44.

Bulkeley, H. (2005), 'Reconfiguring Environmental Governance: Towards a Politics of Scales and Networks' 24(8) *Political Geography* 875.

Capaldo, A. (2014), 'Network Governance: A Cross-level Study Of Social Mechanisms, Knowledge Benefits, and Strategic Outcomes in Joint-design Alliances' 43(4) *Industrial Marketing Management* 685.

Choy. S. (2009), 'Transformational Learning in the Workplace' 7 *Journal of Transformative Education* 65.

Clifford, M. and T. Edwards (2012), *Environmental Crime* (2nd edn, Burlington, MA: Jones & Bartlett Learning).

Davidson-Hunt, I. (2006), 'Adaptive Learning Networks: Developing Resource Management Knowledge through Social Learning Forums' 34(4) *Human Ecology* 593.

Dawes, S. (2012), 'Transnational Public Sector Knowledge Networks: Knowledge and Information Sharing in a Multi-Dimensional Context' 29 *Government Information Quarterly* S112.

Du Rées, H. (2009), 'Can Criminal Law Protect the Environment?' in R. White (ed.), *Environmental Crime: a reader* (Cullompton: Willan Publishing).

European Union Implementation and Enforcement of Environmental Law (IMPEL) (n.d.) website 'Cluster i: Improving Implementation of EU Environmental Law (Permitting, Inspection, Enforcement and Smarter Regulation)', accessed 10 April 2015 at http://impel.eu/cluster-i/.

Freiberg, A. (1987), 'Reconceptualising Sanctions' 25 *Criminology* 223.

Freiberg, A. (2010), *The Tools of Regulation* (Sydney: Federation Press).

Garvin, D., A. Edmondson and F. Gino (2008), 'Is Yours a Learning Organization?' 86 *Harvard Business Review* 109.

Gunningham, N. and P. Grabosky (1998), *Smart Regulation* (Oxford: Clarendon Press).

Hartley, J. and J. Benington (2006), 'Copy and Paste, or Graft and Transplant? Knowledge Sharing through Inter-organizational Networks' 26(2) *Public Money & Management* 101.

Heiss, R. *et al.* (2011), 'International Hazardous Waste Inspection Project at Seaports: Results and Recommendations' in *INECE, 9th International Conference on Environmental Compliance and Enforcement: 24 June 2011, Whistler, British Columbia, Canada: Proceedings.* (Washington, DC: INECE).

Holling, C. and G. Meffe (1996), 'Command and Control and the Pathology of Natural Resource Management' 10 *Conservation Biology* 328.

Huntjens, P. *et al.* (2011), 'Adaptive Water Management in a Changing Climate: A Formal Comparative Analysis of Eight Water Management Regimes in Europe, Africa, and Asia' 21 *Environmental Policy and Governance* 145.

International Network of Environmental Compliance and Enforcement (INECE) (2011), *The Operational Guidance for the Takeback of Detected Illegal Shipments of Waste* (Washington, DC: INECE-SESN, 2011).

International Network of Environmental Compliance and Enforcement (2012a) *Manual for Creating and Sustaining Regional Environmental Compliance and Enforcement Networks* (Washington, DC: INECE-SESN).

International Network of Environmental Compliance and Enforcement (2012b), *Second International Hazardous Waste Inspection Project at Seaports: Results and Recommendations* (Washington, DC: INECE-SESN).

Isett K *et al.* (2011), 'Networks in Public Administration Scholarship: Understanding Where We Are and Where We Need To Go' 21(1) *Journal of Public Administration Research and Theory* 157.

Ison, R., C. Blackmore and B. Iaquinto (2013), 'Towards Systemic and Adaptive Governance: Exploring the Revealing and Concealing Aspects of Contemporary Social-learning Metaphors' 87 *Ecological Economics* 34.

Knight, L. (2002), 'Network Learning: Exploring Learning by Interorganizational Networks' 55(4) *Human Relations* 427.

Knight, L. and A. Pye (2005), 'Network learning: An Empirically-derived Model of Learning by Groups of Organizations' 58(3) *Human Relations* 369.

Liebregts, T. and R. Kramers (2008), 'Doing the Right Things: A Step-by-step Guidance for Planning of Environmental Inspections' in INECE, *8th International Conference on Environmental Compliance and Enforcement*: 5-11 April 2008, Cape Town, South Africa: Proceedings (London: Cameron May Ltd).

Marshall, G. (2013), 'Transaction Costs, Collective Action and Adaptation in Managing Complex Social–ecological Systems' 88 *Ecological Economics* 185.

McGuire, M. and R. Agranoff (2011), 'The Limitations of Public Management Networks' 89(2) *Public Administration* 265.

Milward, H. and K. Provan (2006), *A Manager's Guide to Choosing and Using Collaborative Networks: IBM Center for the Business of Government* (IBM Report on the Business of Government).

Moynihan, D. *et al.* (2011), 'Performance Regimes amidst Governance Complexity' 21(1) *Journal of Public Administration Research and Theory* i141.

Newig, J. and O. Fritsch (2009), 'Environmental Governance: Participatory, Multi-Level – And Effective?' 19 *Environmental Policy and Governance* 214.

Nicholson, M. (2011), 'Networking in Europe: How Networking and Cooperation have Helped Respond to Environmental Compliance and Enforcement Challenges in Impel Member Countries' in INECE, *9th International Conference on Environmental Compliance and Enforcement: 24 June 2011, Whistler, British Columbia, Canada: Proceedings* (Washington, DC: INECE).

O'Leary, G. and D. Lynott (2011), 'The Effective Use of an Environmental Enforcement Network in Ireland' in International Network for Environmental Compliance and Enforcement, in INECE, *9th International Conference on Environmental Compliance and Enforcement: 24 June 2011, Whistler, British Columbia, Canada: Proceedings* (Washington, DC: INECE).

Ostrom, E. (2000), 'Crowding out Citizenship' 23(1) *Scandinavian Political Studies* 3.

Pahl-Wostl, C. (2009), 'A Conceptual Framework for Analysing Adaptive Capacity and Multi-level Learning Processes in Resource Governance Regimes' 19 *Global Environmental Change* 354.

Pahl-Wostl, C. *et al.* (2007), 'Social Learning and Water Resources Management' 12(2) *Ecology and Society* 5.

Pahl-Wostl, C. *et al.* (2011), 'Societal Learning Needed to Face the Water Challenge' 20 *AMBIO* 549.

Patton, M. (2006), 'Evaluation for the Way We Work' *Non-Profit Quarterly* 28.

Patton, M. (2011), *Developmental Evaluation: Applying Complexity Concepts to Enhance Innovation and Use* (New York: The Guilford Press).

Pfiffner, J. (2004), 'Traditional Public Administration versus The New Public Management: Accountability versus Efficiency' Festschrift for Professor Klaus Konig of Speyer, Germany, in A. Benz, H. Siedentopf and K. Sommermann (eds) *Institutionenwandel in Regierung und Verwaltung: Festschrift fur Klaus Konig* (Berlin: Duncker & Humblot).

Phelps, C., R. Heidl and A. Wadhwa (2012), 'Knowledge, Networks, and Knowledge Networks: A Review and Research Agenda' 38 *Journal of Management* 1115.

Pink, G., Building regulatory capacity in environmental agencies: Through tailored training. In INECE *8th International conference on environmental compliance and enforcement: 5-11 April 2008 Cape Town, South Africa, Proceedings* (Cameron May Ltd, 2008).

Pink, G. (2010), 'Environmental Enforcement Networks: A Qualitative Analysis', Australasian Environmental Law Enforcement and Regulators NeTwork (AELERT) (7 December).

Pink, G. (2011), 'Assessing the utility of environmental enforcement networks: Maximising benefits to members' in INECE, *9th International Conference on*

Environmental Compliance and Enforcement: 24 June 2011, Whistler, British Columbia, Canada: Proceedings (Washington, DC: INECE).
Pink, G. (2015), 'Environmental enforcement networks: their 'value proposition' during times of reducing resources and budgets', in M. Faure, P. De Smedt and A. Stas (eds), *Environmental Enforcement Networks: Concepts, Implementation and Effectiveness* (Cheltenham, UK and Northampton, MA, USA: Edward Elgar) 153–171.
Pink, G. and J. Lehane (2011), 'Environmental Enforcement Networks: Development of a Network Evaluation Matrix' in INECE, *9th International Conference on Environmental Compliance and Enforcement: 24 June 2011, Whistler, British Columbia, Canada: Proceedings* (Washington, DC: INECE).
Pink, G. and J. Lehane (2012), 'Environmental Enforcement Networks: their role in climate change enforcement' in R. White, *Climate Change, Crime and Criminology* (Berlin: Springer-Verlag).
Podolny, J. and K. Page (1998), 'Network Forms of Organization' 24 *Annual Review of Sociology* 57.
Popp, J. *et al.* (2013), *Inter-organizational networks: A critical review of the literature to inform practice*, accessed 10 April 2015 at http://research4children.com/data/documents/NetworkLiReview-Feb27-2013-Final.pdf.
Powell, W. (1990), 'Neither Market nor Hierarchy: Network Forms of Organization' 12 *Research in Organizational Behavior* 295.
Prieur, M. (2012), 'Non-regression in Environmental Law' 5(2) *SAPIENS Surveys and Perspectives Integrating Environment and Society* 53.
Provan, K. and R. Lemaire (2012), 'Core Concepts and Key Ideas for Understanding Public Sector Organizational Networks: Using Research to Inform Scholarship and Practice' 72(5) *Public Administration Review* 638.
Provan, K. and H. Milward (2001), 'Do Networks Really Work? A Framework for Evaluating Public Sector Organizational Networks' 61(4) *Public Administration* 414.
Provan, K., A. Fish and J. Sydow (2007), 'Interorganizational Networks at the Network Level: A Review of the Empirical Literature on Whole Networks' 33 *Journal of Management* 479.
Reeve, R. (2002), *Policing International Trade in Endangered Species: The CITES Treaty and Compliance* (Abingdon: Earthscan Publications).
Salamon, L.M. (2002), *The Tools of Government, A Guide to the New Governance,* (Oxford: Oxford University Press).
Sanderson, I. (2002), 'Evaluation, Policy Learning and Evidence Based Policy' 80(1) *Public Administration* 1.
Schulz, K. and S. Geithner (2010), 'Between Exchange and Development: Organizational Learning in Schools Through Inter-organizational Networks' 17 *Learning Organization* 69.
Senge, P. and J. Sterman (1992), 'Systems Thinking and Organizational Learning: Acting Locally and Thinking Globally in the Organization of the Future' 59(1) *European Journal of Operational Research* 137.
Shipan, C. and C. Volden (2012), 'Policy Diffusion: Seven Lessons for Scholars and Practitioners' 72(6) *Public Administration Review* 788.
Silvia, C. and M. McGuire (2010), 'Leading Public Sector Networks: An Empirical Examination of Integrative Leadership Behaviors' 21(2) *The Leadership Quarterly* 264.
Slaughter, A. (2004), *A New World Order* (Princeton: Princeton University Press).

Stanley, T. (1995), 'Ecosystem Management and the Arrogance of Humanism' 9(2) *Conservation Biology* 255–62.

Stas, A. (2011), 'The Flemish High Council of Environmental Enforcement – A Coordinated Environmental Enforcement Policy' in INECE, *9th International Conference on Environmental Compliance and Enforcement: 24 June 2011, Whistler, British Columbia, Canada: Proceedings* (Washington, DC: INECE).

Sterling, S. (2011), 'Transformative Learning and Sustainability: Sketching the Conceptual Ground' 5 *Learning and Teaching in Higher Education* 17.

Stone, D. (1999), 'Learning Lessons and Transferring Policy Across Time, Space and Disciplines' 19(1) *Politics* 51.

Taylor, E. (2008), 'Transformative Learning Theory' 119 *New Directions for Adult and Continuing Education* 5.

Thorelli, H. (1986), 'Between Markets and Hierarchies' 7(1) *Strategic Management Journal* 37.

Thorgren, S., J. Wincent and D. Örtqvist (2009), 'Designing Interorganizational Networks for Innovation: An Empirical Examination of Network Configuration, Formation and Governance' 26(3) *Journal of Engineering and Technology Management* 148.

van Tol Smit, E., E. de Loë and R. Plummer (2015), 'How Knowledge is used in Collaborative Environmental Governance: Water Classification in New Brunswick, Canada' 58(3) *Journal of Environmental Planning and Management* 423–44.

Waddell, S. (2002), 'Six Societal Learning Concepts for a New Era of Engagement' 3(4) *REFLECTIONS* 18.

Westley, F. *et al.* (2011), 'Tipping Toward Sustainability: Emerging Pathways of Transformation' 40 *AMBIO* 762–80.

White, R. (2008), *Crimes Against Nature: Environmental Criminology and Ecological Justice* (Cullompton: Willan Publishing).

Wijbenga, B. *et al.* (2008), 'Environmental policing in the 21st century – Background, organisation and experience in the Netherlands' in INECE, *8th International Conference on Environmental Compliance and Enforcement: 5-11 April 2008, Cape Town, South Africa: Proceedings* (London: Cameron May Ltd).

Wilner, K. *et al.* on behalf of the Coastal CURA Team (2012), 'Transformative Learning for Better Resource Management: The Role of Critical Reflection' 55(10) *Journal of Environmental Planning and Management* 1331.

Woodhill, J. and N. Röling (1998), 'The Second Wing of the Eagle: The Human Dimension in Learning our Way to More Sustainable Futures' in N. Röling and M. Wagemakers (eds), *Facilitating Sustainable Agriculture: Participatory Learning and Adaptive Management in Times of Environmental Uncertainty* (Cambridge: Cambridge University Press).

Wright, B. and S. Pandey (2010), 'Transformational Leadership in the Public Sector: Does Structure Matter?' 20(1) *Journal of Public Administration Research and Theory* 75.

Index